# Sharkeyes

# Sharkeyes

# Diane Marger Moore

A tiny corpse, determined detective and a novice prosecutor
— a true story

*Bink Books*
Bedazzled Ink Publishing Company • Fairfield, California

paperback 978-1-945805-79-0

Cover Design
by

Bink Books
a division of
Bedazzled Ink Publishing, LLC
Fairfield, California
http://www.bedazzledink.com

*To my friend and respected homicide detective*
*Leslie Van Buskirk who never gave up.*
*But most of all, my thanks to the Indianapolis Fire Investigation Unit*
*and the Indianapolis Police Department's homicide detectives*
*for their skill and tenacity.*

# Chapter One

IT WAS COLD and gray as only an Indiana winter day can be. It had been an uneventful morning when my telephone rang. It was my boss, chief trial counsel for the Marion County Prosecutor's Office.

"D'you know anything about Brian Poindexter dismissing an arson murder case against a guy named Wise, who supposedly killed his eight week old baby?"

"I didn't even know that Brian had an arson case. He's never mentioned it to me and I certainly didn't agree to dismiss, anything. What's this about?" I asked.

My boss was to the point. "Some bitch of a police detective wants a meeting. Fifteen minutes in the conference room."

He hung up.

Unbeknownst to me, of course, that call was the beginning of a treacherous and testing quest to bring to trial, and to convict a despicable murderer, represented by capable defense lawyers, who planned and executed the unspeakable death of his own, living, breathing, son, an infant only eight weeks old.

The dead baby's name was Matthew Dean Wise and it was for his soul that we were seeking justice.

The unaffectionate nickname the homicide detective gave to the killer, the baby's father, William Wise, was "Sharkeyes," because she recognized the pitiless, remorseless, deadliness in his unblinking black eyes.

A FEW MONTHS earlier I had been appointed by the newly elected Republican prosecutor as the chief deputy arson prosecutor for Marion County, Indiana, which includes Indianapolis, the state capital. I took over all pending arson cases and worked directly with the fire investigation unit.

The unit consisted of veteran detectives and fire investigators-fighters who teamed up to examine crimes that involved fire or explosives. I was the supervisor of all lawyers working on arson-related cases.

It was me who decided which cases would be "filed," meaning that the accused would be criminally charged. And I also had the authority to dismiss arson cases—which I was rarely inclined to do.

My predecessor was a lawyer with maybe two years of experience. She felt "empowered" by her possession of an official police radio. She talked like a TV cop.

As far as I knew, she also had never won a case. She hadn't a clue how to investigate or try an arson offense. While her willingness to go to scenes and faithfully file charges against suspects had made her a well-liked part of the arson squad, her credentials as a trial lawyer/prosecutor were a vast relief to anyone charged with arson.

The chances of being convicted by her were so low that even plea bargaining an arson case had been a very hard sell for the Prosecutor's Office during her stay. Even so, there was a less than enthusiastic response to my appointment. I was summarily cast by the local legal gossips as a "silk stocking" lawyer who had worked mostly for people of significant wealth. I was hired by the election-winning "new Republican boss" for a challenging job that provided more personal satisfaction for me than just a paycheck. And I brought with me a great deal of trial experience.

I was offered almost no advice nor direction from the office's so-called "experienced prosecutors," and to them I was a complete unknown who had no history of criminal prosecution and definitely wasn't from "around here." The arson unit was similarly chagrinned with the substitution.

The ill feelings were never acted out in the open. It was more puerile. There would be a two a.m. radio or telephone call about, say, a house fire. I would leave our snug bed, throw on jeans and a tee shirt and a seasonal coat, climb into my un-garaged car and listen to the police radio. The fire investigation team communicated over the air using numerical "codes" that no one shared with me.

I guessed they wanted to see if I would faint at the sight of a char-broiled body or balk at driving into the most violent neighborhoods. They were disappointed. I managed to locate the fire scenes, listen carefully to whatever the team had to say, even if the fire was obviously accidental and had absolutely nothing to do with arson. I'd keep my annoyance to myself. Then I'd head back home.

Brian was not assigned to the "arson unit" but was one of the mid-level "good ole boys" in the Prosecutor's Office. He had been a prosecutor for quite a long time. He was mildly good looking, his lawyer wife worked for a big firm and she earned the bulk of the family's income. Brian kept a Glock semi-automatic pistol stuffed in his waistband even when he was sitting at a computer. I guessed that screening cases could be dangerous—the computer could explode, you could get a paper cut, whatever.

When I saw the unrestrained pistol wobble around his beltline when he sat down and got up, I wondered what the odds were of him leaving all three safety latches open and blowing off his do-dah. I guessed it was fairly high since he had the pistol in his belt, this meant that, in his mind, he needed to be able to get to his gun and fire fast, and to unlatch a Glock's three safeties would, in his mind, take too long. My presumption was that his Glock was almost always loaded and all safeties were off.

In the months that I had been in the office, no one had ever mentioned that Brian Poindexter was assigned an arson case.

I dialed Brian's extension figuring that he could fill me in on the details of what was up. He didn't answer. So I was going in cold.

Fourteen minutes later, I sat in the cramped conference room. It was a windowless, narrow, longish space with a table and about ten chairs jammed under it with little room to squeeze around. The table and chairs were metallic, scratched, bruised, shaky, and at least a generation old. There was a small TV glowing soundlessly in the corner. Florescent lighting overhead was bluish cold like almost everything else that I had experienced since joining the Prosecutor's Office.

Cale was already seated on one side of the table and beside him was a trim, white-haired man who I guessed was a law enforcement officer. Beside him an attractive and slender blonde woman about ten years younger than my forty-two years, dressed in a flowery skirt and white blouse. Disturbingly, she seemed primed and ready to pounce across the table. I figured she had to be the "bitch."

What the heck was it? She radiated what I can only describe as pure hatred and visceral loathing. As I entered the room, she gave me a laser zap with her espresso brown eyes. For a long time she never took her eyes off of me.

At the end of the table, opposite "the bitch," was Brian Poindexter. A skinny manila folder lay on the table in front of him. He looked dead-eyed at the wall and said nothing. I noticed, with a certain amount of relief, that he did not pack the Glock.

Cale introduced me to Sgt. Steve West, the gray-haired cop, and Detective Leslie Van Buskirk, the bitch.

No one moved as much as a shoulder or nodded a head and no hands were shaken.

Cale started the meeting by asking me, "What do you know about the William Wise case?"

I honestly responded, "Nothing; absolutely nothing." I glanced at Brian, who remained "not here" and silent.

Cale looked at Brian. "Well you know then, Brian. What's the case about and why should it be dismissed?"

Brian looked at me with mild scorn lines around his eyes and lips. But I also saw a glint of alarm in his eyes. His haughty tone attempted to make it clear that it was I who needed clueing in.

"Before you arrived," Brian started, seemingly referring to the new political regime as a whole, as well as to me, "it was decided that we were dismissing this case because it can't be won. There is conflicting evidence. The arson investigator waited too long to decide that the fire was intentionally set and the defendant has retained counsel. The case would be totally circumstantial and it's too messed up to try."

Cale almost swallowed his tongue as he tried, and badly failed, to maintain a level-headed tone.

"So why did you hold on to it for this long? And why didn't you discuss it with Diane?"

There was no response.

To be fair, it was not unusual for one elected prosecutor's "regime" to hold over dismissals and to dump them all on the desk of the next prosecutor after a lost election.

The custom was that the newly elected prosecutor would take the heat for losing these cases, and even might be accused by the former prosecutor of being afraid to try the "tough ones" if a case was dismissed. The new prosecutor could also be branded as incompetent if the new deputy prosecutors tried and lost the cases.

Cale understood such politics far better than I did, but I certainly got the gist.

I had no idea if this was or would be a high profile case or not, since I'd never heard of it.

I glanced at the bitch; her face was flushed, her neck muscles were strung out, her fingers were tensed. I thought of a cartoon dragon with steam puffing out of her ears. I have excellent hearing. I heard a low, warning growl emit from the back of her throat. The bitch seemed to be reaching a boiling point.

Brian directed his comments to Cale. "I didn't think I had to discuss this case with anyone . . . not until I read the memo you sent out yesterday. So I left you a message. I've already told Jimmy Voyles that the case will be dismissed . . . I gave him my word."

The bitch's head snapped back.

James Hugh Voyles was a well-known Indianapolis criminal defense lawyer who was as smooth and charismatic as they come. He wore elegant well-tailored suits, white starched shirts and oozed charm. He was revered in the courthouse for both his legal prowess and political prominence.

He was lower lip deep in Democratic Party machine politics. The Democrats had been in control of county and state offices for decades. Scott Newman, the newly elected prosecutor who had hired me, was a Republican and had wrested the office from very long-time Democratic control.

I had met Voyles only once. I didn't much like his plastic smile, big paw handshake, or his solicitous yet condescending attitude. I had never tried a case against him, but I had tried cases with and against his ilk for years.

The "I gave him my word . . ." part of Brian's explanation was like a lighted match tossed into a big puddle of aviation gasoline.

The bitch shot up out of her chair and the chair's legs squawked loudly against the linoleum flooring. She caught me off guard with that move, and my mouth may have dropped open at the fury of her attack.

"You hoping to get a fuckin' job from Voyles?" she roared into Brian's face.

I saw the fine spray of her spittle in the blue light.

"That's got to be it!" the bitch shouted. "You sure don't give a rusty fuck about the kid Wise murdered."

I felt better that Brian did not have his Glock in his belt. But while he seemed a bit taken aback by the attack, he was not overwhelmed. I wondered whether other women in his life got in his face in a similar manner.

In fact, there was gossip that Poindexter was preparing to leave the office and to move to more lucrative private practice. This is customary for top ranking prosecutors, but line deputy prosecutors like Poindexter were rarely fired, and most like him continued semi-competently in their jobs from one administration to another.

But I was puzzled. Was it possible that the bitch actually knew something about a job offer for Poindexter? I really doubted it.

She slipped around the table and dropped a fifteen by eighteen inch photograph in front of me. It looked mostly black with shades of gray. It was of a room burned from the ceiling to the floor. I could virtually smell the stench.

I looked closer. I saw piled grayish ashes that reached to roughly five or six inches above the floor.

The bitch loomed over my shoulder. She pounded her forefinger into the photograph in front of me.

"*Where's Waldo?*" the bitch demanded of me.

I looked closer.

"*Where the fuck is Waldo?*"

As a parent of two daughters, I was familiar with the children's books of busy drawings of people and places with a camouflaged and hidden little boy/man with glasses, a horizontal stripped shirt, and a knit cap, that you are challenged to locate in the drawing. That's Waldo.

I looked more closely at the color photograph. It was dreadful to imagine that a two-month old child had been incinerated in this room. I scoured the picture, trying to gain a sense of the room itself. I noticed a small bit of white and maybe some pink in the upper corner. I took off my glasses so that I could more meticulously inspect the little specks of light material.

I saw what looked like a tiny baby penis and some white, maybe diaper material, directly below it.

There were no arms or legs attached to this miniscule portion of an infant boy's genitalia because almost the entire body was burned down to baked organs and ashes. Only a slight amount of lower abdomen, a small appendage, and a burned out half of an infant's head was what was left of Baby Matthew.

I swallowed. The bitch was still standing over me pointing to the photograph.

She said in a very clear and accusative way that was not lost on Brian, "He killed that baby and Poindexter wants him to get away with it!" She shared some additional salty and sexually demeaning characterizations of Poindexter, never taking her eyes off of him. She then turned to me and demanded to know, "Have you got any balls?"

Well, I don't, and never did. But balls are not what win arson cases. I took my time, and then I told the bitch in my most tactful way, so I didn't sound too ballsy. "We don't dismiss murder cases, especially arson murder cases, unless there are good reasons to do so."

I pushed the photograph across the table to where Cale could see it. He was the one with authority to make the decision.

To Van Buskirk—*(Oh, Poop! That's the first time I thought of her as anything except "the bitch.")*—I asked, "What was Wise's motive?"

"Who the fuck knows?" Van Buskirk responded. "I think he hates kids. This guy is really sick. Wait until you see the video of his interview from Elkhart. He's got shark eyes. He has no conscience, no respect for life or the law, no remorse. The man is a killer who never blinks."

Something is odd, I thought. I asked, "Why would there be an interview in Elkhart?" I was thinking, If Wise's baby had been killed in Marion County, which is Indianapolis, there would be no investigation in Elkhart.

Van Buskirk explained, "Before our infant was killed, Wise was the prime suspect in the homicide and feticide of a teenager and her unborn twins. About a year before his marriage and the death of Baby Matthew, Wise was dating an Elkhart teenager who became pregnant with twins. Wise was the last person to see her alive. He claimed that they met the evening of her death and after spending a few hours together, she dropped him off in a parking lot. The girl never made it home.

"Wise volunteered to talk to the police, he gave a video tape recorded interview and told the detectives that he wanted to help find the missing teenage mother. When the body of the teen was found later in a wooded area, she and her twins were dead. Blunt force trauma—she was beaten to death. The killing of Rae Ann Symons was ruled a homicide. Wise was the best and only suspect, but the Elkhart police could not make the case and it remained unsolved. Wise's current wife, Michelle, was his 'alibi' in the Elkhart case."

I was surprised and half-way pleased by the way the former bitch presented her facts. I sat thinking for a few seconds longer than I usually do. To Van Buskirk, I guess, it seemed that I was unimpressed.

"Well?" she demanded.

I looked at Brian Poindexter. He avoided my eyes. He was writhing and I didn't mind that. Cale was pokerfaced and said nothing. Van Buskirk's partner was slyly amused but mum.

I turned back to Brian and in my most judicial tone and no-appeals-accepted voice, I said, "You're off this case. Thank you. You will have no further responsibility for what happens, so you can leave now, unless Cale has anything for you."

Brian, with a sneer on his lips, lifted himself out of his chair slowly, took a deep breath while he struggled to mind his tongue, and glared venomously at me. He turned to Cale. "I gave Voyles my word this case would be dismissed," he blurted. "I also told Judge Barney that I would be dismissing the case and explained why I intended to dismiss it."

He dropped the file with a noisy slap on top of the picture in front of me, turned, and walked out of the conference room. He contemptuously left the door open.

No one uttered a word.

After Poindexter was gone, I got up, walked over, and closed the door. "I don't want anything we say to get back to Voyles."

I quick-studied their faces. I did not believe that secrecy would be a problem.

# Chapter Two

CALE MADE IT clear the disposition of the Baby Wise case was my decision.

Politically, he explained, the case should be tried. A newly elected prosecutor hopes to solidify relationships with the local police department and prove his ability to show the former prosecutor that he can win convictions.

On the other hand, if the case is lost, it will reflect badly on the current prosecutor, which is exactly the way it was planned by the former one.

The only way through for me was easy: "Own it!" Make the disposition of the case my decision alone, and hence my loss and not the Higher-Ups' loss if the jury acquits. Cool for them. And fine for me, too. "Own it!" works.

Since I was not an elected official, and an unlikely candidate ever to be elected to anything, I would make my decision based entirely upon the evidence as I saw it, not the fraught demands of a law enforcement officer or department or politician.

I was the one who must try the case and I must prove it. I didn't care if it would be hard or if I could lose. What I cared about was whether I would become convinced, beyond all glimmer of doubt, that William Wise murdered his son.

I pensively exited the conference room and returned to my small window office. I asked myself again, "Why would a father kill his own eight week old son? Can I prove it if he did it?" Far more troubling, "What if I can't prove it and he gets away with it?"

I would not allow that grim possibility to remain for an extra millisecond in my mind.

Instead, I thought about my husband Steve's face when each of our two daughters was born. He was in the operating room with me and the instant he saw the girl's tiny face that look crept into his eyes. It was pure unadulterated love.

What would provoke any parent to kill her or his own child?

I reminded myself that the State does not have to prove the Why?—motive. Despite all of the television and murder mystery novel emphasis on motive, the motive is not an element of the crime of murder. I was not required to prove why William Wise killed his son Matthew, only that he did it.

What will Van Buskirk and our witnesses have to prove—to me and for me alone—that would enable me to persuade a jury to convict a deliberate and cruel monster?

No need now to go into why, but I've long relied upon the law to light my way. The law lets me know what I am required to prove if the case goes to trial.

Later, I will have to consider what additional facts a jury will insist upon before it will convict.

"The jury always wants more than the law requires."

That is a truth the best trial lawyers know, and that I do not underestimate.

I printed out the legal requirements and put the page on the metal ledge near my window that served as the only personal space in my cramped office.

"A person who knowingly or intentionally kills another human being commits murder, a felony. IC 35-42-1-1."

This meant that I had to prove that William Wise: (1) was a "person;" and (2) knowingly or intentionally; (3) killed; (4) Matthew Wise; and (5) that Baby Matthew was a "human being."

I thought about it. Of course Wise was a person and Baby Matthew was a human being. How would I prove that Wise "knowingly or intentionally" killed the infant?

Harder yet, how would I prove Wise's reason for killing his innocent child? Although I had no legal obligation to prove motive, the jurors, or at least one of them, would want to know why.

From our short meeting, it seemed to me that Van Buskirk hadn't a clue as to motive. Her unsupported hunch that William Wise "did not like children" wasn't going to cut it. Not nearly enough.

I urged myself to focus on whether there was sufficient evidence to prosecute the crime. But I kept drifting back to motive.

As so often happens when the physical and intellectual going gets really rough, an urgent craving for chocolate swept over me. I reached into my stash of M&Ms and munched as I pondered.

To prove motive may have been impossible before 1994 when a dreadful woman named Susan Smith entered the public knowledge. Smith was the mother of two boys, one a three-year-old toddler and the other a fourteen-month-old baby, both healthy and adorable.

She put the children in her car, buckled them in their car seats, and slowly let the car roll into a lake. The children drowned. I cannot fathom their terror and wonder if they could have seen their mother watching as they fought for breath and lost consciousness.

Smith infamously appeared on television to beg the "black man" who she claimed had carjacked and kidnapped the children to release them.

Soon her story completely fell apart; Smith confessed to the murders. The public was stunned as this tragedy played out, particularly since the public's heart had been at first with Smith, the mother, a white woman, and against African American males in general.

Few could imagine the truth. But with her confession and conviction, the public could no longer plausibly deny that there are some people, even parents, who are killers of their own children.

Even so, no murder prosecution of a parent is easy. Few jurors are willing to believe that parents with malice aforethought will kill their own children. Jurors are notoriously resistant to the notion that this kind of gross deviance from the expected is even humanly possible.

I thought to myself, "I must simply prove that a parent killed his child, in a most horrible way, by burning him to death."

I tried to convince myself of how much I love a challenge. I began to read the fire investigation report that was in Poindexter's file.

The fire investigation report was written by David Lepper, a fire investigator from the IFD arson squad. I'd heard about Lepper, although I had never prosecuted a case with him before. What I had heard was uninspiring. Word was that Lepper was adequate and nearly ready to retire. That meant that he may have given short shrift to the investigation, although it was hard to imagine that Van Buskirk, in her scary bitch role, had not pushed him to the max to determine the cause of the fire.

Usually the reports that I received from the fire department were spread sheets with the time of call out, time of response, personnel on the vehicle (by numbers), certain activities indicated by a very brief or numeric description and then the time of recall. But this case included a complete write-up of the investigation in addition to the usual chronology. Lepper's grammar and syntax were less than perfect, but I got the point.

Which was as follows:

If we believed what the department was told by William Wise, the fire lasted a total of sixteen minutes from start to finish.

More precisely, William Wise looked at his watch at five a.m. when he went to the bathroom. From that time, to the time that William and Michelle Wise claimed to have first heard the fire alarm to the time when the fire department arrived and extinguished the fire was sixteen minutes. I had to repeat this to myself because the time was so very short. I recalled the photograph.

Everything in the room, and I mean everything, wood, metal, flooring, everything, was burned beyond recognition and to ashes.

The Fire Department put out the flames of the fire, which was only in Baby Matthew's tiny bedroom area, in less than three minutes.

What they saw shocked and immediately raised concerns among the firefighters. The fire had been burning at an alarm-detectable level for less than thirteen minutes yet everything more than six inches off the floor was burned beyond identification; the crib, the changing table, other furniture and lamps in the room.

All the firemen knew that such complete burning doesn't happen in an accidental fire. It didn't take an arson investigator to realize that something was wrong. Still, the report concluded that the fire was merely "suspicious."

Lepper was required to choose among three official ways of describing the fire. He could call it a) accidental, b) suspicious; or c) arson. He had designated the Baby Wise fire as "suspicious."

That posed a problem. If the fire investigator couldn't determine on the scene that the fire was intentionally set then how could I prove beyond a reasonable doubt that it was?

I looked at several additional photographs taken the morning of the fire. These were the only photographs in the file.

I made a note to self: "Where are all of the other photographs and other information?" I knew there would probably be a video taken at the Wise home as the investigators dug out the debris and sifted through it. Photographs would be taken at every stage in the investigation of the death of an infant. There would also be an autopsy and photographs from that autopsy. Nothing in Poindexter's file. Note: "Check with Van Buskirk."

Sixteen minutes, one death, two parents.

I looked to see when the parents had called 911. No phone call from the residence. I wrote another note in the margin of the report. *"Why didn't they call from their house? Why didn't they take the baby with them when they left the house? What the heck? Were either of them burned trying to save this child?"*

911 calls had come in from neighbors' houses. One call was from Michelle Wise, Matthew's mother, made at 5:09 a.m. Another call came from a different neighbor's house at 5:10 a.m. That call was made by William Wise. Note: "Where are the 911 call tape recordings? What did the parents say? Why weren't they together? What about the house phone?" The fire was extinguished by 5:16 a.m.

I also wondered why Poindexter really wanted to dismiss the case. Did the former prosecutor approve the dismissal of the case as Poindexter claimed, and if so why? Was it about losing the case or about something else?

I called my husband Steve at his office.

"Will you please check all of our smoke detectors when you get home?"

Steve did not even ask questions. He recognized that my job as an arson prosecutor had heightened my concerns about house fires. He did not yet know anything about the Baby Wise case. Yet, at my insistence, he had already installed smoke detectors in every room in our home including the garage, laundry room, and attic. He promised that he would check every one as soon as he got home. I told him for the umpteenth time that I would be home a little late. We said I love yous and hung up. I would explain the situation to Steve after we put the kids in bed.

I called Lepper and asked to meet him at the unit. He agreed but seemed surprised when I told him that it was about the William Wise case.

"I thought that Poindexter was dropping that case," Lepper volunteered.

"Why, do you doubt that Wise killed the baby?" I asked.

Lepper didn't hesitate. "Hell no, he did it, I just don't know if we can prove it."

My jaw ached from the effort not to say what I was thinking out loud. "Well, that's my problem not yours," I thought, "Just the facts Lepper, just the facts."

When I reached the arson unit, Lepper had his file laid out and sat down with me. He was a tallish man with short military style hair. He seemed in good shape but had a stoop. I identified it immediately as back pain. Many firefighters suffer back injuries while carrying people or animals out of fires, or being hit with fire debris, or from moving heavy objects and holding high velocity water hoses or from falling during their efforts to extinguish a fire. The fireman's stoop is called an occupational hazard.

I respected this man who had risked his life and his health for decades to rescue people and pets. The pay was low and the risks very high. Inhaling the smoke and toxic fumes, falling, burns, back and neck problems, all were part of the daily grind of working firemen everywhere. Whether he was a great investigator or not, he had earned the respect that I gave him.

Lepper spread his report out on the table and we examined it together. He said that the first firefighters at the scene did not realize that an infant had been in the nursery room and so the fire was put out quickly but without a real search for a living soul.

Within a few seconds they were advised to look for an infant in the room and it took them some time to isolate the tiny white material, body part and charred extremities.

Lepper said, "Everyone knew that this fire was no accident. Too fast, too hot, too little left. Too horrible that this child was incinerated nearly to nothingness."

The fire investigation unit was called in. Later homicide would arrive to take control of the scene, but not before it was cleared and signed off on by the fire department and the fire investigation unit.

Lepper explained how he conducted his investigation.

He started outside the Wise house and worked his way inward to Wise Baby's bedroom.

"I always go from the area of least burn to the area of most burn."

He said that the fire was located only within the confines of the baby's room, which was the size of a small walk-in closet. No more than, say, eight feet by five feet.

Once in the room, he sifted through the debris with the same equipment that a gold miner might use. "I looked at every piece that could be examined and then sifted through the rest looking for any possible source of the fire. Once I sifted through the debris, I threw it out the bedroom window into the yard for further examination."

I'd been to several fire scenes as a prosecutor and previously as a defense lawyer, both civil and criminal. You never forget the smell. It lingers, even days after the fire is extinguished. Char stench—it gets into your hair, clothing, shoes. Even worse, the smell of burning flesh is instantly, sickeningly recognizable. It almost smells of agony, although most victims of a fire succumb to the smoke and lack of oxygen, not from burning. That ghastly cooking odor is never forgotten. I wondered if this child had died before he was burned to death. It was not likely. Not enough time. Just sixteen minutes.

Lepper continued to describe his actions. Unlike most fire scenes, the sifting only took a few hours because there was so little left to look through. He had sifted about six inches of charred debris.

The remains of Baby Matthew were covered with a small tarp or cloth so that the investigator knew where the remains had been found after the fire was extinguished. But because of the burst of water that had been used by firemen to drown the fire, the location of the baby's remains was not a reliable indication of where he had been at the time of the fire. The water or firefighters could easily have moved the corpse, if it could even be called that. The lifeless remains, both human and inanimate, were documented in photographs and a video recording.

When the debris was painstakingly removed from the floor of the room, Lepper inspected the floor for burn patterns that might help him determine where and how the fire started. To locate the source of the fire allows the fire investigator to look at possible accidental causes, and other purposeful causes.

Although there was evidence of burning on the floor and even a pattern, Lepper explained that he did not want to give his opinion of how the fire started until he had additional information.

If an accelerant was poured on the floor of an area, there might be tell-tale markings known as a burn pattern. This is evidence of the type of burning caused by an accelerant. Lepper identified a burn pattern but wanted to be cautious about making a hasty determination about the cause of the fire.

"That's why I called it suspicious and not intentional," he told me. "I wanted to have all accidental causes ruled out by an expert, like an electrical engineer. This was a homicide and I didn't want to be accused of calling it arson before I had ruled out every possible accidental cause. Especially since Wise was one of us."

"One of *who?*" I asked without comprehension.

"He worked for IFD, didn't you know that?" Lepper asked.

"Wise was a firefighter?" I asked incredulously. Up to this point I had no idea who Wise was or what he did for a living.

"Wise worked for the Indianapolis Fire Department as a dispatcher. He was IFD—one of us."

I painfully realized how much I needed to learn about this case. The facts that everyone took for granted, and I didn't know, could be extremely important.

My head ached at my own ignorance (or was it hyperglycemia?), but I nevertheless began to think about how fires actually start.

A fire can be started by a number of accidental events or an act of nature. A fire can be started by faulty wiring, a lit cigarette, lightning, forgetting to turn off the stove, the heat from electrical appliances (coffee pots and curling irons are frequent causes) or from other unintentional means.

Because there are many unnatural but noncriminal ways of a fire starting, to prosecute an arson case first requires the State to prove that the fire was not caused by lightening or wind or any other act of nature. Then the prosecution must prove that the fire was not an accident. Only after proving that the fire was not an act of god or accidental can a prosecution move forward to prove the intentional act of arson.

Finally, after all of that, the prosecution must prove who started the arson fire.

In fact, most arsonists are caught because they burn themselves in the fire. They may leave a container with the accelerant in the area, which is then traced back to them, or brag about the fire later and get caught through their admissions. The identities of arsonists are frequently confirmed when scene photos are reviewed and the suspected arsonist is in the crowd watching the fire and the firefighters extinguish the blaze.

Most arsonists love to watch a fire burn. Many have a history of setting fires, from playing with matches as a child and setting things (and pets) on fire, to the real thing—burning down a car or a building. But the very worst of them use fire as a weapon, no less deadly than a gun, to kill another human being.

Lepper said that he inventoried the items that he was able to identify in the room. Several blobs of plastic were found, melted and degraded but blobs nonetheless. In the meantime, they interviewed witnesses, searched the rest of the house and spoke with the dead newborn's parents, Michelle and William Wise.

Lepper's IPD partner had worked with him to take statements from everyone involved.

William and Michelle Wise were asked to describe Matthew's bedroom and everything in it so that the debris could be matched with the room's contents.

Although they were interviewed shortly after Baby Matthew's body was found, Lepper said that William Wise was calm, cool, and anxious to help. Lepper knew that William Wise was a dispatcher for IFD but knew nothing else about the man. Lepper had not met him before.

I asked Lepper to describe the house.

"It was a split floor plan with three bedrooms, a bath, kitchen, and living area on the top floor and downstairs was another living area and a bedroom. There was a fire alarm system installed in the house. It was there in the house when Bill and Michelle bought it a few months before. Matthew's room was the first door on the left as you entered the upstairs bedroom hallway."

Lepper said that despite all of the work he had done, at first he could not explain how the fire started.

He said, "I had suspicions, but no conclusions. I ruled out any electrical defect. No lightening or other natural event caused the fire. The rest of the house was intact; it had not even been damaged much by smoke because the fire was extinguished so quickly."

I really couldn't fault Lepper for wanting to be certain before labeling the fire arson. Still, I wondered if his hesitancy was because William Wise worked for the Indianapolis Fire Department.

"I'm always looking for a hidden agenda," I scold myself, "because there usually is one."

After his physical inspection of the property, but before he released the scene or finalized his report, Lepper had wanted to hear what the occupants said about the fire. So he and his partner interviewed William and Michelle Wise.

Lepper's take on the interviews were that William Wise was more than strange; he was disturbing.

"Tell me what the Wises are like," I asked.

"Bill is small. Not just short, but thin and wiry, with very dark eyes. His face was blank when we talked to him. Like, no expression, no guilt, no grief, no nothing."

Lepper thought a moment and I could tell that he was reliving the interview.

"Wise answered our questions and seemed to have thought about his answers before we asked them. He like, *ummm,* seemed like he was enjoying the attention."

"What about Michelle?" I asked. I really wanted to know about this mother who didn't try to save her son.

"Michelle is a real dog—fat, swollen looking face, stringy brown hair, no makeup, and thick legs. I mean the kind of woman who no one asks out." His tone was dismissive. As they said at school, "Too stupid to live, too mean to die."

I left the Unit annoyingly puzzled. The fire must have been accelerated but testing of the debris failed to reveal any of the usual accelerants. There had been no gasoline, kerosene or lighter fluid found in any of the debris, although William Wise was a smoker and there were matches and lighter fluid in the home. Dave Lepper told me that he was convinced that it was an arson fire. It appeared to him that the fire started in the middle of the nursery. Michelle Wise had said that the only things in the middle of the room were the child's crib and the baby monitor.

I drove home thinking about that little room and the fire that had incinerated Baby Matthew. I intended to hug my girls before bed, tonight and every night from now on.

# Chapter Three

THE BABY WISE case was not my only case at the time. I was responsible for every arson case in the county, and I also had half of a "regular" case load in one of the six major felony courts.

I was assigned to Criminal Court Five, so I had about thirty run of the mill serious felony cases including armed robberies, attempted murders, aggravated assaults, and aggravated battery cases, as well as the arson case load and a few other murder cases that I'd inherited or adopted.

Every case was important to me, but the Baby Wise case woke me up and troubled me in the middle of the night.

Poindexter did not return my calls or messages. I noticed that he was friendly with my supervisor, John Commons, a Marine (one of the "There are no former Marines") who still wore his hair as if he were in the Corp. Commons was about as glad to have me as part of his team as I would have been to meet a band of armed street thugs in a dark alley. After the conference room situation, I saw Brian speaking with Commons in Court Five. As soon as I walked into the room the conversation abruptly ceased.

Apparently Brian had no intention of discussing the Wise case with me. Que sera, sera. I had no time to play cat and mouse with him. I doubted that he had anything of value to tell me anyway. But I had to interact with Commons. I felt my already cool relationship with him chill significantly.

I thought a lot about Baby Matthew and those sixteen minutes. I even mentioned the case at dinner with Bruce, my mother's husband ("stepfather" was not in my vocabulary).

My mother married Bruce shortly after my high school graduation. Bruce was tall, maybe six-three, very thin, with thick salt and pepper hair that he brushed back. He rarely spoke, but when he did it was heartfelt and intelligent. There was something very gentle about him.

Bruce and my Mother had decided to move to Indianapolis to be closer to us. Although Bruce had been a member of the family for nearly twenty-five years, I had never lived in the same part of the country as he and my mother, so our relations were limited. They bought an adorable cottage in Beech Grove. Bruce was redoing the bathrooms to my mother's specifications. When they were finished, she would move in.

Bruce immediately took an interest in the Baby Wise case, which surprised me. He had watched the news and read a great deal, yet I had never really shared my work with him. But Bruce was a good listener and talking to him helped me organize my thinking.

It was now time to telephone Van Buskirk. It had been about a week since our first meeting and I was sure that she was fuming that I had not gotten in touch with her. But I'd been doing my homework and she needed to know that I planned to be in charge. The telephone rang.

"Van Buskirk, homicide," she answered.

"Let's discuss the Wise case," I said.

"About time," she said.

She agreed to meet me in my office. I asked her to bring her entire file.

"I'll be right down. Clear your desk."

To clear my desk was a challenge. My entire office consisted of a door, a metal desk with faux wood veneer on top and three drawers on the left side. The desk was pushed up against the window wall. I had a metal chair for me, one metal client chair and a file cabinet near the doorway. The remaining space could accommodate one very lean person standing and no more. The desk supported a large computer screen, the top of which held photographs of Steve and my girls, and two white legal pads, plus several accordion folders filled to the brim. There was also the skimpy manila folder labeled "Wise, William" that I had received from Poindexter.

I heard a knock at the door, which I always kept closed. I do not like surprises. I need quiet to work and that is hard to come by in the crowded Prosecutor's Office. When I opened the door there was Van Buskirk and a flat-bed cart loaded with two or three banker's boxes of files. She lugged them into my office.

Van Buskirk glided like a dancer on long, graceful legs. She was slender, with incredibly long eye lashes, a pretty face, and a manner that was almost elegant, although tempered a little by her amazing ability to swear and curse and cuss with greater intensity, vision, and precision than any person that I had ever met. She dropped into the client chair. She was quiet as I looked into the boxes.

I scanned the contents; I smiled when I saw that Van Buskirk had ordered the 911 tapes from MECA, the Metropolitan Emergency Communications Agency.

MECA is housed in its own building in a run down and poor section of Indianapolis. It is fenced and gated, although the gate is rarely closed. The interior of the building contains various sections, but the dispatch area is separate and each dispatcher has his own cubicle. The cubes are located in a circular formation with the open end of the cubicle accessible to all of the other cubicles. The dispatchers have a screen, computer keyboard, headphone, and multiple incoming call lines.

Every call in and out of MECA is recorded. The computerized equipment also shows all calls received by the center where there is no contact with the caller, so if a 911 call is placed and no one speaks, the fact that a call is made is recorded and a follow-up call or dispatch will be made.

With this configuration, one dispatcher can listen to the caller while also sending fire engines and emergency responders to the scene.

Few people knew that MECA tape recordings were only kept for thirty days and then they were recorded over. If a detective failed to order the recordings from a particular incident promptly, the recordings were forever lost. While the time stamped printouts remained part of the permanent record, to hear the caller's voice was often important evidence, especially where, as in this case, the suspect made the call himself. Many arsonists call 911 to report the fires that they set.

Sometimes these recordings are hard to understand because there are sirens and other background sounds like shouting, whimpering, coughing, sobbing or other noise reflective of the emotional impact of a witness's observations. Because the large majority of calls are not related to a crime, the tape recordings are not maintained for long. Only knowledgeable investigators order the tape recordings preserved or order transcripts made from the recordings. There is no automatic system to obtain transcripts and they are only ordered when approved by higher ups, because of the cost.

For me, just finding the MECA request was a major point in Van Buskirk's favor. Maybe this detective knew what she was doing.

I noticed that no tapes of the 911 calls were in the file and no transcripts of the calls either. I wanted to hear what the voice of William Wise sounded like on the morning he killed his son.

I wanted to hear what Michelle Wise sounded like when she called to report the fire, yet failed to mention that her child was still inside the burning house.

"Okay," I said, "tell me everything and start at the beginning."

Naturally, Van Buskirk did not do as I asked. She instead started by saying (and I will not directly quote Van Buskirk lest I wear out the f and the u and the k on my keyboard) that William Wise had been "out on bond" for more than a year.

"*What!?*"

I was astounded. Murder is a capital offense in the state of Indiana, as it is in most jurisdictions. Bond is rarely granted for accused murderers and, if bond is permitted, the accused must post a cash bond for the entire amount of the bond or pay a bondsman a fee for the bondsman to post the high dollar bond amount. Even where a high dollar bond is set, the court is likely to place conditions on the release, such as home detention, an ankle monitor, pretrial services reporting, and other means of the state keeping an eye on the accused. Most accused murderers remain in jail until trial.

"Brian Poindexter, representing your office, agreed to Wise being released on like a ten-thousand fucking dollar bond," Van Buskirk said disgustedly.

I suffer from red face and neck syndrome, meaning that as my temper rises so does the flushed scarlet color from my chest up. I usually wear high collared blouses to cover this tell but that day my consternation was obvious. I could see that she was pleased that I had reacted so strongly and negatively to Wise's release status. She had obviously wanted to see my reaction, too.

Well, nothing now could be done about his being released. William Wise had apparently been walking free for nearly two years. No judge was going to lock him up just because the case was now assigned to me.

"So what do we know about William Wise?" I asked. "What has he been doing since he made bond?"

"What do you mean?" she asked.

"Look," I said, "Guys don't kill their kids for no reason, even sickos have some imagined reason for the killing, so I want to know everything about this guy including what he and the missus have been doing since he was released on the murder charges. Everything."

"On it," she said. I again asked her to tell me what she knew in chronological order.

"Detective, do you know what I mean by chronological order?" I asked.

Van Buskirk shot me what would become her trademark glare and then she began to tell me what she knew from the beginning. She consulted a reporter's notebook that she apparently kept for every investigation. She had more than one notebook for the Wise case. I sat back to take it all in.

My phone kept ringing but I barely heard it. I was intent on listening to what Van Buskirk was telling me. Once or twice my door opened, but I signaled that I was busy.

John Commons opened the door. "I expect you to answer your phone," he said. He nodded at Van Buskirk and she nodded to him. I told him that I was busy and would get back to him later.

So I learned for the first time that William Wise had no life insurance on his son (an obvious motive that didn't exist) and that he had little to gain from the loss of his house since he and Michelle had just purchased it a few months before the fire. The house was mortgaged and the insurance company, Allstate, had conducted a full investigation.

Unlike Lepper, the investigators for Allstate had ruled out all accidental causes for the fire immediately and therefore had called the fire arson. Allstate had been so thorough in their investigation that they had interviewed William and Michelle Wise, looked at the room and the debris, and had built a model of Baby Matthew's room and done a test burn.

"*No!* Oh my God," I blurted. I was astounded.

A test burn is extremely costly and this house was insured for a small amount, less than sixty-thousand dollars, most of which was owed to the bank and would have to be repaid whether the fire was arson or accidental. A test burn required building the room to scale, filling it with a similar burn load, meaning the same type of things as were in the actual room, having engineers or fire investigators determine whether it was similar and then perhaps videotaping before, during, and after the fire. Most insurance companies would not spend the money, but apparently Allstate did in this case. I had never seen a mock-up before. This was amazing.

"Well, what was the result?" I asked.

"Apparently the whole thing was video tape recorded, but I don't have all the tapes. I have one, but I didn't get the rest because the case was being dismissed. As far as I know the room has been stored at Barker & Herbert laboratories near Ft. Wayne. They concluded that the fire was not an accident. *Duh.*"

I had never before heard of an insurance company spending tens of thousands of dollars to build a replica room and to conduct a video tape recorded test burn. The fact that Allstate had also paid to store the room for two years was even less believable. Ft. Wayne was about a two and a half hour drive from Indianapolis. I added a visit to Barker & Herbert to my to-do list.

Although I had never seen the test burn room, I knew that after sixteen minutes of burning, even under the hottest of conditions, most of the furnishings would still be standing after the fire. It would look completely different than did Baby Wise's nursery. A jury could use their own eyes to see how a fire would have actually burned in Baby Wise's nursery. They would be able to see what the firemen saw.

"Now, if only they did it right and I can use the test burn room as evidence," I thought to myself.

Some evidence that police find or that is available, like this burn room, can almost never be used at trial because of protections in our Constitution.

For example, the jury would never know that William Wise was the prime suspect in three homicides, or that Michelle was his alibi. That is because it would be too prejudicial and he was not the proven murderer in that case. This is a Constitutional protection.

Exclusion might also occur if the burn room was not similar enough to the actual room, or, if the testimony of the guys at Barker & Herbert laboratory was not proven scientific evidence, Wise's lawyers could have it excluded from the trial.

Also, if the information that was used to build the test room had been illegally obtained (such as without a search warrant or given involuntarily by Wise or his wife) then it could be excluded.

There were lots of ifs, but all of what Van Buskirk had to say suggested a thorough and intensive investigation. That's what I needed. It was my job to put the evidence in front of the jury in an interesting, comprehensible, and persuasive manner. It was also my job to know what was admissible and to get what was into evidence.

One of my mottos was, "The one who knows the rules of evidence best, wins." There are many ways to get a particular item of evidence admitted at trial and a good lawyer must prepare for objections and have a strategy to get important items properly presented before the jury.

Van Buskirk gave me the name Jerry Shulte and said that he was the investigator or adjustor for the insurance company. She supplied his telephone number. I dialed it.

"Mr. Shulte, my name is Diane Marger Moore. I am the chief arson prosecutor for Marion County, Indiana," I began.

Shulte told me that Allstate knew that the fire was intentionally set. They also knew that they would have to pay off the mortgage and that there was little to gain financially in investigating the claim.

"But someone killed that baby and I just couldn't let it go," Shulte explained. With his company's approval, Shulte had retained a well-respected laboratory to scientifically determine formally the cause and origin of the fire.

"After speaking to Wise, I knew that he killed that child," Shulte continued. "As a father myself, I just couldn't let it go. His wife was pathetic. She let him kill their son.

"So I asked Allstate to build the test room, hire Barker & Herbert and conduct a test burn to prove it. At the same time, I told them they would have to pay the mortgage company for the loss."

"Wow!" I thought gratefully. This Shulte was some kind of do-right guy.

Shulte and I talked a while longer. He gave me the names of two Barker & Herbert employees: Steve Shands, the fire cause and origin expert, and Jim Finneran, an electrical engineer.

"Will you call them and authorize them to share their investigation with me—everything including the burn room?" I asked.

"I'm very glad that you asked. You are the reason that we have paid to store the burn room for all of these months. I'm really pleased to learn that the investigation is moving again. I felt certain that Detective Van Buskirk would keep pushing for a prosecution."

"She's sitting right here, Mr. Shulte. I'll give her your regards."

Jerry Shulte agreed to contact Barker & Herbert. He also assured me of full cooperation.

Before I hung up the phone, Jerry Shulte asked, "You've heard about the lawsuit haven't you?"

"I'm just getting up to speed, Jerry. Why don't you tell me about it?" I glanced at Van Buskirk who shrugged.

"Yep, Bill and Michelle are suing Fisher Price and Wal-Mart. They claim that the baby monitor caught the room on fire and killed Matthew. Wise is asking for millions of dollars. He just filed the lawsuit in the United States District Court, in Indianapolis, a few days ago."

Van Buskirk and I both looked amazed at each other. Suddenly there was motive.

I thanked Shulte profusely for the information and all that he had done to seek justice for Matthew. He gave me the case number of the federal lawsuit, the lawyer's name who was representing Fisher Price and his promise to call Barker & Herbert as soon as possible to let them know I would be calling.

Van Buskirk and I discussed the timing of the federal lawsuit. It was no surprise that William Wise was trying to get millions of dollars for Matthew's death. Obviously he waited until Poindexter had agreed to dismiss the case.

There is a two-year statute of limitations for product liability cases in Indiana. This means that if you believe that a product of some kind injured you or someone in your family, you must file a complaint before the last day of the second year after you learn about the injury or death.

William Wise had no choice; he had to file his lawsuit before the end of the second year after Matthew's death or he would never be able to file. He had to have known that Poindexter intended to dismiss the case and probably thought that no one at the Prosecutor's Office would find out about the lawsuit.

He was almost right.

I decided then and there that I would not agree to dismiss the case, at least not until I knew a whole lot more about the facts.

I told Van Buskirk as much. I also sent a message to Cale Bradford and Brian Poindexter. My decision was made. The case would not be dismissed for now. Finally, I warned detective Van Buskirk that there was a great deal of work to be done on the case.

"If I try this case, then I intend to put William Wise in prison, for a very long time."

"Allfuckinright," was all she said.

She was almost smiling.

It was late. We were evidently alone in the office and Van Buskirk offered to ride down to the basement parking lot with me. It was always pretty creepy going down there alone after all of the other cars had vacated their assigned spots.

I had, once again, lost track of time. I hoped that the girls were not asleep, but I knew that they had been in bed for hours. It was after midnight and I had a hearing at eight-thirty a.m. the next morning. But there was no way that I would let this detective escort me to my car.

"Thanks, Detective. I'm fine."

Everyone was sleeping when I arrived home safely a little bit late, again. As I tried to fall asleep, I mulled all the things that I wanted to do and all that I didn't know I didn't know and needed to learn.

# Chapter Four

I DECIDED THAT I needed to see the house where it happened. I wanted to see the test room at Barker & Herbert. I wanted to see Wise and Michelle, in person. I wanted to learn everything that was collected up to the moment. And I wanted it all yesterday or sooner.

I decided that I should start by reviewing all of the documents and materials that Van Buskirk had hauled into my office.

There were photographs, fire investigation reports, police reports, statements that William Wise had given to investigators and to Allstate and to the first reporting officers.

Apparently, Wise never heard of the Fifth Amendment—or the best legal advice that a suspect can receive from his lawyer: "Keep your mouth shut." He had been talking to everyone and giving sworn and unsworn statements willy-nilly.

Although William Wise was called Bill by people with whom he interacted, I just couldn't force myself to use a nickname for the man. When he wasn't Sharkeyes, he was William Wise to me, and he would continue to be that. I taped a small copy of the "Where's Waldo?" photograph on my window. I found the only baby photo of Matthew in one of the Van Buskirk boxes; I taped it on the window next to the other photograph.

I searched through the boxes and collected the written statements that Wise had given. I placed them in chronological order. I wanted to find out what Wise claimed happened that morning. The math was clear: Only three people knew the truth. One couldn't tell us anything since he was dead. The other two were Michelle and William Wise.

Although I knew that he had probably spoken to law enforcement officers at the scene, and to someone at the hospital, no formal statements were taken from Wise until about two weeks after the fire. The police probably waited until after Matthew's funeral to take Sharkeyes' statement.

There's a delicate balance to be maintained when the parent of a dead child is a suspect. Police officers are trained to try to show respect for a parent and a family's loss while still keeping the investigation fresh. It creates needlessly bad publicity to interrogate the parents while their child is in the morgue, especially if it's later determined that they had nothing to do with the death.

During our meeting in my office, Van Buskirk described the small starter home where the Wise family lived before the fire. The house was a split foyer.

You enter the house through a front door and as you come in there is a small platform, or landing, that forms a space that may be called a foyer. There is a wooden staircase of six steps that lead up to the living room and bedrooms and six steps that lead down from the landing to a semi-below ground level where Wise and his wife's master bedroom was.

There is only space on the landing for two or three people to stand comfortably together and there is a panel for the fire alarm and a light switch on the left wall as you enter. There is a light fixture hanging from the upstairs ceiling that illuminates the upper stairway.

On the upper level of the house is the living area, with a galley kitchen, dining room, and living room all to the right of the stairs as you come up from the front door. On the left of the stairs is a very short hallway containing what Van Buskirk said were the smallest bedrooms she had ever seen.

Two of the bedrooms were on the left side of the hallway. On the right hand side of the hallway was a bathroom and the remaining bedroom. Matthew's bedroom was the first door on the left. There was a window in it that looked out on the front yard and street. The nursery was the closest room to the stairway and the living room.

Downstairs is a basement level. There is some living space on the right of the stairway and to the left of the stairway is the utility closet with the heating unit, water heater, utility connections, and washer/dryer. To the far side of the basement is a makeshift master bedroom apparently used by William and Michelle.

I looked at the first statement given by William Wise. The statement was not taken by homicide detectives but by Hubert Rethmeier and David Lepper of the fire investigation unit (arson squad). Note to self: Why didn't Van Buskirk take the statement? Was she watching it?

Hubert Rethmeier was about forty years old at the time, baby faced, roly-poly, tired, and seemingly not too bright. Rethmeier had a great deal of experience, I knew, and I had not worked any cases with him. Maybe looks were deceiving. He and Lepper were a team. Although a voluntary (not in-custody) form was used for the statement, I noticed that Wise had not signed the statement after it was typed up from what I assumed was a tape recording. Hmmm . . . would it be admissible?

Wise was asked his date of birth, (May 1, 1965), where he worked and what he did for a living. Wise said that he worked from noon to midnight as an Indianapolis Fire Department dispatcher. The night before the fire he got off work at midnight. By 5:16 a.m. the next morning his son was dead. This was important because that meant that we could focus on a five hour and sixteen minute window of time—from midnight to 5:16 a.m., when the fire was extinguished and Matthew's charred remains discovered. I hoped that we could narrow it down even more because five hours can be a very long time.

Wise claimed that when he got off at midnight he spent some time speaking with someone in the break room and then drove home. Darn! Rethmeier didn't ask Wise for the name of the someone. I hoped he would get back to it.

Sometimes questions are asked in a disorganized manner on purpose to throw the witness off or to keep going back over the same information to see if the responses change. Or, sometimes, the questioner just forgets to ask. The last person who spoke with Wise on the night before the fire might prove to be a key witness. He or she could give us some insight into Wise's mood, appearance and anything else unusual about his behavior that evening. Did Wise plan to kill the child or was it a spur of the moment decision?

Wise said that when he got home, his wife Michelle was on the upstairs couch with Matthew. He and Michelle talked for about a half hour and then he put Matthew in his crib. The crib was in the nursery on the upstairs level of their home, just a few steps down the hall from the living room couch. Wise recalled that he put Matthew in his nursery at about one to one-thirty a.m. He covered Matthew in blankets before leaving the nursery to return to the couch.

According to Wise, within a half hour or so, Matthew woke up again. He and Michelle had already gone downstairs to their bedroom and taken the receiver part of the monitor with them. He said he and his wife both knew that the baby was awake because they heard him cry over the baby monitor which was on the nightstand near their bed downstairs. Wise said the transmitter was in the nursery under the crib.

Why under the crib?

Why would anyone put the baby monitor under the crib? The monitor was intended to pick up sound and movement of the child. Under the crib those sounds would be muted by the mattress, and besides, why was he so specific in describing its location? All Rethmeier asked him, after Wise said that the receiver was in the downstairs bedroom, was if there was another part to the baby monitor. Unbelievably it seemed that Skip Rethmeier did not know what a baby monitor was or how it worked. Really? Was this just an act to get Wise to talk about it? I really wasn't sure.

I made copies of the statements so that I could write notes on my copy. Wise said that the baby monitor transmitter was plugged into the nursery wall and that there were no batteries in the transmitter or the receiver.

When the baby began to cry, William said that he fetched him from his crib and brought him to the living room couch. Michelle was breast feeding Matthew but this time Wise gave him a bottle and Michelle expressed milk for another bottle to leave in the fridge. Wise said that it took until about three o'clock in the morning to finish feeding the baby. Wise didn't recall if he changed Matthew's diaper, but it took the infant about fifteen minutes to fall asleep. After Matthew fell asleep, Wise said he put the infant in his crib.

Wise did not recall whether he or Michelle brought the monitor receiver upstairs, but it was plugged into the outlet near the couch. Wise told investigators that he wanted Michelle to be able to get some rest, since she had returned to work; so he told her to go back downstairs to sleep in their bed while he remained upstairs on the couch with Baby Matthew.

I thought to myself, "But it was a Friday night. Michelle only worked week days and would be off the next day, Saturday. Wise, on the other hand, was scheduled to work the next day."

Now to the crucial time frame, I thought. Although the format of the statement was question and answer, Wise was clearly telling his story in his own way. Many questions were something like, "So what happened next?"

Wise said that he woke up at about five a.m. and went down the hall to the bathroom. He looked at his watch and was certain of the time. Wise walked from the couch, down the hallway on the same level, past the nursery to the bathroom which was to his right across from the nursery. Wise remembered that the bathroom light was on when he left the bathroom and he looked in on Matthew in his crib as he returned to the living room couch.

Perfect, I thought. Wise now had to explain what occurred in the last sixteen minutes of Matthew's life. There were only sixteen minutes or less between Wise's bathroom excursion and the death of Baby Matthew.

Wise said that there was no smoke or fire in the nursery when he looked in on his way back to the couch, but he did not go all the way into the child's bedroom. Wise confirmed that Matthew's bedroom door was always kept open. So no fire at 5:01 a.m. or 5:02 a.m., assuming that Wise was actually quick about it. He said that it only took him a couple of minutes to use the bathroom and return to the living room.

Wise then volunteered, "I was about asleep and then Michelle had come upstairs to make sure that I was, or to make sure that Matthew had been put back to bed."

When asked if Michelle checked on Matthew, Wise equivocated. "Not that I know of."

Sneaky bastard. Subtly imply that Michelle could have done it. Wise claimed that Michelle asked him if he needed anything and put an Afghan over him because it was cold.

He claimed that Michelle sat on the couch for another five to ten minutes when their smoke alarm went off . . . well, not actually a smoke alarm but an audible alarm on the wall. "Could have been the burglar alarm which had gone off before," Wise offered.

Apparently both William and Michelle got off of the couch and walked down the stairs to the landing to check the alarm panel. All of the signals were illuminated and blinking. William stayed put at the alarm panel while Michelle went to the panel in the downstairs bedroom to try to turn it off. Wise just stood there waiting for her to return. Neither one of them checked on Baby Matthew.

When Michelle came back up to the foyer level they remained at the landing.

William Wise said that it was only then that they input the numeric alarm code that he had memorized. (You hadn't been doing that?) The alarm kept sounding.

I tried not to imagine Baby Matthew, shrieking and terrified by the loud noise, alone in his nursery. When Michelle returned to the landing, Wise, also, apparently for the first time, turned on the light that hung from the upstairs and saw smoke near the ceiling. He claimed that the dark cloud hung down three to four feet from the upper level.

"So. . ." I say to myself. Yes, I do talk to myself, a lot. I practice closing arguments in the shower, organize my cross examinations in my head while getting dressed and gesticulate while driving. I assume that passersby are either amused or terrified.

In this instance I say to myself, "Are you kidding me? This horrible siren is going off—and neither one of you goes to get the baby? Really, a convention at the alarm panel? Freaking unbelievable—not human. Two parents, one eight-week old infant, in a very small house and no one makes any attempt to save the baby?"

The transcript continued. Wise explained that after Michelle returned to the landing, he went upstairs to the living room. He turned right at the top of the stairs toward the living room instead of going left to Baby Matthew's room. He grabbed the portable telephone that he had left on the table and returned with it to the foyer level. By then the smoke was thick at his height, which he described at five foot eight inches.

I can imagine that both investigators wanted to shout, "Why'd you get the phone instead of your kid, [expletive]!?" Instead, Skip asked Wise if, when he was upstairs, he was able to see down the hall to the nursery. "I don't think I looked" was Wise's reply. Wise did not see any fire either.

Apparently Wise and Michelle were still standing at the landing. William claimed he tried to call 911 but did not get a dial tone. He tried a couple of times and then he sent Michelle across the street to call for help.

Before she left the house, Michelle went downstairs to look for her shoes and a coat and then left for a neighbor's house across the street. Michelle never returned to their house until the fire was out.

After Michelle left the house, Wise claimed that he first went back upstairs, got down on the floor and "followed the baseboard to see if I could get back to the room to the baby."

By then, Wise claimed, the smoke was so thick that he couldn't see. Despite the intense smoke and heat, Wise claimed that he got to the bedroom and could feel the heat coming out of the baby's room. He could not see any flames and he retreated back down the stairs and then went upstairs again. On his second try he got into Matthew's nursery, about two feet into the room, where the dresser is, when the window broke. He saw flames when the window broke, but it had been very dark before then even though the bathroom light was still illuminating the hallway. He said that his hair and mustache were singed when he entered the burning room the second time.

Wise said he saw flames between the changing table and the south wall and pointed to a drawing that he had been making during the interview. He said he saw flames on the east wall. He also saw flames, in his exact words, "underneath the crib, going underneath the bottom of the mattress, that's what I'm trying to say. Ah, under the mattress and up the back side of the wall of the south wall and out from underneath the foot of the bed and out the window."

He drew a sketch of the room.

Wise claimed he then backed out of the room, went downstairs, looked for Michelle and, not seeing her, found a neighbor's light on and went to the house. He knocked and was eventually admitted to the house where he called 911.

Wise said that after making the call, he returned to his house where a nondescript black man was trying to kick out the windows in the lower level of the house. Wise went into the house and grabbed "an old fire jacket that I had hanging on the wall and the helmet that ended up being a friend of mine's that didn't fit me. I put those on" and then he told the man to follow him.

According to Wise, he made another attempt to go upstairs but it was too hot and they retreated. Wise said that he and the black man had gotten as far as the nursery door and there were flames coming out so he threw a three legged stool through the bedroom window.

No way! There are three things that every fire needs: fuel, heat, and oxygen. This is called the fire triangle and pretty much everyone from elementary school on is taught about the triangle. Every firefighter, from the most basic training to the most sophisticated, knows that without all three of these elements a fire will exhaust itself. No one with any fire training would try to break out windows allowing more oxygen to get into a burning room.

Rethmeier knew this and asked Wise why he threw the stool. Wise said he hoped to clear the window so that when he reached the baby he could throw him out the window.

My neck was a deep shade of magenta by now and getting redder. Wise said that the mysterious black man left and that at the bottom of the stairs at the front door Wise met an Indianapolis Police Department officer, in uniform.

Wise told the policeman, "I'm with IFD, there's a baby upstairs."

No mention of Matthew. Using the officer's mag light flash light, Wise and the IPD officer went up the stairs. Wise claimed that he got to the room and was able to see "where the fire was and what was happening in the room."

He said he saw the crib and changing table engulfed in flames. He claimed that right after seeing into the room he "met someone from IFD," a firefighter.

Wise told the firefighter where "he was at and what room it was and what side" before going outside where he put snow on his hands, neck and face.

Lepper asked some more questions to try to pin Wise down to the time frame of the fire. That's also when he started asking Wise about the MECA radio that Lepper had found hidden in Wise's downstairs bedroom. (Wise had a radio? A MECA radio is the bulky, black, rectangular equipment with a small rubber antenna that police and fire personnel use to communicate. It's generally referred to as a police radio. It's the same one as I carried 24/7. Why would a dispatcher have a radio at home? Van Buskirk had not told me about the radio.)

That radio could have been used in a fire emergency to summon a fire truck to the Wise home in less than three minutes. But it was not used to contact the police, or fire department. Was Wise afraid that he would get in trouble for having it at home that morning? He freely admitted that he showed it to Michelle and that they listened to various channels, although he did not have permission to have the radio at home.

He did not say whether he kept the radio frequently or if it was a first time. He gave no excuse. Note to self: What channel was the radio on when Lepper found it?

Lepper asked Wise the obvious questions. No finesse, but then—nothing wrong with being direct, I guess. "How do you think the fire started, Bill?"

Wise replied, "Possibly in the monitor."

*Whoa! The guy thinks the fire started in a baby monitor. Where'd he get that idea? Why?*

Lepper also asked about the front door. None of this stuff was in Lepper's report so I paid close attention.

Apparently either Wise or Michelle left the front door open during the fire. More oxygen for the fire—a bigger, hotter fire with more oxygen. Wise said he thought Michelle opened the front door when she went to call 911, but he did not explain why it remained open from the time she left the house to whenever Lepper or someone else observed it in that position.

Lepper asked Wise if he had been back to their house since the fire and Wise indicated that both he and Michelle had. Lepper asked him if, in looking at Matthew's room, Wise had an opinion as to where the fire started. "I want to say around the electrical plug" on the east wall.

"He's determined to blame it on a baby monitor," I mumbled. (Okay, I have to admit that I used a Fisher Price baby monitor when each of my daughters were infants and into their first years of life. I really didn't remember if it was a single monitor that we used for both girls or if they were different ones, but they were incredibly precise and captured even the slightest sound or movement.) Maybe I just didn't want to believe that a baby monitor, especially the one that I had entrusted to my children's care, caused the fire. Maybe.

# Chapter Five

ON THE DAY that Wise was first questioned, Michelle was also asked to give a statement. Normal procedure requires that all witnesses be questioned separately so that their recollection is not tainted by hearing the other witness's account.

Michelle's statement was similar to her husband's in almost every detail. I scanned her statement for even the most minor differences. If the statements were identical then, in my mind, it meant that they had discussed, planned and maybe even memorized their stories.

On the other hand, if their statements were not exactly the same, the differences might lead us to additional evidence and set the stage to separate and conquer. I hoped that the statement would flesh out some of the many questions that I had after reading Wise's statement. I had hoped that Michelle would give us more information that might point to motive. What about the baby monitor? I found some discrepancies and focused on them.

But I was playing catch-up. It was two long years after the fire. If I had been involved from the beginning, right when the fire happened and Baby Matthew was killed, I could have asked questions, watched the interviews, and directed the investigation. I was pretty sure that Voyles would never let me speak to William Wise now. I mean, he could allow it, but I sincerely doubted that he would.

Even if I couldn't interview Wise, Voyles might decide to put Wise on the stand during the trial. But Voyles was very unlikely to do that. Way too risky. Usually the jury really wants to hear from the defendant and almost every time that the defendant testifies he helps convict himself. No, it was not going to happen. The time for me to get to question William Wise face-to-face was long past.

We could try to speak with Michelle, but she was solidly supporting her husband. Technically, Michelle and Matthew were the victims of William Wise's crimes, but Michelle was opposed to the prosecution. The entire Davis family (Michelle's maiden name), at least the ones we knew, were also backing Wise. So was the Wise family, but that was more predictable. Didn't the Davis family want to send Matthew's murderer to prison? Apparently not. Who was going to fight for Baby Matthew? We had as much information as we were going to get from Michelle and William Wise. I needed to read, reread and really understand those statements.

Fortunately, William Wise had wanted to talk about the fire. Not about Matthew. He never talked about Matthew in any of the interviews unless very specifically asked and then it was as abbreviated a response as possible. Neither did Michelle.

I read the other statement that Wise gave to law enforcement. No great discoveries there.

The most in-depth statements had been taken by Allstate Insurance. Because Michelle and William Wise made a claim on their insurance policy, Allstate hired an excellent defense attorney to take what is called their sworn statement in proof of loss. There was a transcript of the detailed interview in the file. All together Wise had given a statement to Lepper and Rethmeier, an informal statement to Allstate, and a sworn statement in proof of loss. Michelle had provided statements each of these times as well.

Allstate also hired, either on the day of the fire or shortly thereafter, experts to inspect the house and assist investigators. These experts probably worked with the defense lawyer to formulate some of the questions that Wise was asked at his statement in proof of loss.

Allstate's experts, employed by Barker & Herbert Analytical Laboratories, sent Steve Shand to examine at the house. His job was to figure out where and how the fire had happened. They call this a cause and origin expert. In essence, Shand's job was the same as Lepper's had been. Because Wise wanted the insurance company to pay off his mortgage and possibly pay him for his losses, he was obligated to let Allstate investigate the fire. That meant that Wise had to allow investigators into the house, to take samples and to ask him and Michelle questions.

The Indianapolis police and fire departments had no right to inspect the house or to compel William and Michelle to respond to questions. While the fire was burning and being extinguished firefighters were allowed inside the residence. Their investigation could be conducted without violating anyone's rights; but once Lepper completed his initial investigation—sifting through debris, taking photographs, washing, and documenting the floor—he was not allowed back onto the property without a warrant. That was one of the reasons that Lepper had attempted to be so thorough.

Allstate had no such constraints. Shand came to the Wise home with Jerry Shulte, the Allstate claims adjustor, Jim Finneran, an electrical engineer and Det. Van Buskirk. William Wise and Michelle allowed them into the house and they did another methodical inspection.

"So, what's the problem?" I wondered.

I checked my watch and I was late for court. None of my arson cases were on the docket, but several cases on my regular felony case load—the ones that John Commons supervised—were on the calendar. I had to hurry. I'd have to read the statement in proof of loss later. I skipped ahead to Shand's final report to Allstate.

Jim Finneran, an electrical engineer ruled out all of the possible electrical causes at the house. Check.

Finneran did not find a baby monitor transmitter and so he could not rule that out. Not great. Shand looked at the room and the rest of the house, remnants on the lawn that had been thrown down by the fire investigators. He reviewed Lepper's report and documentation. Shand concluded that the fire had been accelerated. Good. So what's the problem? Then I saw it.

Shand described what he called burn patterns in a much wider area of the floor than Lepper did. Even worse, Shand opined that because of the shape, depth, and pattern of the burns, a hydrocarbon was used as an accelerant. Uh oh. From the police and fire reports that I had read, firefighters did not smell these accelerants when they entered the room after removing their breathing equipment. No one found any unusual hydrocarbons in the carpeting or anywhere else in the room and no container for gas or kerosene was located in the house. Hydrocarbons include gasoline, butane, kerosene—the usual fire starters' friends. Problem is that Lepper, who also rendered his opinion that the fire was accelerated, ruled out hydrocarbons, saying the burn patterns were not consistent with a hydrocarbon accelerant.

Lepper had smelled alcohol in the carpet as he was clearing the nursery. Lepper had taken a sample of that area of the carpet and stored it in a clean paint can. These cans are used because they tend to keep liquids and gases in place and, if the lid is sealed tightly, the gases do not dissipate as quickly. These samples remain sealed until they can be tested.

While arson cases do not always have a high priority, and therefore their samples have to wait in a long line to be tested, there was an infant killed in this fire. I suspected that the sample was tested as soon as there was available time at the lab.

The Marion County Crime Lab was awesome. Many people don't know that most cities, even large populous ones, do not have their own laboratory where samples can be tested. Some cities or counties rely on private labs (frequently expensive and a nightmare because of a lack of proper chain of custody documentation) or on the State or FBI crime labs which can take years to test a sample.

But Marion County, Indianapolis had a top notch lab with the equipment necessary to test debris for chemicals. I had the pleasure of relying on them in several cases and their lab technicians and scientists made excellent witnesses. The lab used the same equipment, gas chromatography-mass spectrometry, to test samples from fires as they did to detect drugs or alcohol in blood or urine. This equipment is very sensitive and if used correctly, gives reliable results. The equipment was well respected and the resulting readings were admissible in court.

I knew that Lepper had submitted one or more carpet samples to the lab, but I did not have the results. Did the lab find anything? If it did, would it support one of the experts? If the lab found nothing, then what would the jury think? More importantly, which of them was correct? Was either one of them right?

"Yes, ladies and gentlemen," I fake rehearsed, "well respected cause and origin expert Steven Shand says that William Wise poured gasoline on the floor. On the other hand, firefighter and Investigator David Lepper says that it could not have been gasoline and that it was alcohol that Wise poured on the floor. Oh, and the crime lab did not find alcohol, gasoline or anything else unusual." Not good at all. I chewed an imaginary hangnail. Can you spell "reasonable doubt"?

I picked up the phone and called Van Buskirk.

"Do you have the crime lab reports on the samples that Lepper submitted?"

I heard her shuffling through her file boxes. Apparently Van Buskirk had copied her files for me but kept the originals for herself—that was policy. She was responsible for the investigation. I should have realized that. I was sorry that I had wasted minutes making copies of the statements—no time to worry about that now. I was beginning to see some serious flaws in the case.

Minutes went by. As I waited I was able to hear Van Buskirk as she searched her files. I learned some new blue vocabulary words. Finally she came back on the line and said that she did not have the [expletive] reports. She couldn't recall if she had gotten them in inter-department mail or even whether she had followed up with the lab. It was kind of all suspended after Poindexter told her about the conflicting accelerant theories from Shand and Lepper. He had concluded, he said, that the case could not be successfully prosecuted.

I was worried. Since Detective Van Buskirk had already checked her files and the computerized documentation that she had stored on the case, I wondered if the lab had ever tested the samples. It had been two years. Thousands of samples were submitted to the lab every year.

I didn't even know if I wanted the results. I would have to turn them over to Wise's lawyers. Did I want the report to indicate the presence of something?

Hydrocarbon or alcohol? But if Wise's lawyers knew that one or more samples were submitted to the lab and we didn't turn over the results they would claim Brady violations, prosecutorial misconduct, and all sorts of other unkind stuff. In other words, we were probably shish-kabobed one way or the other. Best to track down the lab results and turn them over to the Defense. (And to figure out what they really mean to the case.)

As I grabbed an armload of files to take to calendar call in Criminal Five, I wondered, does alcohol even burn? Okay, I know the answer to that, or do I?

I will never forget being at a fancy restaurant with my father and some of his friends as a small child. Dad took a glass of what looked like water and asked me if I had ever seen water burn? When I said no, he lit the contents of the glass. Flames pranced in the liquid. Unfortunately he also spilled a small amount of the fiery stuff and the flames danced up his arm. Dad grabbed a napkin and put the flames out. He explained that vodka and not water had been in the glass. Great trick, Dad, scared the bejesus out of me.

Anyway, that was vodka and this could be rubbing alcohol. Does rubbing alcohol actually burn? Besides, if Lepper was right and it was rubbing alcohol, the fire might have been an accident.

Rubbing alcohol is a common household product. If there was a bottle in Matthew's room at the time of the fire, and it burned, or somehow accelerated the fire, then there was no case because it could have been an accident. Dad's vodka was sounding pretty good about now.

Van Buskirk and I had agreed to meet a few days later to go to the evidence room to look at the stuff that she and Lepper had collected, then go to the crime lab to try to locate our results and for me to get a look at the Wise residence.

Van Buskirk was resistant to the idea of going to the house. It had been two years and the property had been repaired and sold. It was unlikely that the new owners knew that a child had perished in the fire that damaged the property. Van Buskirk did not want to have to tell the new owners about the tragedy.

"What if they have an infant?" she had implored.

"Look, Van Buskirk, they had to know about the fire. Or if they didn't know when they bought the place, surely the neighbors have told them about it by now. Just say that we are with the fire investigation unit and that we need to look at the house. I hope that it is in the same configuration as it was when Wise lived there."

She agreed to make an appointment to see the house. We would get together at the end of the week to work on our to-do list.

I rushed to get to court. Although I was loaded down with files, I took the stairs down one floor and then used the walkway over to the Criminal Five. I thought this would be quicker than taking the elevator.

"Glad you could grace us with your presence," was all that John Commons had to say. But the judge was not yet on the bench so I was "on time."

I didn't sit next to John but at the other end of the State's table with the pile of files in front of me. I had several armed robberies, a couple of attempted murders, and an assortment of other cases, most of which involved violence and weapons.

A calendar call (wryly referred to as a cattle call by some prosecutors) is a time when the court requires everyone involved in cases that may go to jury trial in the next month or two to show up at the same time. The prosecutor, defense lawyer and defendant for each case are expected to be present and to explain to the judge why the case hasn't been resolved either by a guilty plea or a dismissal.

The calendar call is really the time that the judge stares harshly into the eyes of the defendants and warns them what may happen if they go to jury trial. Then he similarly warns the prosecution that unless they offer a decent plea bargain to the defendant, they may lose the case. This pressure is actually pretty motivating. A lot of cases get resolved at calendar call.

After the judge does his thing, he gives everyone time to think and leaves the courtroom. Lawyers confer with their clients and prosecutors offer up the best deals they intend to offer. Those cases that are not resolved are given numbers and they will be tried based upon the priority of the number given to the case. I was grateful that all of my cases were newish and so the court continued them to another calendar. I needed the time to work on the Baby Wise case.

As I was packing up my files, a bailiff from Judge Barney's criminal court upstairs was waiting for me. I did not know him, although I knew most of the bailiffs in the major felony courts.

In Marion County, there were a large number of criminal courts. There was a traffic court that handled the minor driving offenses called ordinance violations. There was a drug court that handled all drug related offenses and had some treatment alternatives to incarceration. There were D felony courts. These were the most minor felony cases and included car theft, commercial burglaries and other lower level offenses. All of the more serious cases were in major felony courts and there were six of those courts. Murder, Rape, Arson, Armed Robbery, Kidnapping—these were the felonies tried in major felony court.

As the chief arson prosecutor I had cases in all of the courts, but I had never been in front of Judge Barney. Word was that he was capable, experienced and, would let you try your case. The bailiff said that the judge was waiting for me on the Wise case.

"You got to be kidding?" I said to myself. "I haven't yet even entered an appearance in the case so I didn't know that the case was set for hearing. Funny, Poindexter hadn't mentioned this hearing date."

When I entered the courtroom, it was empty except for Voyles and a small man that I assumed was William Wise, plus a couple of females in the audience area and a felony prosecutor assigned to judge Barney's court. The judge was on the bench. He did not look happy.

Judges can be as late as they please, but they do not expect to have to wait for lawyers, especially when said lawyers have an office in the building. Judge Barney was physically fit, older, white haired, and had an endearingly pleasant face. He wore a blue starched button-down shirt and dark tie beneath his black robe.

I took a seat next to the line deputy prosecutor. He whispered that a hearing was scheduled on the Wise case for that morning and that everyone had been waiting for me. I took a deep breath.

"Good morning your honor, Diane Marger Moore for the State. I apologize for the delay, I was at calendar call with Judge Miller . . ."

The judge motioned for me to stop talking. He looked at his court reporter to see if she was ready and called the case by stating the name of the defendant and the case number.

Jimmy Voyles stood up and announced that he was counsel for William Wise who was present in the courtroom. I looked carefully at Wise for the first time.

He was scrawny with thick hair that was dark and straight. He looked childlike next to Voyles, a far larger man. Wise did not look at me. There was absolutely no readable expression on his face. The room felt damp and cold.

I looked behind me. Two women were seated behind Wise.

As if in answer to my curiosity, Voyles told the judge, "Also present in the courtroom are Michelle Wise and Jeanne Wise, Mr. Wise's mother." I turned again to look at the two women.

Michelle was young, overweight and homely. Her hair was shapeless, and unflattering, hanging loose and stringy against her doughy complexion. She was large-boned, small eyed, and had such a slouched posture that it was obvious even while she was seated. She wore a shabby, wrinkled dress that was tight on her, the waist band stretched to its limits, with dark, cheap shoes—the whole outfit looked like it came from an old dime-store catalog.

Jeanne Wise, the mother, was older, petite, and nicely groomed and dressed. She had a sour expression and glared directly at me.

Jim Voyles did not introduce these women for my benefit. He was using their support to show the judge that Wise was "a good guy, with a loving wife and mother."

I turned back around in my seat. Judge Barney's voice was booming in the empty courtroom that was one of the largest in the building. He asked me if I was the new prosecutor handling the case. I said that I was but had not had a chance to enter an appearance. He asked me if I knew that the case was scheduled for trial in three weeks.

"I was unaware of the trial date your honor, but since I just got the case I cannot be ready in three weeks."

I glanced toward Voyles; he was enjoying this.

Voyles told the judge that he and his client had been told by a senior member of the Prosecutor's Office that the case would be dismissed today. Voyles feigned surprise that I was taking over the case, but then conceded that Brian Poindexter had contacted him days before to explain the situation.

The judge turned to me. "I also understood that the case was going to be dismissed by the State."

The judge then addressed the defense table.

"Mr. Voyles will you be ready to try this case in three weeks?"

I held my breath. There was no way I could have the case ready in that time. Voyles had me and he knew it. He hesitated. He looked at me and there was a glimmer in his eyes. Then he leaned down and whispered to Wise. A few moments passed as they discussed something.

"No, your honor, we will need about six months to prepare for trial. We expect that Mr. Wise will remain on bond during that time."

The judge had no intention of giving either side six months to prepare for a case that was already a year old.

It had taken Van Buskirk a year to collect enough evidence to convince the Prosecutor's Office to file charges against Wise. So although the fatal fire had happened two years before, the court case was only a little more than twelve months old.

The Supreme Court of Indiana maintains statistics on how many cases a judge tries every year, and the age of their cases. If a judge falls behind in his or her stats then the court publicizes the data which usually results in a newspaper article making thinly veiled characterizations of the judge as lazy or slow, or both.

This was considered an old case. Judges did not like to keep old cases on their docket. The judge gave us three months and set a firm trial date.

Judge Barney looked down at me. "I hope you know what you are doing, young lady."

I smiled and nodded. I thought, "Thanks, Judge, so do I."

His tone implied that he was fairly certain that I did not.

I waited for Wise and company to leave the courtroom. I took a deep breath. It was not my shining moment.

I walked back downstairs and across the hall to collect the files that I had left on the State's table. I rarely leave prosecution files on a desk, but because I rushed across the hall, I had forgotten to take them with me. I knew that the deputies assigned to our courtroom would make sure that the files were not touched. I was glad to find that the large, heavy, solid oak doors to the courtroom were still unlocked. Usually the courtroom was empty for the lunch hour and if the doors had been locked, I would have come back later in the afternoon. I hurried in, with my mind on Wise.

John Commons was in the courtroom leaning against the wall near the door. I really didn't think much about it because I had plenty of other things on my mind. I went and collected my files and headed back out the way I had come.

John cornered me near the door and closed in until my back was against the wall. He stood uncomfortably close to me with only my files hugged to my chest between us.

I thought I smelled alcohol on his breath. My neck was hot scarlet.

"How dare you think you know more than Brian Poindexter?" he snarled in his deep, fierce, Marine's voice. "Who the hell do you think you are? The Wise case should be dismissed!"

He was addressing my face. His narrowed eyes intended to bore into mine. I could see specks of yellow against his blue corneas and dilated pupils.

I looked sidewise to see if the deputies were in the courtroom. No one was in the cavernous room except for the two of us.

I stood as still as I could for a few beats. I lowered my eyes. I was already exhausted. I was sweating. I took a long, deep breath.

Then I burst out laughing.

This day was just too much for any sane person.

John looked astounded and then confused. He backed up a step.

"I'm sure that you've been laughed at before, John," was all I said, as I slipped around him and out the door.

# Chapter Six

I IMMEDIATELY CALLED Van Buskirk and told her about the new trial date.

"We have to get me up to speed. And fast. There's so much to learn and to digest," I complained.

She responded in her usual profane way. I gauged the positivity of her happily thrilled reaction based upon the extra length and creativity of the expanse of expletives she explicated.

When I hung up, I called the fire investigation squad and told the commander that we would need Lepper and Rethmeier for the trial. I also asked him to make arrangements for me to see all of the evidence that was stored in the evidence room. I remembered to ask if he had a copy of the lab results on the carpet samples. He told me that he had the report somewhere and that it had confirmed the presence of alcohol. I had no immediate reaction.

I wanted all of the available information and so I called a detective with whom I worked frequently and liked a great deal. Detective Will Wilson was not as experienced as some of the investigators in the unit but he really cared about doing the job right, and was not afraid to roll up his sleeves and work a case.

Will was pretty standoffish when we first met. He was one of those great looking black men that kept everything to himself. He was about six foot three, very broad shouldered, clean shaven and always had the faint smell of a man who had just gotten out of the shower. He did not talk much and was a serious listener. You could almost see his focus as he conversed with witnesses.

His street slang and our age difference (I am ten years older) created some comprehension issues.

Sometimes I had to ask him to speak English. He generally obliged.

We never listened to the radio, except for the police radios that both of us were obligated to carry. Det. Wilson once described his Detroit neighborhood growing up. "You either went to prison or to the military." He chose the Air Force and was still in the reserves.

His partner was a firefighter who could talk enough for both of them. Will was the kind of guy who saw everything and said nothing. I would go into the worst neighborhoods with him in the early morning hours and feel completely safe. When I asked Wilson to find a witness, he would scour the bars, street corners, any place and everywhere and sure enough, that witness, even a homeless man that I needed to testify in an arson case once, was present in court and on time, even if not well clothed for trial.

I called Will and asked if he was working that evening. He acknowledged that he and his partner, Larry Carter, were at the fire investigation offices and would be taking calls that night. I asked him to find a metal garbage pail and promised to drop by the squad after I left the office on my way home.

I finished reading more of the file and made arrangements to meet Steven Shand and Jim Finneran at Barker & Herbert laboratories in Ft. Wayne the following Saturday. No time to waste.

As I made the appointment I knew that I would be in trouble at home. My girls were Olympic hopefuls and exceptional soccer players at almost two and almost six years of age. While I hated to miss their games, Steve would be there to cheer for both of us. So I told myself that I would make brownies on Sunday, but I already knew that I would probably come into the office before sunrise, work for several hours and then return home—hopefully before the girls got up and noticed that I was gone.

I was meeting potential witnesses, both Shand and Finneran, so I needed Van Buskirk to come with me. A prosecutor never wants to become a witness in a case. For that reason, a prosecutor never puts herself in the position of interviewing witnesses without the presence of a law enforcement officer who can later recount the conversation, if that becomes necessary. For example, if I was interviewing a witness and the witness suddenly confessed, I would not be able to testify about what the witness said and still prosecute him. There needed to be another person present at all such interviews.

I had not reached Shand or Finneran on the telephone, but spoke to a man with a dignified sounding voice who identified himself so quickly that I did not get his first name. I learned that he was the head honcho, owner, and apparently a legend in the field of fire cause and origin. I didn't know if he was Barker Davies or Davies Barker. Since I had no idea how much we could pay for Barker & Herbert's expertise, and I doubted that we could pay their usual rates, I did not want to antagonize him. I just called him "sir."

Mr. Davies (as I learned the next day) said that he was glad to make the guys available to meet with me and he would be in on Saturday and looked forward to seeing me then. He seemed very kind and affable.

I called Van Buskirk to see if she could join me for the two hour drive to Ft. Wayne. She couldn't. She had to attend her daughter's dance recital. Was she married, I wondered? To whom? Did he have a great deal of life insurance? Was he deaf? How many children did she have?

Lepper had already moved to Florida, where, I understood, he was spending time catching bad guys while navigating his golf cart as head of security for a seniors' community. I pictured that, perhaps mistakenly, in my mind. Rethmeier was back on his regular duty, so I decided that I would ask Will to drive me on Saturday.

I left my office and walked down the hall, past the reception area and was buzzed in to the other side of the office, past the conference room, to where the executive offices, which were only slightly more luxurious than mine, were located. As I told Cale about the trial date, Scott Newman came in and asked us to join him in his office. Apparently he had gotten a call from Judge Barney and Mr. Voyles. As the elected prosecutor he had the final word.

Scott Newman had been an Assistant United States Attorney and had worked with Cale, who was also a federal prosecutor. When Scott was elected, he brought in Cale as his chief trial counsel. We sat in Scott's office and I told them both about my hearing with Judge Barney, my observations about the Wise clan and my plans to prepare the case for trial. I omitted anything about my run in with John Commons.

Scott was a remarkable strategist with a brilliant mind. He had some singularly unpleasant traits, but he gave me pretty much free rein and I respected his judgment. Scott told me that Judge Barney and Voyles had both questioned my judgment on the Wise case.

"Are you going to convict this guy?" he asked bluntly.

Before I could respond, Cale spoke up and said that the cops were hot under the collar about the case and we would tick off the police brass if we failed to move forward.

"Are you going to convict the guy?" Scott asked again.

"I don't know if I can convict Wise, but prosecuting him is the right thing to do. He did it. He killed his own child in the most heartless and gruesome way."

Scott made a few pithy suggestions, not as to the arson prosecution, but about how to deal with Voyles. He also told me that Judge Barney was a good judge, that he had been persuaded that there were significant issues with the case and wanted to prevent embarrassment to anyone.

We knew that it would be an uphill battle, even with the understanding of the judge. We spent some time discussing the issues. Although I doubt that Scott had ever prosecuted an arson case, he was astute and had a trove of criminal trial experience.

"What's our budget for hiring experts?" I asked Scott.

"What experts do you mean?"

"Well we'll have to pay Shand and Finneran for their time, get the room transported down here from Ft. Wayne, if they haven't destroyed it, and we may need other experts to rule out the baby monitor as a possible cause of the fire."

Scott said, "Our annual budget for experts is twenty five thousand dollars and we have already spent that—mostly on our child molest cases."

We had a separate division that handled only sex crimes. It had an office downtown, away from the City County Building, fitted with child sized interview rooms and teams that focused on sexual crimes against children. They frequently had experts work with the children to ensure that they were not traumatized by being questioned or further damaged by the criminal prosecution.

Scott said that because he had no idea that this case was on the horizon, he had not budgeted for it. He also told me that the budget is approved a year in advance and so he would not have the budget to pay for experts next year either, even if I could somehow get the case delayed for another year.

"Okay then. No paid experts." I said to myself.

Scott told me to do my best. I knew he would expect a conviction.

Cale and I left Scott's office. Cale walked immediately into his office and was packing to leave before the door closed behind me. I returned to my office, grabbed my purse, and headed down in the elevator to the basement parking. I was fortunate to have been given a space in the building because of the hours that I worked.

I headed to the arson squad, promising myself that I would only stay a few minutes, and get home in time to fix dinner for Steve and the kids. I stopped at the K-Mart that I usually passed on my way to the arson investigation unit. I bought two plastic bottles of rubbing alcohol, one of each of the two available brands, and headed to the arson office.

Det. Wilson and his partner were waiting for me, anxious to discuss our case. I told Wilson that we had a trial date for the Wise case. He whistled. That was a huge emotional response for him. I asked what he knew about the case and the word around the squad. Other than Will's partner, no one else was present. I knew that Will would be candid with me.

"Look," he said, "everyone knows that Wise killed the baby, but Lepper is about to retire and well, Skip is Skip."

I didn't know what he meant, but I didn't interrupt him to ask. I asked Will what he knew about Leslie Van Buskirk.

"She's a ball breaker."

He added that she was divorced from Sgt. Van Buskirk who was in charge of the IPD firing range. He had never worked with her because she was in homicide.

I asked Will's partner, Larry Carter, if he knew whether rubbing alcohol can burn.

"I think so," Carter replied. Not much confidence there.

I pulled out the two plastic bottles of alcohol and asked Will if he had found a metal trash can. He had and I asked them to show me if the alcohol would burn. The labels showed that the bottles contained thirty percent water. I was skeptical.

As we moved outside, Carter, who was a longtime fireman, told me that it was unsafe to try to experiment with a possible accelerant in a container like a garbage can.

"The fumes can build up and possibly cause an explosion."

He explained that it was better to pour the alcohol on the back steps which were concrete and see if it would burn. He, like almost every firefighter that I knew, smoked tobacco or something. Counterintuitive but true. Anyway, he had his matches on him and the three of us went outside to the parking area behind the squad offices.

I poured out the alcohol and Carter threw a match near it, careful that it did not land directly in the alcohol. Nothing. He tried again and *whoosh*, the steps were ablaze with pale bluish flame. We all jumped back and I accidently spilled the rest of the first bottle of alcohol. The fire spread down the steps so quickly that I was mesmerized. Will grabbed my arm and pulled me back a few feet. Pretty convincing. We did the same thing with the other bottle and I was surprised how little alcohol it took to start a flame on the hard surface.

I was still dubious. "Got any carpet?"

We went into the building which was a former IFD firehouse. It was large and high-ceilinged, with a large garage type door on one end and lots of open rooms probably converted from dorms. There was also a men's locker room and men's bathroom and offices for the unit commander and assistant commander. The teams had desks out in the big room.

Command of the unit alternated between an IFD officer and IPD officer with an officer from both departments filling the two top spots. At the time, Mark Froelich, a merit lieutenant with IFD, was the commander. Mark was about to return to the fire service so I searched his office.

He had a little rug under his desk . . . it looked ratty and ready to fall apart. Perfect. I "borrowed" the rug. I would explain this to Mark later—his contribution to the case—but Wilson and Carter shook their heads.

"Not gonna burn the Commander's rug, no, no way." Carter was adamant.

Never having been in the military, I was not as wed to chain of command, but I understood that I was not going to get their help burning the rug unless I had permission. I called Froelich on my police radio. I asked him to call me at the unit. When he did, I asked him if I could burn up his rug. He asked why and I told him what we were doing.

He replied, "You do *not* have my permission to burn down the building, but you can burn that thing under my desk . . . it was left there by someone and is as old as I am. Tell Carter if he catches the squad on fire he'll be riding the back of a fire truck for the rest of his career."

I conveyed all except for the last part to Will and Carter.

We headed back outside. We only had the one brand of alcohol left, but I felt comfortable that if one would burn so would the others. I threw the mat on the steps where we had burned the alcohol. I noticed the brownish burn pattern on the small area. I covered it with the rug.

Carter told me that we had to burn the piece of carpeting farther from the building so we moved onto the cement parking lot. I threw the small piece of carpet down and poured the alcohol on it. This was not a scientific test—I just wanted to be sure. Carter lit and threw a match. In a whoosh, flames rose above the carpet and then the carpet caught fire. We let it burn for a few seconds, but Carter told me that breathing the burning fumes could be dangerous depending on the composition of the carpeting. He stomped the fire out with his boot. I was now convinced that alcohol could accelerate a fire.

But where did the alcohol come from and could we prove that it was not an accidental spill?

I headed home and broke the news about Saturday to my waiting preschoolers. There were some pretty glum faces until I promised to be a "fun mom" on Sunday. Both girls piled on my lap and we fell asleep.

# Chapter Seven

TWO DAYS LATER Van Buskirk called. I had set aside the whole day to work on the Wise case.

"I spoke to the owner of the Wise house," she said. "I didn't say anything about Matthew or the trial. I just told her I was a cop investigating the fire and asked if we could look at the place. I promised that we wouldn't take up too much of her time."

"Great, when do we leave?" I asked.

"I'll pick you up out front in ten." The phone clicked off.

The horseshoe drive of the building was filled with cars and I looked for what I knew would be an unmarked police car. The days of the Crown Vic had long passed and the IPD seemed to have gotten a better deal on Taurus sedans. I was going from car to car when I heard the blast of a car horn. It was emanating from a powder blue monstrosity that looked more like a boat than a car. It was old and while obviously American made, I could not identify its make or model. I was glad that I had worn casual clothes for casual Friday.

"Get the fuck in, I'm freezing out here and we're going to be late." Van Buskirk was in a good mood.

"Who did you have to bribe to get this car?" I joked. "Was it confiscated from like the most pathetic drug dealer in Indy?"

The car looked worse from the inside. It was worn and had been badly abused by its prior users. There were cigarette burns everywhere and the lingering smell of smoke and burgers and fries. The car was spotlessly clean and obviously someone had tried to make it habitable but its past was reekingly evident.

"Yep, had to fuck the chief to get this baby," Van Buskirk said. "I'm lucky to have a car at all these days. Now shut up and let's go."

It was winter with only traces of snow on the ground. The car was unexpectedly cold inside although the heater was noisy and blasting hot air.

The driver's side window was rolled down and I feared that it was stuck in that position. Van Buskirk pulled out of the driveway and headed to the I-65 entrance. The window remained fully open.

Personally, I drive like a maniac. When traveling in cop cars, as I frequently did during investigations, I was used to a fast trip. The badge paved the way. I had never driven anywhere with this detective and was just getting to know her. Still, my experience with many other cops was consistent . . . they drove fast and ignored speed limits.

Van Buskirk drove like a little old lady. The steering wheel seemed too large for her delicate long fingers and arms and she drove slowly with both hands on the wheel. She kept her window rolled down the whole trip. I didn't ask why.

She said, "The lab sent over another copy of the report on the carpet samples that Lepper submitted for analysis. It confirmed that there was alcohol in the carpet. Your copy is in my brief case."

"No gasoline or lighter fluid?" I asked. Maybe Wise poured both. Not likely, but hey, there are suspender and belt guys, so why not?

I didn't tell her that I already had a copy of the report from the arson guys. I had hoped that maybe there was another report with a different result. If there was lighter fluid in the carpeting, the case would be much easier. No such luck—only alcohol.

Both Wise and Michelle had denied that there was alcohol in the area of the room where the sample was taken, but that could change. I was still considering what to do with the information.

Van Buskirk confirmed that the defense already had the lab's report.

As we got close to the house Van Buskirk looked at her watch. "We're early. I don't want to surprise them. Let's just drive around the neighborfuckinghood and I can point out where some of the witnesses live, in case any of them are still around."

"Get on that detective," I said. "I want to re-interview every one of the witnesses. So you need to track them down, get good addresses, and then we can meet with them. Try to group them together—like all of the neighbors as one group, the firefighters at the scene as another, and like that."

"You can't interview them together. What the fuck?"

I cut her off. "No, I mean I want to schedule each witness separately but on the same day or same time of day. It'll make it easier to compare their statements and see where we have problems. I want the interviews to be in their homes. That way we can be sure that they could see what they claim to have seen and get a better feel for their testimony. We don't have a lot of time."

"Who do you want to meet with first?" Van Buskirk asked.

"Well, why not do it chronologically? Let's start with the newspaper lady. What's her name?" I asked.

"Cynthia Neweadde. She was helping her son with his paper route. She worked full time and then drove her kid on his paper rounds. That kid was lucky. Neweadde passed the Wise house the first time at about at 4:25 a.m. and then again at 4:58 a.m. She got out of the car to hand deliver the paper to Wise's next door neighbor and she saw no smoke or fire in Matthew's nursery."

Van Buskirk continued, "She will be a great witness. She timed the route very carefully because her son had to be at school and she had a day job, besides, the kid's pay got docked if the papers were delivered late. She should be easy to find. I'll set it up. Who else do you want me to schedule?"

"Why did she look at the Wise house when she was delivering the paper next door?" I asked. I wanted to be sure that she would hold up on cross-examination.

"She said it was still dark out and she is always cautious. She would park the car, look around carefully to be sure no one was lurking around the house or near the house, and then she would get out and lay the paper on the doorstep. She looked around again before walking back to her car. She was also looking out for her son who was delivering papers a couple of houses down. So she looked at the Wise house before she got out of the car and on her way back to her car."

"Good. Well, the next witness would be the neighbor that let Michelle use the phone to call 911. Then whoever let Wise call 911, and then the cop that stopped to help. Then we get to the firefighters. I want to meet with everyone. I don't want to put anyone on the stand that I haven't interviewed, unless we have to. Besides, it's been a long time and people forget important details. I want to make sure they remember what they told you or some other investigator when they gave their original statements."

I always keep a small leather calendar in my purse. I took it out and Van Buskirk opened her briefcase and pulled out her calendar. We compared available dates and agreed to try to track down and re-interview witnesses. We decided that if we had to, she would have other detectives work with me on the case, including her partner. But I wanted to see and hear every witness myself.

"Poindexter will not be filling in for me," I smiled.

She did not appreciate the puny attempt at humor.

"I mean it. I need to do this myself," I said more seriously, and she knew.

There was at least one other felony prosecutor who was assigned to work on arson cases, but I wanted him to do the paperwork and hearings on the Wise case so that I could prepare the case for trial. Three months sounds like a long time, but it isn't when there are file boxes of evidence and the defense has a year's head start. I knew that Voyles would want to depose our witnesses and I always tried to have someone else cover depositions for cases that I planned to try.

A deposition is an agreed upon time when lawyers ask a witness questions and obtain answers while a court reporter takes down every word that is said and later types it up into a written transcript. Depositions are permitted in civil and criminal cases in Indiana, unlike some other states.

Criminal defense lawyers have the right to find out what every witness for the prosecution would say in the witness box by asking them questions, under oath, before the trial. In most cases, only really important witnesses are deposed because of the expense of paying the court reporter for the time and the charge per page of transcript. But in a case like this, Voyles would want to depose the majority of, if not all of, the witnesses. It would be up to him to ask for the witnesses to be made available by the State.

The State is also entitled to depose defense witnesses before trial, except for the defendant. The defendant has the right to remain silent and cannot be deposed unless he wants to waive that right. Wise, represented by competent counsel, did not care to waive.

Deposition questions in criminal cases are very different than the questions asked at trial. Depositions are intended to elicit information and find out everything that the witness might say at trial. The rules are very relaxed for depositions and so questions can be asked during a deposition that cannot be asked at trial.

One of the reasons that I avoid taking depositions myself is because it gives the witnesses an insight into how I ask questions and where I am going as it might concern their testimony. For adversaries, this can be really helpful for their preparation. When their deposition is taken by another arson prosecutor, I get the information that I need to prepare, without giving up anything about myself, or my methods, or my theory of the case. Of course, I did not yet have a theory of the case so that problem was more theoretical. Jim Osborne was assigned to work under my supervision and I would later ask him to handle the deposition portion of the work.

"Okay, let's go," said Van Buskirk as she exited the Carolinabluemobile. The window on her side was rolled up and she locked the car.

Van Buskirk had parked in front of a petite house with 8404 posted on the siding. It was set back from the street. There were no trees in the front yard and the house was one of the smallest in the neighborhood. There was a cement walk up to the front door. On the left side of the door, facing the house, were ground level and upper floor windows. To the right of the door were a similar set of windows. I hadn't realized from the photographs that the basement was partially above ground. There was no snow now, but I tried to visualize the morning of the fire when there was snow covering the balding yard.

A young woman let us into the house. She was cordial. As we were invited into the foyer area we could smell the remnants of cooked bacon in the air.

I was washed over by a wave of déjà vu. It was almost surreal to step into the house. It was as if I had already been in that house many times before. I had read so much, seen diagrams and memorized the layout. The feeling was most disturbing.

The young woman, whose name I immediately forgot, offered to show us around, but Van Buskirk told her that we would be fine if we could just have a few minutes. She said she would do laundry and went downstairs, leaving us alone on the landing.

It was only one or two steps from the front door to where the alarm panel still hung on the wall to the left of the stairs. It was the usual white plastic box that looked like a thermostat. I assumed it was in the same place as before. The light switch for a hanging light fixture was next to the box.

"Yeah, this is exactly where the alarm box and light switch were. Looks like the same ones," Van Buskirk said. She had been there on the day of the fire, after Lepper or the commander had called for a homicide detective, and apparently several times after the fire.

It was six steps up to the upper level. On the right, where I remembered it, was the living room area. Everything was smaller than I had imagined. Even though everyone had used the words "tiny" or "small," I still imagined it larger.

There was a small carpeted living area with windows facing the street. A sofa, coffee table, and chair over-stuffed the space. There was a small table and chairs in the constricted eating area. There was also a small galley-like kitchen. Compact was too generous a description for these rooms.

Van Buskirk showed me where Wise claimed to have been sleeping on a couch when the fire began. The new owners had rearranged their furniture slightly, but there really wasn't enough room to change things too much. The coffee table, although a different style, was in the same place. Van Buskirk pointed out the wall outlet where the baby monitor receiver had been plugged in.

The inside of the house had been completely repainted, but Van Buskirk confirmed that the layout had not changed. I found myself lingering in the living room.

A part of me did not want to see the nursery—apparently a significant part of me. I had been to several fire scenes, but I had never been to a place after it was rebuilt or in which an infant had died.

We walked down the short hall to the left of the stairs and looked into the first room on the left. As I opened the door I could not believe how small it was. I mean it was too small to have been a closet. I felt as though I could reach the back wall from the hallway although that was certainly an exaggeration. The room was warm and there was no actual odor of fire or smoke, but I smelled it anyway.

Van Buskirk and I stood in that space for several minutes without saying a word.

"Didn't Wise say that he got two feet into this room and couldn't reach the baby?" I asked Van Buskirk.

"Yes."

There was no way. No way. Two feet into the room and the crib would have been so close that you could nearly touch it. The measurements that I had read and the drawings by Wise and Michelle had not prepared me for how doll house small the room was.

"I have to be able to convey to the jury the actual smallness of this room," I said. "They won't understand just from seeing photographs."

"Fucking Poindexter!" was all that Van Buskirk had to say.

We looked at the bathroom, just a short distance across the hall and a bit down from the nursery, and also at the other two little bedrooms. Both rooms were larger than Baby Matthew's nursery.

I backed out and stood at the top of the stairs facing the upper level. I tried to imagine the eardrum piercing howl of the alarm siren, knowing that smoke was hanging down from the ceiling, smoke was filling the house. Coming up those stairs and then turning right to go into the living room to get the portable telephone instead of turning left to get a helpless and perhaps wailing infant. That was William Wise's inexplicable decision.

Van Buskirk and I went downstairs into the lower level but there was nothing much down there that I had not already seen in my mind and in photographs. The young woman asked if we needed anything else. I think she knew what we were doing and what had happened here. I hoped that she would not first find out from reading the newspapers when the trial finally started.

Van Buskirk and I were both quiet on the way back to the City County Building. Neither of us made a single wisecrack. I was imagining the fire in that miniscule room. As we neared downtown I asked Van Buskirk if we could swing by MECA to pick up copies of the 911 tapes. I wasn't ready to go back to the office.

"Hey, did you know that Wise had a police radio at his house that night, umm, morning?" I asked.

"Yeah," she said. "Lepper found it stashed in the downstairs bedroom in some hole over the dresser. That little fucker had to have hidden it when he knew police or fire were on the way. Why?"

"Why didn't he use it to call in the fire? He claimed that he had never taken it home before that night . . . a first. What channel was it on?"

"We know why the fuck he didn't use it. He killed his kid. No rescue required. But we can ask Lewie-Bob all those questions. She's our contact at MECA."

Van Buskirk instinctively clicked her radio and asked whether Lewie-Bob Hiatt was at MECA. She was. We slowly made our way to the dispatch building near downtown Indy.

As we drove in, I thought about how important this nondescript building was. One story, white, cement block with a fence but no gate or lock protecting the parking lot or building. Only the several antennas and dishes on the back lawn and on the roof provided hints that the building was anything other than a warehouse. And of course there were a few marked police cars in the lot.

We parked and got out. Both of us were clutching our radios. Van Buskirk was a completely comfortable with hers while I was self-conscious about mine. I only had it because my position as chief arson prosecutor required me to haul it around so that I was readily available to any fire investigation unit member. I had been issued the radio, battery, spare battery, belt holder, charger, and strap, but nothing else. No instructions at all.

I didn't know the lingo except from my experience watching cop shows on TV. No one had shared a list of code numbers and I did not have the unit numbers that identified individual department members. I had learned a few of the identifiers for the arson guys but mostly I listened to the voices that I knew. I was very uncomfortable with the device and almost never used it, although I always listened to it.

We entered the building and Van Buskirk badged her way into the IFD dispatch area. Lewie-Bob greeted us and apparently knew Van Buskirk, who introduced me as the new prosecutor, no name, and asked about the tapes.

Lewie-Bob was a middle aged woman of average height, weight and brownish hair color. In fact, she looked to me like an average Midwest housewife; proving to me once again that looks can be deceiving.

"Would you show me how the 911 system works?" I asked.

Lewie-Bob agreed and took us to the dispatch area. It was configured in a semicircle. Each dispatcher had his or her own cubicle with a screen, head phone system, and keyboard. I noticed that the head phones had long cords so that someone could stand up or peek into the next cubical.

"When a call comes in," Lewie-Bob explained, "it is randomly assigned to a dispatcher who is not on another call. The telephone number of the caller, street address, and name of the person who gets the telephone bill for that telephone number appear on the screen so that the dispatcher immediately knows the location and possible name of the caller." Lewie-Bob it seemed had given this description many times before.

"Every dispatcher is trained to get answers to a standard list of questions from each caller. Depending on the nature of the problem, he or she will identify the closest equipment and dispatch the correct response. For example, if the caller reports a fire, the closest station will be notified immediately, even while the caller is on the line. Each dispatcher has multiple lines from which to make the call out and can also do it manually by typing in the proper codes.

"Most important is we teach everyone that works here that 'seconds save lives.' It is more than a saying, it is our creed. We know that every second counts."

"How does the dispatcher know what equipment or personnel to send based on a 911 call?" I asked. "Would an operator sitting in a cubicle actually make these life or death decisions?"

"Our dispatchers are trained to obtain the essential information from each caller. Do you see that check list on the desk?" Lewie-Bob asked.

I looked at a set of laminated paper sheets on each desk held together by a single metal ring. The top sheet was a script.

"Every caller is asked about the fire, if there is entrapment, any pets, which rooms are involved, whether the fire has spread to other buildings, the contents of the building—meaning if it is a commercial building, for example, are there tires or men's clothing being stored there—because it's a very different response depending on whether the contents are hazardous. The most important information is what we call entrapment. If there is someone trapped in the fire, the response is obviously more intensive," she explained. "After the initial dispatch, that dispatcher remains the control for that incident. If calls come in to other operators about the same situation, they can look at their screen to find out when dispatch was made and what type of response is on the way. Also, if personnel on the scene need additional call-outs they can use their own operations channel on the radio to request assistance or they can contact dispatch to have the dispatcher locate a person, make a call, or send another unit."

It seemed like a great deal of responsibility for the dispatcher. The equipment looked simple, but apparently wasn't.

"So are all of the communications recorded?" I asked.

"Yes. We record every spoken word and also have a log of the times that every action is taken. The log is completely computerized, recorded and maintained. The spoken word is recorded on a large spool of tape. Because we tape everything, including routine calls and complaints, and because of the cost involved in paying for the tape and storing these large spools, we only maintain the tape recordings for about thirty days and then we tape over them. You wouldn't believe the calls that come in to 911. People use it like an information desk at times, tying up the lines for reports of a loose dog or a stray cat that has been clawing through their garbage."

Lewie-Bob continued, "The computer data is maintained for a much longer time. Usually we provide a print out of the computerized data on request. I am not certain how long the computer stores that data, but I know that it is a lot longer than thirty days."

I had seen the printouts and learned to read them with comprehension. Each sheet had a number identifying the officer or firefighter or piece of equipment or other personnel. It had the time of dispatch, time of arrival, time of departure and several other times in between. The printouts showed the hour (in military time) minute and seconds.

"How accurate are the times on the computer print-outs?" I asked.

Lewie-Bob looked at me with disbelieving eyes. There was complete silence for a few seconds and the only the sound in the room was a dispatch operator on the line giving directions to a caller. Lewie-Bob apparently had to regain her composure and looked to Van Buskirk as if to ask whether I was a recent escapee from an asylum. She looked back in my direction.

"They are accurate to within a millionth of a second," she said. Her tone left no room for further discussion on the subject.

"Can the data be manipulated?"

I had to be sure that the times were right because time was the key to this prosecution.

"No," Lewie-Bob said with finality.

Again Lewie-Bob looked at Van Buskirk who merely nodded. Lewie-Bob continued, "The data is captured by the computer and it is a closed system. As far as I know, it cannot be manipulated."

Lewie-Bob walked past the dispatch area into her office where a huge reel of tape was slowly turning. There was a second reel onto which the tape was winding.

"This is the type of tape that we use. When someone like Detective Van Buskirk requests a copy of a 911 call, I locate the position on the reel based upon the time that the call came in, which I can track from the computer print-out and then record the original on a cassette tape and provide it to the detective."

She handed Van Buskirk four cassettes. "I made an extra copy as you requested."

"Michelle Wise called 911 at exactly 5:09:392 from 8405 E. 37th Place which is across the street from her residence. William Wise called 911 at 05:10:06 from 8413 E. 37th Place. The phone calls were less than a minute apart, exactly twenty-seven seconds apart."

Lewie-Bob continued reading from the print out. "Within ninety seconds IPD officer Keith Williams arrived at the Wise residence. All of the others arrived shortly after that. The print out will show the times and the tape recordings will let you know what each person said."

Lewie-Bob was obviously competent and proud of the job she did. She would make a good and unflappable witness. I confirmed that she was the "custodian of records," meaning that she was the person that I would need to bring to court to authenticate the 911 call records. The timing of the calls was crucial.

Could William Wise have made two attempts up to the baby's room, as he claimed, crawling along the floor because of the heat and smoke and then backing out, gotten his shoes and fire coat on, gone to one neighbor's house and knocked on the door and then before she could answer the door gone to another house where he called 911—all in twenty-seven seconds? If anyone believed William Wise's story, that's exactly what he did.

I wasn't buying it.

I had already listened to the 911 tapes. Michelle had called first. She reported the fire but did *not* say that her child or baby was in the house. Twenty-seven seconds later William Wise called 911. Wise was able to identify the dispatcher by her voice and called her by name. He said, "Jodi, my house is on fire" and then told her that the baby was in the house.

We suspected that Wise was unaware that we had located the first neighbor, the one whose door he had knocked on before going to the house where he made his call. But her testimony would be that Wise came to the door and knocked a few times as she put on a robe, by the time she reached her front door and opened it, she saw Wise crossing the street to another house where she watched him knock, be admitted and go inside.

"Do dispatchers work from home?" I asked.

"No, never. There is no way that a person could provide the information that is needed from any location other than from his or her station," Lewie-Bob told me. "I know this is about Bill Wise. Are you wondering about the radio found at his home?"

"Exactly! What can you tell me about that, Lewie-Bob?"

"I know that Bill did not have permission to have that radio. We keep three spare radios here in dispatch to be used only in an emergency, like, if the computerized system crashed or we had to evacuate this building. Each of the three is assigned a number that comes back to MECA. They are kept in chargers and the supervisors have access to them, but the radios are out in the open."

"Do you know what happened to the radio that Wise had on the night that Matthew was killed?" I asked.

"Yes. It was initially returned to us by Investigator Lepper. We confirmed that it was ours and that Wise had no permission to have it in his possession. We also checked our system and confirmed that no calls were made from the radio and no emergency alert was made on the night of the fire. Afterward, Det. Van Buskirk came over and took the radio. I haven't seen it since then."

"Was the radio fully operational?" I asked.

"Yes, for both IFD and IPD. We found that the battery was fully charged and the radio fully operational. It was apparently set to OPS 2 at the time that it was found by Investigator Lepper. At least that's what he told me."

"What is OPS 2?"

"OPS 2 is a radio channel—Operations channel 2. Every fire district uses one of the operations channels to communicate on the way to the fire location and while at a fire scene. It is intended to be a private line of communication. OPS 2 is the channel that the fire response team was using for the Wise fire."

"Are you saying that Wise was able to hear the fire trucks being sent to his house and what the fire department personnel were saying to each other once they got there?"

I was really speaking aloud to myself.

"Yes. He would have known when they would arrive. He would have been able to monitor all communications. That is, if he was actually listening to the radio. There is no way to know that."

Lewie-Bob had answered another one of my unspoken questions.

"You said something about an emergency alert. What is that?" I asked, knowing that I sounded stupid, even to myself.

"Take that radio that you have in your hand." Lewie-Bob took my radio to illustrate. "See this little red button? If you hit this button it creates an alert in the system. It is perceived as the most dangerous of situations and we do everything in our power to locate the person assigned to that radio and dispatch help immediately. Bill did not press that button on the night of the fire."

Maybe Wise was in a panic and didn't even remember that he had the radio. But then why had he brought it home, for the first time, only hours before the fire? And if he was panicking, would he have recognized the voice of the IFD dispatcher and spoken to her calling her by name?

"Did you know William Wise?" Van Buskirk asked.

"Of course. He worked here and at Wishard for nearly two years."

There was something in the way she said it. Van Buskirk immediately picked up on it.

"Was he a good dispatcher?" she asked.

"No. He was on probation at the time of the fire. That was the last step before being terminated. He had been moved from the night shift to the noon to midnight shift. He never came back to work after the fire."

"So why was he on probation?" Van Buskirk asked.

"That is a personnel matter and I can't discuss it. You'll have to talk to his supervisors."

I whispered to Van Buskirk, "Do we have his personnel file?"

"Yes. He was on the verge of being fired," she responded.

"Is there a direct line into dispatch, I mean other than calling 911? A line that someone who worked here could use to get through immediately?" I asked.

"Of course we have a direct line. It is used by our dispatchers to call in if they're sick or going to be late. It is answered by the shift supervisor."

"Did Wise know that phone number?" I asked her, thinking that there were several ways that he could have gotten a quicker response by the fire department.

"I guess so. Every time that he called in sick, late or with a question he would have used that number."

"Did he know how the tapes are kept or anything about your job of monitoring the calls and printouts?" I asked.

"Funny that you ask that question. Bill asked me if I would show him how the play-back system worked. Dispatchers don't need to know about that. I told him that it was need to know." Lewie-Bob provided no additional details.

"Was it unusual for a dispatcher to ask about the recording process?"

"No dispatcher had ever asked me about it before," Lewie-Bob said flatly.

I asked Lewie-Bob if any of Wise's co-workers were available to speak with us. She said that two of his co-workers were in the building and she would check to see if they were willing to talk.

Both were willing to discuss William Wise. This was an unexpected bonus.

We spoke with the two co-workers. They told us that Wise did not invite anyone to his wedding and they didn't learn about it until maybe two weeks beforehand. The marriage came out only because he was taking some time off of work and they had to divvy up the dispatch duties. Wise told each of them that Michelle was pregnant and each described his attitude as annoyed. As we talked, it became clear that, at least as he had described it to his co-workers, he was getting married to Michelle because of an unwanted pregnancy.

One of the women told us that Wise claimed to be dating several women right up until the wedding. Van Buskirk asked for the names of any of the alleged dates and one of the co-workers said that Wise had gone out with a woman firefighter several times.

"I think her name was Marcie or Maggie, he just said she was on disability while they were dating. He seemed to like her," one of the women said.

Within minutes, we decided that we should speak to these potential witnesses separately. Besides, at least one of them had to be at her station at all times. We asked Kathy Roberts to meet with us and Lewie-Bob loaned us her office.

Kathy explained that she was a dispatcher and she had worked with Wise ever since he was hired by IFD dispatch. Kathy worked the same shift with Wise until he was placed on the noon to midnight shift. She said that Wise talked a good bit to her, although he seemed generally to keep to himself.

"I didn't even know that he was getting married until about two weeks before the wedding. Bill told me that he had to get married. He said that the girl, he called her a girl, had gotten herself pregnant. He didn't want to get married but they were going to do it. He told me that he offered to pay for an abortion but the girl wouldn't do it."

She took a deep breath. She closed her eyes and seemed to be thinking back.

"Months later, he still hadn't said anything about when the baby was due. Some of the other operators and I kept asking him and finally, about two weeks after the birth, Bill told us that he had a son."

Kathy was also mostly unemotional in her demeanor and I wondered whether dispatchers were trained or selected for their ability to remain calm under stress. It made me wonder about Wise. Would it make a difference when it was your own house, your own child?

"What did he tell you about Matthew?" I asked.

"The only thing he told us about the baby was that he cried all the time. Bill complained whenever he mentioned the baby, about the baby crying and keeping his wife awake. He never even showed us a photo of the baby until we had asked him several times and then he showed us one photo, that kind that they take at the hospital." Kathy said that she did not know anything about the fire and had not been the control dispatcher on the morning of the fire.

Kathy went back to her station and Cathy Robinson came into the office. Unlike her colleague, this Cathy was visibly upset.

"I am so glad that you came to talk to us. I feel so guilty. I could have saved that baby. I should have. I have thought about calling the detective many times, but I didn't know who to call. Are you the detective?" she asked, looking at me.

Van Buskirk reached past me and shook Cathy's hand. "Leslie Van Buskirk and I am the detective on this case. Good to meet you. This is Diane Moore and she is the prosecutor. How could you have saved the child?"

"That night—morning—whatever, right after Bill's shift ended, I was in the break room and he came in. I was getting some coffee and Bill was getting his stuff to go home. We had talked before about the baby. Bill said, you know, when he showed us a picture of him, that the kid was ugly. We all said, no Bill, he's beautiful, you know, he's a beautiful baby.

"Bill wouldn't hear it. He said how the child cried all the time, 'all the time,' and just wouldn't stop crying. Bill also told us that he was tired of his wife running to the baby all the time, every time the kid cried. Like, you know, the baby was getting all the attention and he wasn't getting any. That's all he ever said about his wife and their baby. The baby cried all the time.

"But when I saw him on the night or early morning before his house caught fire, Bill was adamant. He said that the kid kept crying all the time and he was not going tolerate that. I should have done something, or warned someone."

Cathy was in tears now and we gave her a moment to compose herself.

"I thought he was just tired and so I told him that I had friends whose babies cried for the first six months and then stopped. He looked angry. 'Six months? No way. I will never tolerate that crying for six months.' I thought my story would calm him down, like, you know, it happens, then it gets better, but it didn't."

I asked, "Cathy, how did Bill say that he wouldn't tolerate it anymore? Was he joking or serious or what?"

She thought a second or two. "He was hard and said it—kinda cold. He looked dead serious. I knew that he meant it. But then part of me said, 'Like no way he meant it.'"

Cathy told us that she couldn't get the image of that newborn, whose picture she had once seen, burning up in a fire. Van Buskirk questioned Cathy about anything else she knew about Bill Wise or the murder, but she knew little more than she had told us. She confirmed that Bill had told her that he was dating a female firefighter but she did not recall the woman's name. Cathy began to cry again and we assured her that we would be in touch.

Apparently Cathy Robinson was the friend who Wise had spoken with on the night before the fire. I could check that mystery off of my list. She was an important witness, as was the other Kathy. It was shaping up to be a good day for the investigation. We had only a few leads about the woman Wise was dating, and I wanted to ask Van Buskirk to try to find her.

I also needed to know more about the relationship between Wise and Michelle.

Van Buskirk dropped me off at the horseshoe. She said that she would park her car and meet me in my office. I went upstairs, asked if the conference room was available, and it was. I reserved it and then dragged my notes and files into the room to wait for Van Buskirk.

# Chapter Eight

I HEARD THE buzz of the entry door and a few seconds later Van Buskirk walked into the conference room with a couple of notebooks. We sat on opposite sides of the table and spread out. Two of us in the Prosecutor's Office were notorious for grabbing the one and only conference room without reserving it. The other deputy prosecuted a lot of homicides, was married to a detective, and did not have kids. She worked late nights. I was more of a morning person, get in to the office at four a.m. and stay until five or six p.m. so we conflicted infrequently.

Van Buskirk turned some pages in her notebook but then began telling me what she knew about Michelle without having to check her notes.

"Michelle Davis, white female, uglier than shit, born in 1964. She's a few months older than Wise. She worked for Banc One in the mortgage division. I interviewed some of her co-workers right after the fire."

She looked up and I nodded for her to keep going.

"She met William Wise on Matchmakers, International. It's an internet dating website. Founded 1986. We discovered that Wise still had an active account even after they tied the knot. They dated for a while and Michelle got pregnant.

"According to her friends, she wanted to keep the baby and Wise pressured her for weeks until she gave in and aborted the fetus. They broke up for a while and then they started dating again. The women at Banc One thought Wise was creepy and didn't understand the attraction. Michelle was quiet and they suspected that she had never had sex before Wise came along. Anyway, they presumed that Michelle was a virgin when she met Wise. During the break up, Michelle moved back home to Elkhart, which is where she was raised. Michelle may have lived with her mother while she was there. After a while Michelle returned to Indianapolis and her job. The women learned that Michelle was dating Wise again when she returned from Elkhart. He lived with her at her apartment."

"Did you speak to these co-workers in person?" I asked.

"Yes, every one of them. None of them was really close to Michelle. One of the witnesses told me that Wise tried to talk Michelle into another abortion when he found out that she was pregnant with Matthew. Michelle seemed really stressed for a few weeks after she learned that she was pregnant for the second time and her co-workers got the idea that Wise was pressuring Michelle to abort the pregnancy again.

"Next thing they knew she was married. No one from Banc One was invited to the wedding. After the marriage, Michelle came back to work until she left on maternity leave."

"Anything else?"

I wondered if Michelle had talked about Matthew when she returned to work.

"Nope. Seems like she was only at work for one or two days before the fire and she was busy getting caught up. She did apparently have a photo of Matthew on her desk. Michelle told the others that she was breastfeeding and that she was not getting enough sleep because she was up with Matthew every few hours feeding him. They said Michelle seemed tired and worn out despite having just returned from maternity leave."

"Where was Michelle when Rae Ann Symons was killed?" I asked the detective.

"She was in Elkhart. When Wise became the target of the investigation into Rae Ann's death and before they found her body, Michelle stepped forward as his alibi."

Van Buskirk looked through her notebook and produced a police report about Rae Ann's murder.

Rae Ann Symons was seventeen years old and dating Wise, who, at the time, was twenty-five. Wise was seeing the teenager at the same time that he was dating Michelle. Rae Ann became pregnant, and on the last day of her life she learned that she was carrying twins. Rae Ann would have celebrated her eighteenth birthday the next day. She left her parent's home in her car and was planning to meet Wise. Wise claimed that they met in a mall parking lot, spent some time together and then Rae Ann dropped him off at his own car late that night. Rae Ann never made it home and was never seen alive again.

I wondered aloud. "So Michelle alibis Wise and then gets pregnant again and he marries her? Did she threaten to tell the police the truth about Rae Ann? Is there any reason to believe that she was involved in Rae Ann's death?"

"Not that anyone can prove."

Van Buskirk finished the story. The gist was that Wise volunteered to help local police investigate Rae Ann's disappearance. Wise suggested that he was the last person (other than the killer, of course) to see Rae Ann and gave a videotaped statement.

About three weeks after her disappearance, Rae Ann Symons was found bludgeoned to death. She was discovered near a riverbed and had apparently been carried to the location in what was described as a fireman's carry. Van Buskirk was reading from the Elkhart Police Report. Michelle told police that Wise was with her after Rae Ann had dropped him off, verifying the time and giving him a partial alibi.

"Did Michelle return to work at Banc One after the fire?" I asked.

"Apparently she did return to work, about two weeks later for a short time. She and Wise moved to Las Vegas and stayed there until he was arrested. I've looked at the video and spoken with Miles Stacey, the detective assigned to Rae Ann's murder. He is certain that that fucker Wise killed her, but doesn't have enough evidence to arrest him. You need to see the tape. Wise is a stone cold killer."

She produced a video tape and we watched the interview on the television set. The tape recording was black and white but it was clear and the audio portion was easy to understand. It began with William Wise, dressed in light colored slacks and a darker long sleeved shirt sitting alone in a cement block interrogation room. The choice of white trousers struck me as strange. The room was standard issue with a table and two chairs, one on each side of the table, and bright florescent lighting. I assumed that there was a one way mirror facing Wise, but I could not see that side of the room on the video. Wise was sitting at the table calm and quiet. He just sat there and I was struck by how slender he was.

When the investigator entered the room, Wise barely moved. The investigator was dressed in casual clothes and must have been a detective. He asked Wise questions in a slow and deliberate manner.

"Watch the son of a bitch's eyes. He doesn't blink," Van Buskirk said.

I focused on Wise's eyes. They were nearly black. He looked totally unmoved by the questions or the situation. He was staring darkly, emotionlessly at the detective.

"I see what you mean." I responded. Nothing in the interview related to our case. Rae Ann Symons had died in 1991, before Wise joined IFD as a dispatcher.

We watched the tape to the end and I shivered. There was something wrong with this guy. He was totally detached. Zero emotion. He kept repeating that he would do anything he could to help law enforcement. Could it have been a coincidence that Wise's twins were murdered and then a year and a half later his son Matthew was killed?

As we watched the tape, Van Buskirk was completely focused on Wise. She had been a homicide detective for longer than I had been a prosecutor. Wise never confessed to any crime but the cadence of his responses was odd. He waited too long after each question to answer it. It was almost as if he needed to digest the meaning of the questions.

Wise never acknowledged that the Symons' twins were his. He never showed concern for them. I wondered if Rae Ann had refused to have an abortion.

After watching the video twice, Van Buskirk and I walked across the street to grab something to eat. We sat at a table in the Market across from the City County Building and ate our sandwiches. For the second time that day we were both silent. It was a lot to absorb.

It had taken Van Buskirk nearly a year to collect enough evidence to convince Brian Poindexter to file charges. On March 3, 1994, three days before the first anniversary of Baby Matthew's death, Van Buskirk succeeded in getting a warrant to arrest Wise.

This meant that after working with the fire investigation unit, interviewing witnesses and collecting evidence, she prepared a written document, under oath, that contained sufficient facts to persuade the Prosecutor's Office and a judge that there was probable cause to believe that a crime was committed and that the criminal was William Wise.

Wise was charged with murder, felony murder, and arson, as a class-A felony (causing death or serious bodily injury). I had reviewed the affidavit in support of the arrest warrant. Wise was arrested in Nevada and returned to Indiana to face the charges. There was no mention about Rae Ann Symons' death in the Probable Cause Affidavit.

I clearly recalled a part of Van Buskirk's Affidavit that described one officer's observations. This information came from IPD officer, Keith Williams. Van Buskirk had written:

> During an interview with officer Keith Williams he related the following: on 3/6/93, while on routine patrol, he heard the fire department dispatched to 8404 E. 37th place on a reported residential fire with entrapment. He responded to the scene within a minute to a minute and a half. He observed flames coming out an upper window on the south side of the residence. Fire units were arriving as he was. He approached the residence and spoke to a white male standing in the doorway. The door was propped open. The subject was dressed in mismatched fire gear. Officer Williams later learned this was Bill Wise. Officer Williams advised as he entered the foyer Wise stated, "I'm with IFD." Wise then stated, "There's a baby inside."

Officer Williams stated he thought Wise was a fireman and asked where the baby was. Wise gave him verbal directions to the nursery. Officer Williams stated they then attempted to rescue the baby from the nursery. He followed Wise into the residence. Officer Williams stated that he would "never have thought that was his child due to the fact he showed no emotions and was very unconcerned about the "incident." Officer Williams stated Wise never indicated that it was his own residence or his own child inside.

I thought about this IPD officer who had come to the scene of a fire, and without even knowing the family or the child, had risked his life to try to save Matthew. He described William Wise with the same demeanor that we had just seen on the Elkhart video. Officer Williams would undoubtedly make an excellent witness. He couldn't believe that Wise was calm and unmoved while his son was dying or dead.

"What else do we know about William Wise?" I asked Van Buskirk. "Does he have any juvenile record?"

I knew that Wise couldn't have an adult record because he wouldn't have been hired to work at MECA. On the other hand, background checks can be faulty and I wanted to be sure that we knew everything available.

"No criminal history that we could find," she said. "But I didn't get to look at his juvie record. What are you looking to find?"

"Arsonists usually have a history of starting fires," I said. "It's a sexual thing, like a fetish. So we need to check on any fires where he lived, animals that were found burned, things like that. Maybe Miles Stacey can help. Elkhart is a small enough town that everyone knows everything about their neighbors. Arsonists start young and progress. Fires may be the key to figuring out this guy."

I took a long breath. I was thinking as I talked.

"Besides, the fact that he was wearing fire gear is pretty interesting. When did he have time to put on a fire coat and hat? Where did the coat and hat come from? Was he trained as a firefighter? If so, how much fire training had he received anyway?

"These are all really important things that we need to find out. If he had any training at all then he knew that propping the front door open was a no-no. Even Keith Williams recognized how significant it was and told you about it."

She said, "Wise was a fireman somewhere in Florida before he came to Indianapolis. He got the full training, something like two-hundred forty hours, plus. I already requested his personnel records from that job."

This was essential information. If Wise was a trained firefighter he knew that throwing a stool through the bedroom window and leaving the front door propped open would feed in air and speed up the fire.

I was again impressed that Van Buskirk had contacted several of Wise's past employers and requested his personnel files. She told me that the Florida fire department had been very cooperative and sent Wise's entire personnel file. I would start going through those documents next week.

While we were in the conference room, and nearly wrapping up, Det. Wilson knocked on the door. He was dressed in well-tailored slacks, a khaki colored long sleeve shirt; his radio was in his hand. I introduced him to Van Buskirk. She was not friendly. In fact, she was icy. I knew from Wilson that there was no history between them, so was it a black/white thing or just homicide versus arson? No clue and no time to care.

Will told me that he would be able to drive me to Ft. Wayne the next day. We arranged to meet at the fire investigation building at seven a.m. I knew that it was a real sacrifice for Wilson to get up that early. I appreciated his willingness to help out on a case that wasn't his. I also knew that with Will at the wheel, we would make it to Ft. Wayne in time for our nine a.m. appointment. He left and so did Van Buskirk. A few minutes later I left too.

I stopped on my way home at Once Upon a Child on Southport Road. It was a children's consignment store and one of my favorites. They carried used children's clothing, toys, and other stuff. I went immediately to the back where used baby monitors were kept. There was a Fisher Price but I wasn't sure if it was a 1510. It sure looked like it. I paid for it and threw it in the car. I figured that I would take it to Barker & Herbert the next morning.

My children's day care, called Adventures, was only a few blocks from our home. Pick up was before six p.m. and they meant it. I was actually early and got to see the girls playing outside. I buckled them in their car seats; I enjoyed the smell and feel of them. They were giggling and talking over each other regaling me about their day. We went home and for an entire evening I was no longer a prosecutor.

# Chapter Nine

WHEN I ARRIVED early and pulled into the Fire Investigation Unit parking area, Det. Wilson was already in his car in the lot. I wondered if he had gotten up even earlier than necessary or if he was just ending his night. Either way, I grabbed my notes and the bag with the used baby monitor and headed to his car. Wilson got out and opened my door.

On the way to Ft. Wayne, Will wanted me to fill him in on the case and what we had so far. I was glad to oblige. Will was a tenacious investigator with street smarts. Mostly he just listened as I began to lay out the evidence. This helped me a lot too as I began to see how the case was unfolding and to be aware of the many gaps.

"What we know is that the room burned too hot and too fast to have been caused by an accidental electrical fire. Lepper and Shand agree on that. Even the firefighters at the scene were immediately suspicious because of the total destruction of the room."

Will had not seen any photographs and so I described the room after the fire as I had seen it in the photographs, and on the videotape.

"We also know," I added, "that Michelle and Wise were the only adults in the house before the fire and so, if it was an intentionally set fire, either one or both of them had to have done it. Two cause and origin experts have differing opinions as to what type of accelerant was used and each opines that there are burn patterns on the floor that support his conclusion. We can't corroborate one of the opinions with any physical evidence or lab results."

I thought about that. I explained aloud, without any joy, that it would be my job to try to reconcile or figure out why these experts had come to the same conclusion by different routes. I believe the words "you're screwed" entered the conversation.

"Finally," I told Will, "the suspect claims that a baby monitor started the fire." I kept wondering where Wise had gotten the notion to blame such an innocuous baby product.

"So why'd he do it? What's his motive?" Will asked. He kept his eyes on the road and his sizeable and leaden foot on the gas pedal.

I thought about giving him the "I don't have to prove motive" lecture, but instead I said, "He really didn't want Matthew, but just because he wanted his girlfriend to abort the fetus doesn't mean that a jury will buy that as motive. It's a start, but a juror may feel that once Wise actually had the baby, he learned to love it. I mean we may have a juror who thought the same thing and then had the kid. It's a risky motive. Besides, I expect the whole Wise family to march into court to say what a great Dad Wise was, he probably even got the tee shirt."

"Did Wise have life insurance on the kid?" Will asked.

"No life insurance, but they made some money on the fire on the homeowner's policy . . . inflating their expenses and the value of the contents of the house. Not really enough to matter to a jury," I explained.

"But we also know that Wise sued Fisher Price for millions of dollars, but that can be explained away too. I can hear Voyles. 'There was nothing we could do to bring Baby Matthew back, so we sued Fisher Price to prevent even one more child from dying in a fire caused by this dangerous baby monitor . . . blah, blah, blah.' I think Wise waited nearly two years to file the Fisher Price lawsuit until the criminal charges were supposed to be dismissed by Poindexter, but the jury will never know about that, so as a motive, it's weak too."

Wilson knew that the fact that a dismissal of the case had been discussed would not be admissible in court. I could speculate until the cows came home and it would get me nowhere. I had to be able to prove it.

"So what's the plan in Ft. Wayne," Will asked, as we got off on the highway exit that would take us to Barker & Herbert Analytical Laboratories in New Haven, a Ft. Wayne suburb. I gave Will the directions that I had gotten from Barker Davie.

"We maybe find out which expert is right about the accelerant and we find out if the baby monitor caused the fire."

I fretted to myself, "Today only makes or breaks this case."

When we arrived in the Barker & Herbert offices, we were greeted by a middle-aged black man, somewhat short and very articulate. He introduced himself as Barker Davie. His diction was almost British in its precise pronunciation. He was welcoming and genial and invited us inside his office which was littered with awards, plaques, pen sets and all varieties of honors and tributes. I took the time to read some of them and was impressed. Mr. Davie was a chemist and had provided testimony in some very high profile cases. He was a pioneer and apparently a well-respected leader in the field of fire investigation and cause and origin.

"I'm glad that you and Detective Wilson are here," he said. "We have waited for quite a while for someone handling the criminal investigation to contact us. We were beginning to believe that time would never come."

Barker Davie was inviting some sort of explanation, but that would not be forthcoming from me.

"A thorough investigation takes time, Mr. Davie. We are fortunate that you and your team are willing to speak with us," I told him.

He replied, "We are more than willing; in fact, we are at your disposal. We will provide whatever assistance that you require. We have an interest in this case. That child should not have been killed in such a cruel manner. We will do whatever we can to help you."

Mr. Davie was sincere. Truly sincere. I liked this man immediately. I didn't want to lose his cooperation, but because he was so candid and seemed so honest, I wanted to be upfront with him.

"Mr. Davie, I know that your time is valuable and that you bill for your time and for Mr. Shand and Mr. Finneran's time. I also assume you bill hourly and that your rates are not insubstantial. The Marion County Prosecutor's Office does not have the budget to pay you for your time. I hope that you are still as willing to let me speak with your staff."

He said, "I figured that, Mrs. Moore. I have children of my own. Allstate has paid for our investigation to date and is paying and will continue to pay to store the test burn room. We will help you without any charge for now. I cannot promise that we will always be able to do that because we are businessmen, but for now, you may take advantage of our services without charge."

I hope that I properly hid my excitement. I had been worrying about a large bill landing in Scott Newman's in-box and me landing in the street. No time to waste.

Two men had approached the door to Davie's office. One was short, a bit round, and pleasant looking. The other was rail thin, much taller, and just looked like he would be the quieter of the two. I assumed that the short man was Shand, the cause and origin guy and that the other was the electrical engineer. It was the hands and the look for some reason. I am married to an engineer—there's something about them—the concreteness. The plastic pocket protector filled with pens and pencils was also a hint.

Both men introduced themselves and Mr. Davie went back into his office. Will and I were given a tour of the facility. Apparently Barker & Herbert provided training for fire departments and private fire investigators from around the country and other countries as well. We saw the classroom facilities with high tech boards, TV sets and audio visual equipment. I learned that some of our investigators at the Fire Investigation Unit had been trained here. The classes included specialties such as HV/AC fire investigation and specific classes pertaining to certain categories of electrical fires. Steve Shand did most of the talking until it came to the details of electrical equipment and then Jim Finneran filled in the details.

We walked through the warehouse area and it was laboratory spotless. Different areas could be identified by the products stored or being worked on there. There was a long wide bench with coffee makers in varying states of dismantle. There was an area with larger appliances, automotive parts, and other types of electrical equipment. Shand explained the type of work that Barker & Herbert was known for, including major investigations to identify or eliminate possible accidental causes of fires in hotels, truck crashes, and almost every other imaginable situation.

Near the center of the large open area was what looked like a wooden structure or building. I wanted to look inside, but waited until Shand took me over to it.

He explained, "After Jim and I left the Wise residence, where I had taken measurements, we came back here and started to build this room. We had the statements that Bill and Michelle Wise had given Jerry Shulte from Allstate, including their drawing of the interior of the room. We made every effort to replicate the room exactly."

"Did you have the statements that they gave to law enforcement?" I asked.

"No, it was still an ongoing criminal investigation so they were not available to us. We just used what Bill and Michelle told Allstate, including the sworn statement in proof of loss. We figured we had enough to complete the testing. Because Wise said that he saw the fire on the east wall between the changing table and the south wall, we assumed that he was claiming to have seen the fire in the step down transformer that was plugged into the east wall outlet. It was the only electrical source for the baby monitor transmitter because Bill said that there were no batteries in the transmitter."

Shand stopped when Finneran asked me, "Are you familiar with a Fisher Price 1510?"

I nodded. "I've used them but I never understood how they worked or anything about their potential for causing a fire."

Finneran said, "Before we look at the test room, you need to understand how the Fisher Price 1510 Deluxe Baby Monitor and its parts work."

He directed us away from the test burn room to a bench near the opposite side of the lab. I did want to see the test burn room first, but I have learned to allow the story teller to have the floor and tell it in their own way and pace. Shand walked with us but said nothing.

Finneran directed our attention to three empty boxes that had contained Fisher Price 1510 Deluxe baby monitors sitting on the bench. The boxes were white and blue with photographs of smiling infants and children. The pieces of the unit were visible though clear plastic panels in the box.

Alongside two of the boxes were the four pieces required to operate the units. There was a transmitter, a receiver, and two electric cords, in front of each box. The receiver was about 4" x 5" x 2" while the transmitter was about 6" x 6" x 2." The transformers were the size of an ordinary jewelry ring box. The third box sat empty.

"We used one of the monitor transmitters and transformers in the test burn. So I've been examining the remaining ones," Finneran explained.

What I saw were sets that looked like the box, receiver, and power cord found at the Wise house. Both units were similar. Mostly white plastic with powder blue plastic covering over what looked like audio speakers.

"What is a transformer?" I asked. I was fortunate to have squeaked by with a "D" in high school geometry so my science and math education ended in the tenth grade.

Finneran said, "Well, here we are only interested in a step down transformer." He picked up what I would call the plug-in part to show me.

"As you can see there is a very thin cord that gets plugged into the monitor. Both the transmitter and the receiver use the same step down transformer so there are two of them in every box."

"What does it do?" I asked.

"The little box on the part that you plug into the electric socket is the key. As you know, electric current in the outlet puts out one-hundred twenty volts of electricity. These units do not need nearly that much power, so the box takes the one-hundred twenty volts and reduces the amount of current that flows through the thin wire to the monitor. It steps down the electric current from the outlet to the lesser amount required by the product, in this case a monitor or receiver. These step down transformers step the current down from one-hundred twenty VAC, which means volts alternating current, to just nine volts DC which is direct current and then down again to one fiftieth of the power in a nine volt battery, which is what this monitor uses."

He saw that I was lost and did not understand what he was saying.

"There were only two power sources for the baby monitor. A purchaser can use batteries in both the transmitter and receiver or the step down transformer. Bill and Michelle both said that there were no batteries in the monitor. So they had to have been plugged into the wall outlet using the step down transformers. That means that there was not enough electric current in the line to cause a fire. Period."

I took out the used monitor that I had purchased at the consignment store. "Are you saying that the plug—the part with the two metal thingies, the prongs, can't start a fire?"

I was holding one of the transformer cords in my hand.

Finneran was firm but not finger waggling in his reply. "No, I am saying just the opposite. The *only* place that a fire could have started involving the Fisher Price 1510 baby monitor is at the wall outlet. Both Steve and your guy Lepper ruled that out. When there is a fire at the outlet, the receptacle has evidence of close burning. There was no burning or no unexpected burning at the outlet near the changing table in the Wise nursery. The transformer did its job."

"Why couldn't the fire have started in the transmitter itself? That's where William Wise claimed to have seen the fire—under the bed," I asked.

"Can't happen. There just isn't enough electricity going into the transmitter."

Finneran could tell that I was not convinced. He asked if he could cut up the used monitor parts that I had purchased.

"Sure, have at it," I said. He got out a pocket knife and scraped the plastic off of the wire that led out from the transformer.

He plugged the transformer into the wall. "We should have tested this before I showed you," Finneran said, dropping the cord and picking up the other transformer.

"I tested it last night," I said. And I had.

"It's going to be easier for you to understand if I show you from the beginning."

First Finneran picked up the receiver, connected the cord to the receiver. and then plugged the transformer into a wall outlet.

We could see that the red lights on the unit were all illuminated. There was loud static coming from the receiver.

"Oh, if the receiver is turned on and the transmitter is either off or not working, the receiver gets this loud static sound alerting a parent to check on the transmitter. Okay, now you know that the cord is working."

He turned off the receiver and again used his pocket knife to scrape the plastic off of the wire that ran to the unit. There were two bundles of very thin strands of what looked like copper wire.

He said, "Ok. Now watch . . . The amount of electric current that is coming from the step down transformer is so limited that it won't even shock you."

Finneran pressed the two bundles of wires together and put them between his fingers. He gave it to Will to try. Will survived it and looked okay. So when Finneran handed it to me, I grabbed the twisted bundles of thin wires.

There was no sensation at all. This was a pretty persuasive demonstration, but Finneran apparently wanted to emphasize his point. He took the twisted wires and stuck them on his tongue. I cringed.

Nothing. He held it there a few seconds and then took it out of his mouth. "Now do you believe me?" Finneran asked, smiling.

"Let me see your tongue," I asked and looked into the stranger's mouth. Hey, I gotta be me. I usually only believe what I see or hear or perceive myself, and even then I may be skeptical. I saw nothing unusual on his tongue. It didn't look burned to me. I bumped Will and he looked too. I had to be sure. Will shook his head in the negative.

"OK, I am getting there," I said.

Finneran patiently took the other pieces apart and showed me that there was no wiring inside that could cause a fire. My skepticism was waning.

The receiver was slim and looked like a handheld radio with a longish white antenna. There was a black plastic band that extended the width of the receiver and that was where red lights would illuminate when the receiver was plugged in and picking up sound. The sound level was reflected in the number of lights that would illuminate at any given time. There was also a blue volume control wheel on the right hand side of the receiver.

The transmitter was maybe twice as wide as the receiver. It had one narrow red light on the front to indicate that the monitor was turned on. There was an on/off switch and a small tab that allowed you to select one of two channels. The monitor sat on a thin platform into which the transformer attached with a cord and plug. There was a receptacle at one end of the platform that would accept the cord to the transformer which could be plugged into the wall.

I had a few final questions. "Have you been hired by Fisher Price to defend this product?"

If I was going to use Finneran as a witness, I needed to know if he had any credibility issues—like being paid by Fisher Price.

I watched Finneran; he was not taken aback by my question.

"Our only client is Allstate on this case. But I bet Fisher Price pays well, maybe you should refer us."

He was clearly joking. An electrical engineer with a sense of humor; maybe it was my day to win the lottery.

We left the work bench area and walked back to the wood frame, test room. Steve Shand was again in charge.

"Why did Allstate pay you to build this room and do the test burn when they were going to have to pay the claim whether it was arson or accidental?" I did my usual wondering out loud.

"You know," Shand told us, "Allstate has used us on several occasions to determine the cause of a fire. Sometimes it's about subrogation. If Allstate pays the homeowner, they can get reimbursed by the company that manufactured a product that caused the fire."

Finneran added, "Coffee makers and curling irons, left on, and designed with no automatic cut-off switches are currently the two main sources of accidental residential fires. Sometimes the homeowners' insurance company will go after the manufacturer of the product for causing the fire, but certainly not in this case."

Shand completed his colleague's thoughts.

"Allstate's adjustor, Jerry Shulte, was convinced that the fire was intentionally set. He wanted to know, one way or the other, regardless of whether the company would pay off the mortgage. He was insistent that we find out whether the fire was intentionally set. He paid a lot more for our time and work than the claim was worth. He and Allstate just had to know what happened."

This information was pretty amazing and rather inconsistent with my experience with homeowners' insurance companies.

Shand continued, "After we built the room, we furnished it with the same fire load that Wise had described in the nursery. We wanted to see what happened to the room if the transformer started burning like Wise said."

We had reached the structure. From the outside it looked like a wooden box without a lid. I looked inside. The interior dimensions were identical to the size of Baby Matthew's nursery. The size of the room had been a factor in Lepper's opinion that it should have taken forty-five minutes for an un-accelerated fire to have caused the total destruction found in the nursery.

Apparently Shand agreed. He explained that the outside of the room resembled the structure of the house including 2 x 4 wooden studs holding the walls and floor in place. He also said that the contents of the test burn room were intended to replicate the contents of Baby Matthew's room based upon the statements that Allstate had taken from Bill and Michelle Wise. They had tried to duplicate the two layers of carpeting over tile with mastic in between, as well as every other detail of the room.

"So what did you do to get the fire started?" I asked.

Although I had the video tapes, I had not watched them yet. I wanted to see the room and get my questions answered before I watched the video.

Shand said, "We first used a propane torch to try to light the transformer at the wall. Darn thing did not want to light. We had to try for a few minutes before it would catch fire. Once the fire was started, we let it go. We recorded what was happening with the time in the lower corner of the screen. We had flashover in about fifteen minutes. We let the fire keep burning for about thirty-six minutes before we put it out."

"So, when I look at sixteen minutes on the video, I should see the amount of fire damage that I would expect to see in an accidental fire?" I asked.

"Yeah, that's the point," Shand said. "Although the fire in our burn room was started with a blow torch, making it a non-accidental fire, the scenario was intended to replicate an electrical fire starting at the outlet on the east wall. The time could be off a minute or two because the darn thing wouldn't catch fire. But you can see that, even after thirty-six minutes of burning, there is furniture standing and recognizable in the room."

Shand directed my attention to the room.

I was still able to identify most of the contents of the burn room. There was a changing table, crib, slide rocking chair, ottoman, and dresser. The furniture retained its original height. All were charred and obviously burned but still there was enough wood remaining that all were standing. There was a doll that looked like a baby in the crib. It was charred but not totally destroyed. There were other things in the room including a trash can and some other baby paraphernalia and toys. Importantly there was a Fisher Price 1510 Deluxe baby monitor near the crib.

"Is this with flashover and at about thirty-six minutes of burning with the same fire load?" I asked remembering the "Where's Waldo?" photograph in which there was nothing but ashes and debris in the room after merely sixteen minutes.

"Yes. Do you want to see the videos? We've made you copies although Det. Van Buskirk already has a set. Are you working with her?"

Shand had apparently met Van Buskirk.

"Absolutely," I replied. "Van Buskirk is still the homicide detective on this case. Det. Wilson was kind enough to come with me today because Van Buskirk had another commitment." He made no comment.

The test burn room would help illustrate the falsity of Wise's claim to have been two feet into the room without grabbing Matthew, and a variety of other things.

Jurors are used to watching TV so mere words alone cannot be relied upon any longer to convey a picture of the scene to some jurors. We needed visual representations. It would show the location of furnishings and even what happens in flashover. I thought it was very convincing and that the video would be enormously important to the case.

But, I already knew that the test burn room was not "identical" to the actual room. I expected that the defense would work very hard to try to keep it and the videos taken of it out of evidence. I was going to have a major battle on my hands to be able to use it with the jury.

First of all, I was aware that the structure itself was different: the studs in the Wise house were 2 x 2 and in the burn room they were 2 x 4. That was in Lepper's report. Both layers of carpet were new in the burn room, while the carpet in Baby Matthew's room included a layer of old used carpet. The baby monitor was near the crib in the test room, but Wise said it was under the crib. These were minor discrepancies to me, but made the room dissimilar and not identical to the Wise nursery.

Also, there was a doll in the test-burn crib. That fact would drive the Defense crazy to keep it out because it could elicit sympathy, bringing the jury back to the important fact that an infant had been in the crib. There were some other minor differences including the type of diapers on the second shelf of the changing table (the test burn had paper but the nursery had cloth on that shelf.) Every difference between the burn room and the actual nursery would be scrutinized by the defense and raised as reasons to exclude the test burn room.

But of most concern to me was that the Barker & Herbert team had placed a plastic bottle of alcohol on the changing table in the burn room. The bottle, partially melted, was on the floor of the test burn room, even after flashover.

Rubbing alcohol is frequently used on newborns to keep the umbilical cord clean until it falls off. Wise and Michelle both, in their statements, said that they had used alcohol on the baby for that purpose. But they were certain that that the bottle of alcohol was either on the dresser in the nursery (on the other side of the room and away from where the alcohol was found in the carpet) or in the bathroom, even farther away. William and Michelle both said it could only have been in these two places and not on the changing table. If we used the videos or showed the test burn room, the bottle of alcohol could confuse the jury and undermine the lab results.

I worried that the dissimilarities between the test room and the nursery might result in the test room becoming inadmissible as an exhibit. Note to self: Research this issue for trial.

It was getting late, but I had to pose some difficult questions to Shand. I asked if we could sit somewhere, as we had been standing at or near the test burn room for a long time. Shand or Finneran offered to send out for a late lunch, but we were close to done and I didn't want any distractions.

"Steve, you and Lepper do not seem to agree on burn pattern or accelerant, is that right?" I asked this with some trepidation.

"Yes, I'm sorry but Lepper is wrong. There is a great deal of burning at the floor level and in a wide area far beyond the space that Lepper identifies as the 'area of origin.' Alcohol would have evaporated too quickly to have covered such a large area and the markings and patterns are more representative of a hydrocarbon fuel."

He sounded certain.

I was defensive.

"Is there some way to reconcile your findings with Lepper's report?" Hope springs eternal.

"I don't really think so. I mean we both agree that the fire was intentionally set, although he kept the cause as 'suspicious' for quite a while before ultimately concluding that the fire was arson—intentionally set. I'm pretty confident in my opinion. Jim and I have ruled out all accidental causes of the fire."

He shrugged, looking at me as if to say, "Hey, I'm right and he's wrong."

"How would you explain the absence of a hydrocarbon in any of the samples taken from the scene?" I asked him.

"Most of the time the fire burns all traces of the accelerant like it did here. I would be more surprised if there was an accelerant present after that fire," he said.

"Can we agree that both of you identified the same area where the fire started, only your area is wider and larger than his area?" I asked, hoping to reconcile the differences.

"Well, that's true. But if I'm asked, I will have to testify that I do not believe that the accelerant was alcohol. I think it was a hydrocarbon."

Shand was going to stand his ground.

There wasn't a lot more to say. I thanked Shand and Finneran and we all headed back toward Mr. Davie's office. He was already gone. I told them that I would review the videos and then get back with them. I also asked them if they could be available on our trial date.

"How long do you think the trial will take?" Shand asked.

"About two weeks. I would expect to have you testify during the first week if possible."

"We'll clear our schedules, but please let us know if the trial is continued. We have a class that week that we will have to cancel if the trial is a go," Finneran said.

"Will do."

Det. Will Wilson and I left the building. He seemed deep in thought. I was hungry and grumpy. Getting free expertise requires diplomacy. I had been smiling all day and my face hurt.

"Not gonna be easy," was Will's only unsolicited comment on the ride home.

"Finneran seemed great," I said. "He's going to help a lot and the jury should love him."

# Chapter Ten

SPENT ONLY SIX or seven hours at the office on Sunday. Better than usual. While I was there, I called the home number of the lawyer who was representing Fisher Price in the lawsuit that William and Michelle Wise had filed. He was very pleasant for a man disturbed on his day off and called at home. He offered to provide us with as many Fisher Price 1510 Deluxe baby monitor sets as we might need. I was appreciative. I asked him to get them to me the next day so that we could conduct all of the experiments that we wanted.

"No problem. Just let me know if you need more. I will send you units that have been randomly selected from stock. All of the ones that I'm sending were manufactured between 1990 and 1993. I will have a courier deliver them to your office tomorrow."

Since the Prosecutor's Office had no budget for things like baby monitor purchases, not to mention couriers, I figured that I saved myself a bundle by not having to buy them myself. I smiled. Now we would have plenty of baby monitors to use at trial. I would also send some of them to Finneran at Barker & Herbert to test and explore.

I left the office and it was still daylight. Cool peas. I met Steve and the kids at my mother's house for dinner, which was always a great meal and fun for the children. My mother is an awesome cook and her home always has that warm inviting feeling. My Mother's husband, Bruce, had taken a serious interest in the Baby Wise case, listening to me talk about it, reading every newspaper article and watching every newscast. By this time, William Wise and the case against him had garnered a great deal of public attention. Bruce was always up on the latest, as reported in the *Indianapolis News and Star*. I was always pleased to discuss the status of the case and hear his take on what I told him.

Bruce had spent his life as a blue collar worker, servicing aircraft as a mechanic on bombers in World War II and then for Eastern Airlines in jet engine maintenance. He retired after nearly forty years working for Eastern. Bruce had a high school education; he was smart but unburdened with the gray that afflicted the overly educated. Things were black or white in Bruce's world. He watched TV, mostly news, science and nature programs that I avoided.

(Naturally I was a fan of all of the police, private eye, and lawyer dramas and rarely watched anything else, *NYPD Blue, Law & Order,* (the real one), *Murder, She Wrote,* all contributed to my legal and investigative skills first honed on *Perry Mason, The Rockford Files,* and *Columbo.* I confess that I also rooted for *Charlie's Angels* while I was in law school, but then who didn't?)

Bruce was the type of person that we were likely to have on our jury. While our jury pool would include engineers, scientists, and students from nearby Eli Lilly and IUPUI (Indiana University-Purdue University Indianapolis campus, which was only a couple of miles away) most would be those people who worked at the GM plant, or for State government, and who earned a living using their hands and mechanical skills. These are the people that support their political party, work hard, and love their families. They also tended to appear and be willing to serve for jury duty.

As Bruce listened, I explained. "We have to prove several important things and convince the jury of each one before we can even start to point the finger at Wise. First we have to show that there was no accidental cause for the fire. I think that Wise will continue to claim that the baby monitor caused the fire, so to rule out accidental causes, we have to convince a jury that a Fisher Price 1510 cannot start a fire. Even if we can prove that the baby monitor did not start the fire, we still have to show that the fire was intentionally set. Finally, if we prove that it was intentionally set, we still have to prove that William Wise started the fire. In theory we don't have to prove 'how' Wise started the fire— just that he did. So, what do you think?"

Bruce was thoughtful. He took his time to consider before he responded.

"If I was on the jury," he said, "I'd want to know how Wise started the fire. Without convincing me of that, I would not be confident that he started the fire at all. Besides, if the prosecution can't explain how this man started the fire, then I would give him the benefit of the doubt and figure that if they can't say how he did it, it must have been an accident."

"Well, what if the baby monitor didn't cause the fire and you were convinced of that?"

"It would be a good start. How will you prove that?" Bruce asked.

I tried to describe in detail how Jim Finneran had shown me the workings of the step-down transformer, his portrayal of the unscathed wall outlet and the "wire in his mouth" demonstration. I thought it made common sense. But would it go over as well with the jury?

"Pretty good demonstration, but why would a man like William Wise draw so much attention to the baby monitor unless he knew that it could catch fire? He seems to be a planner. Is he?" Bruce asked.

"I agree that he is a planner; we call that premeditation, but I don't know why he focused on the baby monitor except if he wanted to target a deep pocket. I mean, Fisher Price has plenty of money and it could be leveraged to settle for big bucks or pay any judgment that Wise might win."

Bruce seemed to be considering that when Mom called us to dinner. We all sat around the table and the food, as always, was incredible: buttery chicken Kiev, fresh vegetables with homemade bread, and Mom's handcrafted triple chocolate cake for dessert. While everything was great, I loved the smell of the kitchen better than anything. On this night it smelled of fresh baked challah, an egg bread that Mom always under-baked because my daughter loved to eat the nearly raw dough inside. No one had room for chocolate cake, but Steve was glad to grab a to go container filled with half of the cake for later.

The adults talked while the kids played with Foxie, Bruce's dog, and crayoned. It was late and I was tired. I said that it was time to leave. I offered to help clean up, but Bruce stepped to the sink to work on the dishes.

We packed up the kids and were about to walk out the back door when Bruce looked in my direction. "You know I think I saw a program when Kaye and I were still living in Cairo about a baby monitor that caught fire. Maybe that's where he got the idea."

My mind raced. Mom and Bruce had moved to Indianapolis from Cairo, Georgia, only months before. It would have been mid-1994. I wondered if the show aired before or after Baby Matthew's death. Could it have aired in Indianapolis?

"A Fisher Price baby monitor? Do you remember the name of the program, Bruce?" I asked, with hope.

"I'm sorry, Di, I don't remember. I'm thinking that the show was on at night but that's all I can remember. I think I only watched the first few minutes and then changed the channel. I really wasn't that interested."

I thanked him and we left for home. Everyone was well fed and Steve drove as I joked with the girls. We were barely out of Beech Grove heading south toward our neighborhood before the girls were sound asleep in their car seats. All I could think of was that I had to find that show.

I had a short armed robbery trial during the week that followed. That delayed my search for the program that Bruce remembered. As soon as I had a few moments, I started looking for any information that I could find about the Fisher Price 1510 baby monitor. I called Fisher Price's lawyer again, thanking him for sending the baby monitors. I asked him whether there had been other lawsuits alleging that the 1510 monitor had caused a fire.

He assured me, "There have been no such lawsuits against Fisher Price anywhere in the United States claiming a fire caused by the 1510 Deluxe."

I got on my computer and found the government website for the Consumer Product Safety Council to see if there had been any recalls for the Fisher Price 1510 Deluxe. The website offered a broad base of information on almost every conceivable product. Under each product category it contained complaints and recalls. There were no recalls and no complaints suggesting that the Fisher Price 1510 Deluxe monitor had caused a fire, although there were a few that said that the transformer got warm at the wall outlet. It was a dead end.

I knew that I had to be doing something wrong in tracking down the TV fire story, so I kept at it. It took me several days and several tries. But then, finally, I thought I found something. I called Van Buskirk.

"I think I found out where he got the idea to blame the monitor!" I wanted to share my findings with the detective as soon as possible but got her voicemail. "Call me back."

I dialed Finneran. "Jim, have you followed the news about the Gerry 602 baby monitor that may have caused a fire? Apparently it killed a child."

"No, I haven't heard a thing about it. What do you know about it?" he asked.

"Got the information on the Consumer Product Safety Council website, but I think there was a news show that ran something about it. I'm checking *60 Minutes, Primetime, Dateline*, and some others. I will let you know what I find. In the meantime, please find out everything you can about the Gerry 602. I need to know that whatever happened to the Gerry 602 could not have happened with the Fisher Price 1510. As far as I can tell, the Gerry 602 is still on the market."

Finneran signed off and promised to get back to me after looking online at the CPSC website. I knew that he would find more with that lead.

But, I couldn't wait. I left the building, ostensibly for a late lunch, got into my car and drove to Southport Road, parking in the lot in front of Once Upon a Child. I headed back to the area where they kept baby monitors and found an ugly gray and royal blue colored Gerry baby monitor. I checked on the bottom and found nothing, but on the back was GERRY DELUXE BABY MONITOR MODEL 602 and a weird clocklike drawing.

I asked the sales person whether this was an authentic Gerry model 602.

"Yes," she said brightly. She also explained that the circle with numbers inside was the manufacturer's date code. The date code appeared as a circle of numbers, with an arrow pointing to the number of the month and the two-digit year number on either side of the arrow. This baby monitor was manufactured in 1990 (the same year as the Fisher Price Baby monitor that Michelle's mother had purchased for the couple for Christmas in 1992).

The monitor that I had in my hands had two pieces: a receiver and a transmitter. Each had the same little rubber antennas that I had seen on the Fisher Price 1510. But the Gerry receiver and monitor had normal looking cords with two metal prongs. Neither piece had a step-down transformer. I asked the salesgirl about the set to see if I had missed the transformers.

"Why no, the Gerry's are really wonderful that way. You just plug them into the wall. No bother with batteries or anything else. You just plug it in and it monitors and you plug in the other part and you can hear the baby perfectly. It's great."

She was enthusiastic about the monitor so I asked if she had one for her own children. She blushed.

"No kids yet, I'm still in college, I'm a late bloomer. But I hope to have them one day and I will certainly want a baby monitor. This one is quite good, people like them."

"Yeah," I thought, "until they cremate your kids."

I didn't say anything but bought the used Gerry 602. It was obvious that it did not have step down transformers, but I needed Finneran to explain how a Gerry 602 could catch fire when a Fisher Price 1510 could not.

"Can't wait to hear Finneran explain this." I either thought or said (hard to tell at times) as I walked to my car, my cynicism enveloping me like a wet dog blanket, one with a really putrid dead animal smell to it. The letdown to my mind was enormous. In only a few weeks the State of Indiana would be putting Wise on trial for murder. These little questions had to be answered before that trial began.

"Okay, let's figure this out," I said aloud to no one in particular as I walked to my car. "If the Gerry 602 really could cause a fire, then we would have to try to limit the evidence at trial to the Fisher Price 1510."

Before I could try to convince Judge Barney, I needed to be sure that the Fisher Price 1510 was somehow different enough from the Gerry to explain this anomaly.

When Van Buskirk returned my call, I told her what I had found and asked her to make an appointment for us to visit Finneran later that week. I wanted him to have a deadline for figuring out the mystery of the Gerry 602. Van Buskirk said she would drive us to New Haven that weekend. "Great, plan on a three hour trip with the window wide open," I thought.

Van Buskirk came down to my office to look at the Gerry 602 and compare it to the Fisher Price model that I also had in my office.

Since we were only weeks from the trial, the defense had begun to bombard us with motions. There were motions to keep the abortion and argument about aborting Matthew out of evidence, to keep anything that Wise told investigators out of evidence, the physical items collected at the scene out of evidence and, of course, to keep the test burn room and the videos of the test burn room out of evidence.

These Motions in Limine and to Suppress were an attempt by Wise's defense lawyer to obtain a pretrial determination as to what evidence would be allowed by the judge and what information, while perhaps relevant, would be kept from the jury because it would unduly prejudice the defendant.

To keep prosecutors busy responding to motions and handling hearings had the added bonus of using the prosecutor's time that might otherwise be spent preparing witnesses and garnering more evidence.

Jurors rarely know more than half the story in any case. The rules of evidence are intended to protect the defendant from rumors, innuendo, and prejudice. For that reason, evidence of other crimes, prior incidents unrelated to the crime charged and other information that might affect a defendant's character is inadmissible unless the defendant testifies. This is another reason that many defendants don't testify at trial, to wit, it keeps out a great deal of information that might otherwise have a strong impact on the jury.

William Wise and his lawyers wanted to keep the abortions out of evidence. Abortions being highly controversial, they claimed, would distract the jurors' attention from the real issues and cause them to dislike William Wise. We argued that the attempt to have Michelle abort Matthew reflected on his relationship with the infant. We also insisted that the first abortion was important to show that Wise never wanted a child.

The judge split the baby, ruling that Michelle's first abortion at Wise's insistence was not admissible but the attempt to have her abort Matthew could come before the jury.

These hearings were court battles without a jury present. But the results formed the boundaries of the evidence. Although each side was supposed to have an even playing field each wanted their side to be more "even."

While my arson colleagues in the Prosecutor's Office attended most of the hearings, doing an admirable job, I handled the major issues on abortion and the test burn room. Both topics would be admissible unless the judge changed his ruling at trial. This was always possible since Orders granting or denying Motions in Limine were only preliminary rulings.

"I wonder if Wise will use the same experts at his trial against Fisher Price and Wal-Mart. Like a twofer?" I whispered to Van Buskirk at one of the hearings.

"You better fuckin' destroy them, that's your job, why you make the big bucks," she said in her quietest voice.

"Right," I said. "I paid my secretary in Miami more than I make here."

I was being truthful in that, but agreed with Van Buskirk's assessment of my responsibility at trial.

As soon as the court resolved some of the motions, the defense would file more. It was a never ending stream. Of course, we filed some motions of our own. As soon as I learned about the Gerry, I was mentally formulating a Motion in Limine to keep out any mention of the Gerry 602 and any other baby monitors (in case there was some other surprise waiting for us) aside from the Fisher Price 1510 Deluxe. But in order to win such a motion, I had to understand if and how the Gerry 602 could be distinguished from the Fisher Price 1510.

As the trial date approached, Wise's lawyers began taking the depositions of our witnesses, and we were deposing some of their witnesses as well. The defense deposed Lepper, Shand, Finneran, some of the firefighters, Van Buskirk, and a number of other witnesses. Wise's lawyers did not depose the medical examiner or most of the police officers involved in the case. Because of our limited resources, we only deposed witnesses we guessed were key to the defense.

Key defense witnesses were hard to identify because the defendant in a criminal case has no obligation to disclose his strategy. Other than some very limited exceptions, like an alibi, the defendant has a range of options for a defense and that defense may completely change as the evidence comes out during the State's case-in-chief. In most criminal cases, the defendant does not present any evidence, instead relying on cross-examination of the State's witnesses and argument discrediting the State's physical evidence.

Wise only needed one juror to have a reasonable doubt. The State needed twelve jurors to be convinced beyond a reasonable doubt.

We deposed Michelle and all of the defense expert witnesses. These depositions gave us some insight as to the defense *du jour* which was pretty much as we expected. Wise would try to create reasonable doubt during the State's case-in-chief by cross-examination of Shand and Lepper and then would present its own experts who would testify that the fire was accidentally caused by the baby monitor.

In reviewing the depositions of Wise's cause and origin expert, I knew that he had testified that baby monitors could and did catch fire. He had no doubt about it. I hadn't understood the bases for his opinion. He consistently referred to baby monitors during his testimony, without referring to a particular brand or model. The witness was also going to testify that a nine volt battery could cause a fire and he said he made a video tape to show the jury. The defense had not yet given us the video tape.

My guess was that this expert was referring to the Gerry 602. It could have been disastrous testimony. Now, we would have an opportunity to prepare for it and maybe even keep that opinion out of evidence. We had nearly been blindsided.

It was my experience that experts were always good news/bad news for the party that hired them. They would give opinions that supported their client's case, but if asked the right questions, they would be truthful and therefore provide some helpful opinions to the other side. Preparation, preparation, preparation was essential for a good cross-examination.

Van Buskirk continued to locate and interview the witnesses we would call at trial and I met with as many of them as possible. She served subpoenas for trial and worked tirelessly to get the case ready. Both of us had other murder cases to work and I had a stack of other arsons to prosecute.

On the day that Van Buskirk had arranged for us to meet with Finneran at Barker & Herbert Laboratories, she picked me up at the horseshoe. Naturally she drove the blue monster. Van Buskirk had the worst sense of direction. Actually she had no sense of direction at all. While Van Buskirk was one of the best detectives I had ever worked with, she could not find her way out of a parking lot. It made for interesting travel. And she got car sick, even when she was driving. I realized that she always had the window rolled down, just in case, not because the window wouldn't roll up.

The trip went faster than I thought because I used much of the time mocking her kinetosis. It helped keep me calm. I needed the answer on the Gerry 602. I was hoping that Finneran could resolve that issue today.

We eventually hauled up in New Haven. Mr. Davie was out of town, but we met with Shand and Finneran. The men took us on what I hoped would be a quick tour of the facility and the burn room. But Van Buskirk fell in love, with the burn room. She leaned over and whispered to me, "How are we going to get that fucking piece of shit to Indy? It's huge and I bet it's fucking fragile too."

"Well I guess you'll be having oral sex with someone else soon," I suggested pleasantly. She did not seem amused, but it was always hard to tell. Naturally she responded like a stevedore.

Finneran and Shand kept describing the facilities to Van Buskirk who was smiling and gliding along with them.

I keep interrupting. "Jim, just tell me we are okay."

"We are okay."

"Are you sure?"

I was too young for heart failure. I assumed that Finneran knew that I was asking about the Gerry 602.

"Yes. I will show you after we show this lovely lady around," Finneran responded, and Shand nodded in beguiled agreement.

Detective Leslie Van Buskirk, a former ballet dancer, used her looks in ways that were exceptional. She would go to the jail on holidays (when inmates were most lonely and susceptible) smelling of expensive perfume, listening intently, allowing her skirts to reach just above her ankle and got confessions that hundreds of feet of rubber hose would never have elicited. She was able to get witnesses to tell all just with a smile and flirty look. Now if only she could find our way home.

I was neither tall nor blonde, but even at forty-two, I was not exactly chopped liver. I had shoulder length cocoa-brown hair that I had worn down, with my Levi's and blouse. Although I rarely wore make-up, I have large hazel eyes (with long lashes), athletic legs, and what had been described, once, by David Zelkind, a boy I had fallen for in the first grade, as big lips. I thought of them as kissable and voluptuous. While having one of my daughters at forty had not helped with my weight, I carried the extra pounds . . . well.

"I want to know about the Gerry 602 and so does Detective Van Buskirk," I grumbled.

I headed for the bench that Finneran had used the last time I was in the facility to demonstrate the step-down transformers. There, on the bench, were a couple of Gerry 602 units. One was new and in a box. There was another transmitter spread out with both sides detached. It looked like it had been cut open like a butterflied pork chop.

Finneran picked up the transmitter pieces and showed them to us.

"This is the Gerry 602 transmitter. It is the portion of the set that is left in a nursery and transmits sounds to the receiver which is kept by the caretaker."

He picked up the handheld radio-like box showing us what he was describing. "It is the transmitter that is the safety hazard on this baby monitor. Let me show you . . . As you can see, there is no step-down transformer for the Gerry; the cord allows the full one-hundred twenty volts to travel down the copper wires into the transmitter. Of course the transmitter does not take that much electric power to operate. The Gerry designers incorporated the transformer into the transmitter unit itself; that is why I took the unit apart to show you . . .

"Here you can see that instead of stepping the current down to a useable charge at the outlet, like the Fisher Price 1510, this Gerry unit steps down the current inside of the unit itself. That means that if there is a short in the wiring, before the current is stepped down, it will act the same way as a short at the outlet. In other words, there can be a fire."

He wanted to be even clearer.

"Diane, remember when you asked me if the Fisher Price 1510 could cause a fire and I said that it could, but that it would have to be at the wall outlet and there was no evidence of that in the Wise nursery? I explained that one-hundred twenty volts at the outlet can cause a fire but the step-down transformer in the 1510 makes a fire in the unit impossible because there is not enough power to cause a fire.

"The inside of the Gerry transmitter is like the wall outlet. One-hundred twenty volts comes into the unit and can cause a fire if the wiring is faulty and the defective wiring

is located in the section before the current is stepped down. After the current is stepped down, no fire can occur."

I asked bluntly, "So you're telling me that a Gerry can cause a fire but the Fisher Price cannot?"

"No. I am telling you that a Fisher Price model 1510 deluxe baby monitor cannot catch or start a fire in the transmitter unit itself. I am also saying that without a doubt, a Gerry 602 deluxe model baby monitor is capable of starting a fire in the transmitter unit. I am not prepared to condemn or endorse an entire brand of products, only the ones that I have tested."

It was now actually understandable to me. I could clearly see and understand the difference. I needed Judge Barney to understand as well.

"Have you reviewed the available data on the Gerry 602?" I asked.

Finneran shook his head yes and put the pieces of the 602 back down on the table.

"There have been several complaints about overheating in the units and also there is one instance where the transmitter may have caused a fire that killed a youngster. I have requested further information. The 602 is still on the market, but it probably shouldn't be. It's just not a safe design."

I said, "I may need you to explain all of this to Judge Barney because I feel certain that Wise's lawyers hope to confuse the jury by showing that 'baby monitors' can cause fires."

"I can do that," he replied confidently. "These two units are very different." I trusted his opinion.

I looked to Van Buskirk. "Were William and Michelle certain about the type of baby monitor in Matthew's nursery? I don't want to hear at trial that it was a Gerry 602 for Pete's sake."

"Absolutely certain," Van Buskirk said, "and that bastard can't fucking change that. Wise gave us the box for the Fisher Price 1510 deluxe monitor set. We also have the receiver and one of the power cords. It was a Fisher Price

1510 and there is no way that even their scum-shit lawyer can mislead the jury about that. Oh, and we also have a statement from Michelle's mother. She said that she bought the 1510 set at Wal-Mart in Elkhart."

I wanted to switch gears to another subject and was aware of the time. Steve had a conference out of town and I was responsible for picking up our girls.

There was another issue that had come up in a subtle way during the depositions of Wise's experts. It had to do with the transformers that Finneran had tested. All of them had been handed over to the defense. All of them had been manufactured in China. I was really suspicious but did not know where the expert was going with this testimony.

"Jim, did you test the new Fisher Price transformers that we sent you?"

"Yes and I'm really glad that we did. We had only tested transformers manufactured in China, just the luck of the draw I guess, but the 1510 power cords are also manufactured for Fisher Price in Malaysia and Indonesia. The power cord transformers look a little different and importantly there are a different number of strands of wire in the Malaysian cords. The effect is the same, but we could have looked foolish if I hadn't tested all of the different cords. Now I have."

"Okay, another detail down, only a zillion more to go," I thought but said, "Please be sure to bring all of them to court to show the jury. The trial is only a week away."

Both Shand and Finneran had reviewed the transcripts of the depositions that we had taken of Wise's experts' testimony. All of the experts would have reviewed the other experts' testimony before trial in an attempt to prepare for it.

"Jim, what do you think he meant about having made a video to disprove your claim that a nine volt battery can't start a fire?"

"That's an easy one."

He nodded at Steve Shand who walked away. "I guess neither one of you has ever been a boy scout. It's something taught in survival training. You are always supposed to carry a small amount of very fine steel wool and a nine volt battery on long hikes and camping trips. Steel wool offers zero resistance to the nine volt current. When you make contact between the steel wool and both the negative and positive posts on the nine volt battery, the steel wool will get red hot and be able to start a fire."

Steve Shand had returned with what looked like a Brillo pad and a nine volt battery. He demonstrated what Jim Finneran had just described. Bingo!

Finneran went on. "Unless Wise had very fine steel wool in the nursery, there is no way that nine volt current started this fire. Actually not all steel wool will do anyway. It has to be 0000 or very, very fine steel wool most of the time."

Finneran was great at explaining complicated electrical information in simple easy to understand bites.

Shand spoke up. "How are you getting the burn room down to Indianapolis and where are you going to put it?"

"It's on my to do list," I said. "I'll let you know as soon as I can. Are you going to shrink-wrap it or something so that nothing changes?" With the doll, lamps, rocking chair, and other contents, I could imagine everything flying out and about between New Haven and Indy."

"Yes," he replied. "We'll have it ready to ship as soon as you let us know. Remember that it is oversized and you'll need to have permits to haul it on Indiana roads."

"I am keenly aware," I assured him.

I really was aware of the paperwork and expense involved in towing the room from this warehouse, storing it, displaying it to the jurors, if allowed, and then disposing of it.

We had accomplished all that we could and we again thanked Jim and Steve for all of their help. I felt guilty about how much of their time we were monopolizing. I didn't know if Shand and Finneran were volunteering their time or if Davie was footing the bill, but I was grateful for their hard and impressive work.

# Chapter Eleven

I BEGAN CALLING the local network affiliate stations to ask about any television shows that had aired about baby monitors or the Gerry 602 baby monitor. I was at it all morning and I was beginning to question whether I should be wasting the precious hours before the trial on this chore.

But I needed this information to satisfy myself of Wise's guilt. I had gotten to the point that I was sure beyond a reasonable doubt that he killed Baby Matthew, but I wanted to be certain beyond all doubt, even unreasonable doubt. For some inexplicable reason, the issue of how this guy dreamed up the baby monitor as the cause of the fire kept nagging at my sureness.

I really hadn't thought about the number of television shows there were that handled topics like defective products. Finally, after what seemed like an endless stream of television shows and eager young people earnestly telling me they had no way to find out about the program, I managed to connect with someone from the show *Nightline*.

"I'd be glad to try to find out for you, but it may take several minutes," the young man said on the phone.

"I would be pleased to wait as long as it takes," I told the young man and mentally crossed my fingers. What the heck, I actually crossed my fingers too.

While he was searching and I was on hold I looked on my computer and found out that Nightline aired after midnight in the Indianapolis market. It started at 12:35 a.m. I go to bed early and get up early. Aside from my wedding and the late nights cuddling a crying infant or hugging a feverish toddler in my arms, I didn't stay up that late. William Wise, however, was on the noon-to-midnight shift. Nightline would come on just as he returned home and was settling in. Wise had told the fire investigators that he and Michelle watched TV when he got home from MECA on the morning of the fire. Nightline could have been one of his regular shows.

"Ma'am? Are you still there? I think I found something."

"I'm here . . . What did you find?"

"We did a show about a Gerry baby monitor that caught fire in a child's room and killed a little boy. His father was injured trying to rescue him. It aired here in Indianapolis."

"Allegedly caught fire." I couldn't help from correcting him. "Can you tell me the date that it aired?"

When he responded, time stopped for just an instant. The show aired in Indianapolis after the marriage and while Michelle was pregnant with Baby Matthew.

"A plan is born," I thought to myself. If there was any remaining doubt in my mind, this quashed it. William Wise killed Baby Matthew. It didn't matter that I couldn't prove that Wise had seen the program. In fact, I may never have been able to share this information with the jury. But I knew. That's what mattered, at least to me. Of course I shared the news with Van Buskirk. She approved of my investigatory tenacity and further confirmation of what we both already knew.

I decided that I had used so many favors so far in this case that I didn't want to use any more until the trial started. I had a plan of how to get the "test burn room" to Indy, but held off because we wouldn't reach this bit of evidence until at least the third or fourth day of trial.

I didn't know how men get ready for a lengthy trial, maybe by asking their wives or staff to get their suits cleaned and shirts pressed. A male lawyer could come to court for a two week trial and wear the same well fitted suit every day without raising an eyebrow. A different shirt and tie are all that is required.

Female lawyers faced completely different expectations. We were expected by jurors, especially the more conservative Midwestern female jurors that would be hearing this case, to be exceedingly well groomed in a dress or skirt suit, heels (and that meant pumps—nothing open toed or flashy), hose, make up (subtle but visible), appropriate jewelry—nothing flashy or over-the-top, and the cardinal rule was that we could never, ever wear the same outfit twice during a trial. I do not make this up. Jurors commented on such things and failing to meet their expectations could amount to a mark against your credibility. Apparently a guilty man could go free if I refused to comply with regional sexual expectations.

"The man who created panty hose was a sadistic psychopath," I told my daughters, who hopefully didn't understand one word of that sentence.

We were at the Greenwood Park Mall where I was shopping for suits, hose, and blouses for the lengthy trial. I wore pant suits to work most days, but for a jury trial I would dress as my classmates at the University of Georgia Lumpkin School of Law had instructed: hair up (and out of the way) hose (extra pair in your purse—always) a slip under every dress or skirt no matter how opaque, artistic but natural make- up, stud earrings, and mostly dark clothing. A different outfit every day, or else face scorn. I refused to buy different shoes for each trial day but did have pumps in black, red, brown, and navy. I doubted that the red ones would get any use.

On the first morning of trial, a Monday, I left home at five a.m. after kissing Steve and the girls goodbye while they slept. I was dressed in one of my new purchases: a longish, tightish, black dress with three quarter length sleeves, a modest cut in the hemline below the knees and fitted bodice, with cubic zirconium stud earrings. I had placed my Lady Justice gold-plated pin on the collar and wore black high heeled pumps, with all appropriate undergarments and makeup.

I parked in the garage and took the elevator to the sixth floor. I knew that I would be the first one there, but needed the time to collect my thoughts, take a deep breath, and begin.

I am always nervous on the morning that a trial starts—until the first words are spoken in a courtroom, and then I am—at home. It is where I feel most alive—it is my native habitat.

All we would accomplish this day was jury selection so there was no need for witnesses to be present. Still, voir dire is a critical stage of the trial.

Voir dire (vwah-deer) is where the court and the lawyers for both sides are able to question the potential jurors, called the venire. In Indiana, the court asked questions that were to qualify the jurors—to be sure that no one was related to William Wise or his family or was a firefighter on the case or related to Voyles or to anyone else associated with the case, and other disqualifying issues.

After the court asked these statutory questions, the prosecution (we) would be permitted to ask the jurors questions and then the defense (they) had the chance to question jurors. Each side was permitted to ask the court to excuse jurors for cause. Cause was, for example, where a juror admitted that he could not be fair and impartial or knew one of the witnesses and would take that person's word over another witness's word. Each side could also excuse a certain number of jurors for no reason at all—just because they wanted to excuse them. This was called a preemptory strike. The number of preemptory strikes each party had was set by law. Lawyers who did not like the look or sound of a juror would try to get the juror to express some bias so as to remove the juror for cause, thereby saving his preemptory strikes for a really bad juror. If that failed, a preemptory strike was the only method to excuse the juror.

Lawyers use this questioning to press their case to the jury. It is argument veiled as questions. The court would not allow the lawyers to ask about the facts of the case and so we would strive to discuss the pertinent issues without talking about the particular facts of the case about to be tried.

For the Wise case, I had a plan to deal with several of the issues at the earliest possible moment. This is called conditioning the jury. I would try to educate them while gaining insight into the individual jurors.

For example, time was an important element of the Wise case. Sixteen minutes. So, I planned to ask some nominally neutral questions of all of the jurors with the underlying intention of convincing them of the quality of the State's case.

For example, I might ask, "Are any of you good cooks?" This allowed the jurors to relax since the question was not personal or invasive. When a couple of the jurors raised their hands I would select one and address that witness by name. My point was to get the jurors thinking about how an experienced cook could look at an egg and know about how long it had been cooking.

"Okay, Mrs. Breen, do you know how long you have to boil an egg for it to be hard boiled?" If Mrs. Breen was indeed a cook she would probably respond that she did.

"As an experienced cook, Mrs. Breen, if someone told you that an egg had been cooking for two minutes, and you opened the egg and it was hard boiled, what would you be able to tell about that egg?"

Likely Mrs. Breen would say that she could tell that it had been boiling for at least eight to ten minutes.

"And if the egg that you opened was runny but had some solid white could you say how long it had been boiling?"

Mrs. Breen would likely say between two and three minutes (a very soft boiled egg.)

I would use this idea later when I asked the firefighters about what they expected to see in a sixteen minute fire. This technique of getting the jury to think about the essence of the case is important. During this type of questioning you do not ask such questions of someone obviously biased against you, but there are also conditioning questions that you might address to them.

In the Wise case, I hoped to condition our jurors to the fact that this case, like nearly every arson case, is circumstantial. Television shows and mystery books almost always implied that circumstantial evidence was somehow inferior to direct evidence. This fallacy was ingrained into the minds of jurors despite the fact that the law considers both direct and circumstantial evidence as having equal value. Besides, as a lawyer, I was keenly aware that direct evidence like eyewitness identification can be completely unreliable.

But some jurors cannot be convinced that circumstantial evidence is as effective to prove guilt and that is why I nearly always excluded certain categories of jurors from my panels if possible—engineers, mathematicians, and school teachers—concrete thinkers who always wanted every detail proven with a confession, eye witness or DNA evidence. These jurors were unwilling to infer guilt from even the most overwhelming implications of circumstantial evidence.

I had learned this truth about people, not only by having married a mechanical engineer, but also from experience in another arson case. I had been questioning a jury panel in general about direct and circumstantial evidence. It went something like this: "Do all of you know what direct evidence is?"

Some of the jurors nodded, but most just looked blankly at me. "Okay, let me give you an example. If, as you came into the City County Building today, you saw it snowing, would you have any reasonable doubt that it had snowed on Washington Street and Market Street in Indianapolis this morning? . . . Of course not."

I watched for nods of agreement because if even one juror did not agree, then I had to either excuse him or keep talking to him to change his mind.

"Seeing it snow is called direct evidence that it snowed this morning. Everyone agree and understand?" All jurors nodded in agreement.

"Let's assume that it was not snowing this morning when you came in. The streets were dry and there were no clouds in the sky. At lunch time, you leave the building to go to the Market for something to eat and you see two inches of snow on the ground. The snow on the ground is circumstantial evidence that it snowed, because you did not actually see the snow falling down. Would all of you agree that the evidence that it had snowed is just as powerful in the second example as the first?"

Most of the jurors nodded in the affirmative, but one man, dressed in a white short sleeved shirt and gray pants with no tie raised his hand. He was dead serious when he told me, "I would not believe that it had snowed unless I had seen it myself or someone swore that it had snowed."

"How else could the snow have gotten on the ground?" I asked, genuinely stumped.

He didn't hesitate a wit. "You could have trucked it in and dumped it on the ground."

He was an engineer for the local power company, Indianapolis Power and Light. The other jurors looked at him incredulously. He had inadvertently proved my point, and I would never again put an engineer on an arson case jury. He probably worked with my husband, who also worked for Indianapolis Power and Light.

I had a variety of similar ways of bringing out the difference between direct and circumstantial evidence and how we rely on it every day.

"Mr. Pocket Protector, when the judge takes a break in a few minutes and you head to the rest room, how will you find your way?"

"I will look for the sign," Mr. Pocket Protector might say.

"Will you poke your head into the restroom to see if there are urinals before you are convinced that it is a men's room or will you rely on the sign?"

By now, hopefully, the jury would be smiling.

"I will rely on the sign."

"Well if the sign has a male figure on it, that is circumstantial evidence that behind the door is a men's room, would you agree?"

Sometimes I would just let it go. Other times I would show the jury through a number of illustrations that we all rely on circumstantial evidence every day.

I have never written down my voir dire questions, opening statement or closing argument. I just know what I want to ask and to argue. I believed that without trying to read or remember what I intended to say or ask next, I become a better listener.

In thinking about my ideal juror in the Wise case, I decided that I wanted fathers of infants and toddlers on my jury. They would know. They would be my first choice.

Mothers of young children would be next, and then grandparents. I was not worried about the anti-law enforcement bias because everyone loves firefighters. Their job is to save people and they deserve their positive image. Most of our witnesses were firefighters and not police officers. I assumed that Voyles would want a different kind of juror, one that distrusted experts, concrete thinkers who needed absolute proof and would buy into an argument that the evidence was only circumstantial. The defense wanted pocket protector and I wanted Mrs. Breen. Both of us would likely end up with Bruces as our jurors, the inevitable composite ratio of these extremes.

As I left the elevator thinking about our potential jurors I slipped and fell hard on my hip on the just waxed floor.

"Give me a break!" I muttered under my breath as I got up and collected myself. My sister had sent me a card years before that said, "First thing every morning I put on my bathing suit and look in the mirror. From that moment on, my day only gets better."

I smiled. "Today is going to be great."

When I entered our waiting room I saw the morning newspaper on the floor where it was each day. I had listened to NPR on the drive in and nothing had been said about the Wise case. I grabbed the paper and used my key to open the locked door that lead into the hallway to my office.

As I dropped the paper on my desk, I saw an article about the William Wise case on the front page. The article was the lead headline for that day with a large bold caption and a photograph of the Wise house after it had burned. In about the third paragraph there was a description of the Rae Ann Symons case and how William Wise was the only suspect. The date was October 17, 1995.

After I read the article, I called Van Buskirk. She was at her desk. She came down and I opened the door for her.

"Goddamnshitass, who the fuck is that reporter?" was her greeting.

"Look Van B, let's hope that the jurors haven't read the paper or just skimmed it. We should be fine, really."

"Bullshit," Van Buskirk commented.

We went into my office to get ready for what we both knew, from experience, would follow.

The byline on the article was the reporter who covered the court beat for the Indianapolis News. I had frequently met his questioning with "no comment" before a trial, while being much more willing to make "on the record" statements after a conviction. I had never discussed the Wise case with him and had no idea where he had gotten the information.

Although I suspected the answer, I had to ask Van Buskirk, "Did you tell him about Elkhart?"

"Hell no! That's crap. I'm no fucking cowboy." I knew that she had nothing to do with the article so I dropped it.

Van Buskirk was dressed for trial—apparently she had gotten the same memo. She was wearing a floral dress with a dark blazer over it, hose, pumps, and make up. She carried her ever-present briefcase.

"Why is it that I suspect that I am going to get blamed for this?" I asked her.

"Cuz you are. It doesn't matter if Voyles himfuckingself gave this stuff to the press."

To change the subject, we talked about voir dire strategy and I told her that her opinion was really important to me. She was an excellent judge of people and I wanted her candid appraisal of each potential juror.

As we sat there, a wave of sadness washed over me. Out of the corner of my eye I had seen the photographs on my window. Usually, at this hour before a trial begin, I would be meeting with the family and letting them know what to expect. I would be giving them assurances and they would be urging me to convict the person that had hurt or killed their family member.

This morning, Van Buskirk and I would be the only people sitting on the State's side of the courtroom. Baby Matthew's side.

At eight a.m. we entered Judge Barney's courtroom. There is both an eerie quiet and a sort of reverence in walking down the aisle of a crowded but almost silent courtroom.

The pews in the back of the courtroom were filled with people. I saw only a few familiar faces, including Cale Bradford and Shelia Carlisle, the chief felony prosecutor. I guessed that they had read the paper and were offering moral support. It was appreciated. Also in the courtroom, seated directly behind the defense table, were many members of William and Michelle's family. Only William Wise was seated at the defense table.

As I surveyed the courtroom and walked toward the State's table, which is the one closest to the jury box, I passed the author of this morning's newspaper article. He smiled and nodded at me. I glared back. His look in reply was confused but I did not maintain eye contact.

Van Buskirk and I sat down and waited for the session to begin. The Clerk entered through a side door and announced, "All rise, the Honorable Judge John R. Barney presiding."

The judge took the bench and looked around the courtroom. His focus was on the defense table. "This is the case entitled State of Indiana versus William J. Wise, cause number 49G039403CF023557."

Jim Voyles marched into the courtroom waving the morning newspaper with disgust. "Have you seen this?" he demanded of the court. The courtroom buzzed with new energy.

Judge Barney responded evenly but with authority.

"You are late, Mr. Voyles. Please be seated."

Voyles sat down slapping the newspaper gently on the table. I suspected that a harder slap had been choreographed but the judge's tone had moderated the movement.

Judge Barney waited long enough to allow the hot air to disburse and the room to quiet.

"Counsel, I am aware that an inflammatory newspaper article was published in this morning's newspaper. We had already ordered more jurors than we could ever use because of recent events and the notoriety of this case. We should be fine, but I will allow both sides to question the jurors about the newspaper article. Any questions?"

"No, your honor," I said.

"I want you to sanction this prosecutor for this article. I move for a mistrial," Voyles demanded and pointed at me.

I sat silently. Van Buskirk kicked me under the table. I was going to have to put a stop to that quickly or I would be crippled by noon.

"Don't let him get away with that shit" she whispered.

I inwardly smiled.

"When both the law and the facts are against you, attack your opponent."

It was a comic poster that I had hung on my office wall years ago. The printed version was wittier but the point was the same. Voyles was creating a prologue to the trial, an attack on me, a means of getting me to focus on defending myself instead of prosecuting William Wise.

Judge Barney spoke. "Mr. Voyles, the only person quoted in the article was a defense spokesman. Not that there is anything wrong with what you said, but we are putting the cart before the horse. Let's see if any of the jurors even read this mornings' paper. We will ask that question first and then move on. Now, everyone move to the last two rows so that we can seat the jury panel in the remaining rows and the jury box."

Judge Barney motioned to his staff to bring in the jury.

It took several minutes for the clerk to fetch the jurors. On the table in front of us was a list of the jurors by name, address, and zip code. We also had individual questionnaires filled out by the panel.

When the clerk returned to the courtroom, I turned in my chair to watch the jurors enter for the first time. Van Buskirk and I rose to our feet as they entered. The first fourteen jurors would sit in the jury box which had room for twelve jurors and two alternate jurors. The remaining potential jurors would sit in the rows behind the counsel tables, where they could hear the proceedings and wait until their turn in the box.

As the procession of men and women walked into the courtroom, I saw many of them with a folded newspaper. A few had books and magazines and other reading material.

"Crap!" Van Buskirk whispered loud enough for even the judge to hear. He gave her a look that clearly communicated his thoughts. It was my turn to give her a kick.

Jurors' names were picked randomly from all of the jurors who responded to notices to appear for jury duty. The jury pool coordinators select the names from a hopper and placed them in numeric order on a sheet of paper. The prospective jurors were given their randomly assigned number.

This was one of the documents on our desks. They were lined up and entered the courtroom in numeric order. Juror number one was in the first seat in the box, juror number two was in the second seat and it continued in order. Even the jurors in the back of the courtroom had entered the room in the order that they would be called for duty.

"Ladies and Gentlemen, we are about to start the process known as voir dire. Voir dire means literally to speak the truth. It is the only opportunity that the lawyers will have to ask you questions to determine whether this is the right kind of case for you to hear. It is very subjective and the fact that you are not chosen to hear this case should not offend you in any way. We expect this case to take two weeks to try and later I will ask each of you about any reasons you have that you cannot take a full two weeks out of your life to hear the evidence in this case."

This was a speech that the judge gave to every jury panel. Judge Barney was giving his own version of the routine instruction given to all jurors.

"All we hope to accomplish today is to find twelve impartial jurors who can be fair to both sides of this case. This case started with a charging document that is nothing more than a piece of paper and it is entitled State of Indiana versus William J. Wise."

Before the judge could finish his remarks there was an audible gasp from one or two of the potential jurors. Many eyes moved from the Judge to the defense table.

"May we approach your honor?"

Voyles had seen what I had seen and wanted to discuss it with the judge in the front of the courtroom where the Judge sat, but without the jurors or audience being able to hear.

"We move for a mistrial judge. From the jury pool's reaction to the name of this case it is evident that they read the false and prejudicial news article."

"We know no such thing, Your Honor," I responded. "As to Mr. Voyles' Motion, there can be no mistrial since no jury has been sworn. The only thing that would be appropriate is for the court to dismiss jurors who cannot be fair. We sure have no evidence of that so far."

Judge Barney said in his deep calm voice, "Motion denied. Mr. Voyles, let's hear what the jurors have to say."

We resumed our seats. The court introduced me as the prosecutor, Van Buskirk as a detective with the Indianapolis Police Department and everyone at the defense table. This introduction is always made because later the court would ask the jurors if they knew us or were related to us by blood or marriage.

The judge began to ask the jurors questions about their knowledge of the case or about William Wise. During questioning of the prospective jurors many admitted that while they were in the jury pool assembly hall, they read the article out loud. Some also conceded that the potential jurors, while they were waiting to be sent to their assigned courtrooms, discussed the article and shared opinions of Wise's guilt, based in part on his connection to the Rae Ann Symons case. Most of the potential jurors questioned had an opinion of Wise's guilt and told the judge, in some way, about the Rae Ann Symons case. Several of the potential jurors offered to put the murder of the teenager and her twins out of his or her mind and be fair.

Two hours later the judge dismissed all of the potential jurors and told them that they did not have to report back for jury duty during the week. He looked at the rest of the people in the courtroom and said that the case would be continued.

"Judge, we have nearly thirty witnesses subpoenaed and several of them have traveled from outside of the State. Since the court has set aside two weeks to try the case, would you consider questioning another jury panel tomorrow?" I asked, hoping that the publicity would be forgotten by the next day.

"No, Mrs. Moore, I don't think so. We have had a resounding and discouraging response to today's questions. I do not believe that we can select a fair jury in the next two weeks. Mr. Wise you are to remain under the same conditions of release. I will set a hearing to schedule another trial date."

"You mean that fucker is gonna walk out of here again with his bitch?" Van Buskirk growled.

"Wow, you speak English. You should take the sergeant's exam." I shared her frustration but should not have taken it out on her. She had done everything that I had asked and gone far beyond what was expected.

I looked over as the smiling members of Wise's family hugged William Wise, shook hands with Voyles and strolled out of the courtroom. Unlike his family, Wise remained expressionless. He did not look at either of us. He just walked out. Voyles winked at me.

"Did you see that motherfucker wink?" Van Buskirk demanded as we sat at our table waiting for the crowd to clear. We were the last people to leave the courtroom.

Outside, in the hallway, the newspaper reporter, George McLaren, was waiting for me.

"What did I do? I thought you'd love the article. What just happened?" He seemed to be legitimately confused.

"You've got to be kidding." I talk a good game, but except in the courtroom, I am not a confrontational person. But my adrenaline was pumping.

"You want to know what you did?" I snarled. I dragged him to the stairwell so that we could have some privacy.

"Don't you know that the jury cannot know about the Rae Ann Symons case? Even an idiot would know that! And you put it in an article on the day of jury selection. If you had even waited until tomorrow, the jury would have been instructed not to read the paper and there would have been no problem, but you had to do it on the morning of voir dire. You are responsible for the delay of justice for an eight week old infant. Ever heard of 'justice delayed is justice denied' . . . You . . . Goof." My voice reverberated in the (hopefully) vacant stairwell.

I did not wait for him to respond. I opened the door and stepped back out into the hallway. My face was burning as I headed back to the office to tell Scott Newman (who probably already knew) the bad news. We also had to contact all of our witnesses to let them return to their lives until the next trial date.

While no one knows for sure, it is common wisdom that delays in trying criminal cases benefit the defendant not the State. Memories fade. Anger recedes. New cases grab the headlines. Apathy sets in. There is always the exception, the rush to trial without adequate preparation by the State, but in my experience the only things that age well are cheese and some wines. (Okay and George Clooney and Sean Connery.)

I took the rest of the day off, going straight home and cooking dinner for the first time since I had learned about the existence of William Wise.

Then came the inevitable hiatus. Months went by. One day, I returned from court to find an envelope, unopened, sitting on my desk.

The return address on the envelope was the Indiana Supreme Court Disciplinary Commission. Apparently, someone had filed a bar complaint against me. This was very serious because a bar complaint could result in my license to practice law being suspended or cancelled or some other sanction. I waited until I was alone in my office to open the envelope. It was on official looking stationary.

Dear Mrs. Marger Moore,

We have received a citizen's complaint that you have targeted one William J. Wise and have threatened to have him jailed. A copy of the complaint is not enclosed as there is a suggestion that you might target the complainant if his/her identity is revealed. Please respond to these allegations within the time provided by Rule etc. etc. etc. . . .

I was accused of intentionally attempting to put William Wise in jail. A civil lawyer, for example, cannot threaten criminal prosecution as a means of obtaining a settlement or gaining an advantage in a civil case. So, there could have been consequences to that complaint depending on the context of the alleged threat.

Naturally I responded on the official letterhead of the Marion County Prosecutor's Office.

Dear Members of the Indiana Supreme Court Disciplinary Commission:

I am a Marion County Deputy Prosecutor. The Complaint is not true. I intend to prosecute Mr. Wise, to the best of my ability, but I will ask the court to sentence him to prison not jail, hopefully for the rest of his life. His wife, Michelle Wise remains a possible suspect in the case.

I was aware that standard protocol was for the Commission to send a copy of my response to the Complainant. Since I assumed that Michelle or William or one of their family members had written the Complaint, I hoped they had received my reply.

State of Indiana versus William J. Wise did not go to trial for a long while.

The delay had nothing to do with me or Van Buskirk. There were a few more hearings and a couple of depositions and Van Buskirk and I did what we could to preserve the evidence and locate additional evidence for trial. In the meantime, William Wise remained free on bond and was allowed to travel to Florida and other locations as requested by his attorneys. Apparently Michelle Wise stayed at his side.

# Chapter Twelve

"TODAY I INTEND to set a final trial date for this case," Judge Barney said.

He was looking at Voyles and in the direction of the defense table. "There will be no delays and I expect no newspaper articles on the morning of jury selection."

This directive was aimed in the direction of the Indianapolis News reporter who continued to cover the case.

Our little stairwell conference aside, George McLaren was a fair and thorough reporter and during the interim months had covered many of my trials. He was usually accurate and mentioned me by name in his articles.

Although we rarely spoke, I sometimes wondered if I had overreacted and regretted my outburst. He had a job to do and had done it well. It had taken some investigation to find out about the Rae Ann Symons case and some of the other details included in the article that derailed our first trial setting.

Apparently McLaren did not hold a grudge. He reported on another of my "impossible" murder prosecutions. This one involved the death of a four year old child whose body had never been found. The Attorney General of the State, the former prosecutor, had commented to reporters that such a prosecution was nearly impossible because of Indiana's strict Corpus Delecti rule. The rule required that there be substantial independent proof that a person was dead before a confession or circumstantial evidence of death could be admitted in evidence. The rule had evolved from the days of forced and false confessions beaten out of mostly minority and mentally ill people who, under duress, admitted to murdering white folks, later found to be alive and well.

McLaren covered the case which lasted about a week. There was no body of the child, a beautiful and sympathetic Mother, and the State's key witness to the murder charge was a Santeria priestess. After the verdict, McLaren approached me in the hallway (I thought I saw him eyeing the stairwell, but it was probably my imagination) and told me that my closing was the best he had ever heard.

This was a rare compliment from a seasoned trial watcher and although I only shrugged and perhaps mumbled a "thank you," his words meant more to me than I cared to let on. One does not get many compliments as a prosecutor and it was a kind and completely unexpected observation.

Judge Barney said, "The trial will begin on July 31, 1996. Be prepared to call your first witness that afternoon, Mrs. Moore."

The judge resolved a few other matters related to the case, confirmed a final date for motions to be filed and Van Buskirk and I left the courtroom elated.

Of course, witnesses had to be contacted and scheduled. Van Buskirk worked with the paralegal assigned to the case to accomplish the issuance and service of subpoenas, telephone calls and letters.

"Houston we have a fucking problem," Van Buskirk said into the phone as I listened.

"What's up Van B?" What else can go wrong in this case?

I had decided to use both Steve Shand and David Lepper at trial. I would try to blend their testimony and hoped that the jury could tolerate the inconsistencies and reach the right verdict. In reaching this decision I had considered the downside risk if I only called Lepper. I was concerned that, if I did not introduce Shand as one of the State's experts, the defense would subpoena him for trial.

I could imagine Voyles questions to this well respected expert. "Mr. Shand, did you meet with the prosecutor? Did you tell her that the accelerant used in this fire was not alcohol? Did you agree to testify at the trial? But she didn't call you did she? She tried to hide you from this jury!"

It is usually better to embrace your weaknesses and present them yourself, in the best possible light.

So that was my plan. We had our firefighters lined up and Finneran and I had spent hours preparing demonstrations for the jury. We also had our time line down to the second and there was no way truthfully or actually to explain the extent of the actual damage in only sixteen minutes.

"The fuckin' pathologist who conducted the autopsy on Baby Matthew is gone. He doesn't work for the Coroner and has left the State of Indiana. We can't get him to come to court," Van Buskirk reported.

"That may be a good thing, Van B," I said. "I heard that he was a lousy witness anyway. Who's the best forensic pathologist that we have?"

I find it hard to admit, but with all of our preparation I had never even called the Coroner to discuss the case. I had made assumptions about his testimony and availability and was now worried. But I had no intention of telegraphing those concerns to Van Buskirk, who was already nervous. She was not at home in the courtroom as I am.

"John Pless," she offered. "He's on the faculty at the med school and does a lot of work under contract for Marion County. He's not easy to work with, has an opinion about everything, but he's a really good witness."

I asked Van Buskirk to get all of the autopsy photographs, tox screens, notes, everything that the coroner had done in connection with the Matthew Wise autopsy to Pless. I heard her suck in some air. I could visualize the glare. Van Buskirk knew what to do and my talking to her as if she didn't added to her frustration.

I hadn't considered the pathologist's testimony to be critical, but it was a necessary part of every murder case to prove that the victim actually died.

In this case the photographs of Matthew's tiny corpse were compelling, but we had to handle this case with great care. Any missing evidence, no matter how insignificant, could be magnified by defense counsel and made to seem like reasonable doubt. I had no intention of underestimating Voyles.

It was not all that unusual for one pathologist to testify after reviewing the photographs, toxicology, notes, and report of another pathologist. I needed to meet with Pless to be sure that his testimony would be helpful and not susceptible to attack during cross examination.

Other than the loss of the pathologist, the delay had not seemed to cause any harm. In fact, we had gained some valuable information during that time.

Van Buskirk had obtained all of Wise's personnel records from the Marion County, Florida (Ocala) Fire Department. We made arrangements to meet because she refused to hand them over except in person.

Van Buskirk read the documents aloud, interspersing her own comments and summaries, as we sat in my office.

"William Wise worked as a firefighter in Ocala for a year beginning in September of 1985," she recited. "He received full firefighting training. He was fired on November 7, 1986. The Marion County, Florida Commission concluded that Wise was an incredible liar and sneaky bastard."

"Just read me what it says, Van Buskirk, and spare me the editorial comments, please," I pleaded.

"No can do." She laughed and continued, "He lied on his employment applifuckingcation by leaving out that he had seizures. Apparently he quote suffered severe head traumas and had been treated with Dilantin and Tegretol. Unquote."

She continued reading. "'Wise had a seizure after a fire in 1986 and told his bosses he was approved to return to work but his doctor had actually warned him that he couldn't even drive. Wise lied and said he was okay to return to work. About nine months later Wise had another series of seizures including one while he was on a rescue call. The treating doc found that he had epilepsy. Wise knew he would get canned from the job so he lied again and then filed for unemployment compensation, even before he was fucking fired!'"

"Come on," I said, "You have got to be making this up." I hadn't yet read the documents myself and I knew I'd have to.

"Swear to God. Wise went to another doctor and told him that he, Wise, had been overcome by heat and gas fumes. So, Wise reported back to work again. Wise lied to his bosses and they believed that dirtbag. He was still working but the comp claim was investigated and they learned about his first diagnosis. When the department tried to get the doctor's reports about his epilepsy, listen to this: 'After the doctors' gathered the medical records, Mr. Wise requested and received the county's permission to personally pick up and deliver the records to the personnel office. Mr. Wise did in fact pick up the subject records, but refused to turn them over to the county. The records were eventually turned over about one week later, after the county re-requested them from each doctor.'

"Here's their summary: 'Mr. Wise has consistently lied about his health, engaged in cover-up schemes and refused to cooperate with the county's investigation.' They canned him."

"Sounds like our William Wise," I nearly shouted. "That absolutely confirms that as a trained firefighter Wise knew what he was doing when he broke out that window and left the front door open."

I pulled out some of the answers to interrogatories that Wise had signed in the Fisher Price litigation. He was asked to respond, under oath, to many questions including a listing of employment history with the reason for leaving the employment.

Wise falsified his response concerning the Marion County Fire job saying that he worked for the West Marion Fire Department and giving the reason for leaving as transferred to Anthony Fire Department. According to his sworn responses, Wise worked as an EMT and Firefighter for the Anthony Fire Department in Ocala, Florida from the time of his termination by Marion until July of 1988.

We had also had time to take the deposition of Wise's mother, Jeanne. During her deposition she admitted that William Wise, as a youngster, had been the only person at home when a fire broke out in the pantry of their residence. Wise's mother tried to downplay the incident but admitted that it was ruled a non-accidental fire.

Non-accidental meant arson to me.

"Besides" Jeanne Wise added, "Bill was only a child when the fire happened."

"Today is your lucky day," Van Buskirk blurted. Her mood was almost ecstatic. She was laughing.

"I have been trying to get Wise's juvie records but no luck," she said. "But I was able to get my hands on this police report. It's from the Elkhart County

Sheriff, March 1980, when Wise was fourteen years old. He stole a friggin' fire truck!"

I grabbed the report and read it. Her fresh laughter was clearly a release of the risk-ridden, pent up frustrations of the past year.

I read the report carefully. Then I read it again.

When William Wise was fourteen, he decided to run away from home and he convinced a thirteen year old male friend to go with him. Wise planned the trip to Florida (where his father and brother lived). Apparently "Billie" decided that the best method of travel was by stealing a fire truck, which they did. Wise was both instigator and planner. The scheme resulted in the boys stealing and then crashing a fire rescue truck only a few miles away from the fire station.

The police report contained a statement by Wise and the report of the responders to the scene. The first to arrive at the crash was the Baugo Township Volunteer Fire Department, specifically Lt. John Walker, who wrote a lengthy report containing what the boys told him and what he observed.

First he checked on the thirteen year old passenger who was not injured. His report continued:

> I walked to the driver's side of the truck. The door was open and there was another boy lying on his back on the front seat with both legs bent at the knee and hanging down the side of the seat out the open door. The boy was sobbing holding his right hand to his forehead. I immediately recognized him as Bill Wise from meeting with him previously on different occasions. I then walked around the front of the truck to the right side to better look at his head. Climbing into the truck I mistakenly addressed him by his brother's name of Greg. He continued to sob saying his head hurt, until I called him Greg the second time. At that time he stopped sobbing and with a look of disgust said, "I'm Bill." The only complaints of injury from him were that his head and his left ankle hurt.
>
> . . . He volunteered no information but answered freely all questions . . . he did reply, "Yes we did have the red lights and siren turned on."

Wise's friend told Lt. Walker at the crash scene that the idea was Billie's who also concocted the plan. The friend claimed that he asked Wise several times if the plan would work and even tried to back out at the last minute thinking the plan was doomed to failure. Wise told him it was too late to back out. The child described how Wise threw a brick through the firehouse window to gain

*Diane Marger Moore*

entry. The other boy also admitted that they had stolen two fire helmets to take with them in the stolen vehicle.

Lt. Walker's report also divulged that Bill Wise had met with him several times before the fire truck heist, at Jeanne Wise's request. According to Jeanne Wise, her son was having problems at school and wanted to be a paramedic but didn't want to wait.

Both teenagers were arrested and taken into custody. At the station the younger child's parent refused to allow him to make any statements to law enforcement. Jeanne Wise agreed to allow her son to give and then sign a written statement. Billie Wise gave a detailed explanation about what the boys had done that day. He admitted to breaking the window at the fire station and stealing the fire truck. In fact, Wise took credit for everything.

As if that was not enough, the young William Wise also admitted to making several false fire calls to the Baugo Fire Department in the preceding year. The Deputy Sheriff who obtained the statement followed up on this admission by Wise, speaking with the Fire Chief. The Chief indicated that the department had received twenty false reports and that he suspected Bill Wise of making all of the calls. The Chief also told the investigating officer that Wise was suspected of an arson fire at his neighbor's house but he was unable to prove that Wise set the fire.

Apparently, according to the statement, Wise had been in trouble with Elkhart before the theft of the fire department truck, but was not then on probation. Neither Wise nor the deputy elaborated on other charges.

Graciously, in a soft mumble, Van Buskirk admitted, "When you told me that Wise probably had a history of starting fires, I wasn't sure you were right. Sharkeyes is defifuckinglutly a fire bug."

I was talking to myself as much as to Van Buskirk. "Too bad that none of this is admissible at trial."

All the juvenile stuff, suspicions, and admissions, would be kept out of evidence at trial because it was far too prejudicial. The only way that we could bring this information to the jury was if Wise testified in his own behalf.

William Wise was stupid and arrogant enough to think he could fool the jury, but Voyles was not. Still, I would be prepared for anything including Wise taking the stand.

Wise, as a juvenile, was placed on probation. A slap on the wrist. He knew he had gotten away with it.

"Look at the similarities between the fire truck incident and the murder of Baby Matthew," I said. "Wise is a planner. He is able to convince others to join in his moronic plans. He wants to play real fireman. He gives little or no thought to consequences. And he is a very experienced liar."

I took a breath. "It's like a replay, except this time instead of stealing a fire truck he killed an infant. Probably didn't even mean as much to him as the truck."

During our year's work, Van Buskirk and I had also learned of another incident in which Wise shot himself with a shotgun and then claimed that he had been shot by the suitor of a girl he fancied.

Wise fabricated a detailed account of his self-inflicted injury, even giving a description of the assailant. The angle of the wound (not a major injury) and the lack of a coherent story led police to Wise's mother's garage where they found the gun that he had used to shoot himself.

I shook my head in mild bewilderment. Despite all of this evidence, Wise had never been convicted of a crime. No wonder he thought he was invincible. We would soon find out.

"Do you think he talked Michelle into doing it with him?" Van Buskirk asked.

We were still on the fence about what role, if any, Michelle had played in the murder. We ended that discussion as I hurried to keep an appointment with the medical examiner.

I met with Dr. John Pless on the campus of IUPUI, at the medical school. I had never been to the university and it took me several attempts to locate the Pathology Department and then to track down Dr. Pless. He was a pleasant looking, slim built man about sixty years old with white hair and a patrician face. He looked like he had been a lifelong runner.

Dr. Pless was no nonsense. He made it clear from the outset of our meeting that he had limited time to speak with me and let me know that he had read the entire file.

"Will you be able to testify as to the cause of death of Matthew Wise?"

"Of course. He died of carbon monoxide poisoning."

"Does that mean that he was alive while the fire was burning?"

"Yes."

He answered only what he was asked and nothing more, which is an excellent trait in a trial witness; but it did not make for an easy interview.

"Are you aware that the fire that killed this infant lasted no more than sixteen to eighteen minutes?"

I hoped that Van Buskirk had provided a copy of Lepper's report and her Arrest Affidavit.

"Yes, I read the reports and looked at some of the photographs taken at the scene."

"Doctor, how long does it take to cremate a human body?"

I wanted him to know where I was going with this.

"That all depends on the size and weight of the body and also the temperature in which the body is placed. The human body is mostly liquid, including a great deal of water. For that reason, it takes a while for the body to burn. I will have the exact numbers for you at trial as there have been hundreds of studies done on the subject."

"Well, how long should it have taken an electrical fire to have burned Baby Matthew as badly as he was burned?"

"Far longer than the sixteen to eighteen minutes that this fire lasted. There is no way that the injuries to this body were inflicted in a fire of sixteen minutes duration unless the fire was accelerated on the body."

I couldn't believe what I had just heard. We had never suspected this.

"Are you saying that the only way for Baby Matthew's body to have been burned that badly is if somebody poured an accelerant onto him?"

"In my opinion the answer is yes. There is additional evidence to support my opinion. Look at this photograph."

He showed me an autopsy photo of the baby's corpse on a metal examination table. It was hideous and nearly unrecognizable as a baby. There was part of what had been a diaper left in the area of Matthew's genitalia.

Dr. Pless unexpectedly asked me a question. "Do you see that the infant's head has been burnt away along with most of his abdomen, all of his digits and most of his extremities? His internal organs were essentially cooked away and yet his penis and scrotum are still pink, identifiable and intact. The only explanation for that is that these areas were protected."

"Are you saying that the diaper protected Matthew from being burned in those areas?"

"Absolutely not! I am saying that if the accelerant was a liquid and was poured on the infant, that the diaper would have soaked up some of the accelerant. That area would have been protected from the fire when the child was set aflame. I have thought about it and that is the only explanation," Dr. Pless reiterated.

I sat stunned, trying to comprehend this.

If Dr. Pless was right, William Wise didn't just set the nursery on fire, he poured alcohol on Baby Matthew and then set him on fire. I was too stunned to speak for a few minutes.

I had researched Dr. Pless' background before this meeting and his credentials were impeccable. We had listed him as a witness yet the defense hadn't even bothered to depose him. He was a military veteran and forensic pathologist. He was the chairman of the Indiana University Medical School's forensic pathology program, and had received many national and international awards for his work. He had testified throughout the United States for both the prosecution and the defense. Dr. Pless was the real deal.

I carefully constructed my next question. "Dr. Pless, can you render an opinion that if the accelerant had been alcohol, and if it had been poured directly on the infant, that it would have caused the body to have been burned to the extent that is shown in this photograph?"

At trial I would have to use this hypothetical question format because Dr. Pless was not present at the time the fire was started. The rules of evidence required it, even though it would sound stilted to the jury.

I was holding my breath. Would he commit all the way? This was more than a hypothetical, it could be the case.

"I don't know. I have never researched alcohol as an accelerant, although I have testified about the effects of fire on the human body in several cases, maybe more. I will have to think about that."

"Was Baby Matthew alive while he was on fire and before the carbon monoxide poisoning?"

"If, as I believe, he was literally set on fire, then that answer is yes."

I wasn't going to push him.

Dr. John Pless was going to be the most important witness in this case. The defense could not impeach his credentials, his motives, or his opinions. I hoped that he would stand up to cross examination about alcohol as an accelerant.

My time was up and Dr. Pless signaled this by standing up and walking me to the door. As we walked back down the locked hallway to the reception area, we discussed the scheduled trial weeks and his availability (or more accurately his lack of availability). I would have to present his testimony on a day and time when he was available whether or not it fit into my organization. While the timing of his testimony might not prove optimal, what he had to say was so powerful that it shouldn't matter.

# Chapter Thirteen

IN THE DARK, frigid early morning hours, Van Buskirk and I stood on Washington Street, in the courtyard behind the courthouse, to survey our delivery.

The test-burn room was firmly planted on the cement near the parking lane in downtown Indianapolis. It was cordoned off with yellow evidence tape and had a police guard. We had succeeded in getting the thing to Indianapolis and left in a location that could be easily accessed by the jury. Now all we needed was for Judge Barney to allow the jury to come downstairs and walk through the structure. I was hoping that the display would peak the judge's interest and he would allow a jury view.

Naturally, there had been no budget to transport the oversized object from New Haven to Indianapolis. I couldn't bring myself to ask Allstate or Barker Davies, who had already been so generous, to do any more for the State. I had been a deputy attorney general before moving to the Prosecutor's Office and had met a variety of people through that position. I had also gotten to know the State's contracted towing service and even some folks at the Department of Transportation. Voila! Wide body delivery, sans unnecessary permits.

The "Room" had attracted the attention of most of the people passing or driving by. It was about as large as the inside of the public elevators in the City County Building. People stopped for a peek into the big box to see what was in it. The police guard and bright yellow evidence tape increased the mystery. Van Buskirk and I shared a conspiratorial grin. We hadn't shared many of those happy understandings in the past several months and it was a great start to the trial.

I hoped that the test burn room would help the jury understand our point about the sixteen minutes. We hurried into the building then waited in line to get on the elevators to the second floor and Judge Barney's courtroom.

There was no newspaper coverage that morning, although I suspected that the test burn room would grace the cover of the newspaper by the next day. Still, we were ready to prosecute this case.

As Van Buskirk and I stepped off of the elevator to head into the courtroom, we saw William Wise, hand-in-hand with Michelle, sitting on a bench outside the courtroom door. It looked like a pose for a family portrait. I felt a bit of bile rise in my throat.

Van Buskirk was concise. "I think I'm gonna puke."

"More defense stage management," I told Van Buskirk loud enough for the Wise family players to hear. I assumed they hoped to be seen by the press and maybe even a few of the potential jurors.

Unfortunately trials are more about perception than about the facts. As many facts are never known to the jury and they are asked to judge the credibility of witnesses based upon a few hours of watching the person on the witness stand, their notions about the defendant in particular can alter the entire course of a trial. Perceptions can be manipulated.

From the minute a person is called for jury duty, what they see, hear, smell or think becomes a part of the trial. In a close case, how the jurors perceive the defendant, his family, the relationship between the prosecutor and detective and the unspoken opinion of the court all become factors that are considered, whether consciously or subconsciously. This is one of the reasons that incarcerated defendants are permitted to wear street clothes for a trial instead of a jail jumpsuit. It is also why the defendant frequently covers his tattoos, gets a new hair style, and brings what he can of his family to court.

I will not soon forget one of my witnesses being brought into the courtroom to testify about an arson fire. He was an eyewitness, having seen the defendant start the fire. He was wearing a Superman tee shirt. Knowing the young man, that may have been his cleanest, best tee shirt, but the jury did not know that. The defense lawyer berated him for his frivolous clothing choice, and, in closing argument, talked to the jury about how "if the State's only eyewitnesses didn't take the State's case seriously," then the jury shouldn't either. It was a winning argument.

Wealthy criminal defendants attempt to manipulate the public perception long before trial. Can anyone forget the photographs and videos of William Kennedy Smith walking down the beach with his puppy? This member of the Kennedy clan was charged with raping a young woman. After he was charged, other allegations of sexual assault (date rape) were publicly revealed. Roy Black, Kennedy Smith's Miami attorney, working with some of the best jury selection and media professionals that money could buy, did an incredible job of altering the public's perception of Kennedy Smith in the months before the trial.

Immediately after his arrest, Kennedy Smith obviously had a negative public image. (He was, after all, an accused rapist.) The entire case would come down to who the jury believed: Kennedy Smith or his accuser. Most of the carefully staged photographs of the young man, in the months before the trial, showed him with his puppy and dressed casually, the "just one of us" kinds of photographs. Roy Black's strategy was to make Kennedy Smith seem less like a rich, spoiled, "gets whatever he wants" playboy and more like a handsome, young, dedicated, medical doctor. Kennedy Smith's well-loved family members also appeared at the trial and in publicity beforehand which may have, consciously or subconsciously, swayed the jurors. It was effective.

How on earth could a defendant speak about himself to the jury if he didn't testify? Well, he could park himself on the bench outside the courtroom each morning to put on a show for the jury—dress respectfully, have clean neat hair, shave regularly, have loads of relatives and friends in the courtroom, and, if he could get away with it, show the jury that he was "a good family man."

I was confident that the holding hands was an act, but whether it was or wasn't, I would ask the court to direct Wise to have no contact with the jury, verbally or nonverbally. They could snuggle elsewhere, if that's what they wanted to do.

"They'd better enjoy it while it lasts," I told Van Buskirk as we both entered the courtroom.

We saw that the defense table was piled with books and files. Usually I would greet the opposing lawyers and at least shake hands. I had been a defense lawyer for many years and had a close and collegial relationship with the prosecutors against whom I litigated. We were, after all, colleagues. No matter how intense the trial, prosecutors and defense lawyers could walk out of the courtroom and have a beer together.

My attitude was apparently not shared by Voyles. Or he just plain didn't like me. I suspected the latter. Either way, there were no pleasantries exchanged.

Voyles' wink, after the trial was continued months ago, was just one of many slights and discourtesies that I ignored. I had never said an unkind word to the man and had always been respectful to him. Perhaps my unwillingness to kowtow was perceived as arrogance.

The fact that he did not intimidate me may also have annoyed him. He should have been better able to read his opponent. I had no agenda. I did not plan to spend a few years as a prosecutor making a name for myself and then compete with him. I had already been a defense lawyer, and a successful one. Besides, I loved being a prosecutor.

We sat at the State's table until the judge entered the courtroom and took the bench. The clerk called the case and then, after a few housekeeping matters were taken care of, jury selection began.

I noticed that many of the jurors wore watches, an important factor for the sixteen minutes type of questioning. The voir dire went quickly and there seemed to be a kind of congeniality among the jurors, except for two female African American jurors who seemed very wary of my questions. These two women still seemed more Mrs. Breem than Pocket Protector and I suspected that they would be willing to vote with the majority. We had twelve jurors and two alternate jurors. The jurors were a diverse group of Indianapolis residents, about half female, half male.

After lunch, dressed in a navy blue pinstriped skirt suit, with a white silk collarless blouse, and my navy pumps, I gave my opening statement. "Ladies and Gentlemen, this case is about the unimaginable—the death of an eight week old child at the hands of his father."

It lasted for about twenty minutes and I outlined the case that I expected to prove. I did not discuss details or describe the testimony of any specific witnesses, meaning I did not say a word about Dr. Pless.

Voyles made the opening statement for the defendant. He was emphatic about Wise's innocence but spoke in generalities. He essentially decried the prosecution of a grieving family. Voyles was careful to avoid opening the door to some of the evidence about William Wise. He criticized Shand and Finneran as bought and paid for and emphasized that there were no eye witnesses except for Michelle and she would tell them what really happened. He artfully ignored the fact that the other eyewitness was William and that he would not be testifying.

There was a short break after opening arguments and then the jury resumed their seats in the jury box. Finally, nearly three years after Baby Matthew's death and a year after I had been assigned this prosecution, the evidence in the case would be presented to a jury. The jury was ready to hear the evidence and after nearly two years waiting, I was anxious to present it to them.

"Mrs. Moore, call the State's first witness." The judge's commanding voice set the stage and all eyes were on the rear door to the courtroom as I announced the first witness for the State.

"The State calls Officer Keith Williams."

Officer Williams walked into the courtroom in uniform; he was a motorcycle cop and an attractive, well-built, young man. He looked impressively presentable in his pressed navy uniform and black spit-shined boots. He did a good job of setting the scene. He described the neighborhood, the house and William Wise when he found him in the open doorway of the Wise home.

The jurors were attentive. They were listening to every word. My goal was to keep the pace moving so that everyone understood the significance of the evidence without becoming bored by the expert testimony. I hoped to intersperse fact witnesses with experts to keep the jurors' attention.

Every witness called by the State did their job—they testified as to what they saw, heard and in some instances, smelled. After Officer Williams testified, the two firefighters who had extinguished the flames with a three second fog spray came to the witness stand. Both testified that it took several minutes to locate Baby Matthew because all of the debris was black char colored and no higher than six inches off the floor. As they testified I hoped that the jury was visualizing the black steam and smoke rise above the charred remains of Baby Matthew.

The next witness was the newspaper delivery woman whose testimony created an incontrovertible time line. This fire had not started before 5 a.m. The firefighters had already told the jury that the fire was extinguished by 5:16 a.m.

Presenting a circumstantial case to a jury is like building a house. Every piece of information must be stacked piece by piece to create the foundation for a conviction. Each piece must stand on its own or else it will topple the other bricks. After all of the evidence is laid out to the jury, the evidence is solidified with the mortar of closing argument.

I called every witness who had seen or heard Wise or Michelle that night. The defense was not able to shake even one of the fact witnesses. Michelle's co-workers' testimony about whether to abort Matthew seemed to raise some juror eyebrows but would not be a deciding factor.

"Just another brick," I thought of the abortion testimony. "Maybe half a brick."

There was a renewed battle over the admission of the test burn recordings, but this took place out of the presence of the jury. The court admitted the tape, but warned the jury that the test burn room was not an exact replica but merely a similar one used to demonstrate some of the State's testimony.

Lepper testified as to his opinions and we played the burn room video while he was testifying. It was a long tape, lasing at least thirty-six minutes. I hoped that the jury was thinking about the baby in that room for every drawn-out microsecond. At sixteen minutes we stopped the tape and showed the jury what the test room looked like and compared it to the photographs of Baby Matthew's nursery. In the tape, at sixteen minutes, every item in the room was still standing. After nearly thirty-six minutes of burning and flashover, the furniture was clearly still standing. The lamps were identifiable. The room resembled a nursery with charred but recognizable furnishings. Even the diapers were still piled on the shelves of the changing table.

After the jury had seen the test burn tape and heard some of Lepper's observations and opinions, the court allowed the jurors to walk through the test burn room which was still outside on the courthouse plaza.

It was a silent and solemn affair. The yellow evidence tape was removed in the jury's presence by the assigned uniformed officer. The jury had been warned by Judge Barney that they were not to talk or ask questions during the view but only to walk through the room. It took quite a while for the fourteen jurors and alternates to walk into and carefully inspect the tiny room. Many took notes. Judge Barney followed them through the room with his court reporter.

I watched as they walked through but could not tell anything about their reactions. The entire mood was muted although it was a sunny and bright day.

The jury also heard what William Wise had said to law enforcement, Allstate and to the Fisher Price lawyers at his deposition. He did not take the witness stand, but his statements and the transcript of the deposition that he gave in the Fisher Price case were introduced into evidence.

Because Wise was the defendant, his statements were admissible even though he did not testify during the trial. These statements were either read to the jury or the jury was given a copy of the transcript to read to themselves. Naturally not everything that Wise told investigators, detectives or the lawyer for Fisher Price was admissible during the criminal trial. So the transcripts were redacted.

All that redacted means is that the questions and answers (and sometimes comments of the lawyers or objections) are blacked out of the transcript so that the jury would not be able to read them. This process occurred before the trial and both sides knew, in advance, what parts of a transcript would be read and which would be blacked out.

Both sides disagreed with how the transcripts were redacted. I wanted more information to come in for the jury to consider and Voyles wanted more of the information kept from the jury. Judge Barney decided what would and would not be presented to the jury.

The judge directed that the complete transcript or statement would be marked as an exhibit. The redacted version of the transcript or statement would also be marked as an exhibit. That way, if there was a conviction, and the defendant appealed, a higher court could decide if Judge Barney had erred in letting in or keeping out parts of the transcript or statement.

After Lepper answered my questions, he was questioned by Jim Voyles. Voyles landed a few punches, but all in all, Lepper stood up well to cross-examination. He was on the witness stand for nearly three days. I was proud of him.

Next, we called the crime lab technician who testified about finding alcohol in the carpet. Then, Steve Shand testified briefly. He told the jury about building the test room based upon what he saw at the Wise home and the statements that William Wise and Michelle had provided. He agreed that the fire was intentionally set and explained that the fire had not started at the wall. When Voyles asked him about the cause of the fire he said it was arson. No one asked Shand about the alcohol. I breathed a sigh of relief at the end of Shand's testimony. He may not have helped the case, but he did not damage it.

We had won our Motion in Limine and the defense was ordered to discuss only the Fisher Price 1510. There was to be no testimony or comment about any other baby monitor including the Gerry 602. This was a critical ruling and I had to be sure that no one testified in a way that would allow this testimony to come before the jury.

"Why are you fighting so fucking hard to keep the Gerry stuff out of evidence?" Van Buskirk asked during one of the breaks. "It's a whole different configuration."

"Ever heard of 'Where there's smoke there's fire?' I don't want the jury to confuse the two monitors. It's just another issue that we can avoid."

Finneran was an important witness, so I called him to the stand early one morning after Lepper and Shand had testified. The jurors were wide awake and ready to take in whatever testimony was presented. Finneran demonstrated why the step down transformer prevented a fire from starting in the transmitter of the Fisher Price 1510. He illustrated why the Fisher Price 1510 could not have started the fire.

Jim Finneran was a people's engineer. He could explain in laymen's English, without talking down to or over the head of the jury, and we had worked for hours on how to present complex testimony in an understandable way.

Finneran brought all of the samples into the courtroom and went piece by piece over them in front of the jury. Every juror stepped down to look at the monitor, plug it in and listen to the sounds made when turned on and off. The judge gave them as much time as they needed and they took that time to check out all of the pieces of the monitor.

During the pretrial hearings and even when the trial finally got started, Judge Barney was professional but cool to the State. What that really meant was that he was not particularly on my side. But, as the trial progressed, I perceived that he was becoming convinced of Wise's guilt. It was in small increments, a bit with every witness.

Judge Barney listened closely and ruled fairly for both sides, but I could tell that the tide was turning.

The last witness for the State was Dr. John Pless. He was exceptional. His testimony was hard to listen to without a dramatic response. It was hard for the jurors to look at gruesome autopsy photographs, but the State had to prove its case. I never put the photographs on a projector or blew them up to eight by ten inch size, like I did some other photographs. The small photographs were nightmarish enough.

During Dr. Pless' testimony, I was given permission to pass the photographs to the jurors. I did so slowly as if even holding the evidence was painful. The jurors looked at the photographs. A few of them began to cry as they saw what was left of the baby after the fire. I had received permission to show the jurors the photograph of Baby Matthew, taken after his birth, at the same time as the autopsy photographs. When the photographs had been passed from juror to juror and then returned to me, I asked the court to take a break. This had to sink in.

As Dr. Pless reached the end of his direct testimony, I asked him his opinion about the fire and he looked directly at the jury and told them that that "someone" had poured accelerant directly onto a helpless eight week old infant. At least two of the jurors were sobbing. Voyles seemed stunned as Dr. Pless testified that an accelerant had been poured onto Baby Matthew.

"And then the infant was set on fire," Dr. Pless added.

"Would alcohol have caused Baby Matthew's body to have been burnt to the extent that you observed it doctor?" I asked holding my breath.

"In my opinion, yes. There is no other explanation," Dr. Pless said authoritatively, looking at the jurors.

The cross of Dr. Pless was short and ineffective. Dr. Pless was able to respond to every question and to explain his conclusions based on unimpeachable facts and science.

Dr. Pless was the last witness for the State. We had placed more than one-hundred exhibits into evidence: photographs, transcripts, redacted transcripts, statements, pieces of debris found at the scene, the police radio that was found hidden in Wise' bedroom, diagrams, videos, and other materials.

"The State rests your honor."

It was now time for the defendant to present any evidence he chose to present, although he was not required to do so.

Voyles called Michelle Wise, Jeanne Wise and some other friends and family members to testify on behalf of William Wise.

Michelle went through her story of up-the-stairs and down-the-stairs and the phone not working and getting her shoes and running across the street and what she understood Wise was doing. I cross-examined her for more than four hours. She never broke down and never cried. She had a Kleenex in her hand, having undoubtedly been coached to show emotion, but apparently there was none there.

In addition to other family members, the defense called one of the neighbors who testified that he had attempted to go upstairs to save the baby with Wise. This was after the 911 call and far too late to make a difference. I thought he added little to the case.

The defense had hired two expert witnesses. Each seemed qualified and gave their opinion that the extensive damage in the room could have been caused by accidental sources. They were not surprised by the sixteen minute time line or the fatal injuries to Matthew. Instead of arguing about the baby monitor, they focused on the foam mattress, testifying that because it was foam, it acted as an accelerant, burning Matthew and the nursery at an accelerated rate.

The first defense expert, a cause and origin professional, had a video that he wanted to show the jury. It was a segment from the Discovery Channel. This had never been provided to us before the trial but the court allowed it.

The video started. It was a child's bedroom. There were bunk beds with childish comforters and small stuffed animals on them. A fire was started. First the flames were small, but soon, in less than a few minutes, everything in the room began to catch on fire at one time—flashover. The jury stared at the screen. The courtroom was silent with all eyes focused on the screen. It was powerful.

Before Voyles continued his examination of the expert, I wanted to know what was on the rest of the tape. It was clear that the recording was not made by this expert and there was no beginning and no end. I was curious about the origin of the recording. I had never seen this tape and I was obviously concerned after seeing the jurors' reaction to the short clip. I was permitted by the court to ask questions about the video recording.

"Is there more to the recording that you have not shown the jury?" I asked the witness.

"Nothing relevant to my testimony," he responded somewhat smugly.

"He's been coached to say that," I thought. There must be something more to the recording. I asked to approach the bench and the judge permitted the lawyers to move forward to where only he could hear what was said.

"Judge, I have never seen this recording before today and the witness just side-stepped my question. I think we need to take this up while the jury takes a break."

The jury was excused and the judge allowed me to ask the expert a few additional questions.

"I asked you if there was more to the recording than you played to the jury and you did not respond to the question that I asked. Can you answer that question now?" I stared at the witness.

"Yes, there is more on the tape, but it is not relevant to my testimony," he parroted. Well, that was my take on his response.

"Where is the rest of the recording?" I asked. He pointed to his brief case under the defense table. I looked at Voyles who seemed preoccupied with his fingernails.

The court directed the witness to step down and get the tape from his brief case and hand it to me. The court gave us fifteen minutes to review the recording. We took a break and Van Buskirk and I, not wanting to wait for the elevator, raced up the stairs to the Prosecutor's Office to watch the rest of the tape recording.

I smiled at Van Buskirk. "Life is good, detective."

"Ain't that the truth," she responded as we headed back down to the courtroom.

When the jury was returned to the courtroom, I got to play Paul Harvey. I was telling them, or actually showing them, "The rest of the story."

Wise's expert had edited the recording to show only what he wanted the jury to believe. I played the entire recording to the jury and it was evident that the program had been misrepresented. By playing all of the segments of the show, not just the one selected by Wise's expert witness, it was clear that the fire burned for at least fifteen minutes before it reached flashover. By playing the end of the recording, the jury saw that even after everything caught fire it did not burn up like the nursery. By the end of the recording, which was clearly many minutes after flashover, everything in the room was still standing, although it was brown and charred.

Jurors do not like to be misled. They looked at the witness, as I began to question him further.

"Can you tell the jury if there were mattresses on the bunk beds in the Discovery Channel video," I asked him.

"Yes, the jury undoubtedly saw that each of the two beds had a mattress," he responded curtly and in a dismissive tone.

"And those were foam mattresses, correct?" I guessed because the program volume was never on and I hadn't a clue as to what kind of mattresses they were.

"Yes they were," he said evenly. He probably didn't know either.

"Where's the lava from the foam mattresses?" I asked.

"I don't understand what you mean."

"Didn't you tell the jury that the foam in a mattress can melt into a burning liquid and accelerate a fire?"

"Yes, that's what happened here."

"And that's despite the fact that baby mattresses are manufactured with fire retardants to slow the rate of burning?"

"Yes."

"You agree that the room shown in the video was burning for longer than sixteen minutes?"

"Well that's hard to say." He was trying to hold his ground.

"Are you telling this jury that the room in the video burned less than sixteen minutes? Is that your testimony?" I was edging closer to the witness stand and looking directly at him.

"Well, I don't know. I mean, I didn't make the video."

"No sir, you just played a small part of it to the jury didn't you?"

"Yes."

"Let's look at the video again. Not the defense exhibit, the whole tape, State's exhibit 62."

I played the video again.

"Look at the lower right hand corner of the video. Do you see the time?" I used my laser pointer, a technological wonder that I had received as a give away at a seminar I attended. "See the time stamp?"

I thought I saw him gulp, but it was probably my imagination. I kept the laser dot on the time stamp that showed that the fire was burning for a little over twenty minutes at the end. I didn't need a response from him, the jury got it.

"So if we are to accept your opinion, the flame and fire retardant mattress in Baby Matthew's nursery liquefied like lava in less than sixteen minutes, and accelerated the fire, burning the crib to the ground and then Baby Matthew? That right?"

"Yes."

"And the video that you presented to this jury, to explain how that happened shows this." I stopped the video at the last frame with the mattresses intact.

I waited for a response as he sat there silently. I looked at him and then the jury as I walked back to the State's table.

"I guess I have no further questions."

The defense asked him a few more questions and the witness reiterated his opinions. In my mind, the jury was no longer listening to him.

The defendant called another expert witness who showed the jury the steel wool video. Knowing what was coming, I had asked a few of the male jurors during voir dire if they had ever been boy scouts. Two of the jurors had been involved in scouting, one had been an eagle scout. So after the video was shown and the witness finished his direct testimony, I pulled out several bunches of steel wool and a nine volt battery.

"Now you're not suggesting that there was any steel wool in the Wise nursery, are you?" I asked focusing on the witness.

"No, of course not. I'm just showing the jury that the power from a nine volt battery is plenty to start a fire."

"Great, let's show them now." I asked the witness to step down and walked directly in front of the jury box. I handed him a ball of steel wool and the nine volt battery.

"Would you show the jury how a nine volt battery can catch this steel wool on fire?"

He wouldn't do it. "I don't know what kind of steel wool this is" he said eyeing me suspiciously.

"Oh, does that matter? I thought you just told the jury that a nine volt battery could cause steel wool to catch on fire, didn't you?"

"Well, yes, but no one asked me."

"Asked you what?"

"Asked me the type of steel wool that will catch fire."

"Ohhhhhhhh."

"Steel wool is made up of very fine threads of metal, thinner than most sewing thread. Is that correct?" I asked him this question while holding the balls of steel wool in my hands. He spoke to me as if I were a child.

"Yes, but some kinds of steel wool are thicker than others."

"Sure, but all of them are thinner than a single strand of sewing thread," I insisted.

"Yes, that's true."

"So would you please show the jury what you did on the tape?" I demanded.

I handed him all of the bales of steel wool. I walked back to my table so that he, with his hands full of steel wool, was standing alone in front of the jury box.

He looked at each of the rolls carefully. The paper labels had been removed from all of them. He looked slowly at each one turning it in his hand. The jury was watching him. He finally put them all down on my table and said, "None of these will catch fire."

"No, none of them will catch fire when touched to a nine volt battery?"

Now I was demanding. "Only the very finest steel wool, pulled apart, under perfect conditions, will heat up. Isn't that correct?"

I didn't care that he did not respond. He just stood there.

"So in order for it to start a fire, it would have had to be the very finest steel wool, pulled apart, and then put in contact with both strands of wires from the step down transformer, right?"

"I don't know."

I had nothing further of that expert witness either.

The Defense rested without William Wise testifying. The State did not call any additional witnesses. The evidence was closed.

I gave the best closing argument that I was capable of presenting. Because the State had the burden of proof, we had a beginning closing argument, then the defense had the opportunity to argue to the jury and then the State had a final rebuttal closing argument.

After my argument, I watched as Voyles rolled his chair from behind the defense table and sat directly in front of the first two jurors: the two youngish African American women. He was at eye level with the two. I had never seen this before.

All of the lawyers that I had ever seen doing a closing argument had stood before the jury and argued on their feet. This was a new technique.

Voyles' goal may have been to create a mistrial. A mistrial would be declared if the jury could not reach a unanimous verdict. So, if the two women refused to vote to convict, his client would have a new trial. Or Voyles may have believed that the two women could sway the entire panel in his client's favor.

He basically ignored the rest of the jury. His entire closing was made in a conversational tone, directed just to those two women. He made a compelling argument that circumstantial evidence was insufficient, pointed out the conflicts between Lepper and Shand and tried to explain away Finneran's testimony. He also said that there were two people that could have saved Matthew, Bill and Michelle. Voyles did not say one word about Dr. Pless.

I responded, as best as I could, to Voyles' argument. He had hinted that Michelle could have set the fire. He seemed to want Michelle to be the reasonable doubt. I reiterated that Wise had the training, the lack of desire to have this child, lack of patience for Matthew's crying and all of the other evidence. I looked at each juror with all of the passion and honesty that I possessed and urged them to convict William Wise. I stopped speaking, maintaining eye contact with the group, and then slowly returned to the State's table. Jurors one and two would not look in my direction.

The judge instructed the jury on the law and excused them to go to the jury room. He told them that the evidence would be brought into the jury room, in a few minutes. He also instructed them that they should not begin deliberations until the evidence was in front of them. I watched the jurors walk out of the courtroom.

"I did the best I could, Leslie," I told Van Buskirk.

Van Buskirk did not respond. She too was watching the jurors leave the courtroom. As the last juror stepped down from the raised second level of the jury box, he glanced at William Wise.

I was bone-tired. I mean that kind of tired that saying one word or doing one more thing was unthinkable. The kind of tired that only a lengthy trial can cause. I was not the only one exhausted by the trial. Van Buskirk was mentally and physically finished and I suspected that Voyles was worn out as well.

The court reporter spread all of the trial exhibits on a large table in the courtroom. The judge directed Voyles and me to look at all of the exhibits before the bailiff took them in to the jury. The exhibits were extensive, as the defense had added to the large number that the State had introduced. We examined the table and both of us agreed that the exhibits were in order. The bailiff left with the first batch of exhibits and continued to walk back and forth until they were all in the jury room.

I was surprised when Judge Barney said, "Don't go far. I don't think it will take the jury too long to reach a verdict."

Voyles' office was down the street, but not far away. My office was only a few feet and an elevator ride away, but I was starving. I don't eat much during a trial but more than make up for it during deliberations.

We left our pager and office numbers with court staff. Van Buskirk and I went to Friday's to have a late lunch. It was the worst time of the trial, when the jury goes out to deliberate there is no telling what will be said, remembered, misinterpreted, misunderstood, considered or determined. I believed whole heartedly in the jury system and the power of putting all of those minds together, but I certainly was not about to celebrate.

Our food had just arrived when I received a page from Judge Barney's chambers. I called the number. "Mrs. Moore, the jury has a question. The judge would like you back in the courtroom immediately."

I left a twenty on the table and Van Buskirk and I got into the old blue car and returned to the courthouse. I ran in while she parked at the curb in a no parking zone. Leslie reached the courtroom before Voyles returned.

Jurors are instructed that if they have a question, it must be put in writing and passed to the bailiff, who will give it to the judge. It is not all that unusual for the jury to have a question and the procedure is for the court to read the question to the lawyers for both sides, accept suggestions on how to respond and then respond in writing to the jury. The usual response is, "the court cannot respond to your question. Please continue your deliberations" or the universally accepted, "please reread the court's instructions to you."

We waited for the judge to take the bench. This discussion would have to be taken down by the court reporter. Instead Judge Barney's judicial assistant came into the courtroom and asked Voyles and then me to come in to Judge Barney's chambers. Voyles and I wordlessly complied, following her out of the courtroom.

When we reached Judge Barney's inner sanctum he was sitting at his large beautifully carved wood desk. Without looking up from the small white paper he was reading, he gestured for us to sit down. He was reading the question and shaking his head. He put it on his desk so that Voyles and I could read it.

"Judge Barney, Are we supposed to have the transcript that talked about William Wise being a suspect in the murder of Rae Ann Symons and her unborn twins?"

I couldn't believe it. Voyles seemed equally stunned. We hadn't taken the un-redacted transcript from the pile. A juror had read it.

"Well counsel, what do you propose?" Judge Barney asked as if we could find a cure for the violation.

"You have no choice except to declare a mistrial," Voyles said. He knew as I did that a mistrial meant having to try the case again. Two long weeks wasted. We were both at fault for the error and so there would be no double jeopardy in retrying the defendant.

I was having difficulty breathing. I looked at the judge and said, "Maybe only one juror read the transcript. We have two alternates. You could excuse that juror and the jury could continue deliberations or you could question every juror about the transcript."

"That's what I intend to do, Mrs. Moore, but I suspect that more than just the one juror read the transcript. We'll find out soon enough. If they have, I have no choice."

The judge was tired too. It had been an arduous and intense trial.

We returned to the courtroom while the judge donned his robe. Van Buskirk looked as if I had killed her cat when I told her what had happened. "I'm so sorry, Van Buskirk. I looked as carefully as I could at the exhibits."

"Hey, I looked too. Who knew the jury would grab a transcript and actually read it. Damn."

The judge called the jurors into the courtroom. After only a few questions, it was evident that several jurors had read excluded portions of the transcript. The document itself was in the hands of a juror in the back row. Several of the jurors admitted that they knew about Rae Ann Symons' death. Jurors number one and two denied reading or hearing anything about the transcript. They swore that they had not read a word. I believed them.

They had made up their mind. Maybe even before the trial had started.

The court explained to the jury that they were being excused and why.

"Ladies and gentlemen, through no fault of your own, you have reviewed materials that may have influenced your verdict. For that reason, you are dismissed and free to go home."

I watched their faces. They looked at each other and seemed to want a further explanation. One juror raised his hand.

"You mean we do not get to vote again on the verdict?"

"No sir, this case will have to be decided by another jury," the judge told him.

A juror seemed to want to know what all the other jurors wanted to know. "Has Mr. Wise been charged in the killing of the young pregnant woman in Elkhart?"

"You are free to discuss anything you care to with the State, Detective Van Buskirk or Mr. Voyles. On the other hand, you do not have to speak with anyone at all. It is completely your choice. I will be back to the jury room in a few minutes."

That was the only answer that Judge Barney gave to the juror and he nodded to his bailiff. We all watched as the fourteen people who had listened to two weeks of testimony filed out of the jury box.

I was looking at but not seeing the group. After they left, the judge declared a mistrial and with the court reporter taking down every word, explained why the court had done so. No one objected. To do so would have been futile. The court of Appeals would have reversed a conviction.

I asked the court to immediately take William Wise into custody.

"Your Honor, you have now heard the evidence against Mr. Wise and it is overwhelming. He is a risk to the community. He now knows the State's evidence and could even present a flight risk. This man needs to be incarcerated until the next trial. There will be a next trial Your Honor."

I was emphatic about the retrial. No matter what, I intended to prosecute William Wise for the death of Matthew Wise.

"Mrs. Moore, because I have granted a mistrial, the presumption of innocence continues to attach to Mr. Wise. I did hear the evidence and understand your argument. But the State of Indiana agreed to Mr. Wise being released years ago. He has appeared at every hearing and each day of the trial. Mr. Voyles, anything to add?"

"No, sir," Voyles said quietly.

Over my objection, Judge Barney released William Wise. The judge warned Wise to appear at all court dates and then William, Michelle and the family hugged again and walked hand in hand out of the courtroom.

For the second time I sat in the courtroom overcome by exhaustion and failure. My mind was blank. After several minutes Van Buskirk insisted that I get up and leave the courtroom. I went to my car, drove home and stayed in bed for the next two days.

# Chapter Fourteen

DRAGGED MYSELF OUT of bed, opened the curtains for the first time in two days, and took a deep breath. My youngest joined her sister in bed with me and we read a chapter of *Harry Potter*. Steve jumped on top of the covers and we all laughed.

"Time to get up and resume life," I sagely advised myself. The kids smiled their agreement as I got out of my nightgown and into some clothes. It was a weekend and I got to enjoy a few more hours with family.

We didn't discuss William Wise, but he was not far from my mind. I still had many arson and murder cases to prosecute and each deserved my attention. William Wise would wait. His time would come, I told myself, a bit less convinced than before.

Mistrials are unusual in my experience.

In fact, in more than eighteen years of practicing law, I had only experienced one before. In that case a federal jury could not decide whether my client was guilty of a drug related "continuing criminal enterprise" charge. They deliberated for two days. Ultimately they, or at least some of them, decided that the proof was insufficient to convict her. After the mistrial, the United States Attorney's office did not retry my client and the hung jury was a victory.

But Wise was different.

It was a technical error that caused the mistrial. It was a mistake. It was my mistake. As the prosecutor, everything that went on in the courtroom was my responsibility, right down to the exhibits that should go to the jury. Wise's jury never had a chance to work together, to deliberate, to reach a verdict. I was convinced that the jury would have convicted Wise.

On the drive home Steve asked me what I was going to do about Wise. It was the first time he had mentioned the trial since I trudged in on Friday afternoon. I shrugged.

"I don't know, honey. It was a battle. I haven't spent ten minutes with you or the kids in months. I told the press that there would be a retrial, but I haven't discussed the case with Scott. What do you think?"

"Look, babe, this guy killed his son. He should rot in jail. We understand about your trials. Do what you have to do." He reached over and held my hand.

"Maybe I can make it up to you?" I asked in what I hoped was a seductive manner. He broke out laughing.

When I got to work on Monday there were some "So sorrys" and a few shakes of the heads. I had several messages from Van Buskirk, but I wasn't ready yet to do the post mortem. I emailed Leslie:

Need some time to recover. Will call you later this week.

She emailed back:

Bullshit. I'll be right down. Don't leave or I will find you.

I smiled at the message. I waited and, in a few minutes, she appeared.

"I have nicknamed you Ginzu Woman, she said. I didn't get it.

"Is that Japanese for stupid twit?" I asked.

The real reference had been to a popular cutting tool that appeared in Benihana-type commercials, with the Japanese chef cutting vegetables and meats at an incredible speed.

"No, dumbshit, it means that you sliced their exfuckingperts into little pieces and you did it so quickly and effectively that they didn't even feel it. You are my hero."

I briefly thought about hugging her, but she was armed and she was Van Buskirk.

"Thanks," I said. "But what about the mistrial, you have to be disappointed?"

"We'll get him next trial. No doubt."

She continued, "I stayed to speak with the jurors after you left. Jurors one and two would only talk to Voyles, but I spoke with most of the others. They wanted that little fuck to fry. At least one of them asked me about the death penalty. You had them."

"What did they say about Voyles' jurors?"

I really needed to know the criticism of the case more than the positives. We would have a second chance and I didn't intend to waste it.

"Those two thought that Michelle might have killed Matthew. Voyles' not so subtle crap suggestion hit home with them. They thought that Wise might have helped, but they weren't sure he did the dirty deed himself. The jury only took one vote and then they started to look at the exhibits carefully. And you know the rest."

"Oh, someone mentioned that they weren't convinced that alcohol could burn, despite what the witnesses said," she continued. "Dumb asses."

This knowledge was a great help. I knew what to do about the alcohol. We could show them at the next trial. Bring in a bottle of alcohol and a match, some sort of safe container and whoosh! Of course, we'd have the fire department standing by.

I wondered how many of the jurors had gone home and burned some alcohol over the weekend. I only hoped that they hadn't set their houses on fire.

That still left the tricky question of what to do about the possibility that the defense would try to blame the murder on Michelle. It was a pretty good strategy. I needed to consider our options.

Van Buskirk and I agreed to meet up in a few days to regroup. Each of us had cases that deserved and needed our attention. I had messages stacked on my desk from other detectives, witnesses, and victims. We did not have any other cases together, although she had asked me to take over a case that was being handled by another prosecutor. I planned to do so.

The publicity about Wise was dying down, although the news channels had aired several stories during the trial and about the mistrial. There were always other murders to cover.

At home we were trying to regain some normalcy. Steve had been Mother and Father to our children for the past month. Steve told me later in the week that his boss had commented "If your wife would keep her face out of the news, you could spend more time at work." Steve assured me that the comment was mostly in jest but I had my doubts. I spent as much time at home as I could.

About a week after the mistrial, Van Buskirk and I renewed our conversation about Michelle Wise.

I said, "There were only two people that could have killed Baby Matthew. The defense can successfully argue that Michelle killed him. Then Wise could get off. On the other hand, if we charge her, then they can point the finger at each other and we won't have a live witness at trial to describe what happened."

"Do you really think she did it?" Van Buskirk asked. "I mean could she have pulled it off? Or was she just doing what her husband told her to do."

We both thought that William Wise was the killer but Michelle could have been a knowing participant. In Indiana, whether she was the primary killer or assisted the killer, she could be charged with murder.

We decided that it was time to speak directly with Michelle. I had no reason to think that Michelle had hired her own lawyer or even considered that she might be charged as an accessory. So Van Buskirk called her and made an appointment for us to meet with her, without her husband present.

Van Buskirk explained to Michelle that we could not meet with him, because he was represented by counsel. Michelle was very hesitant but Van

Buskirk assured her that we would meet with her either on her terms, or at the police station. Michelle relented.

"Okay, she'll meet with us, but at her mother's house in Elkhart, and after work. She says she needs to keep her job. I wanted to meet at a neutral location but she wouldn't agree to that. I think we're OK."

I agreed with Leslie that meeting on Michelle's turf was not a problem.

"Make sure they don't have cats," I warned. "I'm allergic. No cats."

As I was saying this Van Buskirk was laughing.

"Your Achilles heel. Good to know."

"Chocolate and broad shoulders are my weaknesses. Cats only make me sneeze and stop breathing."

The meeting with Michelle was scheduled for early evening. Van Buskirk and I drove to Elkhart, a four and a half hour drive with Van Buskirk at the wheel. I had offered to drive, but she had declined.

The driver's side window was as usual open the whole way and I thought I would get frostbite.

When we arrived, Michelle's mother met us at the door. Her greeting was as cold as the temperature outdoors. We stepped in and found that there were three other family members and Michelle assembled in the dining room. Mrs. Davis said, "We're not comfortable with you meeting with Michelle without her lawyer present."

"Does Michelle have a lawyer?" I asked.

"Well, Jim Voyles is her lawyer or he is Bill's lawyer and he should be here." She looked at Michelle who had not said a word so far.

"Mrs. Davis, if Michelle has a lawyer that represents her interests then we cannot speak with her tonight. What I can say is that you were in the courtroom when Jim Voyles told the jury, or at least implied, that Michelle killed Baby Matthew. He didn't sound like a lawyer representing her interests."

Michelle had testified at the trial and some of her family members had been in the courtroom most, if not, every day of the trial. Surely the whole family had questions about whether Wise killed Matthew. Maybe we could get Michelle to tell us the whole truth.

Mrs. Davis did not respond, but gestured to two empty seats at the dining room table. She did not introduce the other family members at the table.

"Are you recording this," one of them asked.

"No. We are not," Van Buskirk responded truthfully. I wished we were.

Van Buskirk and I had agreed that she would conduct the interview. There were several reasons that it made sense. First, Michelle really did not like me. No surprise there. But also I had cross-examined her during the trial. She had not enjoyed it one bit. So she really, truly did not like me. On the other hand Van Buskirk had never cross-examined her. Detective Van Buskirk got to be the good cop for this interview. But there were more important reasons for her to do the questioning. I did not want to hear later that I put words in Michelle's mouth and I did not want to become a witness in the case.

"Did you kill your baby?" Van Buskirk asked as she looked directly at Michelle completely ignoring the other people in the room.

So much for the good cop.

"No," Michelle said quietly.

"Then why did your husband's lawyer accuse you of doing it?" Van Buskirk continued.

"I don't know," she stammered. "I didn't know that was going to happen."

"Well, how else did you think he was going to get Bill off? All of the evidence is against him," Van Buskirk spat.

"I, I don't know."

Michelle looked even worse than she had at trial. I hadn't thought that was possible. She had gained more weight and was wearing a two sizes too small dress, un-ironed, and hideous ugly. She wore no make-up and her hair hung in strings around her porky face.

The questions and answers bounced around for a little more than an hour. Michelle claimed that Wise's attorney had coached her and that she had "stretched the truth" at his insistence.

I didn't believe that for a second. I just didn't see Jim Voyles risking his license for William Wise. It was possible that Wise told his wife that Voyles wanted her to exaggerate, but that was to be expected since Wise was a liar and a murderer.

"We can charge you with murder too, Michelle. There were only two of you at the house and your story is very suspicious. Why didn't you save Matthew? Why?"

Van Buskirk really seemed to want an explanation.

Michele pleaded, "I thought Bill would get him. I thought that. Really."

She looked washed out. She kept saying that she cared about Matthew, and, "Bill would never have hurt Matthew."

"He killed Matthew. Don't you see that?" asked Van Buskirk.

She didn't seem to.

It's pretty hard for me to sit quietly under any circumstances. To sit and listen to Michelle's denials made me want to grab her and shake her. Keeping my mouth shut was exhausting. But Van Buskirk was far more experienced in out of courtroom interrogations than I was, and it was her case.

We really did not get far with Michelle or her family. She made no admissions, except about the exaggerations. I discounted her allocation of the blame for that, although I certainly believed that she had exaggerated the amount of affection between Wise and Matthew.

On the ride home Leslie and I had a lively discussion about Michelle's guilt or innocence. We also discussed what we had observed. If Michelle was not a meek, easily manipulated, pawn of William Wise, then she was a potential Oscar winning actress.

I still liked Wise for the one who poured alcohol on Matthew. I couldn't see Michelle having the guts to light the match. William was obviously in charge that night. He was also in charge of the relationship. Yet it was she who had refused to abort the infant. Could she be that good an actress? We decided not to decide whether to charge Michelle. We would make up our minds later.

Van Buskirk wrote a report about the interview, as she was obligated to do. I provided a copy to the defense, as I was obligated to do. It apparently did not go over well. Van Buskirk had accurately reported that Michelle accused Wise's defense lawyer of distorting her testimony. She did not include our assessment of those accusations. Just the facts.

"Ran into Voyles outside Criminal Court Two this morning," Van Buskirk reported when we caught up in the reception area of the Prosecutor's Office. "He's pissed."

"Not my problem," I responded. We both grinned. "It's really the little things that bring joy into the work place."

# Chapter Fifteen

MONTHS WENT BY at berserk speed.

I had a lot of cases and they kept me busy. In Baby Wise, we had a couple of tentative trial dates but, for some reason or another, the trial dates were continued. Judge Barney was forced to retire because of health issues. It was a true loss. I had come to respect and appreciate the man and would miss his elegant humor and even temperament.

John Commons was no longer my supervisor as I had been assigned as the Community Prosecutor for the Sheriff's Department. I worked in the jail building down the block from the City County Building. It was not really my cup of tea, too much diplomacy had to be employed and that was not my strong suit.

I wanted investigators who would work as hard as I did. There were a few of them at the Sheriff's Department, but not many. We put together some good cases though, including the murder of a paraplegic, eighty-year-old, highly decorated WWII veteran, who had been killed in his home. It took nearly a year, but we finally went to trial and obtained a conviction.

I think I was accepted by the men in the Sheriff's Robbery Homicide unit where I worked, but I wanted to be back in the City County Building with its courtrooms and slippery hallways. Scott Newman was not pleased that I wanted to leave the Sheriff's Department assignment. I had not understood the importance of the job to the tense relationship between the prosecutor's office and the sheriff. I apologized but insisted. I was still the chief arson prosecutor and wanted to be more accessible to the Unit. Scott and I agreed that I would stay put until there was an appropriate opening in the felony courts.

Only a short time later, one of the senior prosecutors in the office decided to move on to greener pastures. I asked Cale and Sheila Carlisle to give me her job. The retiree was the Supervisor for Criminal Two. While the position would involve some oversight of other prosecutors, I would also be able to try cases on a regular basis. I would continue as chief arson prosecutor as well. The job seemed perfect to me.

Days passed and I was offered the job—supervising felony prosecutors in Criminal Court Two. I would have the same position that John Commons held in Criminal Five. I learned that John had recommended me for the criminal court supervisor spot. His recommendation was a surprise to Shelia Carlisle (who was our direct boss) and a shock to me.

Sheila had confided, "The Marine said he was wrong, well, not in those words, but apparently he and John Barney decided that maybe you did know what you were doing."

I appreciated the sentiment, especially from Judge Barney.

I accepted the position and dove in. I learned that my predecessor was assigned to prosecute a very high profile case. That was not surprising because the supervisor in every major felony court had the option of handling the most complicated and high profile cases and assigning one of the other prosecutors to assist her. What I had not known is that the case was scheduled for trial in two weeks.

I would be lead counsel with another prosecutor who had been working on the case for quite a while. She had also applied for the supervisor position and had considered herself a shoo-in. She told me that the case had been continued many times that the judge had said that there would be no further continuances. She did not share the notebook that she and my predecessor had compiled nor did she offer much assistance or insight.

The case was State of Indiana versus Shane Allen. Shane Allen was the beloved son of the acting Chief of Police. Chief Allen had worked his way up in the department, starting years before as a patrol officer. He was respected in his role but had a weakness for his children. Chief Allen had one son and two daughters. Both of the daughters worked for the IPD. His son Shane was charged with the murder of his sister's boyfriend while the three were driving in a car.

Chief Allen had done everything in his power to get the case dropped. Since I did not know much about the case, I asked to meet with him and he agreed. Big mistake. He spent the time we had together first trying to cajole, then subtly to intimidate, and ultimately he left me with the strong impression that I would need a Sheriff's escort home if I convicted his son. As a parent I got it, but I also understood that this case would have some serious political implications for Scott Newman.

I worked on the case as I did every other major case: day and night and weekends. I had so little time to prepare that I came in no later than five a.m. every day. On the Friday before trial I got into the office early and, having already commandeered the conference room, began to meet with witnesses and prepare for Monday's jury selection. I had my pager, of course, but after a couple of hours I decided to go across the street to the market for my iced tea and some breakfast.

At the market I met a friend, chatted for a few minutes, and then I returned to the office. Scott Newman was livid and waiting for me in the reception area.

The rest is irrelevant to the Wise case. It was malicious and nasty and I resigned that morning. I packed up all of the case files from the conference room table and saw Will walk by.

"Help me carry this stuff to my car," I said through tears.

With Will's help, I loaded all of the boxes into my car. I intended to try the Shane Allen case on Monday. I was not going to let a murderer get off because my boss was temporarily insane. My resignation was effective at the end of the Shane Allen trial, after the verdict.

A week later I found myself at home, without a job, and with no plans. It was like going from New York City at rush hour to Robinson Crusoe Island.

So, I did what every self-respecting woman would do under the circumstances: I started redecorating my house. Wallpaper changed. I let my fingers do the walking. New paint. Order new Pergo flooring. I also renewed my membership in the Parent Teacher Organization, cooked enough food for a small but hungry army and agreed to serve as Chairman of the Board of one of the nonprofit organizations with which I was involved.

And after about three days of that, I was contacted by a very fine law firm in Indianapolis, the second or third largest in Indiana. They wanted to interview me.

I scanned the newspaper every day to find out about my former cases. I spoke with Van Buskirk and Will and told them the truth about why I was forced to resign and what had happened.

"You have to try the Wise case," Van Buskirk demanded.

We were on the phone. She was talking about some of her recent cases and I was looking at a baking for kids cookbook and lamenting the day that the bakery in our neighborhood had closed.

"Sure Van Buskirk. I will just call Scott Newman and tell him to give me my case. Perhaps you haven't heard: only prosecutors can prosecute people. I understand that Lisa Swaim is the new chief arson prosecutor. She worked with me for a while. She is young and learning, but she is good. You can work with her."

"Bullshit. I want you."

I dusted off my big firm suits and practiced for the application process. After a multiday interview, I was hired to work for the large law firm focusing on insurance defense litigation. I had worked litigating fraud and arson claims for insurance carriers before and so my experience was apparently just what they were looking for at the firm. The firm also knew what I had earned as a prosecutor and so I was offered a salary tens of thousands of dollars more than I had been paid as said prosecutor, but also tens of thousands of dollars below what I was worth. Nonetheless, I accepted.

I had been at Bose McKinney & Evans about a month when I received a letter at home from the Prosecutor's Office. I was stunned.

Dear Diane:

Would you consider handling the William Wise prosecution as a special prosecutor for the Marion County Prosecutor's Office? Lisa Swaim, our chief arson prosecutor, will assist you and handle most of the pretrial litigation, as we understand that you have joined Bose McKinney & Evans. (By the way, congratulations.)

We will pay you $x,xxx for your service.

Please let us know at your earliest convenience if you are willing to undertake this challenge.

Sincerely,

Sheila Carlisle

Special Prosecutor is a rare designation and an honor. It provided all of the immunity that I would have had as a prosecutor, but I would remain in private practice. I didn't know how my firm would feel about my return to prosecution, but I wanted to do this.

The small sum that was offered to compensate me for my service was far less than I earned in a pay period at the firm. I would probably have to use my vacation time. Still, I showed the letter to Steve.

"Just say no! I know you want to handle the case, honey, but do you want to go back after what happened?"

My husband is Mr. Mellow and so his intensity was unusual. But he had seen me after I left the prosecutor's office and knew what leaving the office had cost me.

"I know what you mean," I said. "And I agree. But on the other hand, honey, what if Wise walks? Will I ever be able to look at a baby without feeling guilty? I think I need to finish this case."

Steve and I discussed it again a little later. I also called my mother and told her about the letter. She had some unkind things to say about Scott, but said that she and Bruce had been worried that the Wise case would be dropped without me there to prosecute it.

The next day at work I told my boss at the law firm that I needed to prosecute the Wise case. He said that he understood and gave me permission to accept.

We talked about the time commitment and I agreed to keep my billable hours up to expectations, despite handling the Wise case. I hated my new job and probably would have quit if he had disapproved. I suspected that he knew that.

I replied to the letter from the Prosecutor's Office:

Dear Sheila,

A couple of weeks ago I ordered new Pergo flooring for our home. It cost $x,xxx.xx. I included dollars and cents from the flooring bill. If you are able to increase the compensation to pay for our flooring, then I would be agreeable to working with Ms. Swaim and handling the trial of State v. William Wise as a special prosecutor.

Please advise me at your earliest convenience so that Lisa and I can start working on putting this murderer in prison.

Sincerely,

Diane


A couple of days later, Sheila called me, laughing.

"Really, you had to say what you were spending the money on? I'm glad that you are onboard. We need you for this case. Lisa is ready to do whatever is needed and if there are any problems, just give me a call. You have my pager number."

"Has a trial date been set yet? I don't need another Shane Allen situation," I said.

"Pat Gifford has been babysitting the case as presiding judge but she is going to hand it off. We think that Jane Magnus-Stinson will be your trial judge."

Wonderful, I thought. Judge Magnus-Stinson was in the opposite political party and was a major player in party politics, and she was tough on the prosecution, but she was an exceptional trial judge. Judge Magnus-Stinson had been the jurist on another case that I prosecuted where a parent killed her child. She was fair, knew and applied the law, and was one of the best prepared judges in the county. She was a dream.

"Then it's a definite yes, if Scott is going to pay for my Pergo."

Sheila agreed and gave me Lisa Swaim's telephone and pager numbers. I immediately called Van Buskirk and gave her the news.

"Allfuckingright! This is our case and no one else is gonna get it done. Glad you're back."

We planned out a schedule to meet and get with some additional witnesses. Van Buskirk told me that she had located Wise's girlfriend, the firefighter on disability. We made arrangements to meet with her.

I called Lisa Swaim. I couldn't read her reaction. It could not be easy to have someone else as lead counsel when you are the chief prosecutor and we had never tried a case together. But I thought it would work well.

Lisa was in her late twenties, with long very dark hair, beautiful fair skin, and a can-do personality. I knew that she had found her own way, paid for college and law school on her own and was supporting her mother. She was always well dressed. I knew she had an ego, and God knows so did I, so it would be an interesting time.

I advised Lisa, "OK, so you will do the day to day hearings and all of the depositions. Please don't let them try to depose anyone who's already been deposed, like Van Buskirk."

Most prosecutors have limited experience in deposing expert witnesses because they are few and far between in state criminal cases on the Defense side. I explained what the depositions would entail and ensured that she would order a transcript for every deposition that was taken so that I would know what was going on.

"Van Buskirk is pretty quirky isn't she?" Lisa asked me.

"Why would you say that?" I asked, trying to keep my inflection flat. She dropped the subject. Quirky indeed!

The team was back together with another fair judge. I was a happy camper. I did not like working for the firm, despite the pay raise. I had to dress more formally and deal with spoiled and elitist lawyers and staff. I was amazed at the sense of entitlement of the legal secretaries and paralegals and their smug attitudes. I worked my usual hours and was rewarded with a lecture on fraudulent billing by my boss.

"I worked every hour that I billed, Bob," I told him defensively. Really, I was being called on the carpet for working too much? I was usually in the office long before the staff and it apparently was of concern to our secretary.

"Well, you need to work hours while everyone is around," my boss told me in an eminently reasonable tone.

"Not going to happen, Bob," I said. "I come in early and leave early to have time with my kids."

He said he understood and that I should consider working later anyway. Not in this lifetime, I thought. I had little enough time with my girls and I was not going to waste it trying to save money for wealthy insurance companies.

"I'll see what I can do," I fibbed.

During the next few months I spoke to Lisa Swaim often. She was working hard on the case but was not as communicative as I had hoped.

"Voyles withdrew from representing Wise," she told me. "I guess his money ran out."

"He didn't have any money. I guess his Mom's money ran out. Who's representing him now?" I asked.

"Mark Earnest. But he moved to withdraw when I told him that you were going to prosecute the case as a special prosecutor," Lisa told me.

"Did the court grant his motion?"

"No. The public defender is offering support. So, Tom Leslie and Jennifer Lukemeyer will be entering appearances as well. There's a joke in the office about 'How many public defenders does it take to defend a client against Marger Moore.' Jennifer is with the public defender now but she was with Voyles during the Wise trial. Also, they have ordered most of the trial transcripts."

This was really interesting news. I actually liked Mark Earnest and respected his dedication to his clients. He was tall with dark hair, dark eyes, and dark temperament. There was something brooding yet interesting about him. He had little sense of humor that I discerned. I met him when he represented Michelle Engon Jones, a mother accused of killing her son, Brandon.

For nearly a year Mark could have pleaded his client to child neglect, a class B felony, and avoided a murder conviction. He had never even approached me about a plea bargain. After the jury trial, he had disappeared from the courthouse and no one that I knew seemed to know where he was. I spent several unpleasant hours worrying about the young lawyer. He had done an excellent job defending his guilty client.

I hoped that during the Wise trial I would have the chance to let Mark know that, despite our being on opposite sides of the case, I believed that he had an innate talent, being a defense lawyer was his calling, as they would say in the South.

"Please be sure to order a copy of Michelle's transcript," I told Lisa. "We will also want Lepper and Pless. You should order Shand's too, although I don't think we will be using him for the trial."

"Good that you said that, Diane. I spoke with Shand last week. You know that Barker Davie passed away a few months ago. Shand says that he can't afford to testify or work on this case unless we agree to pay for his time."

"Well, that's not unreasonable at all. Mr. Davie spent a great deal of money helping us and with him gone I can understand that the firm can't keep on lending Shand and Finneran to us. We can make do without Shand, but what about Finneran? We need him. I mean we can't make the case without him."

I was concerned. "Do we have any money to pay Finneran?"

"Not that I know of. I haven't spoken to Jim Finneran, I figured you'd want to do that yourself. Also, the room is still in storage. Are we going to use it again?"

Lisa was already up to speed on the case and I was glad to hear that.

After the last trial, I had learned that Barker & Herbert had additional recordings of the burn test room that were taken long after the fire was extinguished. I had decided that using those recordings was less distracting and a better presentation of the evidence.

"Let's keep the room in storage in case we need it. But right now, I don't think we will be bringing it to the courthouse." We made arrangements to discuss the case by telephone on a regular basis.

Van Buskirk had located the female firefighter that Wise had been dating and said that she had a really great surprise for me, a new witness. She wouldn't tell me anything about the witness until I met with her in person.

Several days later, I broke free from my schedule at the firm and Van Buskirk and I met Margaret Jones at her modest Indianapolis home. She was tall and average looking, with strong shoulders and an athletic build. She had returned to firefighting and we did not ask about the disability that had kept her out of work when she got to know Wise.

"So, how did you meet Bill Wise?" Van Buskirk asked her.

"He was a fire dispatcher and we got to talking one day. We agreed to meet for coffee and then we went out a few times."

"Were you romantically involved?" Van Buskirk was being subtle, which works well at times for those who have a reputation for being blunt. Was she on medication? Had someone filed a complaint? Was she seeking a promotion? I hadn't seen this side of her before. I'd expected something on the order of "so were you fucking him?" Heck I wouldn't have put it past her to ask, "Was he any good?"

"I guess," she replied vaguely. "He seemed more interested in what I did for a living than in dating me. He was always talking about fires and being a firefighter."

"Had he applied to IFD to be a firefighter?" Van Buskirk inquired without mentioning Wise's epilepsy.

Margaret was pondering as she spoke.

"No. He told me that when he rescued someone they would take him. That was like his fantasy. He was going to rescue someone from a fire and the fire department would take notice and hire him. I told him that it didn't work that way, but he didn't believe me."

Van Buskirk and I looked at each other. Was that unshakable fantasy Wise's real motive. Wise's dream of being a hero may have trumped even his monetary motives. He was going to kill two birds with one stone. Rescue a baby, albeit a few minutes too late, and then get hired as a heroic firefighter. The million dollar product liability lawsuit was, perhaps, just icing on the cake.

"We will need you to tell the jury about this dream of his, will that be a problem?" I asked.

"Hell, no. Did he really kill his kid? That's sick. I will be glad to testify," Margaret Jones said unequivocally.

We talked a while longer, but she had already told us what we needed to know. We thanked her and left our cards. We got her current contact information, shared a few more pleasantries and then left.

"Are you up for a promotion or something?" I asked as we got into the blue bomb.

I mimicked her, "Were you 'romantically involved?" I laughed.

"I was being polite," Van Buskirk said. "And yes, wiseass, I am studying for the sergeant's exam. But I suck at taking tests, so screw it!"

"You're really smart, Van Buskirk. What's the big deal? You should be a top choice."

She didn't reply, instead rolling down the window and pulling onto the street.

"Tell me about the surprise witness," I asked, buckling up for the slow lane.

"Unbelievable—good luck for a change," she said. "After the publicity about the mistrial, I got a call from one of Michelle's cousins. She's an attorney with the Indiana Division or Department of Insurance. Who fuckin' cares which. Anyway, she saw Bill and Michelle at a family funeral only two weeks after Matthew was killed. She knew Michelle, of course, but had only met Bill a couple of times. Right at the funeral Bill asks her if she believes that they could win a million dollar verdict if they sued the baby monitor company for the baby's death."

Van Buskirk kept her eyes on the road but I know she wanted to see my reaction.

"They told her, that they had spoken with a lawyer, who told them that they could get a million for the kid's death. They asked her what she thought. Two weeks after the kid died."

"What did she tell them?" I wanted to know.

"She said that she couldn't believe that they were asking that, only a few days after their son was killed. She doesn't remember exactly what she said, but she wanted to get away from them as quickly as possible. She didn't know who to call until she read my name in the paper."

Back at my building I took the elevator to my windowed office on the twenty-seventh floor. I had a spectacular view, beautiful furniture, a company cell phone, and the use of a secretary. There was even a free Coke machine in the break room. And popcorn. But I loathed it.

# Chapter Sixteen

FANCY OFFICE, IN my chair, staring blankly out of the window at the Indianapolis skyline, I wanted to escape. I could hear the rest of the office, at least our floor, begin to come to life, but I had already finished a brief and was staring at another file. I couldn't force myself to start on this new case. I had worked for the firm for several months and it was not a good fit. It was a paycheck. Nothing more and nothing less.

I picked up the telephone and called Lisa Swaim. I hoped that I would catch her before she was off to court. I hadn't seen a courtroom since I'd left the Prosecutor's Office. Lisa had been doing an admirable job of fending off motions filed by the defense, who were re-litigating every ruling and issue that Judge Barney had already resolved. New judge, new hope.

Mark Earnest and the troops had tried to get a different decision on the abortion issue, on the admissibility of the burn room, and to keep out Wise's statements to Allstate and law enforcement. The most significant skirmish was whether to exclude all testimony concerning other baby monitors, including the Gerry 602.

Judge Magnus-Stinson permitted evidence to be submitted as to each issue, heard argument, and then ruled the same way that Judge Barney had ruled on every issue. While I sat in my beautiful digs gathering lint, Lisa was prevailing in the courtroom.

The defense team had decided against using the same experts that had testified in the first trial.

"Ginzu Girl strikes again!" Van Buskirk mused as we reviewed the new witness list. The new experts included some guy from California, Donald Berman, and a local cause and origin expert who worked for a pretty good group in Indianapolis. Lisa took these experts' depositions, and sent me the transcripts.

Over the months, Lisa had done a superior job. But letting someone else, anyone else, make decisions on the Wise case or handle issues at her own pace, was torture for me. Once, when Sheila Carlisle asked me how Lisa was doing, I noxiously complained that she was not doing enough and was dragging her feet. It was an unfair assessment.

Finally, a trial date was set. Judge Magnus-Stinson ordered that the trial would begin on March 2, 1998. Matthew Wise had been dead for nearly five years. William Wise had vacationed in Florida. It was finally time to put him behind bars. There would never be another second chance.

I said goodbye to my luxurious office with a grin and walked to the City County Building. Parking was scarce near the courthouse, so I left my car in the parking garage of the firm's building. I intended to spend the entire week before trial and however long it took to try the case at the City County Building. Lisa and I snagged the conference room as our headquarters (both of us couldn't fit in her office) and began to finalize our trial preparation.

Lisa wanted to be an equal member of the team. She wanted to question some of the witnesses, handle a few cross-examinations, and otherwise serve as co-counsel on the case. It just wasn't going to happen. Every single witness in this case was critical. The examinations required the experience that comes from many mistakes, most of which I'd already made. I was more than hesitant. After months of hard work, Lisa lost her self-control. She rightly felt that she had earned a chance to be actively involved. I had nixed that by saying that I intended to question all of the witnesses at trial.

"You're a control freak! You are impossible to work with! I can't do this."

She tried to slam the door on her way out of the conference room, but it just closed noiselessly.

Lisa was right, of course. I am a control freak. And a perfectionist. I needed her help but could not agree to her requests.

"You're right, Lisa," I admitted aloud when she returned to the conference room. "I am a control freak, about this particular case."

I didn't hand over the reins or anything like that, but I agreed that Lisa would question a few of the witnesses. I told myself it was not really about control as much as technique.

I believe it's utterly cut and dry. Done well, cross examination looks simple. But it's not. A really good cross examination of an expert witness is an exquisite work of art; sometimes more of a Van Gogh than a Monet, but still one of the most important parts of an arson murder case. It requires boundless patience, hyper-acute listening skills, and painstaking preparation, preparation, preparation.

I would handle the cross-examination of William Wise's experts.

Van Buskirk, Lisa, and I discussed what to do about Michelle. It was too close to William's trial to charge her. If we did, it would be characterized as a scare tactic, to keep her from testifying for Wise. Besides, nothing had convinced us that Michelle was the person who had poured alcohol on Baby Matthew.

There is no statute of limitations on murder. So Michelle could be charged at any time in the future. But I couldn't allow the defense to use her to create reasonable doubt either.

"Lisa, will you prepare jury instructions on aiding and abetting. We need to get them to Earnest and the court today. I don't want them claiming that we surprised them at trial."

Lisa came back with a proposed jury instruction that we submitted to the court and to the defense. It was the law in the State of Indiana. It read:

> Every person who shall aid or abet in the commission of a felony, or who shall counsel, encourage, hire, command or otherwise procure a felony to be committed, may be charged by indictment or affidavit, tried and convicted in the same manner as if he were a principal.

"Perfect!" I told Lisa. She went down the hall to ask our, I mean her, paralegal to formalize and file it.

"Earnest is going to go crazy," I predicted to Van Buskirk. "This instruction neutralizes the implication that maybe Michelle was involved. It means that even if the two of them were in it together, the jury should still convict Wise."

My crystal ball was functioning fine. The defense insisted on an emergency hearing that afternoon. Mark Earnest argued that because we had not raised the issue of accomplice liability in the first trial, we should be precluded from doing so here.

I urged the court to consider the facts. There were two adults in the house when the fire was started. Either one of them could have done it. We believed that the evidence against William Wise was strong, but the jury could be led to believe, as Voyles had attempted in his closing argument in the first trial, that Michelle had contributed or caused Matthew's death. The court considered this for a few moments and then concluded, preliminarily, that the State was entitled to the jury instruction.

"A huge victory," I thought. "Let's get this show on the road." So we did.

I had no need for additional shopping, as my wardrobe was complete. The same protocol for the first morning of trial. I got up early, dressed in the dark, walked as quietly as I could on the new Pergo flooring down the hall to kiss both girls goodbye, as they slept. When I left our home for the City County Building it was still dark. I wore the same outfit, neatly cleaned and pressed, including panty hose, as I had worn on the first day of the first trial.

Judge-Magnus-Stinson was already on the bench handling some other minor matters when Van Buskirk, Lisa Swaim and I entered the courtroom. We had brought a cart filled with boxes and exhibits. We stored it behind the State's table. Lisa sat down at the far end of the table with Detective Van Buskirk between us. Van Buskirk was in her trial costume: flower patterned dress with a dark blazer and accoutrement. Lisa looked pretty in her dark suit and blouse. We were ready.

A few minutes later William Wise and his defense team entered the courtroom. The judge was still handling some other minor matters with lawyers not involved in our case. I suspected that a criminal defendant was also at the bench and they were speaking in whispers. Mark Earnest was as dark-headed as ever, especially in comparison to Tom Leslie, who was prematurely white haired with a white mustache and pale complexion.

Tom Leslie had been the chief arson prosecutor years before and fancied himself as an expert on the subject. He had defended an arson case that I had tried some months before I left the Prosecutor's Office. Also in tow was Jennifer Lukemeyer, a young female lawyer who had worked for Jim Voyles. She had moved to the public defender's office and the public was obviously footing the bill for all three of Wise's lawyers. Wise looked exactly the same as he had before.

The William Wise family and friends stepped in after the lawyers. Michelle, Jeanne, Mrs. Davis, and some others took seats behind the defense table. Jeanne and Mrs. Davis both glared at Van Buskirk and me. I smiled back pleasantly until they averted their eyes.

The judge called the case and we selected a jury. We spent some time conditioning the jury, especially about time. From the questions and answers, we thought that we had mostly conceptual thinkers and had weeded out the concrete and hard to convince ones. It's so hard to tell. Some jurors are nervous and others more articulate. It's a bit like speed dating, not very satisfying with a great deal of guessing involved.

For example, Lisa and I disagreed about one of the jurors who had an engineering background. She really liked him and I was concerned about his concreteness. But he was the father of a teenager and, on Lisa's recommendation, we kept him on the jury.

This time the court suggested that we have three alternates. The panel consisted of fifteen jurors and alternates, a good mix of men and women. Some were black and others were white, and a few of them had children. There had been no pretrial publicity and so the selection process went smoothly. We had not brought the burn room out of storage yet. I didn't know if William and

Michelle had revived their hand-holding act, but I doubted it. Judge Magnus-Stinson did not tolerate such cheap shenanigans.

After the judge swore in the jury, she read some preliminary instructions to them. These included instructions about the burden of proof, the nature of the charges against William Wise and other preliminary and housekeeping rules. The jury was cautioned to avoid reading or listening to any news about the case or discussing the case with anyone. The judge also told the jury that what the lawyers say in opening or closing argument is not evidence.

I always disliked that one the most, especially since it was given right before we started our opening statements.

Naturally, I wanted the jurors to take every word I said as gospel. They could ignore the defense lawyers, if they wished.

For decades lawyers were convinced that the closing arguments in a case, the time when lawyers have the most latitude to argue the facts and law to the jury, was the most persuasive part of the trial.

But more recently, studies have proven that many jurors essentially make up their minds about their verdict during opening statements. So what was once considered an unimportant part of the trial had become an essential presentation of the case.

There are many landmines in opening statements that do not exist during closing argument. In opening statement one is expecting that the evidence will prove certain things. This is unlike closing argument where the lawyers know what evidence the jury heard and saw.

For example, let's say that in opening statement the prosecutor promises the jury that an eye witness will positively identify the defendant as the person that committed the crime. Unfortunately, when the witness takes the stand and is faced with the presence of the defendant, she says, "I think it's him, but I can't be sure."

Your goose may be cooked. First, you may lose credibility with the jury and second, you have no eyewitness, despite the fact that you promised one to the jury in opening. Finally, if you make any misstep in opening, the other side may have the opening transcribed and highlight your missteps to the jury in closing argument.

The slick defense lawyer will tell the jury, "Mrs. Marger Moore assured you that you would convict my client based upon the 'positive identification' by Ms. Jones. But Ms. Jones was not certain. She wasn't sure. Not being sure is reasonable doubt. Mrs. Marger Moore exaggerated what the testimony would be, she hoped it would be a positive identification. But, the truth is, the witness had serious doubts about whether my client committed this crime. So should you."

It's a lose/lose situation if you fail to forecast correctly. The danger is far greater to the State than to the defendant. The State has the burden of proof. So a prosecutor must tread carefully, being persuasive and factual without promising too much and delivering too little.

When I stood up from the table, I looked at the judge and waited for a nod, got it, and then looked at the jury as I approached the wood barrier that separates the jury box from the remainder of the courtroom.

I walked up to the jurors and, hopefully without invading their personal space, directed my statements to each and all of them. I tried to maintain eye contact with every juror, at least for some period of time. I sometimes spoke loudly to emphasize a point, and sometimes lowered my voice so that the jurors would have to strain to hear what I was saying. That was another way to emphasize a point. I did not use many exhibits during the opening statement. I only used one: the photograph of a smiling Baby Matthew taken on the day of his birth.

I gave our opening statement, focusing on Baby Matthew and his ghastly death. I described our evidence generally but slowly and methodically. I emphasized the length of time that the fire burned. I wanted to be sure that sixteen minutes was imprinted in the jurors' minds. I reminded the jurors that this child had been killed because his father did not save him. His mother did not save him, or even attempt to save him. I ended by telling the jury that while they could not save Baby Matthew Wise, only they could punish the man that had killed him.

Tom Leslie gave the opening statement for the Defendant William Wise. Tom was far more argumentative than the rules allowed, but I did not interrupt his diatribe. He argued that the investigation was tainted by a ruthless detective, hell bent on destroying the family of Baby Matthew and assisted by a prosecutor who cared little for justice but a great deal about convicting an innocent and grief-struck father for the crime. He pointed out that the State's experts were at odds with each other. And finally, that William Wise and his defense lawyers had brought an expert, all the way from California, to tell them the truth—that the fire was caused by a trusted electronic device—a Fisher Price 1510 Deluxe baby monitor.

He sashayed back to the defense table when he finished and slid his arm unctuously around William Wise's shoulder.

"The State of Indiana may call its first witness," the judge said.

I looked at Lisa, who went to the back of the courtroom, all eyes on her, and brought in the State's first witness.

An exceptionally attractive young man walked into the courtroom behind Lisa Swaim. He was in full navy blue police uniform with shined black boots up to his knees. He had his motorcycle helmet tucked under his arm and strode to the stand exuding confidence.

"The State calls Officer Keith Williams to the stand," I announced as he walked down the aisle.

It was late in the afternoon and Officer Williams would be the only witness of the day. I wanted to end the first day of trial on a strong and positive note for the prosecution.

Under my questioning, Officer Williams told the jury that he had been a motorcycle officer for the Indianapolis Police Department on March 6, 1993. Before he had joined the IPD, Officer Williams had been a fireman in Winston-Salem, North Carolina.

"In North Carolina, we were cross trained as public safety officers. We attended both the police and fire academies. So my background is primarily as a law enforcement officer, but I was called to serve as a fireman many times while I worked in North Carolina." Officer Williams looked at the jurors as he responded to my questions.

"Where were you working in the morning hours of March 6, 1993?"

"I was working in the East Division. I was listening to the police radio and heard that there was a fire with entrapment. I knew the area well. I was very close to the residence," he responded.

"What does it mean when there is a radio call for a fire with "entrapment?" I asked.

"It means that there is a person trapped in a fire situation. Since I was only a minute or minute and a half away, I went right to the scene."

"As you got closer to the house, what did you see?"

"I saw smoke coming from the property, when I was a few blocks away. As I pulled up to the house, I saw fire coming out of the upstairs window that was facing the street. There were two men standing in the doorway of the residence. One of them was a white male and the other was a black male. The white male was wearing turnout gear."

"Officer Williams, why did you respond to the call-out for firefighters?"

"Ma'am, it is my job to help folks in trouble. That was what I intended to do."

"But you're not a firefighter in Indianapolis, are you Officer?"

"No, ma'am. But I was going to get the person out of the house if I could. I could hear the fire trucks behind me, but every second counts in a fire."

"What exactly was the white man wearing? You called it 'turnout gear'?"

"He was wearing a fireman's jacket, helmet, and black boots with pull straps, like firemen wear."

"When you first pulled up to the house, did you notify anyone that you had arrived?"

"No, ma'am. I ran to the front door where the men were standing and the white man said, 'I'm with IFD. There is a baby in the house.'"

"What did you understand 'I'm with IFD' to mean?"

"With his gear, I assumed that he was with the Indianapolis Fire Department."

"The next thing he said was, 'There is a baby in the house' is that correct?" I asked.

"Yes, ma'am. Those were his exact words. I will never forget them. I told him, follow me, we need to find that baby."

"Are you sure that it was you and not the white male who suggested that you go into the house to find the baby."

"Yes, ma'am. I am certain."

"Before you tell us what you did when you entered the house, officer, please describe everything that you noticed about the white man in the turnout gear as you saw him in the doorway."

"First I noticed that the door was open to the house. That was dangerous because the air would fuel the fire. The guy in the turnout gear did not have soot on his face, wasn't coughing or anything, so I assumed that he had arrived right before I did. It didn't look like he had been anywhere near the fire before I arrived." "Objection. Objection!" Tom Leslie interrupted, jumping to his feet, pointing at Keith Williams. "Stop speculating. You don't know whether he was or was not near the fire before you arrived."

Before I could even respond, Judge Magnus-Stinson overruled the objection.

"Mr. Leslie, he is describing what he did or did not observe."

As the trial progressed, Tom Leslie and Mark Earnest would make many of these "speaking objections" which were almost solely intended to divert the jurors from the persuasive witness and to try to distract or detract from the testimony. They became so prevalent that I urged the court to admonish the lawyers to wait for closing argument to try to make their points. The judge did not agree with me.

"Did Mr. Wise have any soot on his face when you first saw him?" I asked the officer.

"No, he did not."

"Did you hear Mr. Wise coughing when you first approached him?"

"No, ma'am."

"As an experienced firefighter, Officer Williams, what do you expect to find if a person has tried to enter a burning room to rescue a person?"

"If the person did not have a SCBA then I would expect to see soot on him. He would likely be choking or coughing and he may even have singed hair and minor burning in and around his face or other exposed areas of his body," he explained.

"What is a SCBA?"

"Self-contained breathing apparatus. It's the tank and mask that you see firefighters wearing, so that they can breathe when they are in a smoke filled building."

"At your direction, did Mr. Wise go into the house with you?" I asked.

Keith Williams had not identified William Wise as the white male. But since no one objected, I called him by name. Williams was no dummy. Although we had not prepared him for his testimony, he picked right up on my rhythm.

"Yes, ma'am. Mr. Wise went up the stairs ahead of me. The smoke was at floor level and it was very hot. When we reached the upper level and turned left, the heat and smoke was too much for me. I started backing down the stairs. As I was on the stairway, I felt a fireman on his way up."

"How long had you been in the residence, Officer Williams?" I asked him.

"A matter of seconds, but it seemed much longer."

"Can you describe to the jury what you looked and felt like when you got outside the door of the Wise house?"

"Yes. I was coughing and gagging from the smoke and heat. I had soot all on my face and hair and my uniform had the stench of smoke."

"Other than what you have told us, did you have any conversation with William Wise that day?" I asked.

"No. I didn't even know that he wasn't a fireman until later."

"Did you ever see Michelle Wise?"

"Well, about fifteen minutes after I arrived, and after the fire was put out by IFD, Mr. Wise was sitting in an ambulance and I saw a woman run across the street and go to him. I figured that was his wife."

"Did you see where Michelle Wise came from?"

"Yes, she was inside a house across the street and when Bill Wise was sitting on the back edge of the fire rescue ambulance, she must have seen him and come outside."

"Was that the first time that you had seen Michelle Wise that morning?"

"Yes, ma'am."

"So, Officer Williams, you risked your life, went into a burning building to save a child that you didn't even know?"

"Anyone would have done what I did, ma'am," he replied.

That was a sentence I hoped the jury would long remember.

Tom Leslie, arrogantly approached the witness. He reminded me of the public defender in *My Cousin Vinny*. He asked Officer Williams questions on cross-examination.

"Now, Mr. Williams, you weren't there to see whether my client tried to rescue Matthew, before you arrived, were you?"

"No, sir. I wasn't there until I was there."

Officer Williams answered in a calm, straight-faced manner that was not mocking. I didn't know how he did it.

"So you can't say that Mr. Wise hadn't made numerous attempts to save Matthew before you arrived, can you?" Tom Leslie insisted.

"No, sir. I can only say what I saw, and that is that Mr. Wise did not have any soot on his face or hands, he was not coughing or gagging, and there was no smell of smoke on him, when I first approached him."

Tom asked some additional leading questions but Williams had the advantage. He was just telling it like he'd seen it.

"Mrs. Marger Moore, do you have any redirect?" the judge asked, knowing that I did.

"Yes, I do, your honor."

I walked nearer to the witness stand.

"Officer Williams, you said that the front door of the Wise home was open, with two men standing in the doorway, when you first arrived. Is that correct?"

"Yes, both the screen door and the front door were propped open. I noticed it immediately because I did not understand why a firefighter would have the doors propped open."

"Why did you question the doors being open?" I asked innocently.

"Leaving a door open gives a fire more oxygen. That means that the fire burns faster and probably hotter."

"How do you know that?" I asked.

"Pretty much everyone knows that, especially anyone with fire training."

I walked back to the State's table and looked at some papers while his testimony settled in.

"No further questions, your honor. May this witness be excused?"

"No" said Tom Leslie, before the judge could respond. "We have a few more questions."

Tom reiterated what he had asked the officer before. Keith Williams gave the same answers as before. Tom Leslie continued to call Keith Williams, Mr. Williams, despite the uniform and that the fact that Officer Williams had risked his life to try to save the Wise infant.

It was a few minutes before five p.m. and I saw jurors looking at the clock. Apparently, the Wise defense team wanted the last word. Not just the last questions for Officer Williams, but every witness throughout the trial.

I did not grace Tom Leslie's re-cross with further questioning. But the State had requested that jurors be permitted to ask witnesses questions.

Indiana has an unusual law that permitted jurors to pose questions to a witness, if the trial court permitted them to do so. I had urged the court to allow juror questioning, in a complex case that I had tried a year earlier. It was a great help.

The procedure was that the juror would write his or her question on a piece of paper, hand it to the bailiff, who would hand it to the judge. The judge would consider each question to determine whether the question would be asked of the witness. The lawyers were permitted to ask questions based on the witness's response to the juror's question.

One juror had a question for Officer Williams. The court read the question silently and then showed it to the lawyers. No one objected.

The judge asked Officer Williams, "Did you ever hear a baby crying?"

"No, I did not."

The silence in the courtroom lingered, until the judge said, "Court will be adjourned until nine a.m. for the jury. The parties will be back in the courtroom by eight-thirty a.m." Judge Magnus-Stinson smiled at the witness as the jury left the box for the night. The courtroom cleared and the three of us left for home.

# Chapter Seventeen

WHEN WE ARRIVED at eight-thirty the next morning, the defense had filed a few more motions and wanted to argue them before the jury was returned to the courtroom. I asked Lisa to handle the arguments, while I spoke with Van Buskirk.

Lt. Vernon Brown and Ed Barnes testified as the first-in firefighters. Their testimony did not vary from what they said at the first trial. Each of them was detached and factual, until Lt. Brown described finding the charred remains of an infant in the destroyed room. His voice cracked as he described what he had seen. He looked at the "Where's Waldo?" photograph and nodded when I asked if it was consistent with his observations. His eyes welled with tears and he did not look up for several seconds. The testimony was short and to the point.

The State's next witness was Lewie-Bob Hiatt, who described MECA and Wise's job there. She explained that Wise was trained to be calm under pressure. With me asking questions, Lewie-Bob and I took the jurors through all of the ways that Wise could have contacted dispatchers if he had wanted to rescue Matthew.

"Please explain to the jury what happened in 1993 when a person called 911."

"Well, it has changed since then, but in 1993, all 911 calls went directly to the Indianapolis Police Department's dispatch operators. IPD shared the same building with us, but had a completely separate group of dispatchers who were housed in a separate area of the building. If the call related to a fire, then the IPD dispatch operator would transfer the call to the Indianapolis Fire Department's dispatch center, which is us," Lewie-Bob explained.

"How long would it take to get a call transferred from IPD to IFD?" I asked.

"That would depend on how quickly the call was answered in the first place, how long the IPD dispatcher spoke with the caller before identifying the call as one for IFD, and then, however long it took for our dispatcher to respond. Several seconds, at least."

"Would everyone who worked at IFD dispatch know that the quickest way to get fire engines rolling would be to call IFD dispatch directly?"

"Of course, our employees would know that, but the public does not have access to our direct lines or to police radios."

"Can you show the jury how this police radio, found in William Wise's bedroom, works?" I asked.

Lewie-Bob stepped down and showed the jurors how the police radio operated. First she turned the off/on knob. The screen showed that the radio was on OPS2. She switched channels and described what each of the channels was used for by the IFD. Then she showed the jury what happened when the radio was turned off and then turned on again. When the radio was turned back on, it was tuned to the last channel that had been tuned-in.

She explained that the red/orange button alerted the dispatchers to the most serious call of all: Officer in Distress. She also demonstrated what happened when the red dot on the radio was pressed. We had agreed beforehand, that it would be more authentic to just push the button in court, without warning the dispatchers in advance.

When Lewie-Bob pressed the button, a dispatcher's voice came over the radio immediately.

"What is the nature of your emergency?" asked the dispatcher. The dispatcher did not even wait for a response before saying that she had the location of the radio and was sending help.

Lewie-Bob hurriedly responded that she was testing the radio. She explained to the jury that her reply had avoided an avalanche of officers/firefighters storming the courtroom.

I noticed jurors looking at William Wise as Lewie-Bob showed them the radio and explained the various ways that Wise could have gotten immediate help for Matthew. Lewie-Bob also testified that Wise had taken the police radio, that night, without permission. To her knowledge, it was the first and only time that Wise had ever taken a radio home with him.

"In addition to using the police radio that he had taken home, were there any other ways that Wise could have contacted IFD dispatch directly?" I asked.

"Yes. We have several direct lines into our operators. Wise knew the telephone number and he could have called that number and saved several seconds," she replied.

"Ms. Hiatt, did the dispatch operators, including the defendant, have a catchphrase that was part of their training?"

"Yes. Seconds save lives. It was the mandate for every dispatcher at IFD. Bill Wise knew that seconds save lives."

"Was William Wise a good employee?" I asked.

"Bill Wise was on performance probation. It was the last step of discipline before he could be terminated," she responded.

"Do you record the 911 calls that come in to the IFD dispatchers?"

"Yes, we do."

"At my request, did you have the taped 911 calls from the early morning hours of March 6, 1993, transcribed?"

"Yes, ma'am. I also compared the tape recordings to the transcripts. They are identical."

"By the way, Ms. Hiatt, do dispatchers have anything to do with these tape recordings?"

"No, they do not. In fact, the only dispatcher that ever asked me to see the recording units was Bill Wise."

"Can you tell the jury when Mr. Wise asked about the recordings?"

"I don't specifically recall the date. But it was after his son was born."

With the court's permission, Lewie-Bob Hiatt read the transcript of the 911 call from Michelle Wise.

"The first call was made by a female caller. It came in at 5:09:39," she said.

"Did the female caller ever tell the operator that a child or baby was in the house that was on fire?"

"No. Absolutely not. She never said a word about entrapment, or anyone being caught in the house."

"Was there a second call to 911?" I asked.

"Yes. At 5:10:06. It was Bill Wise. He called the dispatcher by her name, Jodi."

"So, Mr. Wise was readily able to identify the voice of the operator?" I asked.

"Yes, apparently so," she responded.

"Did he advise that there was entrapment?" I asked.

"Yes, but only after Bill identified the dispatcher, told her that there was a fire at his house, gave her his address, chatted a bit, and then he told her about the entrapment. Seconds save lives, so all of that was wasted conversation— translating into wasted seconds. Bill finally told Jodi, 'The baby is upstairs.'"

"Ms. Hiatt, did William Wise say that his baby was upstairs in his house?" I asked.

"No. He said, 'the baby.'"

"You told the jurors that Mr. Wise was on probation at MECA. Did he have a problem remaining calm under stress?"

"No, not at all. I never saw Bill panic or even get frantic. Bill's problem was with stretching the truth," she said.

"Was that a one-time event, where William Wise stretched the truth?"

"No!" Hiatt said firmly.

"Ms. Hiatt, do you know if William Wise was ever trained as a firefighter?" I asked this as I handed her a document that I had marked as an exhibit.

"Yes, according to Bill's application, he had received the full two-hundred forty hour basic firefighting training in Florida. He also put down that he had additional training after basic. He worked for two fire departments in Florida."

That was all for me at that time.

Mark Earnest handled the cross examination of Lewie-Bob Hiatt.

Earnest asked her, "Are you sure that Mr. Wise knew the special telephone number that you told the jury about? 634-1313?"

"Why would he repeat the phone number?" I wondered under my breath. "Thirteen, thirteen is pretty easy to remember."

Lewie-Bob responded, "He reported sick on the telephone lines in the center before. I'm not sure which number he dialed. There are several. He knew the numbers going directly to IFD dispatch. They're posted on the telephone at each console. They're labeled, the lines."

Earnest also wanted the jury to hear the 911 tapes. ("Smart boy," I thought.) I had not asked Lewie-Bob to play the recordings themselves because Wise, obviously knowing that he was being recorded, sounded pretty shook up about the baby upstairs.

That's why we had transcribed the recordings and just summarized Wise's call. Good call.

Mark Earnest had placed the two recordings on a cassette with William Wise's 911 call first and then Michelle's call. We objected, raised the issue with the court and the recordings would be played in their correct chronological order.

"Please play the tape recordings of Michelle's 911 tape and then William Wise's call to 911," Earnest directed Lewie-Bob.

The jury first heard the tape recording of Michelle's 911 call.

DISPATCHER: Indianapolis Fire and EMS.
FEMALE VOICE: Yes. I need to report a fire.
DISPATCHER: Where?
FEMALE VOICE: 8404 East 37th Place.
DISPATCHER: Okay. Is this across the street . . .
FEMALE VOICE: Yes.
DISPATCHER: 8404.
FEMALE VOICE: Yes.
DISPATCHER: What's on fire?
FEMALE VOICE: The house.

DISPATCHER: Okay then.
FEMALE VOICE: Okay.

The tape abruptly ended.

"Now, Ms. Hiatt, please play the recording of Bill Wise," Earnest directed.

I broke in. "How long after the call from Michelle Wise did the call come in from William Wise." (I had learned from Tom Leslie's antics that the court would tolerate these interruptions.)

"Twenty-seven seconds later," Lewie-Bob responded as she cued up the second recording.

MALE VOICE: Hello.
DISPATCHER: Indianapolis Fire and EMS.
MALE VOICE: Jodi?
DISPATCHER: Yeah?
MALE VOICE: This is Bill.
DISPATCHER: What's wrong?
MALE VOICE: I've got a fire in my house.
DISPATCHER: Okay. What's the address?
MALE VOICE: It's 84—
DISPATCHER: Uh, huh.
MALE VOICE: 04 East—
DISPATCHER: 84 –8404?
MALE VOICE: East 37th Place.
DISPATCHER: It's a single, right?
MALE VOICE: Yes.
DISPATCHER: All right, we'll be right there.
MALE VOICE: Jodi?
DISPATCHER: Yeah? Bill, what's wrong?
MALE VOICE: Oh, God.
DISPATCHER: Bill?
MALE VOICE: The baby is upstairs, Jodi.
DISPATCHER: Okay, Bill. We'll be on our way, okay?
MALE VOICE: Okay.
DISPATCHER: We'll be right there. Bye-bye.

Then silence. The voice hung in the air.

Earnest had no additional questions for Lewie-Bob Hiatt. I had a few.

"Did you hear Mr. Wise coughing, as if he had inhaled smoke, on that 911 call?" I asked.

"No. I did not."

I really just wanted the jury to think about how the voice of this guy, who was supposed to have made several attempts to rescue his child, sounded.

"Did you hear any strider in his voice? Do you know what strider is?" I asked her.

"Yes I do."

"Objection! Ask to approach."

Mark Earnest did not want to argue this one in front of the jury.

"Judge, the jury heard the tape for themselves. These are improper questions," Earnest argued.

"Well, I don't know what strider is, so I can't tell if it's proper or not," the judge responded.

"Strider is something that happens to your voice if you inhale smoke," I summarized.

I'd made my point to the jury (I hoped), so I did not argue much over the issue. The judge told me to move on.

"Ms. Hiatt, you told the jury that the radio in Mr. Wise's possession on the night of the fire was set to OPS 2, is that correct?"

"Yes, ma'am."

I asked, "Other than the communications relating to the Wise house fire, was there any other talk over that channel from midnight until 8 a.m. on March 6, 1993?"

"No. I listened to the tape recording and there was nothing on the OPS 2 channel of the radio, until dispatch sent the call out to East 37th Place. Then, the various fire personnel communicated with each other on that channel. The talk was about responding to the fire. Later the fire personnel used that channel to communicate among themselves."

I asked innocently, "So the only reason to have the radio set to OPS2 would be to keep apprised of when the fire personnel would arrive and what they were doing?"

"Objection!"

Tom Leslie was on his feet, despite the fact that this was Mark Earnest's witness.

"Sustained," the judge said.

No one had any further questions of Ms. Hiatt.

We all took a lunch break. Lisa was going to question the newspaper lady but she was not available until the next day. I hated to start an important witness midday, but had no choice.

Van Buskirk's contribution to the trial team was to try to take good notes so that I could review them each night. She was doing a pretty good job of it, but when she became really interested in or disagreed with the testimony she wrote me little notes. So, I couldn't read the notes until the kids were in bed because Katrina was beginning to read and the notes were not for a child's eyes.

After lunch we called David Lepper to the stand. Lepper had returned from his little vacation paradise and was now working for the Indiana State Fire Marshall. This gave him some added credibility and his enthusiasm for fire investigation had been renewed.

Lewie-Bob had been dry and the only drama had been the 911 tapes. Still, Lepper was the logical next witness, so I put him on the stand right after lunch.

We started by going over Lepper's credentials, his years of service to the Indianapolis Fire Department, his commendations, and his current position as a statewide fire investigator. He answered as we had suggested, only responding to what I asked and nothing more.

Lepper described the nursery and showed the jury photographs of what was left. (I did not have him show the "Where's Waldo?" photograph, although he identified it.) He went into considerable detail about his outside-to-inside search, finding the police radio, and the smell of alcohol in the room.

There were a number of speaking objections by Tom Leslie, but all-in-all the description of the devastation was complete. I could see that the jurors' eyes were beginning to glaze over. It was nearly five p.m. I asked the court to recess for the day.

The judge excused the jury and Dave Lepper, but told him to be back in the morning. As he left the stand, I whispered that I wanted to meet with him in my office after court. I told the judge that we wanted to call Cynthia Neweadde, the newspaper lady, first thing in the morning. I explained that Mrs. Neweadde could only be available at that time. There was an objection from the defense, but the judge said she would allow it. We left the courtroom.

Van Buskirk, Lisa Swaim, and I took the elevator upstairs. I had been on my feet all day and was looking for a place to park myself. Van Buskirk was uncharacteristically upbeat.

I offered a warning. "Look, ladies. We are supposed to be ahead during our case-in-chief. We haven't given them anything to really hit us with yet. They are going to be all over Lepper and Finneran,"

When we had all arranged ourselves in the conference room, I announced that we had to decide whether to bring the test burn room for the jury to inspect or just use the video recordings that we had obtained. I wanted everybody's take on the subject before making the decision. This was a matter of perception and I look at things differently than many people, so every opinion counted. I honestly wished that I could ask Scott his opinion, but we were very definitely still not speaking much. After some back and forth it was decided that we would not use the burn room, instead we would focus on the videos.

Most of the exhibits had been marked as evidence/exhibits for the first trial. Because of that, we were not permitted to let them out of our possession, so I had made copies of the videos for Lepper to review. No matter how prepared as a witness he thought he was, it had been five years since the fire, and a year since the last time that Lepper had testified about the case. I wanted him to do his homework.

"Dave, please review your reports again, and these video tapes. I will ask you questions about them tomorrow. When I'm done, Tom Leslie will be asking the questions. Please know your stuff."

"Will do."

Lepper seemed glad to do it. That made me cautiously optimistic. But putting a lot of our eggs in the Lepper basket made me very nervous.

I hadn't told Lepper, but Steve Shand would not be testifying at this trial. Shand had other fish to fry and was not willing to spend his own time testifying for the State. Even more importantly, the court had no authority to compel his testimony, since he lived in Ft. Wayne and not in Indianapolis. The defense had been trying to force him to come to court, but he had refused to do so. I don't know who he had retained as legal counsel, but I loved the advice he had been given. We were going to trial with no conflict between the State's cause and origin experts.

Finneran could also have refused to testify in the case. He too lived in Ft. Wayne, we were not paying him and, frankly, he had absolutely no obligation to assist us. But, after only a modicum of groveling and pleading by me, and a bit of flattery, Finneran had volunteered his time to continue working on the case. Truthfully, Finneran would have volunteered without much effort on my part, but it was a sacrifice and we wanted him to know that we appreciated him for it. I had requested funds to pay Finneran, but had never gotten a response from Sheila.

"Thank you, Finneran," I thought as I drove to Mom and Bruce's house for dinner. Steve was meeting me there with our girls.

Obviously, food was a major enticement to visit Mom and Bruce. When I was in trial, I devoted all my time to the trial, but my kids had to eat. Steve did not cook. Our nanny had returned to Miami, so the family was subsisting on sandwiches and school lunches. Grandma Kaye's house was like Nirvana for the kids. And Steve. And me too. We didn't stay long. Eat and run was acceptable when I was prosecuting a case.

Bruce was quieter than usual, but still enthusiastic about the progress of the trial. I never thought to invite him to the courthouse and he never came. But he read all about the case, which was back in the newspaper and on the news. He was my silent cheerleader.

The next morning Lisa questioned her first witness: Cynthia Neweadde. Lisa took Cynthia through her testimony. She did not stretch out the questioning to ensure that the jury got the time line, but by then Keith Williams, the firefighters, and Lewie-Bob Hiatt had all done a respectable job of creating a timeline. Neweadde finished the drawing with her testimony. There was no real cross examination and the newspaper lady was excused.

Lepper returned to the stand and we continued telling the story of what happened to Baby Matthew. He told the jury that he had ruled out all accidental causes of the fire and one by one we introduced the outlets from the nursery walls to show how they were not burned from the inside out. He explained how damaged electric receptacles look when shorting occurs at the outlet. Lepper also explained that, as he walked in the room, he smelled alcohol. He took a sample of the mushy carpet and placed it into a clean paint can to be processed.

We then broached the statements that William Wise had given to Lepper and his partner. Michelle's statements were hearsay, which means that because the statements were made outside of the courtroom, they could not be admitted unless Michelle testified. But because Wise was the defendant, his statements were admissible. Each of William Wise's statements and deposition were either read or given to the jury to read.

Many questions and answers were blacked out, but the jury was allowed to read the remainder. The sworn statement under oath was the most in-depth. Before giving the jurors their individual copy of the transcript, I explained that Q stood for Questions, which were asked by Allstate's lawyer. The A stood for Answers, which were given by William Wise.

The jurors then read his statement:

Q. Can you tell me what education you have?
A. Graduated from high school and have gone to Indiana – Florida State Fire College. I'm an EMT.
Q. Did you receive a degree from the Florida State Fire College?
A. It's given in certifications by the classes that are taken. I have several certifications from there.
Q. During the year, year and a half that you were at the Florida State Fire College, share with me the certifications that you obtained there.
A. Basic firefighting. We were trained on self-contained breathing apparatus, other courses on extrication.

Q. Would that involve extrication of persons trapped in a burning structure?

A. That also.

. . .

Q. I want to know what you studied down there.

A. Well, again, basic firefighting. We did study search and rescue in buildings, high-rise building rescues, where we trained on HAZ MAT.

Q. Did you have any course work dealing with the investigation of cause and origin of fires?

A. Some under the—general firefighting basics, and I believe there was a course that was an advance, 240-hour, firefighting other that the basic firefighting there.

Q. Did you take the advanced firefighting?

A. Yeah, that was just another level up to—there's multiple levels of, you know, courses you can take.

. . .

Q. Tell me what course work you remember, if any, about investigation of cause and origin of fires.

A. Cause and origin of fires is basically how they are—how a fire—you know, the origin of a fire. When I took it, there's basically three things that are needed to start a fire, everyone is taught that, I mean.

Q. What were you taught about that?

A. There has to be fuel and heat and oxygen.

Q. Okay.

A. I think that's taught in high school.

Q. Did you have any course work, for example, where you were taught anything about the flammable characteristics of different liquid materials or different hard materials, building materials?

A. Yeah, that was in the basic firefighting, you know. To advance to different levels, you have to know those type of things.

Q. I mean, did you learn things, for example, about the rate of burn of 2 by 4's or carpets, wall coverings or draperies, different kinds of cloths?

A. I would have to answer yes, but I can't remember them.

Q. Okay.

A. It's been a long time since I've done that.

. . .

Q. Did you take any courses dealing with arson?
A. I can't—I can't remember if I took an investigation—I want to say I took like a basic investigation course.
. . .
A. I was down in fire—in Florida with the fire department.
Q. You worked for a fire department?
A. Uh-huh.
Q. Was that while you were in fire school or after?
A. I think just after I had taken the basic firefighting course I was hired there.
Q. What department was that?
A. It was the East Marion Fire Department.
. . .
Q. How long did you work there?
A. I believe a year, year and a half.
Q. And was that a professional firefighter position or a volunteer firefighter position or a combination of the two?
A. It was a paid position.
Q. What was your position while you were there?
A. As an EMT and firefighter. Later I volunteered for the Osolo fire department near Elkhart.

There were several pages to the statement. During questioning, Wise described the layout of the house in detail and drew a diagram of the house. He also drew a diagram of the nursery. Wise described to Allstate's attorney, as he had to Lepper, what he did that morning from the time he arrived home from work.

Q. So there was a monitor in the nursery?
A. Yes.
Q. What brand of monitor?
A. Fisher Price.
Q. Can you show me on the diagram that you've drawn where the monitor was positioned in the nursery?
A. It sat kind of just under the bed on the northwest—
Q. You mean the northeast corner of the crib?
A. Yeah, northeast corner, yeah.
[Witness drawing on the diagram.]
Q. That would be the monitor; is that correct?

A. Yeah, it's the transmitter.

Q. Does that have a cord attached to it?

A. Yeah, for the power.

Q. Does it require a wall outlet or can you use batteries?

A. It can use both.

Q. How were you using it at that time?

A. Just plugged into the wall.

. . .

Q. And then you had a portable monitor downstairs; is that right?

A. Yes.

Q. Did that have to be plugged into anything?

A. Yes.

. . .

Q. Now, why did you stay up in the living room?

A. Because I was—I was going to feed him when he got up. At 5, 5:30 he usually got up, that's when she got up to feed him, and I told her just to stay in bed because she needed to go back to work the next day. She had been up working all day and half the night.

Q. Was she going to have to work on Saturday?

A. No. No, she didn't need to go in that Saturday, but I told her just to go get some rest.

Q. Did you bring the baby monitor up with you?

A. I know it was upstairs, yeah.

Q. Who brought it up?

A. I believe I brought it up. I'm not sure if she brought it up or – after we talked about it, since—since we spoke with you the first time, I believe I did.

Q. Do you know whether you brought it up when you came up at 1:15 or did you go back down and get it at some point?

A. No, I think it was brought up when I came up.

. . .

Q. Had you, on any occasion before those early morning hours of March 6th, ever come upstairs and slept on the couch with the baby monitor before?

A. Usually she slept on the couch upstairs with the baby a lot of times, because I was working and things like that. She was on maternity leave.

Q. Okay.

A. I usually slept downstairs until she went back to work.

Q. Had she actually begun working again before the fire or was she scheduled to go back the following week?

A. I—I should have asked her before we—before we started this. I think she worked the Thursday and Friday. I'm not sure.

Q. Before the early morning hours of the day of the fire had you ever slept on the couch with the monitor before or was this the first time?

A. I'm sure at some point, yeah, I had slept on the couch.

Q. I'm talking about from the time the baby was born up until the time of the fire. Had there ever been occasions where you left her sleeping downstairs and you brought the baby monitor upstairs and slept on the couch?

A. I'm not sure. A lot of the times she would bring it upstairs, you know, like I say, around 1 and 2 he usually ate, that's when she would go upstairs and take it. I was usually asleep in bed and she would just leave me down there sleeping.

Q. And she would stay up there for the rest of the night on the couch; is that right?

A. Yeah.

Q. As far as you can remember, was this the first time that you had taken the baby monitor up and slept on the couch?

A. I had slept on the couch—I guess I want to say yes, that I had slept on the couch, but it was like when I come home from work or on my day off or something like that. A lot of times she—I remember one time she got me up and had me come upstairs with her, you know, she needed a break of getting some rest, that type of thing. I'm not—I mean, as far as what time when we brought him home, those types of things, or a lot of times in the daytime when I would come home or days off. I—I can't positively answer your question, because I just don't remember.

Q. But your best estimate is this may have been the first time that you spent the early morning hours on the couch with the baby monitor; is that right?

A. I want to answer you correctly, but I'm not positive if I had done—if I had come upstairs before, I—I don't believe I ever come upstairs when I was working and fed him in the morning hours like that, mainly because she was off of work.

As the jurors read the lengthy statement, I tried to read their minds. Nothing. But they were reading intently.

Wise described his trip to the bathroom and looking at his watch to learn it was five a.m.

Q. When you got up at 5 a.m. was the bathroom door plainly visible with the light coming out of the bathroom?
A. Yes.
Q. And did that light illuminate the hallway and into the living room so that you could see pretty well.
A. No. It shines back down the hallway to the other bedrooms, that's why I would leave it on, you know, when he was sleeping and if it's nighttime, because it didn't shine in onto the crib, it kind of shined down the hallway the other way.
Q. But it produced enough light that you could clearly see an unobstructed view from the couch to the bathroom as you got up to go to the bathroom at 5 is that right.
A. You could see the light.
Q. When you went from the couch to the bathroom did you notice any smoke in the house at all?
A. No.
Q. Did you smell any smoke at all in the house?
A. No.

. . .

Q. After you left the bathroom did you immediately return to the couch or did you take a couple of steps to your right to look into Matthew's room?
A. Yeah, I just kind of, you know, walked out of the bathroom and stuck my head in the door.
Q. At that time could you clearly see across his bedroom to where the crib was located?
A. Just to where the crib is, that's what I was looking for.
Q. Was there enough light in that room from the bathroom light and from the illumination from outside to be able to basically see into the room?
A. Yeah, kind of like what a night-light would put out, that type of thing.
Q. I guess my point is: That room was not pitch black, was it?
A. No. I mean, I could see enough to see his crib and that, you know he was—that he was not all the way underneath the covers, that kind of thing. A lot of times he would tend to crouch himself down underneath the covers. The covers had a—

Q. But you could actually see him?
A. Yeah.


Wise began, in his statement, to equivocate about the time. He repeated that he looked at his watch, but then said it could have been just before five or a few minutes after. But he was certain about other things.

Q. When you looked into the nursery, where Matthew was sleeping, after you came out of the bathroom, was there any fire in that room?
A. No.
Q. Was there any smoke in that room?
A. No.
Q. Did you smell anything at that time?
A. No.
Q. Did you see anything out of the ordinary in that room at that time?
A. No.


The rest of that statement was nearly identical to the statements that Wise had given to Lepper. He recalled the alarm going off, and Michelle going downstairs to try to turn the alarm off and then him turning on the light on the landing when Michelle returned and then seeing smoke.

He described how he had gone upstairs to retrieve the telephone and when he returned to the landing, he said that Michelle was standing at the door. Then he said she had opened the front door.

Wise had omitted Michelle's second trip downstairs to retrieve her coat and shoes.

Wise said that as he tried to dial 911 from his house, he was halfway in and halfway out of the front door. The smoke was coming out of the front door. He told Michelle to go across the street to call 911 and that he was going to get Matthew.

Q. Did you reach the nursery on this second attempt?
A. Yes.
Q. And how far inside the door did you get?
A. Just like a couple feet. I know I was past the door, and just inside the door is the closet, I know I was past that into the room.
Q. So you think you did throw something through the window"
A. I know I did, whether I did it at that point before I went outside or when I came back. I went outside and called 911 myself by the other neighbor's phone.

Q. So the flashover you've talked about occurred during your second attempt to get to the crib?

A. Yes.

. . .

When asked why he left the house to call 911 when he knew that Michelle was going to call Wise explained that he hadn't directed his wife to tell 911 that a child was trapped in the house.

A. "I mean, being a dispatcher I know I didn't tell her to say he's still in the house, that type of thing. We send a lot different responses when there's somebody trapped in a house."

. . .

Q. Do you have any reason to believe that there were any other persons in your house on the night of this fire other than you, Michelle or Matthew?

A. Not that I know of.

. . .

Q. When was the first time that you notified Allstate Insurance Company about the fire?

A. It was that Saturday.

Q. The same day as the fire?

A. Yes.

When all the jurors had finished reading, the court directed me to collect the transcripts.

We all took a break. Just reading the transcript of that statement, although silently to myself, was draining. I got a diet Coke and Lisa, Van Buskirk, and I headed back to our table.

Lepper was still on the witness stand. I returned to the end of the jury box and asked him my next question.

By standing where I chose, I could be sure that all of the jurors could hear what Lepper was saying and that Lepper would be looking at the jury or in the direction of the jury as he answered.

"Did you tell William or Michelle that you had smelled alcohol in the nursery?" I inquired.

"No, ma'am. I wanted to see what they said about alcohol in the room without letting them know that we'd found some on the carpet," Lepper said.

"I asked both Bill and Michelle about alcohol. They told us the same thing. There had been alcohol in the room when Matthew was only a few days old. They used it on his umbilical cord. But that fell off weeks before the fire. Bill told me that the alcohol was in the bathroom closet. I asked him if there was any other place that it could have been. He said, 'Well, if it was still in the room, it would have been on the dresser.' Michelle said the same thing."

"Why was that significant to you, Investigator Lepper?"

"Because I felt some squish in the carpet. I bent down and smelled alcohol. The location of the alcohol was across the room from the dresser, on the floor, near the far wall closest to the changing table. The alcohol was in the location that Bill and Michelle said that the baby monitor transmitter was supposed to be," Lepper explained.

Lepper also highlighted that William Wise insisted that he looked at his watch while going to the bathroom. He said it was five a.m.

"Wise said that after he went to the bathroom at five a.m. he looked in on Matthew and he was asleep and everything in the room was fine," Lepper told the jury.

Because Lepper now knew that Wise had been trained as a fireman, I asked him what firemen learned even in the most basic courses. He talked about the fire triangle, and that the single fastest way to increase the size and intensity of a fire is to feed it oxygen.

"Did William Wise admit that he fed oxygen to the fire in Baby Matthew's room?" I asked.

"Not in so many words," Lepper recalled. "But Wise was seen by Officer Williams in the doorway with the screen door and the front door open. That would have fed the fire oxygen as it was pulled up the stairs. Bill Wise also said that he threw a chair or stool through the window in order to break out the remaining glass so that he could throw the baby out the window. Both of those actions, opening the front door and breaking out a window, fed the fire. Anyone trained in firefighting, or even about the fire triangle, would know how harmful those actions were."

I stopped my questioning and looked directly at Wise, who was seated silently at the defense table. He did not look at me. I had hoped to see any small flicker of remorse, some humanity, but there was nothing.

The judge had preliminarily ruled on the admissibility of the burn room tapes but had agreed with the defense that she would make the final decision at trial. Lepper would be using the recording to highlight his testimony, so we had decided to only use one view of the room.

The tape was forty-seven minutes long. It began as a blow torch was being used to try to ignite the step-down transformer plugged into the wall and continued filming until long after the fire was extinguished.

I emphasized that the recording was for demonstrative purposes only. This meant that the video would help the jury understand what Lepper was saying by illustrating his testimony. For instance, the tape would show what Lepper meant when he used the term flashover and the phrase burn pattern and some other parts of his testimony. It was agreed that no audio would be allowed.

After some argument and serious paranoia on my part, the court allowed Lepper to play parts of the tape recording to the jury. But the blow torch scenes were excluded (too prejudicial) along with some other footage.

To avoid the jury being confused, before we started, Lepper pointed out, with the tape on stop-frame, the things that were out-of-place in the test burn room. Among them, Lepper showed the jury that the alcohol bottle was misplaced by Steven Shand in the video. The bottle in the video was on the changing table near the wall outlet where the monitor transmitter was plugged into the wall. In reality, the alcohol bottle was either in the bathroom closet or on the dresser. Lepper showed the jury on the freeze-frame, that the dresser was across the room and as far away from the outlet as one could get in this tiny space.

There was also an intense argument, both in front of the jury and outside their presence, about a bottle of alcohol that had been introduced at the first trial.

Mark Earnest and Tom Leslie wanted that bottle to be put into evidence. I did not have the bottle in the courtroom and had no intention of admitting it, during this trial.

Lepper swore that he did not find a bottle of alcohol in the Wise nursery. I had mistakenly introduced the bottle of alcohol at the first trial, unaware that the half melted bottle in the evidence carton had been from the burn room, not from the Wise nursery.

Lepper started the video player. Unlike the silence during the jury view of the burn room during the first trial, I broke up the recording, stopping it when flashover occurred, so that Lepper could explain that flashover means the room had reached a certain temperature and not that everything is immediately disintegrated. We resumed the video and stopped it again when the fire had been burning for sixteen minutes.

With the stop-frame at sixteen minutes, everything in the burning test room was readily identifiable, with colors and shapes. I asked Lepper to hold up an enlargement on poster board of one of the photos of Matthew's room, so that the jury could compare the scenes. After giving the jury enough time to compare the two, Lepper resumed playing the video tape.

At the appropriate junction, Lepper described where Matthew's body was found in the nursery. We then showed the rest of the video, stopping and letting Lepper explain something every few minutes.

After hours on the stand, Lepper's posture became more stooped. He began to give lengthier responses instead of the short, crisp answers that I had so often suggested he provide. Lepper was becoming fatigued.

I asked Lepper about finding the police radio in Wise's bedroom. Lepper described where and how he found it. He said the radio was switched off when he located it. When Lepper switched the police radio on, it was tuned to OPS 2. Lepper testified that he knew this type of police radio intimately, it was the same brand and type that he had used for years. He said, based on the radio being tuned to OPS 2, that Wise had been listening to the fire department response to the fire at his residence.

I had run out of questions. David Lepper had done a good job. I couldn't think of any more ways to stall the inevitable, it was time for cross examination by Tom Leslie.

# Chapter Eighteen

TOM LESLIE TOOK his time getting to the podium in the center of the courtroom.

Tom had apparently once worked with Lepper when he was a prosecutor, and I could see that there was some tension between them. Tom glared at Lepper, who seemed to shrink in his chair.

Tom started by asking Lepper about his recent employment history. Lepper said he had worked for the Indiana State Fire Marshall for five months. Before that he had worked for four months as a process server for the Marion County Sheriff's Office. Before that Lepper had been employed with Midwest Forensic Services, as an investigator, where he had investigated more than one hundred fires in the six months that he worked there. Lepper also responded that prior to working for Midwest, he had worked for Florida Design Communities as head of security. (Lepper did not volunteer that he did so from a golf cart.)

Leslie had Lepper testify in reverse chronological order. It was confusing and suggested that Lepper couldn't hold a job. Before moving to Florida, Lepper testified, he had worked for the Indianapolis Fire Department for nearly a lifetime. Lepper had no formal education beyond high school and was not an electrical or any other kind of engineer or engineering technologist.

"Did you keep a log in the case involving William Wise?" Leslie asked.

"I'm not sure of the term 'log.'"

"A . . . a written record of the evidence collected."

"There is a written list that is given to the property branch by me. I don't keep the evidence. I have to turn it in . . ."

"Well . . ." Leslie cut Lepper off.

" . . . and I get a copy of, of that record," Lepper responded.

"I think by log what I mean is not merely a list, but comments that go with the items collected showing where they were found, when, what state, things like that."

"No," Lepper said.

"How do you label the evidence you find at a location?" Leslie demanded.

"Well, it's put in some type of a container, and then the container is sealed, and then I put some type of a label that is provided by the city . . . as for the, I believe the day of the fire, the case number, the investigator, and I'm not sure what else is on it."

"Do you place on that label the exact location where the item is found?"

"No, sir."

"How do you know where it comes from?"

"Well, I do make some kind of a, a notation. Usually I'll do a diagram or something for notes, and I will note that I picked this up in this area or that area," Lepper explained.

"On your diagram, then, do you show where the item was found by measurement?" Leslie asked.

"No, sir."

"Have you ever heard or learned in your training and experience that when placing something on a diagram that you measure from two walls?"

"Some people do."

"And do you follow that protocol?"

"No, sir."

"What do you use to determine exactly where a piece of evidence is located in a fire scene?"

"I usually make a note or draw it on a diagram, and maybe will mark a number 1, 2, 3, 4, 5."

"Your diagrams are always to scale, are they?" Leslie asked sarcastically.

"Never."

"And so you would not really know where the items is if you simply draw it on a diagram, is that correct?"

"I put it in an area, yes, sir."

"As far as feet and inches, we don't really know," Leslie stated.

"No, sir," Lepper agreed.

Defense counsel was making a fair point. How could Lepper pinpoint where the alcohol had been found without having a very specific drawing? After a few more questions on the subject, Tom Leslie turned his attention to how Lepper had collected the carpet sample for lab testing.

But Leslie came back again and again to this topic. Most of the time he asked Lepper the same questions and sometimes the questions were framed somewhat differently. The answers never got better.

"How many carpet samples did you take?"

"One."

"How large was the one carpet sample that you took?" Leslie continued.

"Six by eight inches."

"Who tested that?"

"Marion County Crime Lab," Lepper replied.

"Did you send any other carpet samples out for testing?"

"Just the carpet? No, not to my knowledge."

"Did you send anything to Barker & Herbert Laboratories for testing for accelerant?" Leslie asked the question although Lepper had already answered it.

"No."

Tom Leslie asked questions about when Lepper had arrived at the Wise residence (5:51 a.m.) and what he observed. He showed Lepper photographs and used them to show the placement of the sun upon Lepper's arrival. This was a useless point as there was no obstruction from the sun. Apparently just a ploy to confuse Lepper.

Tom also attempted to showcase his knowledge of fires by identifying V patterns, which are blackened areas in the shape of a "V" made by a fire as it goes up and spreads outward, in some of Lepper's photographs.

Leslie's questions almost always contained the answer. That is proper on cross-examination as these are leading questions. He walked Lepper through the description of the debris outside the house. Lepper concluded that no mattress had been found either in the nursery or in the debris, but the metal crib springs had been found in the pile of debris outside of the nursery window.

Some of Tom Leslie's questions were intended, in Van Buskirk's words, "to throw some shit and see if any of it sticks."

"Were you able to rule out burglary as a cause in this case, or as being a cause in this case?" Tom Leslie asked.

"There were no signs of forced entry," Lepper said looking suspiciously at Leslie.

"Don't you start every fire investigation with the presumption that the fire is accidental?"

"I start every investigation presuming that a fire has occurred and that I am to investigate it," Lepper replied.

Tom Leslie continued to ask Lepper questions about what he did when he first arrived at Wise's home and about his observations. Why had Lepper gone into the basement when it was obvious that the fire had not started there? These questions were intended more to harass Lepper than to obtain favorable testimony for the defense.

"I was looking at the electrical panel to see if there were any signs of arcing or sparking or shorting in the electrical service panel. There were several fuses and some that had been discarded. I don't recall if there was a blown fuse, but I think there was."

I noticed immediately that Lepper answered more than he had been asked. If Dave Lepper had only answered Leslie's question, all would have been fine.

But because he added the last sentence—"I don't recall if there was a blown fuse, but I think there was"—totally volunteered it, he gave Tom Leslie ammunition. Leslie pounced on the admission.

"Could that have been a fuse for the nursery?" Leslie asked.

"It could have been," Lepper conceded.

"Did you ever determine whether that blown fuse, which resulted in a short, was for the nursery? Did you send it out to be inspected by an electrical engineer or anyone else?" Leslie asked in rapid fire.

"No." Lepper looked at me for help.

But Leslie jumped from one subject to another so quickly that Dave Lepper was lost in the dust. He was becoming agitated and that was dangerous. Leslie focused some questions on the bathroom light. Lepper testified that the bathroom light was illuminated when he arrived at the scene, but that there was no exhaust fan sound or feel from that light.

Lepper admitted that fire could have gone through the fan and into the attic where it would have gone out one or the other side of the house, if the fixture had a fan attached.

I hadn't considered the bathroom fan, and it had not been a factor in the first trial. Lepper and I had never discussed it, so this was new territory. My rapt attention was on Lepper's testimony. Lawyers are permitted to ask hypothetical questions of expert witnesses and a chill ran up my spine. David just wasn't a man who could think quickly or logically on the fly.

"If, hypothetically, if the fan had been on in the bathroom, and there had been smokiness, or smoke starting to build in the baby's room at any time, might that fan in the bathroom have pulled smoke across and vented it up into the attic?" Leslie hypothesized.

"If? Yes, sir."

"And, I mean in the very—and, and this is a hypothetical, too. In the very early stages of any kind of smoldering, or any kind of fire beginning where the smoke is very hot, it could very well have been pulled across through that, that fan, is that right?"

Leslie had neatly reframed the question.

Lepper caught on. "No. I don't see—not, not that way. I thought you meant the smoke that was in the bathroom itself."

"No, I meant the very first smoke that may have come from this fire, however it started," Leslie clarified.

"No," Lepper concluded.

"It would not have been exhausted with that bathroom fan?" Leslie implied that it would.

"I believe that the smoke went up, and once it banked down probably eighteen inches off of the ceiling, then it could have gone out into that room," Lepper said.

"Is there something that would have held smoke in that baby's room?" Leslie asked argumentatively.

"Yeah, the wall coming down from the ceiling above the door," Lepper responded. But his architectural picture was hard to follow.

Leslie questioned Lepper about downed drywall, the condition of the nursery when he arrived and the condition of the rafters above Baby Matthew's nursery. The rafters remained in place and they could be seen from the bedroom because the ceiling had either fallen or been pulled down. The fire had burned up and out the window and into the attic. The roof was still intact.

"Is it your contention that what remained in this room after the fire is wholly related to how long the fire burned?" Leslie asked.

"Not how long it burned. How fast it burned," was Lepper's prompt response.

"I think we are saying the same thing, are we not?"

"Then, no," Lepper replied quickly.

"How long did this fire burn?" Leslie asked.

"I would say not more than twenty minutes. The call came in to MECA, I believe at 5:09 and the firemen said that the fire was out at 5:16 a.m."

"Isn't that the time they arrived at the scene?" Leslie asked.

"I don't believe so. I believe they arrived at 5:15." Lepper held his ground on that response.

Tom Leslie kept asking Lepper about heat release rate of the fuel load (furnishings, furniture, diapers, and other items in Matthew's nursery), but Lepper never varied from saying that he did not understand the term and didn't know.

Leslie approached it in several ways, but Lepper never wavered. I assumed that this was intended to serve as a foundation for the defense experts. I knew that there was a risk that Lepper did not sound professional, but I far preferred that he sound a bit more fireman than say something stupid.

Leslie also kept trying to attack the time line. He implied that the fire burned for longer than it did. Knowing that the records were exact as to arrival and departure from the house, he tried to add time in other ways. When Lepper said that the first engine arrived at 5:15 and the fire was out at 5:16, Leslie asked him, "How long does it take the firefighter to get from the truck to the scene with a hose?"

"Probably thirty seconds," Lepper opined.

Lepper held up on cross, but obviously gave the defense some helpful responses. I thought that Leslie was finished and that we could release Lepper. I was about to sigh with relief, but Judge Magnus-Stinson looked at the clock and decided to break for the day.

That meant that I could not talk to Lepper overnight and that Tom Leslie would have the whole night to think up some more questions for him. I smiled at Lepper sympathetically as he left for the evening.

My pattern had been to leave right after court was recessed, head home, have dinner with the family and then get to sleep early. I usually went to bed at the same time as my preschool children. Standing all day thinking had that effect on my nocturnal habits.

We—Van Buskirk, Lisa Swaim, and me—would resume very early in the morning, usually meeting in the conference room. I didn't like walking from my firm's parking garage to the City County Building in the dark, but did it the first day or two. Then, without my asking, Van Buskirk started picking me up on the corner near the firm's high rise building at about six a.m. each morning.

"A new day, a new witness," I hoped.

The judge said, "Good morning, Ladies and Gentlemen. Today is the fifth day of trial and the case is moving along as we had expected. Has anyone read or heard anything about the case over night?"

All heads in the jury box shook in the negative. Lepper had already taken the stand.

"Mr. Lepper, you are still under oath," Judge Magnus-Stinson warned. "Mr. Leslie?"

Tom Leslie approached the podium and looked at Dave Lepper. I immediately pictured a matador facing down a bull. I wouldn't have bet which was which.

Leslie asked his first question. "Remember yesterday we were talking about certain things you found in the fire room, certain things you found in the house as you made your inspection, and that eventually you made a determination about this fire?"

"Yes, sir," Lepper responded warily.

"I believe you testified that it was incendiary in nature, meaning somebody, some human element was involved, is that correct?"

"Yes, sir."

"And you stated that you couldn't find any accidental causes. Was that part of your finding?"

"Yes, sir."

"Aren't you actually charged with eliminating all accidental causes of a fire?" Leslie asked.

"Yes."

"So you're telling this jury, then, your conclusion is you couldn't find any accidental causes, meaning you could eliminate all accidental causes."

Whenever you hear the phrase, "So you're telling the jury . . ." look out for a curveball.

"At what time are you speaking of?" Lepper asked. Did he not understand the question?

"Just say yes, Lepper!" I screamed in my head.

He gave you plenty of rope, now hang him. But instead Dave Lepper had equivocated. Darn.

"As of yesterday," Leslie said.

"Yes, sir."

Leslie switched subjects again, keeping Lepper off balance. From the looks of Lepper, he hadn't slept well and it was beginning to show. Tom Leslie went through a group of photographs where there were black markings on the floor in the nursery. He asked Lepper if someone had poured accelerant all over the floor where the marks were.

Lepper tried to explain that he only testified to an accelerant pour in the small area near the east and north wall. Lepper explained that the remaining burned floor was the result of flashover.

"Have you eliminated all accidental ignition sources?" Leslie asked, as if for the first time.

"Yes, sir."

"Have you found any that are not accidental sources?" Leslie asked.

"Other than the suspects, no," Lepper responded.

"So what did you finally determine was the burn time of this fire, what was the maximum, what was the minimum?" Leslie asked, ignoring Lepper's last response.

"Well, the documented burn time that I can go with is sixteen minutes," Lepper repeated.

"Sixteen minutes?"

"Sixteen to nineteen. Sixteen to twenty at the most," Lepper equivocated.

"Sixteen. Is that your opinion of the burn time?" Leslie asked for the umpteenth time.

"Yes. I wasn't there, sir. If an accelerant had not been used, it would have taken forty-five to fifty minutes to burn to the length that I observed in that nursery," Lepper declared.

Leslie jumped back into his mattress questioning. Even my head was spinning as Tom sprang from subject to subject. He was a jabber rather than a knockout punch artist. But several of the jabs were landing and Lepper seemed too tired to raise his arms.

Lepper testified that he was told that the mattress in the crib was foam and that it was never found. While Lepper had refused to go into burn rates yesterday, Leslie led him down that path today without employing the specific phrase. Leslie got Lepper to agree that a foam mattress would burn much faster than a cotton mattress. Lepper volunteered that most foam mattresses are made of petroleum products and help accelerate a fire.

"Don't volunteer, Lepper," I silently raged.

I had only told him that every time we had met over the last several years. "Just answer the question asked and do not volunteer anything."

Leslie asked Lepper if foam, like in a mattress, first turns to a liquid when heated and then to a vapor which will burn. Lepper said that he didn't know. But he did volunteer that if the foam mattress turned to liquid it would follow the heat and flow in the direction of the heat.

I was ready to volunteer to kick Lepper in the ankle. I sat helplessly at the State's table looking down to prevent the jury from seeing my consternation.

Leslie kept on. He was annoying and obstinate. He asked whether Lepper had investigated the particulars relating to the foam mattress that had been purchased as a gift for Baby Matthew. For example, had Lepper identified its composition, whether it was flame retardant and to what extent, if any, it had met standards for flame retardancy.

Lepper admitted that he had not investigated the mattress and repeated that answer for each of the related questions asked by Leslie.

Then, turning on a dime, Leslie switched to questioning Lepper about the test burn room and how it was inaccurate. He pointed out that the room in the test burn had been ignited by Steve Shand holding a blow torch to the outside of the step-down transformer until it caught fire.

He asked Lepper, "That's not how the fire in the Wise residence was started, was it?"

I looked at Lepper and saw a twitch. "Oh, Lord, he's going to get cute."

I'd seen that twitch before in the first trial. Lepper said he didn't know.

"Wise could have started the fire with a blow torch, but not at the wall outlet where the fire was started in the test burn room."

At supersonic speed Tom Leslie moved to another subject.

Was he losing the jury or convincing them? I had no idea.

Leslie kept going back and forth to testimony that had already been given multiple times. He focused again on the fuse that was blown and Lepper's lack of investigation of that particular fuse. Even I was beginning to wonder about the darned fuse. Note to self: ask Finneran to discuss the fuse.

Lepper identified a glob that he found attached to remaining carpet about one foot from the east wall and two feet from the north wall. Shazam! Leslie changed gears, asking Lepper about arcing and whether when electrical arcing (a short) occurs it leaves a bead of metal on wiring. When Lepper conceded that it could, Leslie asked him if he had tested the glob and looked for arcing or beading. Lepper said no.

"Another issue for Finneran," I told myself. "Will this misery ever end?" Leslie wasn't even winded.

"Sir, what do you know about isopropyl alcohol?" Leslie asked him.

"Very little."

"Does it ignite when you put a match to it?" asked Leslie.

"The vapors will," Lepper replied.

"At what temperature?" Leslie demanded.

"I, I don't know."

"Does it evaporate?"

"I'm sure it does," Lepper conceded.

"Does it evaporate rapidly?" Leslie kept asking.

"I don't know."

"What does anybody use it for?" Leslie asked.

"Well, one of the things it can be used for is to accelerate a fire," Lepper answered defiantly.

I didn't laugh or give a high five sign, but after some bad information coming out, it was nice that Lepper kept his sense of humor and fight.

But I didn't want him to seem argumentative and rigid, and I wanted him to avoid being "cute." He just could not pull it off.

"Is that what people buy it for off the store shelf at Revco?" Leslie asked viciously.

"I'm sure some, I'm sure some people do, yes, sir," Lepper replied.

"They do? And in your experience what percentage of the population goes to Revco to buy a bottle of that to start a fire?" Leslie asked in a nasty tone.

I objected as argumentative, but the court allowed it. I wished that Lepper would get back on course. I asked to take a break.

"Denied," the judge said.

"No idea, sir."

"They use it for rubbing alcohol, do they not?" the defense lawyer suggested.

"That is one of the uses, yes, sir," Lepper agreed.

Now it was Tom Leslie who began to get cute. He asked Lepper to compare isopropyl alcohol to Jim Beam. Lepper said that he couldn't compare the two because he'd never seen a bottle of Jim Beam up close. I winced. Question after question, Tom Leslie asked Lepper about alcohol, its water content and how it compared to other accelerants.

Leslie went on and on. He dragged several boxes of burned debris into the courtroom and asked Lepper to identify each item. The defense and prosecution knew that these boxes were the rejects from the first trial. These items had been kept in much better shape before the first trial. But this jury would never know about the first trial and the condition of the boxes with globs and debris thrown in looked sloppy and unprofessional.

Lepper pulled out a glob of plastic that he had guessed was the baby monitor. It was a radio. Another blob he identified as a radio turned out to be a telephone. There it was. Lepper was tired and angry. Having finally gotten Lepper where he wanted him, even though it had taken nearly two days, Tom Leslie pounced.

"You based your opinion that this was an intentionally set fire on the absence of accidental causes, correct?"

"Yes."

"Yet you say you could not rule out the baby monitor."

"Not at that time," Lepper replied lamely.

"And, you've not been able to rule out the baby monitor since, isn't that correct?"

"I, I was, I didn't find the baby monitor," Lepper mumbled.

Somewhere in the courthouse, ghostly enemies were grinning. I was not.

In my opinion, Leslie had all he needed. He should have stopped questioning Lepper then and there.

But Leslie kept on trucking. He asked more questions about a variety of things including the fact that Lepper never used the word "alcohol" in his report. Leslie was so excited by the word's absence from the report that he admitted it into evidence.

I didn't object. While the report didn't mention alcohol, it listed the items collected (including the carpet sample) and some other observations that were good for the State.

Leslie's last series of questions related to Wise's claim of throwing a stool through the window of the baby's room. That again, was a total change of subject. Lepper agreed that a stool had been thrown through the bedroom window by Wise. The stool was part of the debris that was piled in the front of the house.

I guessed that Leslie would later argue that this was proof that Wise had tried to rescue Baby Matthew. I would counter that Wise had thrown the stool on his only attempt to get to the nursery, when he was ordered to do so by Officer Williams.

Throwing the stool ensured that the fire would decimate the room.

I really wanted to get Lepper off of the stand. His nonverbal gestures were "Get me outta here!" But, I had to try to rehabilitate some of his testimony. So, I asked a few questions on redirect examination.

I tried to boost Lepper's spirits before I broached the more difficult issues. I also needed to sound confident for the jury and disguise my concern about Lepper's admissions and mistakes. I smiled at Lepper encouragingly and spoke in my usual confident voice.

"When defense counsel started yesterday he asked you some questions about your background. Would you tell us why you left the fire service with the Indianapolis Fire Department?"

"I was retired on disability."

"How did you get hurt?" I wondered.

"On a fire in 1975," Lepper recalled.

"And, what happened to you?"

"I fell off a roof and broke both my heels and injured my back and my neck."

"What were you doing at the time that you fell off the roof?"

"Chopping a hole in the roof," he said.

"Did there come a time during the course of your service, that you were no longer able to do all of the things necessary of you?" I wanted the jury to know that Lepper was a real fireman who had a great deal of experience and was injured in the line of duty.

"Yes, ma'am."

"Is that the reason you left the Indianapolis Fire Department and the investigation unit as you described to Mr. Leslie yesterday?" I asked.

"Yes. I was retired."

Hoping that Lepper had regained some of his composure and credibility, I got to the essential and most serious part of my re-direct examination.

"There's been some talk about what happens when a foam product or a petroleum product, as you described it, breaks down in the process of a fire, is that correct?" I asked.

"Yes."

"Is it true that when a plastic or foam or that type of petroleum product, after it breaks down during the fire, if it remains, it would cool off. Is that correct?"

"Yes, ma'am."

Anytime that I was making an important point, Leslie objected, to try to distract the jury. He did this several times during my redirect examination. But the court mostly allowed the testimony.

"What happens when the item cools off, that petroleum, the plastic, or the foam, or whatever?" I asked this trying to give him the chance to explain more completely.

"It usually stays in whatever shape that it was when it cooled off," he replied.

"So, if, for example, some petroleum product, like State's Exhibit 42 (I picked up the blob/glob that Finneran had recently concluded was the baby monitor and showed it to Lepper) had moved into an area that was protected, how would you expect to find it after the fire?" I asked.

"I would expect to see a hard rigid item," Lepper said. He was catching on.

"In the point of origin that you identified to the jury, which you found to be on the east wall, as you looked under the baseboard and saw the low burning, and smelled alcohol, did you see anything that appeared to have been something like a plastic or foam petroleum product?"

I hoped the question was understandable.

"No, ma'am. It was clean," he said.

I also wanted Lepper to explain the damage that he observed along the east wall. Tom Leslie had made some points describing the east wall as more damaged than the other walls. Lepper had testified that the wall receptacle was not badly burned, and that proved that the transformer cord did not start the fire. But the issue raised by Leslie was how the wall itself was burned so badly.

I had to ask Lepper directed questions, because I could tell that he was having a hard time listening. I also needed him to address this molten mattress issue raised by Tom Leslie. He answered my questions pretty well.

"My opinion was that after the foam mattress had been ignited and was starting to be consumed that it did drip down into a plastic washtub and eventually ignited that washtub, that was under the bed, and stayed in that one place, and kept burning upward, which exposed that outlet to heat for a longer period of time than other places in the room," Lepper explained.

I asked a question at the same time I showed him the poster-sized drawing. "Is the metal wastebasket that you think protected the alcohol in the carpeting shown in Michelle Wise's drawing?"

With a laser pointer in his hand, Lepper showed the jury Michelle's diagram. He pointed out the wastebasket that protected the alcohol soaked carpet.

Lepper was becoming more confident. "Yes, that is it, south of the electrical outlet and between the changing table and the baby's bed near the east wall. The blob that Mr. Leslie asked me about, the one that was a foot from the east wall and two feet from the south wall, was a telephone. That was consistent with what Michelle drew in her diagram."

"Did you examine every item in the room that had any wiring in it?" I asked.

"Yes."

"And you did, in fact, examine the blob that Mr. Leslie showed you?" I asked, as I showed him Exhibit 42, the glob.

"Yes, ma'am."

Of course, I knew that Finneran would identify this blob of plastic as the baby monitor transmitter. But I hadn't told Lepper about the other witness's testimony. "Just the facts, Lepper. Please stick to the facts." I silently pleaded.

I wanted to be as brief as possible on re-direct examination. Lepper said that he carefully examined the wall outlet where the monitor was supposed to have been plugged in and was able to rule that out as a source of the fire.

"Did you believe that there was anything electrical near the point of origin in this room that could have caused the fire?" I said, pointing at Michelle's drawing of the nursery.

"No, ma'am," Lepper said again.

Lepper testified that he took more than one-hundred photographs at the scene and that I, as the prosecutor, had selected which ones to place into evidence. I ended on the following question and answer. "After all of the questioning by counsel, do you still have an opinion as to the cause of this fire?"

"Yes," he said firmly. "My opinion is that it was an intentionally set fire, and that a flammable liquid was poured and ignited on the floor near the east wall."

Tom Leslie was allowed by the court to ask another series of questions. All of them already had been asked and answered. Lepper repeated that he had not found the baby monitor.

In my final questions, I asked Lepper if he had found anything out of place at the Wise residence. He testified that William Wise smoked and used a disposable lighter, except, on occasion, he would use a book of matches. On the morning of the fire, Lepper found a book of matches on the floor of the empty bedroom, next to the nursery, just down the hall from the bathroom.

Finally, Lepper was excused. He left the courtroom, limping slightly.

# Chapter Nineteen

I HEARD THE judge excuse the jury for lunch and saw them as they silently filed out of the jury box. None of the jurors looked in my direction. The lunch break was going to be longer than usual because the judge had other matters that she wanted to handle before the Wise trial resumed. I sat at our table, sullenly, thinking about what had just happened. Several minutes apparently went by and then Lisa Swaim touched me on the shoulder.

"He could have been worse," Lisa said, trying to be upbeat. I didn't respond.

Van Buskirk was sitting beside me and she too was quiet. That would have worried me had I been paying attention. My mind kept repeating some of the incredible things that Tom Leslie had elicited from Dave Lepper. I wondered if the trial could be salvaged.

"Let's get something across at the market?" Lisa suggested, although she knew that I rarely left the courtroom during a trial. She or Van Buskirk had been bringing me lunch each day from the Market: toasted bagel with light butter and a slice of Swiss.

I needed to clear my head, suck it up, and get on with the trial. The thought of Wise walking free entered my head for the first time since I had asked Poindexter to leave the conference room so many months ago.

"Fuck it." Van Buskirk said. "Let's get out of here." And so we did.

We went downstairs, out the front door, and into a sunny but cold spring day. The courtroom had no windows, none of them in the courthouse did, and so we never knew what we would find outside. Today we discovered the sun, a coldish breeze, and not a cloud in the sky.

"I think Tom Leslie made a few good points," Lisa continued as we walked across the street. Before Van Buskirk could say (or do) something to Lisa, I responded, "The understatement of the day, Ms. Swaim. Let's figure out how we're going to recover from it."

We walked away from the Market toward Monument Circle and my favorite chocolate shop. The aroma of the homemade candies wafted through the air. You could smell that wonderful scent a block away.

Across the circle from the chocolate store was an Episcopal church with beautiful stained glass windows and the quiet ringing of bells that sounded as if they were on a faraway hillside. I considered how these sounds and smells called to me. I didn't know which I needed most, a priest or a chocolate bar.

I stopped abruptly, got out my cell phone and called Jim Finneran. "Jim, I need you to come to Indy this weekend. I probably won't put you on the stand until Tuesday, but we have a lot more work to do. Can you make it?"

Jim and I made arrangements to meet at the prosecutor's office on Sunday morning. When I hung up I asked Van Buskirk to bring exhibits 38 and 42 to the office Sunday morning for Jim to look at with me.

"No friggin' problem, I'll be there as soon as my kid is done with dance class."

"So, what's for lunch?" I asked, veering off toward Washington Street right before we reached the big stuffed bear that was both greeter and guardian of the chocolate shop. I walked a little faster as we headed to a small sandwich shop. "Maybe they have bagels and Swiss," I thought as we sat down. They did.

About an hour later our trio was fed and feeling a lot fuller and more satisfied. It was Friday afternoon. We would have the whole weekend to decide how to handle the debacle.

Dirk Shaw was the next witness. He would only take about ten minutes. We discussed the afternoon line up. I wanted to end with Amy Strati, Michelle Wise's cousin. That meant that we would have four witnesses testifying this afternoon, but we could make it work.

Fortified, we walked back to the courtroom. Jeanne and Michelle Wise looked happier than I'd seen them since the trial started as they sat outside the courtroom. They were not supposed to know what the witnesses had said, but it was obvious that the Rule of Sequestration had been loosely applied by someone in the defendant's camp.

Inside the courtroom, William Wise sat stoic at the defense table. I announced, "The State of Indiana calls Dirk Shaw."

Dirk Shaw was a chemist who worked at the Marion County Crime Laboratory. He briefly summarized his educational background and work history with Marion County. He described the equipment that he used to determine the composition of each sample. He had done this type of analysis hundreds of times before. It was hard to glam up Dirk's testimony. He was a scientist and testified to this testing several times a week. But the jury was listening closely.

"Yes, I received a sealed paint can with a label signed by Investigator Lepper," he said in response to my question. "When I opened it, there was the smell of isopropyl alcohol."

"Why were you able to identify isopropyl alcohol by smell?" I asked.

"We always have it in the house. It's a common smell."

"Do you know whether isopropyl alcohol sold at K-Mart has water in it?" I asked.

"Yes. The kind that anyone of us would buy at K-mart or a pharmacy would be about thirty percent water."

I wanted to be the one to tell the jury about the water content in alcohol. Credibility is everything.

"What was in the can that you opened?"

"It was a piece of carpet that smelled of isopropyl alcohol. The label gave me a case number which represented that the sample was taken from 8404 E. 37th Place, nursery."

Dirk Shaw tested the sample using gas chromatography/mass spectrometry and found that it contained isopropyl alcohol. The chemist opened the can and showed the jury the piece of carpet inside the can. He explained that it no longer smelled of alcohol.

Tom Leslie cross-examined Shaw.

"From the label on the can, Mr. Shaw, you cannot tell us where in the nursery this sample was taken, can you?"

"No, sir," Shaw admitted.

Leslie asked Shaw a series of questions about the equipment he used to test the sample. Leslie stretched out a few questions into an hour's worth of questioning about the testing equipment. Then he asked Shaw about mastics like the ones used to keep carpet in place and the burn temperature of various chemicals including mastics, hydrocarbons, and alcohol.

"So, I take it the water content in over-the-counter isopropyl alcohol inhibits its burning capacity?" Tom asked.

Naturally, we had anticipated this question.

"You know," Dirk Shaw responded, "I wondered that myself, so I took some to my house and poured it on some scrap carpeting to see how it would burn. I lit it with a match. It burned very easily."

Dirk Shaw didn't mention who was with him at his house burning up the carpet, but then Tom Leslie hadn't asked him.

"How volatile is alcohol?" Tom Leslie asked him.

"Extremely volatile," Shaw responded, looking directly at the jury.

"Would kerosene or alcohol burn faster?" Tom asked.

"Alcohol would burn much more quickly," Shaw replied.

Leslie suggested that the alcohol was not in the carpet, but could have been placed into the can before the carpet was stored there. Shaw said that the only two things in the can were the carpet and alcohol but admitted that the alcohol could have been put in the can before the carpet. Shaw doubted that was the case.

Dirk Shaw was not intimidated by Tom Leslie and it showed. Leslie kept asking questions and receiving answers that were less than helpful to his client.

"How long could alcohol be in the open air before it evaporates?" Leslie asked the scientist.

"It would depend on the quantity of the alcohol poured and the conditions. If you poured an ounce, half an ounce on a carpet, I can only surmise that it would be gone in a few minutes, an hour, two hours, a few hours."

Tom Leslie persisted, "Well, you said a few minutes or a couple of hours."

Shaw was unfazed. "It depends on how well it was trapped in the carpeting, how thick the padding, and several other factors."

Although Tom Leslie had slung some poo, it was undisputed that there was isopropyl alcohol in the carpeting taken from the Wise nursery. We had three statements from William Wise and two from Michelle swearing that there was no alcohol in the area of the room where the alcohol was found. That is, if the jury believed Dave Lepper's imprecise description of where the alcohol was found.

Dirk Shaw was excused.

"The State calls Doris Gilbert," I said as Lisa headed to the back door.

In a moment, Doris Gilbert, in uniform, entered the courtroom and headed for the witness stand. She had very short brown hair worn straight. Her uniform was navy blue work pants with pockets at the waist, hip and knee and blue collared shirt. She had what looked like the end of a pair of scissors in the pocket of her pants. She took long steps and seemed to hurry.

"Ms. Gilbert, who do you work for and what do you do?" I asked.

"I work for Wishard Ambulance Service," she said. Then she described her experience and training, first as an EMT and then as a paramedic. She had worked for Wishard Ambulance, as a paramedic, for six years. She studied for nearly two years and passed a statewide certification examination. She testified that her primary responsibility was to assess potential patients.

"What is an assessment?" I asked.

"It's looking at them and trying to figure out what kind of distress they're in. We look at their airway, their breathing and their circulation." She also described the lighting conditions in the ambulance.

"The ambulance has six interior lights in the passenger compartment. It has to be that well-lit so that we are able to see the patient and tell what kind of, how they're looking, their skin and such."

Gilbert testified that in March of 1993, she was the paramedic on a big box truck, ambulance. During the time that she had been a paramedic, she had treated several firemen and a few civilians who had been exposed to fire conditions. By March 6, 1993, she knew what to expect from someone who had been exposed to severe heat, smoke or fire.

"From those observations, can you describe to us what you expected, and what you had seen in the past, from individuals who had been exposed to smoke, heat, and fire?" I asked.

"A lot of times they had a very hoarse voice, very difficult to speak," she began.

"Do you know why someone who's been exposed to heat or fire had that hoarseness about them?" I asked.

"Because of the fumes, the gases. They're so hot that they dry out your airway, your breathing tract," Gilbert explained.

"Is there anything else about one's breathing that is a sign that they'd been exposed to that heat, and smoke and fire?" I continued.

"Sometimes the toxic fumes will cause your airways to decrease in diameter, causing a wheeze. A lot of times when someone is having difficulty with breathing they'll posture—they'll throw their chest out so that they can breathe easier and better."

"Can you tell us whether there's any relationship to someone coughing and having been exposed to heat, or smoke, or fire?"

"It's a normal reaction to try to get the toxic fumes out. It's involuntary, you can't help it. You're just coughing to get the stuff out."

Gilbert was matter of fact. She spoke loudly enough for the entire courtroom to hear without needing to be encouraged. She made excellent eye contact with the jury.

"Can you tell us what stridor is?" I asked.

"Stridor is an upper airway reaction, it comes when the vocal cords get singed or, or hurt. They'll swell, and then you'll get a sound that's almost like a rooster crowing when you try to breathe in. It's also an involuntary reaction of the body."

"What else would you look for in assessing someone who had told you that they'd been involved and subject to intense heat, smoke and flames?" I asked.

"I look at hair around the airway. Nose hair, facial hair, mustache, eyebrows, any place where you could have significant burning going on."

"Why would looking at hair around the airway help you assess a patient?"

"It gives you an idea of just how much heat they were exposed to, and how much they've sucked down into their lungs, how much they've dried their airway out," Gilbert said.

I wanted to give the jury a clear picture of everything that a paramedic would look for to determine whether a person had been subjected to smoke, heat, and fire. So, I continued to draw these descriptive factors from Doris Gilbert.

"Is there anything about the interior of anyone's mouth, or things that you'd observe aside from just their physical characteristics that would be a telling sign for an assessment?" I asked.

"You look inside the mouth to make sure that their gums are pink and moist. It's a normal way that our gums are. If someone has breathed in a great deal of hot smoke, their gums can dry out and become very blanched looking, very pale looking."

I kept focused on each item that a paramedic might examine to confirm a patient being subjected to fire conditions.

"Aside from what happens to the gums, does anything happen to one's tongue during the course of, of being exposed to heat and smoke?" I asked.

She was patient with me. "Usually you can get a lot of soot on your tongue just from being exposed to the black heat and smoke. You breathe it in."

Naturally, Tom Leslie was on his feet objecting, trying to break the rhythm of Gilbert's description.

He knew where the soot and black tongue testimony was going and so he tried to derail it.

"Let's talk about somebody who'd been exposed for a period of four or five minutes. Would you expect to smell anything about them?"

"Yes," she said.

"What about three, three or four minutes?"

"Plenty," she responded.

"What about two or three minutes?"

"Yes."

"What is it that you expect to—tell us about the odors—and, by the way, are odors part of your assessment?"

"Sure."

"Tell us about odors you'd expect to find in, in a person who's been exposed to that significant smoke, heat or fire?" I asked.

"You can have smells if, if flesh is burned, you can smell it, and it's extremely noxious smelling. Hair also stinks when it's burned, and you can smell it. It's a stench that stays on you."

She scrunched her face as she spoke.

"Did there come a time on March 6, 1993, that you were called to 8404 E. 37th Place in Indianapolis?" I asked.

Doris Gilbert explained that when the ambulance approached the front of the Wise residence there were flames shooting out of the upstairs window. The fire engines had arrived ahead of the ambulance. She saw a person on the curb in front of the residence.

Ms. Gilbert recounted that the person she had seen was William Wise. She described what the defendant was wearing in the courtroom identifying him as the man she saw on the morning of the fire.

She said she put Wise on a gurney, because that was protocol, and wheeled him over to the ambulance.

"Did you speak to him before you placed him on the gurney?" I asked, looking at Wise.

"He said his face was burning. But nothing else. He wasn't slumped over and he was conscious," she recalled.

"When he told you that his face was burning, were you able to understand him?" I asked.

"Yes."

"Did you hear any coughing?"

"No."

"Did you hear any stridor?"

"No."

"Any respiratory distress?"

"No."

When they reached the well-lit ambulance Doris Gilbert said she was able to hear and to see William Wise very well. She shut the doors of the ambulance so that she could hear better and make her further assessment. Gilbert was in the back of the ambulance with Wise for at least fifteen minutes. She described her observations. "He was able to speak to me. There was no hoarseness in his voice. I asked him where he hurt. He said his hands. I looked down at them."

I wanted to be sure that the jury heard every word. So I tried to ask very short questions that would be answered in short definitive responses.

"Did you observe any burns or even redness on his hands?" I asked.

"No."

"Did you hear him coughing at all?"

"Not much. He coughed every now and then."

"How is that, as compared to what you would have expected to have found in someone who'd been in a hot, smoky house for a period of, of minutes?"

"I would have expected him to find it hard to speak, because he would have been coughing so much," she told the jury.

"Was it hard for Mr. Wise to speak from what you heard?"

"No. No."

"What about the stridor you described, the—"

"None of that was present." She had anticipated the question and answered before I finished.

"What about any other respiratory conditions that you described, did you listen with a stethoscope?"

"Yes, I did, but he had no wheezing."

I asked about any other indicia that she had described to the jury.

"I looked at his mustache and it was intact."

"Why did you look specifically at his mustache?"

"Because it was right in between the nose and the mouth, both places where you breathe," she responded logically.

"Did he have any severe burns on his face?" I asked.

"Not that I could see."

"Was there any redness?"

"No."

"What about his gums, did you look inside his mouth?"

"Yes. He had a small amount of soot in the center of his tongue."

"Did William Wise tell you what he had been doing, did he tell you he'd been in the house?"

"Yes."

"Based on his description to you of what he had done, did he appear to have the physical signs of having really done that?" I asked.

"No."

"Was his physical appearance consistent with what the defendant told you he had been doing for the several minutes before you arrived?"

"Not that I could see," she said.

As I asked more questions, Doris Gilbert described Wise as having nice pink gums. He was alert and oriented and was speaking in a normal speaking tone. Although she was able to smell a small amount of smoke on him, it did not hurt her nose to smell him. There was no singing of his nose hairs. She gave Wise oxygen because, "Oxygen is good," and not for any other reason.

Wise allowed Gilbert and the other paramedic to take him to the hospital. Gilbert observed that, if the patient is willing to go to the hospital, protocol is to take him.

Although Tom Leslie had been making the objections, it was Mark Earnest who asked Doris Gilbert questions. This type of double teaming is rarely permitted, but Judge Magnus-Stinson did not seem to mind.

Mark entered some hospital records and questioned the paramedic. First he suggested that Gilbert was not as well educated as some of the hospital personnel. She agreed that she only had nearly two years of training to be an EMT and paramedic and two years of college. Then he asked her about William Wise.

"Now he told you that his hands were hurting, right? Was it the palms of his hands, you dressed his hands, so you saw them?" Earnest asked.

"He told me that and I dressed his hands but they were not red."

"When was the first time that you spoke with Miss Marger Moore, or this detective?" Earnest asked this question as if speaking with me or Van Buskirk was a crime.

"A gentleman called the firehouse about a month after this happened."

Earnest abruptly switched to another subject. He asked, "Was his hair scorched?"

"He had a quarter sized singe in the upper right side of his head," she told him.

"You just can't get that standing fifteen or twenty feet away from where the fire was blazing, right?" Earnest asked her.

"Right, I agree," she said.

The hospital records had suggested that there was some singing on Wise's nasal hairs and identified a bit of soot on his face. But Doris Gilbert stuck to what she saw and the defense did nothing on cross to shake her recollection.

The next witness was going to be questioned by Lisa Swaim. I got a few minutes rest for my aching feet. I always wore heels to trial and suffered for it. I was glad to sit back and listen as she called Gary Triplett to testify for the State.

Gary Triplett was an accountant who lived in Indianapolis and was married to Michelle Wise's cousin. Wise had called Triplett from the hospital after the fire. Triplett learned, after he arrived at the hospital to pick-up Bill and Michelle, that

Baby Matthew had died. Triplett and his wife had invited Bill and Michelle to stay at their home for four or five days.

While Bill and Michelle Wise were staying with the Tripletts, they examined the Fisher Price baby monitor that the Tripletts were using in their daughter's nursery. There was some sort of minor problem with the cord to the transmitter and they heard static on the receiver at times. Aside from the static, the monitor did not smoke or get hot and there were no popping sounds.

Triplett described the relationship between Wise and Michelle during those first few days. At first Wise cared for his wife, who cried several times a day. After a couple of days, Wise seemed more interested in finding a cause for the fire than about his wife's crying.

The cross-examination was brief. Triplett agreed that people grieve differently. Other than relieving my foot pain, the witness added little to the trial.

Our final witness for the day was Ami Strati. She had not testified at the first trial and we had never met. I only knew what she had told Van Buskirk. I also knew that lawyers are notoriously bad witnesses. This is because they tend to anticipate questions instead of listening to the questions themselves, they talk too much and generally are difficult if not impossible to keep on track.

"The State calls Ami Strati," I announced. She was seated and sworn.

"Ms. Strati, would you tell the jury where you work?" I began.

"The State of Indiana Department of Insurance," she said.

"Please tell us how long you've worked for the Department of Insurance and what you do there."

"I am an attorney and have worked for the Department for five years," Strati said.

"Are you related to Bill or Michelle Wise?"

"Yes, Michelle is my husband's cousin."

"Did you know Bill and Michelle before Baby Matthew was killed?" I asked.

"Yes. Through the family, yes."

"And had you seen them on prior family occasions?"

"Yes."

"About how often?"

"I'd seen Michelle a couple of times a year, several times a year, and I'd seen Bill a handful of times," Strati responded.

"The first time that you saw them after Baby Matthew's funeral, do you recall when that was?"

"Yes. It was at the funeral of another family member in April."

"So it was within one month of Baby Matthew's death?" I asked.

"Yeah. I think it was about a month."

"Would you tell the jury what you discussed with William Wise after the funeral of another family member in April 1993?"

"It was regarding Bill and Michelle's conversation with an attorney in Indianapolis," she said.

"What did Bill tell you about meeting with a lawyer? Did he tell you why he'd met with him?" I asked.

"Yeah. They said that they had met with a lawyer regarding a suit involving Matthew's death against Fisher Price."

She was looking directly at me as she spoke.

"And what, what question did he want to know? I mean, what was the apparent purpose in asking you about this meeting with a lawyer?"

"They'd been told that, if successful, they would be able to recover maybe a million dollars, and they wanted to know if that was a reasonable opinion that they had received."

"Was money their main concern in speaking with you?" I asked.

"Yes."

"And this conversation, ma'am, you remember it quite distinctly, don't you?"

"Yes."

"Why is that?"

"I thought it was kind of unusual." She glanced at William Wise, but only for an instant.

I had no further questions for Mrs. Strati.

Jennifer Lukemeyer was taking the cross-examination. She looked young and a bit frightened. She asked Strati about her job at the Department of Insurance. She then tried several times, over my objections, to imply that an attorney had first contacted Bill and Michelle about their claim, rather than Bill seeking the information on his own. Lukemeyer eventually was permitted to imply that lawyers were chasing after Wise to file a case against Fisher Price instead of Wise contacting them.

"I was not told anybody contacted them. I was told they had a conversation. I don't know who instigated. I just know they had a conversation with an attorney," Strati responded.

"They came to you, or they wanted to know whether it was reasonable, this discussion about a lawsuit?" Lukemeyer repeated.

"No. About the amount of money they could recover," Strati replied flatly.

"They just came straight to you and said, what about this amount of money?" Lukemeyer said incredulously.

"Correct," said Strati matter-of-factly.

"And they had asked you about the conversation that they had with this attorney, whether or not this conversation and the contents of it were reasonable . . . and . . . and . . . and responsible?" Lukemeyer stammered.

Strati clarified. "Not responsible. They asked me if that amount of money was an, was a reasonable amount. I told them that I didn't practice in that area of law."

"Is this the first time any family member or friend has come to you and asked you for general legal advice or to get your opinion?" Lukemeyer asked her.

"No."

The defense indicated that it had no further questions. I did.

"Is this the first time that, within weeks of someone's death, family members asked you whether they could get a million or two million dollars as a result?" I asked sounding incredulous at the dollar amount.

"Yes," she said, looking from me to the jurors.

Lukemeyer objected to the question. The judge said, "I haven't heard any testimony about two million dollars, so I'll sustain the objection."

"What was the dollar amount that they asked you about?" I asked.

"One million dollars," Strati said.

"All right, one million dollars," I repeated, looking at Lukemeyer.

"No further questions, your honor."

It was right at five p.m. and Amy Strati was the last witness of the day.

"One million dollars," I repeated to myself silently. "One million dollars is a lot of motive." I was hopeful that the jury would consider a million dollars overnight.

We broke for the weekend. There was a lot to accomplish before Monday morning.

# Chapter Twenty

AFTER WORKING ALL weekend, and spending Sunday with Jim Finneran, I was psyched for Monday morning. As far as I could tell, my children still recognized me when I woke them to say goodbye each morning.

Van Buskirk had popped in and out of the conference room and Lisa had been there for the entire weekend. She had helped a lot with witness coordination, preparation and was always upbeat and willing to do whatever was asked of her.

On Monday morning, I was wearing my best suit, a navy pinstriped number with matching Jones of New York white cotton men's shirt. My navy pumps were on and I had pearl earrings and choker. Today would be a serious day and I hoped that I looked the part. My shoulder length hair was up and out of my way. I had even put on some cranberry lip gloss, although it would probably only last through my morning iced tea.

The first witness of the week was Kathy Roberts, one of the women who worked with William Wise at MECA. She told the jury about her job, described MECA, and said that she was assigned to train William Wise. Roberts identified Wise as the defendant sitting in the courtroom.

"Did you have an opportunity during the course of his employment, to observe Mr. Wise under stressful conditions of dispatching fire engines, ambulances, and the like?" I asked.

"Yes."

"Would you describe to the jury how he reacted under stress?"

"He handled it very well," she said.

She told the jury that she and Wise had been friendly. She also told them what she knew about Wise's dating, including his seeing a woman named Julie, who worked across the hall from IFD dispatch. I asked Kathy to describe Wise's engagement.

"Could you tell the jury what he told you about this engagement?"

"He told me that his soon-to-be wife was expecting, and that the marriage was, was, was going to happen."

"Can you tell us whether he expressed to you any feelings about his impending nuptials?"

"He wasn't very happy about it," she said.

"Did he indicate to you his feelings about the pregnancy?" I asked.

"He wanted an abortion to be done, but was told by her, his wife-to-be, that she was not going to have an abortion."

Kathy Roberts had not been invited to the wedding. She did not know of anyone else from dispatch invited either.

"After you learned from him that he had become married, did you hear very much about his relationship at home during the course of the months thereafter?"

"No, not unless we posed a question to him," she responded.

"Did there come a time when you learned that his wife had delivered their child?"

"Yes."

"How did you learn that?"

"We asked him if she had had the baby yet." Kathy Roberts looked in Wise's direction.

"Aside from you asking him, did the defendant ever volunteer any information about having had a child?" I inquired.

"No."

Roberts said she had asked to see photos of the baby, but Wise said he didn't have any. Later, after she and other dispatchers pestered Wise to show them a photo of the child, he brought one in.

"Did there come a time when William Wise made remarks to you about the baby?"

"Yes. We would ask him from time to time, how, you know, how was the baby doing, and he'd complain about the baby crying all the time," Roberts said.

"Could you describe to the jury the intensity of the complaints?" I asked.

"He was not happy about it. I mean, it was like the baby was a bother, maybe. He complained about the baby crying all the time, and that's, that's the main gist of his conversation about the baby."

"About how many times, from the time that you learned that Baby Matthew was born, until you learned that Baby Matthew was killed, did Bill Wise complain about his constant crying?"

"Whenever you asked about the baby. 'The baby cries.'"

I had no further questions.

Mark Earnest stood to question Roberts, who told him that she had worked at MECA for nineteen years and was third in command. Earnest pointed out that Matthew was killed in 1993.

"When was the first time that this information that you've just related to the jury, that you've spoken to somebody, police officers, investigator, about this?" Earnest asked her.

"In the last three or four months," she replied. "Maybe longer . . . before December 1997."

Kathy denied having discussed her testimony with Lewie-Bob Hiatt. The court did not allow further questions on the subject. Earnest asked Roberts about Wise's demeanor when he described Matthew's crying.

"When he spoke to you about the baby crying, and not wanting to have a baby, what did he look like?" Earnest asked.

"He looked like he always looked. He didn't—it wasn't any overt expression. He, he was not ever, he, he just said the baby cries."

"All right," Earnest said.

"You know, he wasn't angry. He, he just was not pleased."

"He wasn't angry though?" Earnest highlighted.

"He wasn't pleased," she replied.

Earnest took some photographs of Wise with Baby Matthew in his arms and showed them to Roberts and the jury. "Did he look similar to the way he looks in this picture with his wife, and they're holding the baby, did he have the same smile . . ."

"Objection!" I said, but Earnest kept going.

" . . . on his face when he was telling you that he, he was upset and angry at the baby."

I objected again and the court sustained the objection because the photographs were not in evidence. I had never seen them. She also struck Earnest's question, meaning that the jury was instructed to ignore the question. "Un-hear what you just heard," was the essence of the instruction to the jury.

There were no further questions, answers or skirmishes over Kathy Roberts. She was excused and Margaret Jones took her place in the witness box.

"Ms. Jones, can you tell us where you were working in 1991 and 1992?" I asked.

"I was with the Indianapolis Fire Department on light duty. I was working in the dispatch office at that time."

"Prior to coming on light duty, what was your employment with the Indianapolis Fire Department?"

"I was a firefighter and EMT," Jones said.

"During the time that you were on light duty did you meet the defendant, William Wise?"

"Yes, I did."

I asked her to identify the defendant and she pointed to Wise as he sat at the defense table. He was dressed in a gray suit and tie. She also said that she and Wise had gone out a few times outside of work.

"When you went out with him, did you observe anything unusual in his car?" I inquired.

"Yes, ma'am."

"What did he carry with him at all times, ma'am, that you observed him?"

"Fire gear from a volunteer fire department," Jones said.

"How did you learn about him carrying his fire gear?" I asked.

"He opened the trunk of his car when we were at the apartment, and I noticed it in there, and it just seemed strange to me to be carrying fire gear from a town that's not close enough to respond to a fire."

"At the time, you were a firefighter?"

"Yes, I was."

"Did you ever carry your fire gear around with you?"

"No, ma'am, unless I was changing stations."

"To your knowledge, is it routine for firefighters here with the Indianapolis Fire Department to carry their gear with them?"

"Not unless it's a sub that's going to be changing stations."

"In showing you his fire gear, did Mr. Wise also tell you about any aspirations that he had?"

"Yes, ma'am. He told me that he carried the gear because he felt that he would see a fire, come upon a house fire, and be the first one in and be able to make a rescue." Margaret Jones shook her head in the negative as she repeated what Wise had told her.

"What did he say about making that rescue, ma'am?" I asked.

"That the Indianapolis Fire Department would then award him a position in the department."

"Did he indicate to you, that he wanted to be a firefighter?"

"Several times."

"And that was the method that he told you he thought he would achieve it?" I asked.

"Yes, ma'am. He never once spoke of going through the process of hiring."

"Did he ever talk to you about his feelings about children?" I asked.

"Spoke on it briefly. Once he asked me if I was interested in having children, and my response was that it wasn't a big deal one way or the other. I've raised nieces and nephews, I feel like I've raised my own, and the only response back from him was that he, he said that kids could be a real pain."

"At any point did Mr. Wise talk to you about going on a trip or to meet anyone with him?"

I had slowly walked to the end of the jury box so that Jones would talk to or at least in the direction of the jurors.

"The only trip he talked about was after we'd went out the first time, was he wanted to take me home to see his mother, to meet his mom. This was in 1992."

There was nothing further for me.

Mark Earnest asked a few questions of Margaret Jones. His tone was condescending.

"I didn't catch it. Are you still working for fire dispatch?" Earnest asked.

"No. I am disabled. I'm on a pension."

"When did you quit working there?" Mark asked.

"November '92 is when I was pensioned off."

"When was the first time that you spoke with an investigator or a police officer or prosecutor about the information you just testified to?" Earnest asked, as he had of every witness.

"A year maybe, year and a half," Jones said.

"In your experience working for the Indianapolis Fire Department, are you familiar with whether or not they regularly or occasionally hire somebody who has become a hero after rescuing somebody in a fire, is that the way that they hire their firefighters?" Earnest asked.

"They always have to go through the hiring process. It's anywhere from nine months to a year," Jones replied accurately.

"Yeah," Earnest said as he walked back to his table.

I didn't get it. Was Earnest implying that Jones had fabricated the conversation? Why would she have done that?

Apparently Van B had a similar impression. She leaned over to me and whispered, "So Wise is a fuckin' moron, does that make him not guilty?"

"I hope not," I thought. I didn't respond to Van Buskirk.

The court excused Margaret Jones and asked who the State would call as its next witness.

"Coming down the home stretch," I thought nervously. I looked at Van Buskirk who gave me a thumbs-up roll of her eyes.

"Your honor, we have one short witness who has been delayed. We would ask to skip that witness, but take her out of order as soon as she arrives."

The court asked the name of the missing witness and I responded that it was Tamara Snyder. Mark Earnest denied that Ms. Snyder was on the witness list and I responded, at the bench, that she had testified in the first trial.

The court decided to take the matter up when the witness got to court and she allowed the State to call its next witness.

"The State calls James Finneran."

The jury had become accustomed to these announcements and those that were taking notes had their pads and pens ready to write the name of the witness. The jury stirred, because they already knew that Finneran was our electrical engineer.

Jim Finneran walked down the aisle with a large closed box in his hands. Finneran was tall and, as ever, with a glint of humor in his eye. He seemed to be mildly amused at life and his place in it. He wore a dark pair of Levi's with a button down shirt that was well pressed. He did not wear a tie.

Finneran told the jurors in his quiet but authoritative voice that he was employed by Electrotech Consultants and had worked there for two and a half years. Before that he had worked for Barker & Herbert Laboratories in New Haven, Indiana. Finneran testified that his expertise was in origin and cause investigation, product failure analysis and forensic electrical analysis.

"What is forensic electrical analysis?" I began.

"Basically it is looking at electrical products that have been suspected of causing a fire, and analyzing the product to try to make a determination whether it failed or not, and then ultimately going to court to testify on the outcome of that examination, if necessary."

Finneran spoke directly to the jury and never looked away from them.

"What is product failure analysis?" I asked.

"Basically, it's the same thing, except I deal with products that aren't just electrical. I will look at almost any type of product that would be in your home, for instance, that may have started a fire, or allegedly started a fire, and try to make a determination if that product failed and caused the fire, or caused an injury. I do a lot of shock and electrocution cases, also."

Finneran received his degree in electrical engineering technology from Purdue University. He attended a multitude of seminars and training programs over the years and listed and described many of them.

Finneran also talked about his twelve years at Barker & Herbert Labs and what he did there. He trained fire department investigators and was the engineering laboratory manager. He specialized in electrical fires, whether caused by a coffee pot, curling iron, washer, dryer, stove or the branch circuit wiring in the structure.

Finneran taught seminars in fire cause and origin and excluding electrical causes of fires. He trained engineers from other companies, and Alcohol Tobacco and Firearms agents, other governmental investigators, policemen, firemen, and insurance investigators. It was a broad spectrum of training geared toward the need of the agencies. There were only two instructors for all of these programs.

Finneran taught the electrical aspects of fire investigation and product failure and his partner taught the gas aspects of failure, such as with a gas dryer or stove. They would even do live demonstrations of how a particular product would fail. He estimated that he taught more than twenty-five of these two-day training programs.

In addition, Finneran taught basic electricity and product failure analysis to the ATF national response teams. He repeated this training program annually for six or seven years.

He liked to explain things and he was great at it. He went on to explain, "Arcing, for instance, there's a lot of misconception about arcing, and we would show arcing in a fire situation compared to arcing due to the failure of a product, or failure of a branch circuit. And it really was a live demonstration, so the classroom was limited to thirty students, and they would all get to see what was going on, and there was a lot of teacher-student interaction."

Once Finneran told the jury about his education, training, and experience, I asked him questions about the Wise case.

"In March 1993, I was working for Barker & Herbert and was a salaried employee," Finneran said.

"And was your salary based upon the determination that you made one way or the other?" I asked.

"No, it was not."

"Were you asked to do anything in regard to a residence at 8404 E. 37th Place, in Indianapolis, Marion County, Indiana?"

"Yes, I was. I was asked to come out and look at the alarm system that was involved in the residence, and also look at the electrical system. There was a question with the alarm system about a, a seizure of the phone line, and I had been involved in other alarm systems, either failures or alleged failures, and was asked to evaluate the system and try to determine why the phone line was seized and didn't make the call."

Finneran said that he went to the Wise residence on March 12, 1993. He said the scene had already been investigated by IFD and an investigator from Barker & Herbert by that time. He walked around, and went from the outside to the inside to try to figure out what happened and to evaluate what was going on with the alarm and electrical systems. He described exactly what he did at the residence. After changing into boots and coveralls he took exterior photographs and then interior photographs. He started in the basement and worked his way up to the room with the most damage. Finneran examined the alarm system.

"The alarm system," he said, "was my initial job, to look at it, and the alarm system was downstairs, I believe in the utility room, and there was a phone jack right next to the alarm system, and the phone plug was disconnected from the jack."

Finneran showed the jury a photograph of the alarm and the phone jack with the cord unplugged.

"Was the fact that the telephone cord was disconnected of any significance to you in your investigation?" I asked.

"Yes, it was."

"Could you explain why to the jury?"

"Well, it was my initial impression that it was connected and when I found it disconnected I just assumed that a fire department investigator had disconnected it."

"Did you determine whether that was the case?"

"Yes. It was never connected."

"Based on your investigation, did you reach a conclusion as to whether or not, because of the alarm system, the telephone at the Wise home would have been taken out of operation?"

"Yes. The alarm system would not have taken the telephone service out of use."

He also explained that the hardwired smoke detector would continue blasting an alarm noise even if the detector part itself had melted.

"The smoke detector, once it's activated, the only, only way to reset the system is to go to the control panel and shut it off. So no matter what happens to the smoke detector during the fire, once it's activated the siren is going to be sounding. The smoke detector will never shut off the siren. It has to be manually shut down."

"Did the alarm system have anything to do with the cause of this fire?"

"No, it did not." Finneran was firm but there was no arrogance in his voice.

Finneran next examined the service panel, which is a fuse panel, located downstairs. There was no fire damage in that area. The panel was intact. Only one fuse was blown.

"Based on the fact that the fuse was blown, did you believe that was any evidence at all in regard to the cause of this fire?" I asked.

"No, I did not. The fuse did its job. The fuse did blow, and at what time-frame, there's no way of telling how soon the fuse blew, but it functioned and there was no evidence of any electrical damage to the writing that was connected to the receptacle."

Again we showed a photograph of the electric panel, blown fuse, and the receptacle.

One by one, Finneran ruled out all other possible accidental causes of the fire. He had investigated the furnace and water heater and ruled each out as a potential source of the fire. He said that if an accelerant was poured away from the furnace, say on another floor, it would have no effect at all on the furnace, even a gas furnace.

"Does the fact that there was no damage to the gas furnace in the Wise home as a result of burning or an accelerant prove that no accelerant was used in the nursery?" I asked.

"No, it does not."

Finneran exuded a certainty while still being humble.

"In looking at the downstairs of the Wise home, was there any possible electrical source for this fire?" I asked.

"No, there was not," he said with confidence.

He continued his methodical outside/inside course. Finneran moved on in his descriptions to the upstairs of the Wise home. He had inspected every appliance in the kitchen, but with no fire in that area, these appliances were easily ruled out as potential causes of the fire.

With the kitchen excluded, he focused his attention on the nursery.

"Everything in the upstairs was ruled out as a potential cause for the fire, except for Matthew's nursery," Finneran said.

"Basically," he added, "the room had already been investigated twice prior to me getting there, so there was really nothing in the room as far as contents. The fire department had already removed any remnants of the furniture that had been in the room, and the floor was, had been swept clean. So my investigation pretty much was just looking at the burn patterns in the room, looking at the wiring in the walls, just to see what was there. Ultimately, we did wash the floor down again while I was there, and some carpet remnants were set back into place, but there was nothing of the furnishings left to set back into place. The outlet on the east wall and the south wall had already been removed by the fire department. The outlet on the west wall was still present."

Finneran was able to make a determination about whether there had been an electrical cause for the fire because the circuit wiring remained in the wall. There was no evidence of any type of damage in the wiring. Finneran showed the jury photographs of the inside of the walls in the nursery. These photos illustrated that the interior wiring was undamaged.

As we had discussed, Finneran also explained that arcing could occur on wires that were not the cause of a fire.

"It's normal," he said. "As the fire progresses in a room, you're going to burn the lamp cord, for instance, the potential for arcing occurs because of fire burning the insulation, it's likely to occur. It depends on how quickly the circuit breakers are going to react. It depends on how the fire spreads."

I asked, "Well, how can you tell whether arcing is caused by the fire itself, externally, or whether it was the wire that caused the fire?"

"That's very difficult to do. There are some very interesting conversations going on, the chicken and the egg syndrome, which is really what this amounts to. What you look at is the potential for this arcing to start a fire. Fire induced arcing is very common. It's one of the ways that some fire investigators do their origin and cause investigation. They will look at arcing on conductors and do what's called arc mapping. And what you're doing is you're looking for all the damage to the conductors, and then moving closer and closer to the service panel."

"Do you look at the wiring itself, taken out of context, or do you need to look at where the wiring was and other evidence in order to conclude where the fire started?" I asked.

"Oh, you have to put, take everything as a whole. You can't just say, 'Oh, I found arcing on a wire, that's the cause of a fire.' It's very difficult to start a fire in an arcing situation. It's not impossible, but it's very, very difficult. So you have to look at it. You have to look at the degree of damage. Because you have an arc on a wire clearly does not mean it started the fire."

Tom Leslie made some objection. His primary objection, in my mind anyway, was that Jim Finneran was persuading the jury.

"Mr. Finneran, did you determine whether or not the wiring in the nursery had anything to do with this fire?"

"Yes. The wiring had nothing to do with this fire."

Finneran looked at the jury as he responded.

"Did you determine whether the fire came from the inside of the wall out, or, outside the wall to the extent it went in?"

"The fire came from outside the wall, from the living space of the room, and penetrated the wall."

"Is your opinion based just on your inspection of the wiring?"

"No," he assured. "It included my inspection of the wiring, and the fact that there was no arcing in the walls of the nursery. Then I started with the sheetrock. I looked at the studs that were used to make up the walls and the very limited damage to those studs."

Finneran demonstrated what he meant by showing another photograph that he had taken. He showed the photographs and spoke slowly, allowing the jury to absorb his testimony.

"I looked at the sheetrock that was still there and the absence of sheetrock, what some people call gypsum board. You see a wide edge here, and then this is the sheetrock that's intact."

Finneran showed the photographic proof to the members of the jury. "You can see the fire damage discoloration on the sheetrock itself, and then you actually look at the studs and see that there is very limited damage to the studs, they're hardly charred. If the fire started within the wall, we're going to see a lot more damage to the studs themselves."

"Which wall had the most damage in the nursery?" I interjected.

"The south wall had the most damage. The sheetrock was missing over almost the entire wall, and the studs were more charred. The east wall would have been next."

"From looking at all of those things that you've described to us, did you form an opinion, as to whether or not the fire had started anywhere in the walls?" I asked.

"Yes, I did."

"What is your opinion?"

"It was my opinion that the fire did not start in the walls," he said. "And the burn patterns on the floor helped me come to that opinion."

Finneran methodically excluded each of the nursery's wall outlets. The one on the west wall was still there and showed only external damage. Later Finneran examined the two other outlets taken by the Indianapolis Fire Department from Matthew's room. Each outlet had been labeled and placed in a clean paint can. One was labeled "south wall" and the other was labeled "east wall."

Finneran took the actual, labeled, paint cans, stepped down, and walked directly in front of the jury. He took the outlet from the south wall out of the can and showed it to the jury, as he explained why the damage did not come from a plug or cord or short in the outlet. As he described what he observed, he held the outlet so that jurors could see what he was describing. He repeated what he observed several times, as the jurors stood or gathered to see what the outlet looked like.

When he had discussed the south wall outlet, I asked him, "Were you able to determine whether the outlet from the south wall was the source or in any way connected to this fire?"

"This outlet (Jim still held the outlet in his hand) was neither the source nor connected to the fire."

Then I asked Finneran about the east wall outlet. He did the same thing with the paint can and receptacle.

"Well, you can easily see the difference between the amount of damage, not only to the receptacle body itself, but also to the junction box that it's sitting in. Again, the Romax conductors coming out of the top are intact, they have been cut off, there's no heat damage to it. We also have a blade or a prong in one of the receptacle openings.

"There should be a mate sitting next to it. Takes two prongs to have anything operate."

I asked, "Based on Bill and Michelle Wise's statements to Allstate, that you read later, did you know that they claimed that a Fisher Price 1510 Deluxe baby monitor was plugged into the east wall outlet?"

"Yes."

"Based on what you observed in the outlet, did it appear that the transformer portion of the baby monitor had been in the east wall outlet?"

"Yes. The remains of this one prong and this little tab that comes down are indicative of a component within a step-down transformer."

"Did you receive information that the only thing allegedly on the east wall in the plug was a Fisher Price 1510 baby monitor?"

"Yes, I did," Finneran replied.

"In fact, were you given the opportunity to look at the receiver portion and transformer portion of the baby monitor that was taken from the Wise residence?"

"Yes, I did."

I showed Finneran a paper bag with the receiver and transformer that had been found at William and Michelle's home on the morning of the fire. Finneran identified the two objects for the jury.

"When you got that exhibit, did you do anything to test it?"

"Yes, I did."

"What did you do?" I asked.

"I powered it up. I plugged it in to make sure the cord, the transformer still worked and the unit would light up, and it does."

"Would you describe the portion that you have in your left hand?" I asked.

"This would be the receiver. This is what would be remote from the nursery, or baby's room, or wherever you're going to use this, and this is what you would hear sounds from. There's a counter-part to this, which would be called the monitor or transmitter, and it would pick up the sounds that are generated and transmitted to this device so you could hear what was going on."

Finneran held the unit as he spoke and showed the jury.

Slowly we went through everything that Finneran had done to test these items. It started with his inspection of the cord, plugging the cord into an outlet, turning on the receiver, checking the volume and such. Finneran determined that the receiver was functional, that it was set to volume level three. This was consistent with Wise's statement.

Finneran identified a transmitter and transformer from separate bags that I handed him. He also identified another receiver and step-down transformer that were of the same make and model.

"During the course of your investigation did you analyze the baby monitor, the type of baby monitor that you learned or believed was in the Wise residence, in order to render certain opinions in regard to its relation or lack of relation to the fire?" I asked.

"Yes, I did."

Finneran said that the pieces would help him illustrate his testing to the jury. And so the step-down transformers, transmitter, and receiver parts of a Fisher Price 1510 were allowed into evidence and shown to the jury. One pair were made in Taiwan and the other in Thailand, but both had the same UL listing numbers and appeared very similar. Nothing, even on an assembly line, was identical, according to Jim Finneran.

"At some point, did you focus your investigation on a baby monitor?" I asked.

"Yes, I did."

"Why did you shift your focus to the baby monitor?"

"Because Bill Wise said that he saw the fire in the area of the baby monitor. Later, I was also requested by the Indianapolis Fire Department to do so. So, first I looked at the box that Mr. Wise provided as the box from the monitor that was in Matthew's bedroom."

We showed the jury the box that had remained at the Wise residence. "It clearly identified the baby monitor as a Fisher Price 1510 Deluxe baby monitor," he said, reading from the side of the box. He also showed the samples to the jury so that they could see that they were the same.

"Did you know how the baby monitor worked or did you try it out?" I asked.

"I had a pretty good idea of how it worked. But I also tried it out."

"Could you show the jury how the transmitter and receiver work?"

"There's two ways to use the receiver," he explained. "You can either use it attached to a step-down transformer—when I refer to a step-down transformer, I'm talking about taking one-hundred twenty volts, which is what the receptacle is, down to nine volts. This will operate on nine volts. Which means if we don't have the transformer we could actually just put in a nine volt battery in the back of it and this would work without having to be connected to your AC circuit."

Finneran was standing in front of the jury box. As he talked he held the receiver and showed the jury.

"Did Bill and Michelle Wise indicate whether or not there were batteries in either of these two, the transmitter or receiver, at their home?" I asked.

"Yes, they did. There were no batteries in the transmitter that I call the monitor, or in the receiver. They were powered by the transformers."

"So, batteries were not an issue in regard to the baby monitor in the Wise bedroom?"

"That's correct."

"Could you power up the receiver and show us how that works?" I requested.

"When you plug it in, you turn it on," he demonstrated.

"Could you put the volume up to three, sir?"

I wanted the jury to know just how loud that receiver was on the setting that Wise had it on. It was distressingly loud.

"It's on three right now," Finneran said. "And you hear static. You can also see the LEDs flashing across. The LEDs, LED is light-emitting-diode, all it is is an indication of the amount of reception that's coming in. You notice when I first turn it on it jumps all the way across, and then if I turn it up to three, I have static. The static doesn't go away until the transmitter part of the monitor is turned on. Then you have a relatively clear channel between the two to hear what's going on."

Finneran talked and demonstrated, walking back and forth so that every juror saw how it functioned.

"One can hear [sounds] over that receiver?" I asked.

"Right. Now you can only hear static because the transmitter isn't turned on."

"Now, that portion that you've identified as a receiver. What does it receive?"

"It receives sound waves that are transmitted by the monitor. It could also receive sound waves that are transmitted by something else also. This is—there are cases where you could pick up a walkie-talkie and pick up information off this also, but its intended purpose is to pick up whatever is transmitted by the monitor."

"Does the transmitter portion of the monitor also use a step-down transformer?"

"Yes, it does."

"You mentioned it briefly, but can you tell us again what a step-down transformer does?"

As he spoke, Finneran took the transformer cord in his hand and showed it to the jury.

"In this particular case, this step-down transformer takes the one-hundred twenty volts that you have at a receptacle and steps it down to nine volts DC.

So we're changing AC to DC. Also within this enclosure are four diodes and a capacitor, and what that does is it rectifies the AC and changes it over to DC so we can operate this as if it was battery operated. The transformer also limits the amount of current that is available. There's markings on the transformer that gives its output, which is nine volts DC, and says one-hundred milliamps."

"What's the purpose of stepping down from the amount of current that you have at a wall outlet to that nine volts?"

"Well, in this particular case it makes the device a dual purpose. It can be operated off of batteries or off of a transformer. It also reduces the risk of fire or shock. At nine volts you don't have the potential to be shocked, and under ideal circumstances you would have a situation for a fire, but normally you would not have a situation at nine volts to have a fire situation either."

This, of course, was intended to steal the thunder from Wise's expert who was going to show how very fine steel wool could be heated by a nine-volt battery. Better coming from us than from them. As I've mentioned, credibility is everything.

I asked, "In fact, there is only one circumstance that is ideal in which a limited amount of output could start a fire, is that correct?"

"Yes. If I would strip the wires off of this transformer and bring it in contact with steel wool, it would actually ignite the steel wool."

"Why?" I asked innocently.

"Steel wool is a very fine gauge wire, and it doesn't take much current to have the wire glow red hot. It's a demonstration that's used a lot with nine volt batteries. A nine volt battery, if you touch it to steel wool, it would ignite the steel wool. As a boy scout it was something that they gave us to start a fire. I mean, if you couldn't get matches to work, you could get a nine volt battery and steel wool to work. So a lot of campers or hikers are aware of a nine volt and steel wool. And that's a very unique situation.

"It's not often that you'll have steel wool come across the contacts of a nine volt battery."

"To your knowledge, was there any steel wool in the Wise nursery?"

"There was none when I was there."

"And from any statements that you received, was there ever any steel wool in the room?"

"No, there was not."

"Other than under those circumstances, if you touch a nine volt battery to cloth would it ever start a fire?"

"No, it will not."

"Ever?"

"Never."

"What about to carpeting?"

"No."

"Now you're talking about stepping it down, and before you do that, can you show us, because we want to see the difference between what would come out of an electrical cord not stepped down as compared to what would come out of this cord based on the step-down transformer, is there a demonstration that you can show us, the amount of electrical power that comes out of a power cord that's not stepped down?" I asked.

"Yes."

"And what would that demonstration be?"

"It would actually be plugging in a, a lamp cord or any type of power cord and touching the ends of the wires together to show the type of current flow, arcing. What you're going to get is a, a bright light and some metal displacement at one-hundred twenty volts. If you do the same thing on a step-down transformer, realistically you get nothing. You may see a little tiny spark on occasion, but the difference is dramatic."

I asked him to get the electric wire. Actually, I had given it to him. It was attached to the cutest Baby Mickey and Minnie lamp that I had ever seen. My youngest had outgrown the lamp and it reminded me of her nursery. While Finneran went to the box that he had brought with him, the judge asked us to come up to the bench.

She told us that Tamara Snyder had arrived and that she would take her out of order, if we wanted. Tom Leslie took the opportunity to try to block the demonstration.

"I'm going to object to the relevance of this. There's been no testimony that a high voltage cord did anything in this case. Everything's from a transformer, to, to a cord that's dissimilar to what he's going to do. Are you going to demonstrate electricity today or are you going to . . ."

Tom Leslie really liked to talk.

The court interrupted. "I think he said he's going to demonstrate the difference between the two."

Leslie countered, "Well what's the relevance of that? I mean, what's he going to bring in next, a linear accelerator?"

"As the defense has pointed out several times, your honor, we have the obligation to rule out all accidental causes. . ." I began, but was interrupted by a somewhat repetitive Leslie.

"What are they going to try to demonstrate next, an atomic bomb, or a linear accelerator?"

Leslie's face was red and his voice was rising. He was serious and adamant. It was all I could do not to grin. The intensity of his argument was hysterical. The judge looked like she was exercising restraint as well.

Straight faced, she said, "I don't think we're going to deal with an atom bomb."

"Well, this is just as relevant," Leslie complained.

Some judges would not have tolerated Tom Leslie. Judge Magnus-Stinson just looked at him and said, "Okay, thank you."

Our demonstration was a go. But first Tamara Snyder was going to testify. It was anticipated that her testimony would take less than fifteen minutes. Lisa Swaim was going to question her while Jim Finneran set up for his demonstration.

"Good morning, Ms. Snyder." She was a middle aged woman, who looked to be athletic. She was dressed in a skirt and blouse and looked at the jurors as she settled in. "Will you tell the jury where you lived in March 1993?" Lisa asked.

"Yes. I lived at 8420 East 37th Place, Indianapolis. I still live there."

On the diagram that we had introduced previously, Ms. Snyder showed that her house was two doors down, on the same side of the street, as the Wise residence.

Snyder testified that on March 6, 1993, she and her husband were asleep when they heard their dog barking. Then they heard someone banging on their front door. She grabbed her robe and walked quickly to the front door where she heard banging and a man's voice hollering, "Help, my house is on fire."

Lisa took Ms. Snyder through the layout of her house, which was similar to the Wise split foyer plan, to show how long it took Snyder to get to the door. It was important because Wise claimed to have made two attempts to rescue Baby Matthew before being overcome by smoke and heat, leaving his home to call 911. Since his call came in only twenty-seven seconds after Michelle's 911 call we hoped to show how some of the twenty-seven seconds was expended.

By the time that Mrs. Snyder got to her front door, the man was still in her yard but running diagonally across the street to another house. Mrs. Snyder did not see where he went.

Wise had to cross the street, bypass the house where Michelle was making a call (which probably had lights on) to knock on another neighbor's door at 8415 East 37th Place. It was there that Wise made his 911 call.

Mark Earnest cross-examined Mrs. Snyder, asking her about her employment and prior employment. (Really? Who cared?) She said that a few minutes later she saw the same man come back toward the burning house.

Earnest also asked about whether Mrs. Snyder had given a statement to Det. Van Buskirk. She said that both she and her husband had given statements. It was some time after the fire. I didn't get the point, maybe I was missing something. Mrs. Snyder was excused.

Finneran was still in the courtroom. Before the demonstration, I asked him whether he had formed an opinion concerning possible accidental causes for the fire, after inspecting the Wise residence on March 12, 1993. He said that he had. He based his opinion on the branch circuit wiring, his inspection of the fuse panel, the circuits, the remaining outlet, the burn patterns, and the nursery room, as a whole.

"Were you able to rule out all accidental causes?" I said loudly and clearly hoping to capture the jurors' attention.

"Yes, I was."

"And what was your opinion on March 12, 1993?" I asked.

"After my initial investigation, it was my opinion that the fire was an intentionally set fire."

"Were you able, after looking at the room itself, to come up with any opinions or conclusions as to how the fire had been set?"

"It was my opinion that a liquid accelerant had been poured in the room and ignited."

He said this quietly and deliberately.

"Well, after coming to that conclusion, was there any further investigation as to other potential causes, including the baby monitor?" I asked.

"Yes, there was. We were requested to look at all of the electrical items, and the fire department had retained several pieces of evidence from that room, and it was part of my work request to look at those items and determine if there was any evidence of a failure with any of the items that had been retained."

"Particularly in regard to the baby monitor?" I asked. "Why did you focus on that?"

"Well, the baby monitor initially became a focal point as the cause of the fire."

"A focal point by whom?" I asked.

"By the homeowner," he said.

"By that you mean, the Defendant William Wise?"

"Yes, ma'am."

I asked him to step down and demonstrate how the transmitter worked. He reminded the jury that when the transmitter was turned off there was static on the receiver.

Finneran plugged the receiver into an outlet right in front of the jury. He held the receiver and I took the transmitter to the farthest corner of the courtroom near the door and plugged it into the wall socket.

Finneran turned on the receiver and showed the jury the LED lights, the volume control and the static noise. Then I plugged the transmitter into the outlet and turned it on. The static from the receiver immediately stopped. When there was no noise, the LED lights were dark.

Then I whispered "I'm whispering, can you hear me?" into the transmitter, and the LED lights lit up and the microphone picked up every word of my whisper. We did the same with me just walking around a bit.

Finneran pointed out how the lights illuminated and the sound of movement was captured by the receiver. I spoke normally and it roared through the receiver. I unplugged the transmitter and walked back to the center of the courtroom. Finneran retook his seat.

"If, for example, at the Wise residence, the transmitter had for some reason stopped functioning, would anything have been heard on the receiver out on the couch in the living room?"

"Yes. If the transmitter stops functioning, and no longer has power for whatever reason, the receiver will go into a static mode."

"Can you show the jury what would have been seen or heard?" I asked.

"I have set it to number three, where Mr. Wise said it was set that morning. All the LEDs light up, and all we get is static over the receiver."

He demonstrated.

The jury could hear the static loudly. The LED lights were evident, even in the well-lighted courtroom.

I had hoped that Finneran could also testify as to how quickly the smoke sirens had gone off in the burn room. However, because the smoke detector in the Wise house was destroyed, Jim could not testify that any of the three used in the test burn room were similar. Score for the defense. The test burn alarms had gone off immediately after the flame from the blow torch had first touched the transformer. But the jury would never hear that testimony.

Finneran testified that he had researched the flame retarding ability of the transformer. We showed the jury parts of the test burn video that had not been shown before. These included the part where the fire was actually started. It had taken five minutes, with a blow torch, to get the transformer to catch on fire and that, in part, occurred because a night light in the receptacle above the transformer caught fire and kept dripping down on the transformer. There hadn't been a nightlight in the Wise nursery.

"Mr. Finneran, can you show the jury how much current comes from a regular one-hundred twenty volt cord, using Baby Mickey and Minnie?" I asked.

Finneran stepped down from the jury box and placed long, thick, bulky gloves on both hands. They covered his arms from fingers to elbows.

"First, let's be sure that the cord is functioning properly."

He plugged the lamp into the outlet across from the jury. The light bulbs glowed brightly.

"Okay. I am going to cut the cord from the lamp." He unplugged the lamp and took a scissor-like tool from his box and cut the cord from the lamp. Then he scraped the plastic coating from the cord with a pocket knife and there were two bundles of copper wires. He explained as he worked.

"I have brought a portable breaker box with me so that we don't cause a problem in the courtroom."

He plugged the safety-assuring breaker box into the outlet. Then he plugged the cord from the Baby Mickey and Minnie lamp into the breaker box.

"Now I will touch these two wires together and you will see the power from the outlet. This power can always cause a fire."

He gingerly moved one wire toward the other. BOOM! A thunderous boom shook the courtroom. We were thrown into pitch darkness. All of the lights in the windowless courtroom went black. My teeth rattled. It was completely silent. And then I heard Finneran's quiet whisper, "Oops."

I thought I heard a chuckle from one of the jurors as the emergency exit lights, which were battery operated, came on. Unlike the juror, the judge did not look amused.

We took a break. The judge looked at me as if to say, "I hope you plan on rectifying this . . . oops," as she followed the jury out of the courtroom. Fortunately, we had only blown the breakers (all of them) in the courtroom. It was promptly corrected.

When the trial resumed, Jim had taken off his gloves. He apologized for the blackout and the failure of his circuit breaker. I was glad that he was still alive.

I asked him to step down to demonstrate the same thing but with the power stepped-down by the Fisher Price 1510 transformer. I could feel the tension in the room.

He plugged in the transformer and attached it to the receiver. The lights immediately illuminated like a pianist playing a light scale, up and down the front of the receiver. There was also static.

"Okay, Mr. Finneran. Please turn the receiver off," I requested.

I watched him unplug the transformer from the outlet. He also unplugged the transformer from the receiver.

"Before we do this demonstration, can you tell the jury whether this transformer has a United Laboratories, UL rating?"

"Yes, it has a class two rating."

"And what does that rating mean?"

"They say that a class two transformer does not have a risk for fire or shock hazard."

He was scraping the plastic coating off of the transformer wiring. There were two separate bunches of wires. They were far less numerous and thinner than the Baby Mickey lamp cord.

"Could you plug that in? Tell the jury what you are doing as you do it," I instructed.

Finneran did not have gloves on. The jury watched as he plugged the transformer cord into the outlet and with his fingers touched the wires.

Nothing.

"I can touch both conductors and nothing happens," Finneran said. "There's no shock hazard . . . I don't know if you've ever tested a nine volt battery. If you don't have a meter to do it you can touch it to your tongue to see if there's any energy. Your tongue is very sensitive, and there's moisture there. You can do that same thing with this, and you could feel that there's current flowing through. But there's no potential. I mean, there's no shock hazard."

He held the two wires between his fingers. Then he took the two wires and placed them on his tongue. I winced. He didn't. He left them there for several seconds and then removed them to answer my next question.

"What about potential for fire?" I asked.

"There's no potential for fire hazard either."

"When you put those two together, do you feel anything when you hold them?"

"No. If I'm holding them I don't feel any heat generated at all. The only time I would feel anything is if I touch it to my tongue."

He continued to hold the two wires together in his fingers.

"Your Honor, we'd request that if jurors want to feel this, that they're able to step down to feel it."

The court agreed and told the jurors that anyone that wanted to feel the wires could step down to do so. The first juror stopped at the bottom of the step and looked right at me. I nodded. He stepped over to the wires and held them in his hand. He tilted his head and walked back to the jury box. By then, the rest of the jurors and alternates had lined up to try it. Each one took his or her turn and then returned to the jury box.

"Do you feel anything at all, Mr. Finneran?" I asked, as he resumed holding the wires.

"No.

"Why is that?"

"Because of the amount of voltage and current limitations that the transformer is designed to provide. This is the way the product has been designed to operate."

I said, "The jury saw what happened when you shorted a standard light cord, one that was not stepped down. Could you do that same thing for the jury in regard to putting the two ends together?"

I had stumbled slightly over my description.

"If I actually brush the conductors across you may see a little tiny spark. Actually, you can probably hear it more than see it."

He demonstrated. There was the smallest clicking sound. "That's the magnitude of what's going on. Now, if I would short them together." He was showing the jury.

"What does that mean, to short it together?" I asked.

"I'm actually touching the conductors together," Finneran replied.

"Are you able to hold them twisted together?"

"Yes, there's no heat generated at this point, which is important because to create a fire situation we have to have sufficient heat to ignite something, no matter what it is. Some type of combustible. So we have to be able to generate enough heat to either decompose the insulation that's on the wire and ignite it, or whatever is in its vicinity. And if there's no heat here, there's no potential here. It cannot start a fire."

Jim Finneran had the riveted attention of every juror.

"Would you put it together, the way you said was the worst possible scenario, could you do that? Can you hold that?" I asked him.

Finneran twisted the wires together and held them.

"How long could you hold those wires twisted together?" I asked.

"I can hold it forever."

"Does it ever get hot?"

"No."

"Does it ever cause a shock?"

"No."

Again, I asked if the jurors could step down and cross the center of the courtroom to where Finneran had plugged the transformer into the outlet. The jurors again felt the transformer's twisted wires.

"It's still plugged in, isn't it?" I asked.

"Yes, it is. He showed the jurors the wire in his hand and the cord where it was plugged into the live wall outlet."

"Why is it important to know this, where someone had claimed that this product might have caused a fire?" I asked.

"To have the potential to cause a fire, we have to have enough energy to do that, and during a product failure analysis, no matter what the product is, you have to determine the ignition source. So by looking at the components that make up the baby monitor, anywhere from the monitor to the transformer, you have to have enough energy that will start a fire."

"Do you have that amount of current flow through there?" I asked, pointing to the transformer that Finneran was still holding in his hands. It was still plugged into the outlet.

"No, I don't."

I asked him whether he had tried these same experiments on more than one Fisher Price step down transformer. Leslie jumped to his feet, arguing in front of the jury.

"Objection!" Leslie hollered. "There's no evidence any baby monitor or transformer was taken from the Wise evidence, or Wise residence."

Judge Magnus-Stinson said, "He's testified as to the remnants of what was in the . . ."

Leslie cut her off, as he was continuing to do. "He indicated the same one, the same transformer, that was taken from the Wise residence, and his testimony has been there was none taken from the Wise residence."

My turn to interject. "Your Honor, we have a receiver, we have a transformer. Mr. Finneran has testified that the transformer that goes to the receiver is the same make and model per pair as would have been with the transmitter."

"Right. He has," the judge confirmed.

Leslie speechified, "She said it is the same as the one in the Wise nursery. We don't know that. It's not in evidence."

Judge Magnus-Stinson replied, "Well, we do know that one was taken. We don't know about the one in the bedroom. We do know one was taken from the receiver in the living room, and his testimony was that the transformers to the receiver and the transmitter on the models are the same."

"I still have an objection, but I guess it is overruled," Leslie concluded.

Judge Magnus-Stinson looked at him.

"Overruled, correct."

"Can you answer my question, Mr. Finneran?" I asked.

"I forgot the question."

"That makes both of us."

Leslie had succeeded in confusing both me and the witness. Probably even the jury. It happens. I moved on.

"In your opinion, is there any way that the current that flowed through that transformer wire, through the transformer wire in the Wise residence, going from a transformer similar to the one that you've shown the jury to a transmitter similar to the one we've shown the jury, could that under any circumstance start a fire?"

Finneran was confident. "Based on the wire coming out of the transformer to the unit, no, it cannot."

"You told us earlier that there's something in Boy Scouting about starting a fire with a nine volt battery and steel wool, is that correct?"

"Yes."

"How does the current output from a Fisher Price baby monitor compare to the output from a nine volt battery?"

"Well, a nine volt battery output is, under a short circuit condition, greater than five amps, and under short circuit conditions with the transformer, this is a tenth of an amp."

This was the first engineering lingo that Finneran had used so far.

"Huh? I'm sorry, I didn't understand a word of what you just said," I said.

"The nine volt battery has fifty times more electric output than this transformer," Finneran clarified.

"Can you prove that to us with a demonstration?" I asked.

I used to love show and tell in second grade. This was the epitome of that. The jurors, especially our "show me" Midwestern jurors, needed to see it to believe it.

"Yes, may I?"

He looked at the judge. She nodded and he stepped down. He picked up the transformer cord again.

"I'm going to strip more of the wire off, and then cut it, and take one single strand, and use the one single strand across both of these terminals, and then place one single strand across the terminals of a nine volt battery to show the difference."

"How many strands are there in the cord of the step-down transformer?" I asked as he stripped the coating off of the wire.

"Approximately nineteen wires."

"So, why are you using a single strand for your demonstration?"

"One of the potential failure modes of a cord is, if you were breaking off enough of the strands, that only one or a couple strands was carrying the amount of current that the load was pulling, load meaning the lamp, or a motor, or a fan, whatever it might be, that the one single strand could overheat. And by demonstrating that, the short circuit of this, we've shorted all the strands together, and there's no overheating. I can do it with one single strand, and, and we're still limited in the amount of current, so it doesn't get even one single strand hot. And yet a battery with one single strand will make the wire glow red and part."

"So it shows that this transformer could not even set a strand of steel wool on fire?" I asked.

"Exactly."

Tom Leslie interrupted. I don't know how the jury felt about that, but I was tired of his rude and inappropriate comments and questions. He said, "That's not exactly what he testified to. He said under short circuit conditions, I believe there is a difference, is that right?"

Finneran answered, "When you touch the two wires together they're being shorted."

Finneran stripped the transformer cord, cut off one strand and placed it between the two sets of wires. "When I plug this in, there will not be enough heat or current to do anything to this strand of wire."

"Before you plug the transformer in, Mr. Finneran, would you show us what happens when you put the strand between the two terminals of a nine volt battery," I asked.

The court permitted four jurors at a time to step down to watch what Finneran was demonstrating. As the four looked on, Finneran took a strand from the transformer cord and placed it across the two terminals of a nine volt battery. "By placing the strand between these two terminals, I am creating a short."

The strand did not get red or smoke, but the strand did melt in two. He then left the battery on the table and picked up the transformer, which had been plugged into the outlet. Finneran placed a single strand of wire between the two groups of wires from the transformer. Nothing happened. Finneran repeated this process until all of the jurors had seen the demonstration.

"Were you convinced that nothing from this transformer wire could have caused this fire, because of a lack of current flow?" I asked.

"That's correct."

"You've also told us, that in your opinion, the transmitter did not cause the fire either, was that your testimony?"

"That's correct."

"Did you do any investigation to determine whether this transmitter, one like the exemplar in my left hand, could have caused this fire?"

"Yes, I did."

Finneran explained that he opened the unit and determined that there was no additional electric source beyond the current that flowed from the transformer. Then he demonstrated what would happen if the transformer shorted out.

He plugged the transformer into the wall outlet and into the transmitter. He showed that the transmitter was working. He again illustrated the static sound that came out of the receiver when the transmitter shorted and was turned off.

With a second transmitter unit in hand, Finneran described the inside of the transmitter. It was a simple piece of plastic with a small amount of metal inside. He reiterated that Michelle and William Wise denied that there were any batteries in the unit and none were found at the scene. He described the interior of the unit, in detail, including the circuit board, capacitors, and transistors. He compared it to a little radio.

Finneran also said that there was an antenna on the transmitter and showed it to the jury. He then identified an identical antenna in one of the globs that was placed in evidence by Dave Lepper. At great length Finneran described the testing that he did to the transmitter. He told the jury that no matter what he did, if there was a short in the transformer, the transmitter just turned off.

Finneran said in a clear authoritative voice, "In my opinion the Fisher Price 1510 Deluxe baby monitor in Baby Matthew's room could not have caused the fire."

Finneran then testified as to his examination of every other glob, item or piece of an item that was found in the nursery. Some of the items were subjected to X-ray analysis, and he was able to identify several globs, as the boom box radio, telephone, a VCR tape housing and some other items. He found that none of these items had any connection to the cause of the fire.

"My opinion is that there is no accidental cause for this fire."

"As a result of all of your testing, the examination of all of the evidence, and all that you have shown us today, do you have an opinion as to what caused this fire?" I said gravely.

"Yes, I do."

"What is that opinion?"

"It is my opinion that the fire at the Wise home was intentionally set when a liquid accelerant was poured in the room and ignited."

He looked at the jury with finality.

A short break was taken before cross-examination. I did not know if Jim Finneran would collapse in the late afternoon as Lepper had done.

I warned him, "Hang in there Jim. Don't give an inch more than you have to. Be honest, but don't go out of your way to teach Tom about fires."

I don't bite my fingernails, but I thought I saw Van Buskirk gnawing on one of hers. I didn't want to discuss the direct. To do so is a jinx. I held my breath and waited for the onslaught.

Tom Leslie started.

"You can't tell us under oath today with any reasonable degree of certainty whether the baby monitor in William Wise's residence suffered from any manufacturing defect, can you?"

"No."

"You can't tell us under oath today with any reasonable degree of certainty whether the baby monitor in William Wise's residence suffered from any workmanship defect, can you?"

"No," Finneran said again.

Then, having gotten those admissions, if one would call them that, Leslie tried to impeach Finneran's credentials.

"You have an electrical engineering technology degree from Purdue University, correct?" Leslie asked.

"Yes, I do."

"And that's not the same as an electrical engineering degree, is it?" Leslie said.

"No, it is not."

"How many fires have you investigated as to cause and origin?" Leslie said. He perceived himself as relentless.

"I'd say probably close to two thousand," Finneran said, calm as ever.

Finneran told him that he doesn't use a diagram, but documents the scene through photographs. He didn't take measurements in this case either.

"Isn't it important to diagram and take measurements, when investigating a fire scene?" Leslie demanded.

"It can be, it depends on the situation," Finneran conceded.

Tom Leslie had a book on his table, it was a set of guidelines by NFPA. There was one very controversial section, 921, that suggested methods of investigating fires. These were the same guidelines that he had asked Lepper about, but it was the 1995 version, which I knew had changed dramatically over the earlier editions. Each time Leslie asked the electrical engineer a question, he would hit the book with his other hand, to draw the jury's attention to it.

Like Lepper, Finneran said that it was his practice to photograph every item in the room, in place and then label it. Finneran did not take measurements of where the items were found.

Leslie took Finneran over the same ground we had covered. He asked him about where he started his investigation and through his observations. He did this at length.

There are several reasons for a lawyer to ask lengthy and repetitive questions. Sometimes the lawyer hopes to confuse the witness, or to wear the witness down so that the witness will be more submissive and make admissions helpful to the lawyer's case. Sometimes the lawyer wants to waste time to avoid another witness taking the stand. And sometimes the lawyer just doesn't' have the skill to ask a short effective question.

Then Leslie asked Finneran about the area of the fire's origin. He asked Finneran to show the jurors that area and he showed an area between the east wall and the south wall.

"Does that conflict with Mr. Lepper's area of origin?" defense counsel asked.

"I don't believe it conflicts with Mr. Lepper's. I believe mine is broader than Mr. Lepper's."

"You testified it was a liquid accelerant, is that correct?" Tom asked.

"Yes."

"And do you have an opinion as to what that liquid accelerant was?" Leslie persisted.

"No, I do not."

"Do you know how much liquid accelerant it was?" Leslie queried.

"No, I don't."

"Less than two ounces?" Leslie asked. Where'd he get that? I wondered.

"I have no opinion," Finneran responded.

"It's a pretty wide area of origin, isn't it Mr. Finneran?"

"Not for a liquid accelerant, it's not, no."

Finneran looked at Tom Leslie without emotion. Leslie was getting nowhere and so he switched lines of questioning.

Leslie asked about the construction of the burn room. Finneran responded that the mastic was not necessarily the same as that in the Wise residence and without hesitation agreed that there were other differences, although every attempt had been made to simulate the actual nursery. He also went through the lack of specifics about the kind of mattress in the baby's room. This time it seemed rote and tired.

Finneran said that the fire in the test burn room was extinguished after thirty-five minutes of burning. Leslie did not allow him to describe how the room looked at that point, but we had the video.

Leslie continued to question Finneran about the same issues. Although Jim continued to respond with equanimity, I was getting bored and the judge was less accepting of Leslie's interrupting me as I tried to make objections. She also seemed fed up with Leslie's attempting to testify instead of making an objection. Because Leslie wasn't able to get Finneran to agree with his argumentative statements, his face became so flushed that it was red ripe persimmon colored.

At one point, as Leslie was taking Finneran through his inspection of the nursery for the fourth or fifth time. Finneran testified that he found a lot of damage on the south wall of the nursery. He also identified the baseboard trim on the east wall as damaged, burned down to floor level.

"Okay. And you're aware, are you not, that that's where the baby's bed was?" Leslie claimed.

"Yes. The baby's bed was in the southeast corner," Finneran said.

"And that's where the mattress was."

"Yes."

"That's also where the baby monitor was identified by Mr. Lepper," Leslie said.

"Objection, Your honor, as to what Mr. Lepper purportedly identified. Mr. Lepper indicated that he relied on things that were told to him," I said.

"Mr. Lepper investigated this fire, drew some conclusions. He said he talked with Mr. Lepper," Leslie said. He was trying to convince the jury that Lepper had identified the location of the transmitter instead of his client.

The judge concluded, " . . . and Mr. Lepper said what Ms. Moore said he said, and I think the jury can sort through that."

Finneran had listened carefully. "It's my understanding that Mr. Lepper never found the monitor. He positioned it based on what he was told, not on what, not on any physical evidence."

Leslie's bait and switch tactics were not working on Finneran. He would switch from one area of inquiry to another with Finneran keeping up admirably. One example was when Leslie tried to get the electrical engineer to minimize his testimony about burn patterns on the floor.

Leslie said, "I believe your testimony was that this was simply an unusual pattern, is that right?"

"Yes, it, it is an unusual pattern. It's indicative of a liquid accelerant pattern."

Leslie asked Finneran about UL testing, but Finneran was only able to give a general explanation. Leslie pointed out that the transformer was marked UL but did not show that it was a class 2 transformer. Finneran explained that it was not marked, but the UL number was a code that helped identify the class of electrical cords.

Leslie asked Finneran if there could have been a short in the cord for a long time. Finneran agreed that it could have been there for a long time, but that if the cord had shorted, the monitor or appliance, or light would not have operated.

Finneran was an expert in every sense of the word. He did not argue. He did not get defensive. He just answered the questions from his experience. I was very glad that he was testifying for the State. And that we had worked hard on anticipating the questions that would be asked of him.

Tom Leslie showed Finneran some photographs of an alcohol bottle and asked him if he could identify it. Finneran agreed that it was an alcohol bottle, isopropyl alcohol. When asked about the bottle, he said he did not know where it came from but did know that alcohol was found in a carpet sample.

"What causes beading on a wire?" Leslie asked.

"Several things can cause beading. Arcing is certainly one of them, short circuiting. Fire can cause a bead to appear on a wire. Also, alloy can cause beading on a wire. When you look at the wire, no one can tell which of these caused the beading."

The defense asked Finneran to pick through all of the evidence that the State had entered into evidence and used an inventory prepared by Barker & Herbert to show that not every item listed had been placed into evidence. After going through many items, Leslie asked Finneran about Exhibit 42, a glob.

"Did you look at Exhibit 42?" Leslie asked.

"Yes, I did. Sometime after March 12, 1993."

Leslie asked him if he tested Exhibit 42, how he tested it, and what he found. Finneran said that he received it and tested it and took microscopic photographs of it. He said that he turned the photographs over to the prosecution about ten days before.

Leslie was livid.

He demanded a conference outside the presence of the jury to complain that the State had not turned over the photographs. His real emotion undoubtedly emanated from the fact that the State had anticipated the defense ambush over Exhibit 42.

"This is exculpatory and it should have been turned over to the defense. There is beading on this wire and it is proof of arcing on the wire," Leslie argued.

The court asked the witness, "Does it show that, Mr. Finneran?"

"No, it does not," Finneran responded.

Leslie interjected, "Shows beading."

"No it does not," Finneran replied.

The judge said, looking at me, "If you've had this, Brady may have required that you turn it over."

I said, "This case is four years old. The evidence itself, your honor, has been turned over. The defense has had the evidence since the beginning of this prosecution. Exhibit 42 has been examined by the defense expert witnesses and we saw, right here in the courtroom, Mr. Mang taking microscopic photographs. Those have not been turned over to the prosecution. I guess they don't believe they need to disclose them, because we have the Exhibit, as they do. The actual item is the important issue, your honor. They've had that for years."

"That's absurd," Leslie spat.

Judge Magnus-Stinson said, "I don't think it's absurd. The evidence has existed for that long."

Leslie continued to argue. The judge asked whether the photographs that she saw the defense expert take of Exhibit 42 had been turned over to the defense. Both Leslie and Earnest answered simultaneously.

"We haven't seen them," they echoed.

"And they haven't been turned over," I said.

In Brady v. Maryland the United States Supreme Court ruled that the prosecution must provide a criminal defendant any information in its possession that could arguably be helpful to the defense. Leslie was claiming that Finneran's inspection photos were exculpatory and should have been turned over. I disagreed because the actual glob was made available.

The judge decided that we had endured enough for the day and that we would break for the evening. She did not rule on the objection. The defense expert was supposed to be in court in the morning so that we could take up the issue of microscopic photography of a glob of plastic. Of course, we all knew that Exhibit 42 was the melted baby monitor transmitter from Matthew's room. No one let the judge know, probably because the defense apparently hoped to surprise the State with microscopic photographic evidence. The judge was very smart. She had probably figured it out.

Leslie seemed shocked and awed that we had anticipated the defense. I didn't understand his incredulity. He had been focusing on Exhibits 38 and 42, so we had taken a much closer look as well.

The next morning we resumed after resolving nothing. The defense was still arguing over the alcohol bottle that was in evidence from somewhere.

It looked like the court was going to admit the bottle. No decision yet. No decision on the microscopic photographs either.

Tom Leslie resumed his cross-examination of Finneran. He continued to cover the same ground. Finneran confirmed that the Wise nursery reached flashover when the temperature reached eleven hundred degrees.

"What happens to room temperature after flashover?" Leslie asked.

"Immediately after flashover you go into what's called full room fire, or full room development, and the temperature will increase depending on the combustibles that are in the room."

"For how long?" Leslie inquired.

"That's difficult to say. There are variations on how long. It can be a couple of minutes that the temperature will increase, and then it will start to decay. Depending on the fuel load that's in the room it can be sustained longer than that."

Leslie asked about various temperatures but Finneran had few answers. Leslie also asked again whether the transformers had UL class 2 marked on them and Finneran said that they were UL rated but that the rating was not on the transformer.

When asked additional questions about the transformer, Finneran offered an exemplar that he had cut open to show the jury. He described the items inside and identified it as a Taiwan transformer. Leslie and Finneran started a colloquy about currents and windings and voltage.

It was far over my head and I hoped the jurors' heads as well. After the lengthy discussion and various hypothetical questions, Leslie asked the witness, "Okay. These things that I've just discussed with respect to a short, or arcing in that transformer, your testimony would be, your testimony would be that as far as you could find, the design would permit something like that to happen, is that right?"

"No," Finneran responded. "The design doesn't permit something like that to happen."

Leslie's point became obvious. There could have been a fault in the baby monitor. Finneran said that there could, but that it was not probable. Leslie spent what seemed like several hours asking Finneran about kinds of arcing.

Leslie's last question to Finneran on cross-examination was, "You have never been a fireman have you?"

Finneran answered, "No."

On redirect I approached the issue of the alcohol bottle. Finneran recalled that the defendant and Michelle had both indicated that if there was a bottle of alcohol in the baby's room, it was on the dresser and not on the changing table. I asked Finneran, "Hypothetically, if it were on the changing table, would that alcohol bottle have survived in that area of origin?"

"I don't believe so, no," Finneran said. He went on to say that he didn't think that a plastic alcohol bottle could have survived this fire no matter where it was in the room.

"And, Mr. Finneran, if alcohol in that plastic bottle had somehow miraculously survived the fire and been kicked over or spilled by a firefighter, would it have caused low burning under the baseboard as identified by you and Mr. Lepper?"

"No, it would not. And it couldn't have caused the burn pattern on the floor either."

As to the boxes of materials in the courtroom, Finneran testified that some came from the nursery, others, taken by IFD, were from other parts of the house. One example was the telephone that Wise claimed was inoperable. He got it from the living room. It was dumped in a box with materials from the nursery and from the test burn room. I hated that we looked so sloppy. But, things had been thrown into boxes after the first trial and had never been properly sorted.

I asked on redirect, "In a room the size of Baby Matthew's nursery, with the furniture of the type that you've been told was in Baby Matthew's nursery, how long, in your opinion, after flashover, would it have taken an un-accelerated fire, one that didn't have a poured accelerant, to have caused the damage that you saw in the photographs to the Wise room?"

"Based on my experience we're looking at times greater than forty-five minutes, maybe up to an hour."

"And that's after flashover?" I queried.

"Yes."

"Does any of the information that you've discussed with defense counsel or any of the evidence alter your opinion as to the cause and origin of this fire?"

"No."

"And what is that opinion?"

"It's my opinion that the fire was intentionally set."

Leslie was permitted to ask some additional questions. Jim Finneran's answers were consistent from day one through the end of the second day on the stand.

The jurors also had a few questions. The judge asked Finneran the questions that the jurors posed.

"Mr. Finneran, in your opinion, is the viscosity of melted polyurethane foam mattress material such that it could flow through carpet and under the baseboard?"

Finneran answered without hesitation. "No, it cannot."

The court read the next juror question. "Can photos with readily identifiable objects such as C cell batteries be used to establish scale or distances in photos?"

"It can be."

The judge read from a small slip of paper.

"How many Fisher-Price 1510 transformers were tested?"

"Approximately twenty," responded Jim Finneran.

"Can we see the one-hundred twenty volt input prongs from the cutaway transformer?"

The court asked, "Does this mean that whoever asked the question, wanted to see the prongs again?"

The juror said, "We were never shown the prongs in the first place."

"Okay," the judge said. "We will show them to the jury."

Lisa whispered to me, "Wow, we have some smart jurors."

I nodded. I suspected that these questions were being asked by the juror that she had selected.

The final juror question was whether the location of the telephone jack in the nursery could have caused a short and the phone to seize. Finneran responded that it could have happened that way.

James Finneran was excused. His testimony was complete. It was about 11:45 a.m. The court asked if we had a witness to call. Cathy Robinson had not yet arrived. She and Dr. Pless were our final witnesses. We apologized for the delay but asked to take an early lunch recess.

# Chapter Twenty-One

IT IS DAY eight of the trial.

Van Buskirk was waiting for me when I walked out of the garage. "Well, how do you think it's going?" she asked and waited for a reply. I gave it some thought.

"Finneran was steady, but the questions from the jurors threw me off. Honestly, I have no clue. How do you think it's going?"

"Fuck if I know. The ups and downs are making me nauseous."

The trial was nerve wracking. "Are you getting heat on this one?" I asked.

"Why should this case be any friggin' different than the rest?" she asked. But we both knew that this case was different. If we lost, it was our loss and no one else's.

I said, "Dr. Pless will either make or break the case. So let's hope he's eaten his Wheaties this morning."

We digressed, discussing each of the witnesses, who we either lauded or cursed. They were our bricks. "We'll know by Friday, Van B. Today is Wednesday and the case will be over by Friday, the judge will make sure of that."

Lisa was in the conference room when Van Buskirk and I arrived. The discussion resumed and she seemed as on edge as we were. "Listen, Lisa. You've been great and I will be sure that Scott knows it. Win or lose, you're an asset to this office and I am very glad that we're working together."

She beamed. I'm not exactly generous with honest professional praise. When I do complement a fellow lawyer, it is because it is well deserved and from the heart. Hopefully it is more meaningful than a bouquet of throwaway pats on the back.

The three of us, in mismatched suits today, walked down to the courtroom together.

The defense squad was already in place and Michelle Wise was in the courtroom. She had been outside the courtroom for the entire trial because she was a defense witness. But today she would be questioned by the judge about her willingness to testify on behalf of William Wise.

We had advised the court that we reserved the right to charge Michelle Wise with murder, or any other offenses, including conspiracy to commit murder, at a later time. We had also agreed that we would not make a scene in the courtroom by arresting her during William Wise's trial. As a result of that warning, the judge had requested that the conflict lawyer for the public defender's office meet with Michelle and advise her of her rights. He was in the courtroom this morning as well.

Michelle looked her usual frumpy self but she had an attitude of determination that I may have underestimated. She glanced in our direction as I walked toward the center of the courtroom. Michelle Wise was sworn and took the witness stand. The court did the questioning.

The judge began. "Present with you in the courtroom today is Mr. Mark Inman, is that correct Mrs. Wise?" Mark Inman was a lawyer who sometimes served as the Public Defender's conflict counsel.

"Yes," Michelle responded.

"And has he consulted with you concerning your rights that you have under the State and Federal Constitutions to not testify against yourself, and also your right to counsel?"

"Yes."

"All right. And the defense has indicated in the case that they intend to call you as a witness, but before that I wanted to make sure that you felt properly advised of your rights."

"Yes."

"Okay. And that you, that you did not wish to invoke your privilege against self-incrimination."

"That's correct."

"Okay," the judge said. "And so you're willing to testify voluntarily?"

"Yes." Michelle said, looking at Wise, who was sitting at the defense table. Wise was dressed in the same or very similar suit and tie as he had worn every day of the trial. He looked in her direction but without facial expression. She showed neither affection nor fear as she looked at her husband. This woman was a disturbing enigma.

Judge Magnus-Stinson spoke to Michelle in a quiet but authoritative tone, looking directly at her, maintaining eye contact and speaking slowly and clearly. The judge instructed and questioned Michelle Wise.

"All right. I indicated to them at a hearing last Friday, there is no, no guarantee that charges couldn't be filed against you in the future, regardless of the outcome of this case. Do you understand that?"

"I understand that," Michelle said.

"Okay. And for a charge of murder there is no statute of limitations, do you understand that?"

"I understand that."

"All right. And knowing all that, do you still intend to testify voluntarily?"
"Yes."

What was wrong about this woman, aside from her horrible choice in men? She had convinced us that she was manipulated and conned by Wise, but she was the one with the college degree and a responsible job, who insisted on testifying, having a baby, getting Wise to marry her.

She was excused from the courtroom. So now we were sure Michelle would testify, but not until the State rested its case. We had two witnesses to go.

Our next witness for the State was Cathy Robinson. She was in her early thirties, casually dressed in slacks and a blouse, and had the "no discernible accent." Cathy testified that she had worked at MECA for eleven years and that she was William Wise's trainer and supervisor. It was evident that she was nervous and had never before testified in court. She fidgeted and mostly looked at the floor when answering a question.

Robinson identified the defendant as the person she knew at MECA. We went through the fact that she had not known about the wedding or pregnancy until after Matthew was born. She had asked several times to see a photograph of the infant but Wise had never shown her one.

"Did the defendant ultimately produce a picture of his child?" I asked.
"Yes, he did."

"Could you tell us what he said in regard to your request to see that photograph?" I continued.

"Just the comment that it was an ugly baby, but here's a picture," Robinson testified.

I asked her whether Wise was joking when he described Matthew as ugly. Her reply was, "That was always hard to tell with Bill."

I asked her about the conversation that she had with Wise on the night before Matthew was killed. She said that she had spoken with Wise and he complained about the infant and his wife.

"He cries all the time, mommy runs to him all the time."

I stopped her to interject, "Did he indicate to you his feelings about 'mommy running to Baby Matthew all the time'?"

"He didn't like that."

"What else did he say?"

"Just that the baby cried a lot and so I told him that I had a child that cried for six months."

"How did he respond to your suggesting that your infant cried for six months?"

"He said that he would not 'tolerate' it," she said.

I repeated her answer—"He said that he would not tolerate it"—because her voice was quiet and I wanted to be sure that the jury heard what she was saying.

I had no further questions.

Mark Earnest stood to cross-examine her. He started out somewhat friendly to the obviously uncomfortable witness.

"This conversation first took place in March 1993?" he asked.

"Yes."

"But the first time that you told anyone about that conversation was when you were approached by Ms. Moore about a year ago, right?"

He pointed at me accusingly.

"About a year and a half ago, probably," she said.

Earnest asked a series of questions about me. How I came to the witness's workplace and had spoken to her at least three times since the original interview. He became more heated with every question, and was standing close to the witness stand.

He demanded, "Could you tell the jury, please, why somebody who doesn't like to hear babies crying would lay on the couch and listen to a baby monitor of his child in another room?"

I objected and Earnest stomped back to his chair, glaring at the witness.

I asked the witness gently.

"Why is it that about a year and a half ago, you were still able to remember so clearly those two conversations that you had with Bill Wise? What was it about the conversation on the night before Matthew died that kept it in your mind?"

Cathy Robinson began to cry. "Because when I came back to work the next morning and learned that there had been a fire and the child had died, I thought to myself, 'Did I say something to cause that?' And that has been on my mind for a long time."

Tears streamed down her face.

I asked, "In regard to the tone that Bill Wise used when he told you that he wouldn't 'tolerate' any more crying, could you tell the jury what that was and why that meant something to you, if it did

She said, "It was just a very cold, hard, calculating comment. I just stopped the conversation with him."

"And is that why you remember that conversation so well?"

"Yes."

Now Mark Earnest was all-out angry. He leaped to his feet and as he was walking toward her growled, "It bothered you so much you didn't say anything about it for three years, until she came to talk to you?"

She whined, "Because, I, at that time, it took a long time before anything ever came out that it was even going to go to trial. I had no idea what was going on until we were talked to later."

"You knew that he'd been arrested in March of 1994?" Earnest demanded. "Yes."

So no good deed goes unpunished, I thought. I hoped that her feelings of guilt came through to the jurors. It's impossible to read these folks.

Robinson was excused. The State announced its next witness.

"The State calls Dr. John Pless, Marion County Medical Examiner," I said.

Dr. Pless walked into the courtroom wearing dress slacks, a button down white shirt, flowered tie, and a brown corduroy blazer. His grey temples and eyebrows were in stark contrast to his dark brown hair. He looked every bit the college professor that he was. His hair and skin were impeccable but not fussy. He had a file in his hand and made himself comfortable in the chair before looking up at me to signal that he was ready to testify. He was sworn to tell the truth before he took his seat. He had given his name to the jury. Dr. Pless had undoubtedly testified more times in a courtroom than I had tried cases.

"Dr. Pless, by whom are you employed?"

"Indiana University."

"And in what capacity?"

"I'm the director of the Division of Forensic Pathology, and Professor of Pathology. I am a forensic pathologist."

It was evident that Dr. Pless had answered these questions hundreds of times before, but he looked at the jury and back to me. He made it sound interesting. We had only gotten to speak briefly before this trial but I had every reason to believe that he would be well prepared.

"What is a forensic pathologist?" I asked.

Dr. Pless described slowly and clearly, checking the jurors' faces for comprehension.

"Pathology is the study of disease," he said. "A pathologist is ordinarily a hospital-based position who runs the hospital laboratory. He manages the technologists who do the laboratory tests, and he helps the doctors in the hospital to interpret the significance of those test results. He examines specimens from patients by biopsy or at the time of surgery to determine the presence or absence of disease in those tissues. And he also does autopsies, or postmortem examinations, to determine the factors related to deaths of patients in the hospital. Forensic is a Latin word which means, forum, or to debate. A forensic pathologist takes the tools of medicine and pathology and he uses those in the determination of the causes and mechanisms of sudden, unexplained death and violent injury. He analyzes injuries, develops opinions about his observations, and then submits those opinions to the adversary system and cross examination in a court of law."

I asked Dr. Pless to describe his educational background. He told the jurors that he graduated from Indiana University in 1963 and did his residency in the state. He was a research investigator with the United States Army doing clinical toxicology and clinical pharmacology research from 1964 through 1966. He then worked for four years at the South Bend Medical Foundation Laboratories in South Bend, Indiana. In 1970 he became a Fellow in forensic pathology at the University of Oklahoma where he was also an assistant medical examiner. For the most recent decade he had been the director of the Division of Forensic Pathology and professor of Pathology at the I.U. Medical School.

He explained that the Indiana University Medical School had a contract with the Marion County Coroner's Office to conduct medical examinations. He frequently relied on the work of other physicians when rendering opinions regarding the cause and mechanism of death.

"Could you explain to the jury why and how you rely on the work of other physicians?"

"Periodically we review the reports of other doctors, pathologists primarily. Occasionally we're asked to testify in their stead when there're not available."

He had been qualified several hundreds of times as an expert in the area of forensic pathology. This qualification had included forty or fifty times where he had testified in regard to autopsies conducted by other physicians. He also testified that he had examined at least two to three hundred fire victims.

"Are there differences in how a body would appear after an accidental fire as compared with how it would appear after an accelerated fire, meaning a fire using a liquid accelerant?" I asked.

"Yes."

"Could you describe what those differences would be?"

Dr. Pless was an accomplished teacher. He used those skills as he explained, "In an ordinary house fire the body burns relative to the closeness with which it is to the . . . to the flame. If it's in direct contact with the flame, the body is more severely burned, and if it is further away from the flame, it shows more of the effects of radiant heat, or more of a baking of the tissues. When, when a body is exposed to accelerants, or flammable substances, the burning on the body is more concentrated in one area than in another, and there may actually be portions of the body that are completely spared."

"What do you mean when you say that portions of the body might be spared?" I asked, letting Dr. Pless lead me to my next question, as I expected he would.

"I mean that there's a significant differential, or difference between the amount of burning in one part of the body or the other. Some areas that are exposed to the accelerant directly can be completely burned away, while other areas may not show any effect of heat. There's also a difference in the kind of burning through the body as well. The surface of the body tends to be much more severely burned, while the interior of the body shows very little effect of heat."

I asked, "You indicated that there is something that one might observe, you described it as sparing. How does the pouring of a liquid accelerant create a spared part of the body?"

"Well, if the body is, is covered with cloth or material which is porous, the accelerant may accumulate in . . . in that material. That material then acts like a wick, it burns on the surface, but very little heat effect is seen underneath."

"Can you tell us approximately how much time it would take in an accidental fire, or non-liquid accelerated fire, for parts of the human body to actually burn away?"

I asked this trying to give the jury a preview of what testimony was ahead.

"Well, it depends on how close the body is to the fire, directly to the fire, and the source of the fire in a room," he said. "It may take as long as forty-five minutes to an hour for a body or parts of the body to be completely consumed by the heat which is generated in a house fire, which is ordinarily about twelve hundred degrees. So that it may be forty-five minutes to an hour. If the, if the fire, or the origin of the fire is very close to the body, it could be as rapidly as thirty minutes, but probably no, no faster than that."

"Can you explain why it would take forty-five to sixty minutes to have any actual destruction of the body in a non-accelerated fire?"

"The body has quite a bit of water in it. The body is very, very high in, in liquid. The water has to literally boil out of the body before the tissues can, can burn. You also have to literally burn away the, the skin before other parts of the body such as fat and muscle can be burned. Bony tissue is very firm and hard, made up primarily of calcium. It also has to be desiccated and completely dried out before it can flake away."

I asked, "Based on the degree of burning, or what you actually see in autopsy photographs, can you begin to determine whether the fire was either accelerated, or the length of the fire?"

"By looking at the body, you can make a judgment with regard to the amount of radiant heat which would cause cooking or baking of the tissues inside the body. So if the body is exposed to high temperatures over a long period of time, the interior of the body burns. You can also look at the parts of the body that are burned away, and which parts are spared, to try to get an idea of where the origin of the fire may have been relative to the body."

"Dr. Pless," I asked, "what types of things might protect the body if an accelerant had been poured on them? Please focus on an infant. What type of materials might be porous enough, if an accelerant was poured on it, that would preserve some portion of the baby's body?"

"Well, the first thing that comes to mind is a diaper."

"And why is that?"

"Because most babies have diapers on and that material is porous and could act like a wick."

"If a baby had been wearing a diaper, and if an accelerant had been poured on that diaper, could you explain to the jury, what you would expect to find at the autopsy or reviewing photographs of an autopsy?"

"I'd expect to see burning of the parts of the body that were exposed directly to the accelerant and less burning over the part of the body that was protected by the diaper."

"And in the case of a diaper, what part of the body would be protected?"

"It would be the groin."

Dr. Pless then focused on the case at trial and described his examination of the photographs taken at the autopsy and the complete report of the autopsy by Dr. Thomas Gill.

I marked the autopsy photographs and Dr. Pless said that he recognized them as authentic. I also showed him the "Where's Waldo?" photograph that was blown up to eight by ten inches. He identified that photograph as well. Each of the autopsy photographs also had a coroner's identification number on it. Dr. Pless compared the number on each photograph with the autopsy report.

These were photographs of Matthew Dean Wise.

"Would you describe to the jury, Dr. Pless, the physical injuries that you observed in the photographs?"

He looked at the photographs as he described the infant's injuries. "The extremities, the arms, legs, a major portion of them are burned away. The entire body, except for portions of the groin, is extremely charred. The skin has been burned away, and the underlying soft tissues, muscle, bone, are exposed to the surface. The head has been burned sufficiently so that the bones of the skull have been destroyed, and portions of the interior soft tissues are burned and charred as well. The muscles of the abdomen are completely missing, and the internal organs of the abdomen are exposed to the outside."

William Wise sat at the defense table apparently unmoved. The jurors look stunned. I noticed one juror who had hidden her expression by covering her mouth with her palm. Another juror was slowly moving his head from left to right as if saying "no." There was complete quiet from the jurors and no pens were moving.

"Is there any area of that body that is spared, as you've described it previously in your testimony?" I asked.

"Yes."

"Could you describe what that area is to the jury?" I asked.

"The area is primarily the groin, including the genitals, and insides of the thighs surrounding the genitals," Dr. Pless said.

"In your opinion, could a non-accelerated, or accidental, fire, in a period of fifteen to twenty minutes, have caused the type of destruction and incineration of that infant that you just described to the jury?"

His voice was authoritative and firm.

"In my opinion, no."

"Do you have an opinion as to the type of liquid that could have protected these areas of Baby Matthew Wise?"

"That liquid could have been urine."

I looked at him for a moment trying to keep the emotion from my face. He continued, "It also could have been an accelerant."

"Do you have an opinion as to which liquid it was in this case?"

I was trying again.

"No."

"Is what you observed consistent with liquid accelerant having been poured on Baby Matthew?" I was persistent, if nothing else.

"Yes."

I asked Dr. Pless to step down and show the jury the photographs of Baby Matthew's protected groin area. He did. All of the autopsy photographs were passed to the jury. Before I gave the photos to the first juror, the judge warned them about what they were about to see.

The judge said, "Let me warn you, ladies and gentlemen, these photographs are gruesome."

I waited at the end of the jury box as each juror looked at the photographs. They were gruesome, but necessary. The look of shock and horror was evident. I saw at least one juror look over at Wise who sat impassively next to Mark Earnest.

I picked up the loathsome stack from the last juror several minutes later and put them face down on the State's table.

"In your opinion, Dr. Pless, was the destruction and the incineration of Baby Matthew's body, as illustrated in those photographs, caused by a non-accelerated or accidental fire of only sixteen minutes duration?"

"No," he said conclusively.

I waited for a few seconds looking at the physician. "We have no further questions, your honor."

Then, I returned to my seat.

The mood in the courtroom was somber. There was complete quiet as Mark Earnest approached the witness stand. I wondered if he would try to attack Dr. Pless overtly as he had every other witness that he had questioned during the State's case.

Earnest greeted the doctor and then reiterated that Dr. Pless had not done the autopsy himself but had reviewed the work of Dr. Thomas Gill. Then Earnest asked about my use of the word porous in describing the infant's diaper.

"And it's, you're saying that it's possible that had an accelerant been poured on the diaper it would have served, a porous diaper, it would have served to protect the groin area, thus explaining the lack of burns in that part of Baby Matthew's body?"

"Yes," Dr. Pless agreed.

"Matthew Dean Wise died as a result of carbon monoxide poisoning," Earnest stated. Dr. Pless agreed.

Earnest challenged Dr. Pless to admit that it would take longer to destroy an adult than an infant. He did, without any defensiveness.

"What does thirty-one percent carbon monoxide tell us about Baby Matthew?" Earnest asked. He was reading from Dr. Gill's autopsy report.

"It's a sufficient amount in and of itself to cause death," Dr. Pless replied.

"When a person is exposed in a fire, to the smoke and the soot and the things that cause carbon monoxide, how is that ingested into their system?" Earnest asked.

"Every time you take a breath, whatever is in the air, whether it be soot or toxic acids from the flame, is breathed into the lungs and, therefore, the soot is trapped in the airway. It can be seen both grossly at the autopsy, as well as in microscopic slides."

Earnest asked Dr. Pless if evidence of an accelerant could be detected on autopsy or microscopic slides.

"Only if some cloth or other material that was on the body was analyzed," Dr. Pless responded.

No analysis had been done on the small bit of diaper that remained on Baby Matthew because Dr. Gill had not requested that analysis.

Right then, Mark Earnest pulled an infant mattress from a bag and showed it to Dr. Pless. We had never seen this before. It was out in full view of the jury. I just watched. Dr. Pless agreed that the tag on this particular mattress identified it as one-hundred percent polyurethane foam.

"Would you have an opinion that if one hundred percent polyurethane were used as the mattress for Baby Matthew's bed, but perhaps that mattress was an inch thicker and a little bit longer and a little bit wider, what effect, if any, would that have had in relation to the injuries suffered by him?" Earnest asked.

"It could act as an agent which would burn under the body," Dr. Pless responded.

"Hypothetically speaking, if polyurethane such as this, when it burned could reach a temperature of two-thousand six hundred degrees, up to two-thousand six hundred degrees, would that explain, in part, or in all, some of the injuries suffered by Baby Matthew."

Mark stared at Dr. Pless.

"It could," Dr. Pless replied.

"And you would agree with me then, that the burning of a foam mattress can serve as an accelerant substance?"

Mark Earnest asked the question seeming to expect that Dr. Pless would disagree.

"Yes," Dr. Pless said.

Earnest whipped out two infant Pampers brand disposable diapers and showed them to Dr. Pless. Earnest stood in front of Dr. Pless with the folded infant diaper in one hand and a bottle of water in the other. He poured the water on the outside of the flattened diaper.

"Could you tell the jury what we just saw?" Earnest asked Dr. Pless.

"The liquid substance splashes off the plastic surface," Dr. Pless said.

"Okay. Take the other diaper," Earnest instructed. "Could you note for the jury what happens when I pour the water, liquid substance, into the inside of the diaper?"

"The liquid substance stays in the diaper," Dr. Pless responded.

"Now is that what you were referring to hypothetically had the child, we're talking about Baby Matthew, urinated, that, assuming this was urine, that this would also serve as a protective effect on his groin area?"

"Yes," Dr. Pless said.

Mark Earnest walked back to his table. But not before he looked at me smugly.

I guessed that the point was that the diaper had a plastic exterior that prevented water from getting inside, as it was poured onto the folded diaper.

Wow! Earnest (who was single) had apparently never diapered an infant, something with which I was rather familiar.

I walked to the defense table and asked Earnest if I could borrow the diaper and bottle of water. He smiled and said, loud enough for the jurors to hear, "Sure, have at it."

I wanted to show the jurors that the plastic surface didn't matter when the diaper was around the baby instead of folded flat. I wanted to put it on something to make the point.

I took the infant diaper and put it on the only available "baby" I could think of, a video tape that I had on my table. (Where were Katrina's American Girl Dolls when I needed them?)

"Dr. Pless. These disposable diapers, after a baby had been wearing them for a period of time, are they sealed tight and flat against their tummies?

"No, not necessarily," he said.

I poured the water on the black video tape and it rolled down into the diaper. I did it again to show the jury. "And so, Dr. Pless, if someone had poured an accelerant on a diaper, with a baby in it, would you expect that accelerant would be in that porous diaper, would serve as the protection that you've described to the jury."

"Yes."

"You've told the jury that you thought Baby Matthew died as a result of an accelerant being poured on him. At the time that you rendered that opinion were you aware that the infant was likely on a mattress that was made of foam or polyurethane materials?"

"Yes," Dr. Pless confirmed.

"And were you also aware, when you rendered your opinions to the jury concerning Baby Matthew's death, of his size and general age?" I asked.

"Yes."

"So, Doctor, when you told the jury that it was your opinion that the damage to Baby Matthew could not have been caused by a sixteen minute accidental or non-accelerated fire, had you taken all of those facts into consideration?"

"Yes."

"Has anything that Mr. Earnest asked you today changed your opinions, sir?"

"No."

"And in your opinion was this destruction of Baby Matthew's body as a result, or likely result, of an accelerant being poured on him and set afire?" I asked.

"It is consistent with that, yes."

Earnest asked some more questions implicating the mattress in the child's death. He ended his examination on the fact that Matthew died of carbon monoxide poisoning that could have occurred in his sleep.

The last word was mine.

"It could also be that Baby Matthew was alive as that room was burning, and that he was awake."

"It's possible," Dr. Pless agreed.

The jurors had no questions for the pathologist. I had no idea of how to interpret their silence.

"Your honor, the State of Indiana rests."

# Chapter Twenty-Two

JEANNE WISE, THE mother of the defendant, was the first defense witness. Lisa Swaim was going to question Mrs. Wise and so I relaxed to listen. First, Jennifer Lukemeyer asked questions of the witness.

Jeanne Wise said she knew her son, Bill, all his life. She retired from Miles Laboratories several years before and had been a forecast analyst for the company for eighteen and a half years. She was working part-time making wedding dresses from her home. She knew Bill's wife Michelle, and made her wedding dress when they married in July of 1992.

Jeanne testified that she, her mother and her brother were present on January 15, 1993, when Matthew was born. By that time, Bill and Michelle had moved into their new home on 37th Place that they had purchased in November or December 1992. Jeanne stayed with Bill and Michelle the second week after Matthew was born because Bill went back to work after spending a week at home with Michelle.

When asked how her son interacted with Matthew, Jeanne testified, "He had him all the time if the baby was awake. He used to hold him on his chest if he was fussy, and they'd sleep together on the couch. He helped bathe him and changed him and carried him around, held him a lot."

She testified that Bill fed Matthew a lot, even though Michelle was breast feeding. Bill and Michelle came to Elkhart where she lived. They stayed with Michelle's mother. Then, on the Wednesday before the fire, Jeanne Wise and her mother visited Michelle and Bill at their home. They stayed over on Wednesday night on their way to Florida.

"Did you notice anything unusual when you were in Matthew's nursery on the fourth and fifth?" Lukemeyer asked.

Jeanne Wise testified, "Before we were leaving, we had bathed him, and I took him in and put him in bed and stood by the crib and patted him until he was asleep, and I heard a pop down beside me on the floor, just a loud noise. It was, I thought it might wake him, but it didn't, and I just patted him a little longer."

After that she and her mother left and arrived in Florida at her other son's home. They met at a bowling alley and her son Greg, told her about the fire.

She and her mother went to her grandson's band contest and then, that night, flew back to Indianapolis.

Jeanne Wise testified that Bill was crying on Saturday and very upset. Michelle was upset too. A few days later they buried Matthew in Elkhart. Jeanne said her son, Bill, was a very loving father.

Lisa's cross examination was short and to the point. She established that Jeanne did not tell anyone about the pop she heard in the nursery. That is, until sometime after she returned from Florida. I wouldn't have bothered asking her any questions, but she was Lisa's witness, and, I was pleased that she limited her cross and was kind to this woman, who was still the accused's mother.

One of the jurors had a question for Mrs. Wise. The court considered the question and asked Jeanne Wise, "Please clarify. Did you attend a band contest after hearing about the baby's death?"

The judge read the question from a piece of paper.

"Yes, we did because it was in St. Petersburg, and that's where my son was taking me to the airport, and I hadn't seen that grandson, and we didn't know when we'd get back to Florida. So we went there to, to see him and to go to the airport. His high school was . . ."

The court interrupted her response there, and asked if the defense had any follow-up questions. Jennifer Lukemeyer asked some questions.

"Were you upset about baby Matthew and the news?"

"Oh my, yes. Yes."

"You didn't go to the band contest to avoid getting back?" Lukemeyer asked.

"No. There was a time lapse, and we were on our way to the airport, and I wanted to see my oldest grandson, also, he was there with his high school class."

"You had just lost your newest grandson."

"Yes."

Jeanne Wise was excused.

I shot a glance at Van Buskirk. She was trying to keep a straight face.

"You've got to be kidding," I whispered.

"Well the juror got it, even if Lukefuckingmeyer didn't," Van B quipped.

Jeanne Wise had given Van Buskirk and me the evil eye every time we had seen her over the past few years, so we were not fans.

The next witness for the defense was Joanne Davis, Michelle's mother. Mark Earnest was questioning Mrs. Davis, and with his usual finesse, his first question was, "How old are you?"

"I'm sixty-one years old," she said.

Mark asked her about her children and she had two: Michelle and her son, Michael. She was employed for a company for whom she had worked for about ten years.

Mrs. Davis and her husband and son had come to the hospital the day after Matthew was born. She described the look of love on Bill's face when Baby Matthew was brought into the room. She had never seen him look like that. He was a proud father.

Mrs. Davis spent the first week after Michelle came home from the hospital with the family. She never heard Bill complain about the baby crying too much. Never.

A few weeks later, Bill and Michelle took the baby to Elkhart to meet Mrs. Davis' sister who was dying from breast cancer. Mrs. Davis also testified that at Michelle's baby shower, before Matthew was born, Michelle got a baby monitor.

Earnest had no further questions. I cross-examined Mrs. Davis.

"Your daughter and Mr. Wise had a rocky relationship over the several years before they ultimately married, hadn't they, ma'am?" I asked.

"Somewhat."

"They'd been engaged, and they had broken it off at least once."

"Yes."

"And, in fact, the first person that your daughter told about being pregnant with Matthew, was you."

"I feel I was, but I don't know that for sure."

"You knew, and you certainly learned, that the defendant pressured your daughter to have an abortion of Matthew?"

I asked this question before Earnest objected and the court ruled that an answer would call for hearsay.

"Once he moved to Indianapolis, the defendant told you that the only person that he was dating was Michelle, isn't that right?"

Mrs. Davis did not respond.

"Ma'am, during the time that, after the defendant moved to Indianapolis, did he tell you that he was dating other women, while he was living at your daughter's apartment?"

"No, he did not."

"There was no wedding planned before Michelle was pregnant, was there?"

"I don't know. They were living here in Indianapolis. I don't know what they were doing or saying or planning. I live in Elkhart, they live here."

"And that's the way it is with kids, ma'am, you lived there, and they lived here, and you just can't know what's going on all the time, can you?" I asked.

"Why should I?" she demanded.

"And, ma'am, the same was true after Baby Matthew was born, wasn't it? You still lived in Elkhart, didn't you?"

"Yes, I did."

"And you don't know, ma'am, what went on after your first week in their house, do you?"

"Everything was fine."

"Ma'am," I asked in my most reasonable tone, "do you know what went on in that house after you left?"

"How can anyone know everything?" she asked grudgingly.

"You did know, however, that your daughter worked days for Banc One?"

"Yes."

"Did you know that Bill Wise specifically asked for the night shift at his job?"

"I'm not sure when he worked."

"That baby monitor that you purchased for your daughter was a Fisher-Price 1510, is that correct?"

I asked this as I handed her the box that was in evidence.

"All I can tell you about the baby monitor . . . is that it was Fisher-Price. I don't know anything about those numbers."

"Would you look at the box, it's in evidence, it came from Michelle's home. Is that the baby monitor that you gave her?"

"Ma'am, as far as I can tell, and I definitely do not remember, it was over five years ago, this looks like the monitor, but I couldn't say absolutely positively."

"You purchased the Fisher Price baby monitor new?" I asked.

"Yes, ma'am."

Mark Earnest asked another irrelevant question about how I was handling the case as his last question to Mrs. Davis.

I had finally had it with the sniping. I didn't understand the personal animosity. I know that Earnest had been devastated by the conviction of his client, Michelle Jones, months before. But other than that case, we had never spoken, never had a cross word, and I thought he was a nice young man, underneath the anger. Still, after a while, the hostility was so evident, that it confounded me. I asked and the court instructed him that his parting shots were inappropriate. I doubted that it would make any difference.

The defense's next witness was Wayne Edwards, an older gentleman from Wise's neighborhood. Mark Earnest was questioning Mr. Edwards. Earnest had a hard time asking direct questions which elicit testimony from a witness in an open ended manner. Most of the questions that he asked were leading. Leading questions are really a statement of the desired answer, which the witness merely confirms.

To illustrate, a leading question might be, "It happened on Thursday?" The same question, asked without leading, might be, "On what day of the week did it happen?" Or even, "Did it happen on Thursday or Friday?"

I couldn't tell if Earnest was intentionally leading his witness or just couldn't properly phrase the questions to avoid leading. Defense lawyers usually win or lose a case on cross-examination and have far less experience in direct-examination. It is always a temptation to lead a witness to be sure he or she says what you want him or her to say.

Mr. Edwards told the jury that he lived at 8413 East 37th Place across the street and catty-cornered from the Wise residence. He showed the jury the location on the diagram that the State had prepared. He worked for General Motor for nearly thirty years. In 1993, he worked the six-thirty a.m. to three p.m. shift and so he woke up very early each morning.

He testified, "Approximately around five a.m. I heard a banging on my front door, sounded as if someone was breaking in. So I peeked out of the window to see, you know, if I could see a person at my door, but when I peeked out of the window I saw across the street from my house, I saw fire, that the house was on fire. I saw fire and smoke from 8404."

Mr. Edwards continued to describe what happened that morning.

"Well, when I saw the fire I assumed it was someone from the burning house, and so I opened the door, and this guy came in and said, 'My house is on fire, I need to make a phone call.' So I direct him to my bedroom where the telephone was, and he was dialing 911, but he was having a problem because I don't think he could. He was excited, he couldn't get the right numbers, and I was going to attempt to, to dial 911 myself, but it, after a while then he had got through."

Mr. Edwards described William Wise. "He was dressed in a, in a jacket, seemed to be a fire department jacket. When I got home that afternoon, I noticed that there was like soot or smoke on my wall and on my telephone."

After Wise made the 911 call, Mr. Edwards asked him if there was anyone in the house on fire. Wise never answered him. Wise just left and went back to his home.

When Mr. Edwards finished dressing and was ready for work, he went outside and walked over to the Wise residence. It was then that Wise told him, "My baby is in there, and I, I got to go in and get, and get the baby out."

Mr. Edwards described what he did next. "It was dark and we couldn't see. So I went back to my house to get a flashlight, and got a flashlight and went back, and we both attempted to crawl up the steps to try to get in, but the heat was too intense."

Mr. Edwards had been a volunteer fireman in the eighties in New Jersey. He had volunteered as a fireman for about five years and had also been a special police officer. He had responded in those years to ten or twelve fires.

He testified that Wise looked like someone "who had been in that house when it was on fire." Mr. Edwards said that the two had not gotten far into the house when he had stopped trying. He claimed that Wise continued to try to get in the house. Mr. Edwards later saw firemen bringing Wise out of the residence and saw him lying on the front lawn.

On cross-examination, I highlighted the fact that Wise had been wearing a fire coat and pants when Mr. Edwards first saw him. Mr. Edwards agreed that Wise had known the name of the operator when he dialed 911. He also conceded that it took him about four to six minutes to get dressed and leave his house to go across the street.

"Now you indicated that you asked the person as he came to your house, whether anyone was left in the burning house, am I correct?"

"That's correct."

"And he didn't answer you?"

"No," Mr. Edwards replied.

"And so you took your time to get dressed, and—well, not take your time, you got dressed, and then several minutes later went across the way, is that right?"

"That's right," he agreed.

"When you got there, the door was wide open at that house, the burning house. The front door was open?"

"Yes."

"So that we are clear on it, when you got back to the Wise house, there were no other people there other than you and the defendant, or whoever this person was?"

"Correct."

Mr. Edwards could not identify the defendant as the person who had been to his house. It was not an issue as far as I was concerned.

Mr. Edwards had never seen a black man trying to kick out the basement windows. William Wise had told investigators about this black man, but had never mentioned Mr. Edwards, who was white.

"You sure weren't the black civilian that was kicking anything anywhere, were you?" I asked the white Mr. Edwards.

"No."

William Wise's sworn statement under oath had been read by the jury. In that statement Wise claimed that he had gone into the house with another man and gotten as far as the upstairs hallway (and maybe thrown the stool through the window).

"So if a statement had been made, that you went into the house with this man, and got as far as the upstairs hallway, all the way inside the house, that didn't happen, did it?" I asked.

Mr. Edwards looked genuinely confused. "I, I, I don't recall us all the way in. We, we was going through the front door entrance."

"You said you got to the front door, that's right, sir? But you sure didn't go up those stairs and into some hallway, did you?"

"No, I didn't go."

Mr. Edwards became a tad belligerent. It was obvious that he thought that Wise had really been trying to save his baby.

"If the statement was made, that there was a conversation between you and the defendant and that police officer who arrived while you were there, that didn't happen, did it?" I asked.

Earnest objected and Mr. Edwards said that the only person he saw that morning was a lady from across the street from his home. She was standing outside.

I had no further questions for Mr. Edwards.

Mark Earnest led him through another series of questions. Mr. Edwards testified that William Wise was very panicked.

"Did you believe that he was going up there to try to save that child's life?" Earnest asked.

I objected as irrelevant.

This was the third time that Earnest had asked the question and each time the judge had sustained my objection.

Earnest responded, in front of the jury, and indignantly, "It's the only thing that is relevant, in this case."

The judge said, "His belief—it's for the jury to decide. Objection sustained."

The jurors had a few questions.

"During this period of time, where was Bill's wife, Michelle?" the judge asked reading from a juror note.

Mr. Edwards responded, "The only time I saw her is when, after I came out after I was ready for work. She was standing on the opposition side of the driveway with the neighbor next door."

"Did you ever hear a baby crying?" the judge asked.

"No, I didn't," Mr. Edwards said.

"Did you hear the alarm going off?" (What a great question. Why hadn't I thought of that?)

"I don't recall that, no," Mr. Edwards replied.

"Was your last answer you don't recall an alarm?" The judge sought to clarify his response.

"Yes."

"How low was the smoke in the house?"

"I, I can't tell you exactly how low the smoke was, but the fire was pretty low."

"Okay. The next part of the question is, we know it was very hot, but were you able to breathe maybe enough to reach the baby?"

"No."

Earnest had no additional questions for Wayne Edwards. Mr. Edwards was excused.

Now Michelle Ann Wise took the stand. She was sworn as a witness. Jennifer Lukemeyer stood to question her on behalf of the defendant.

# Chapter Twenty-Three

MICHELLE TOOK THE stand looking as dowdy as ever. She smiled affectionately at William Wise as she settled into the witness chair. Lukemeyer asked Michelle about her background. Michelle was born and raised in Elkhart, Indiana and graduated from Hanover College in 1987. She married Bill Wise on July 31, 1992 in the Elkhart Calvary United Methodist Church.

Lukemeyer did a competent job of personalizing the family for the jury. She had Michelle testify to her intimate wedding and the special guest, her pregnancy with Matthew. Michelle said that she and Bill did some soul searching and decided they wanted to raise the child together. Lukemeyer spent nearly a half hour asking Michelle questions about the wedding itself and who made what for the big day.

They bought their home for about fifty-five thousand dollars and moved in before Thanksgiving 1992, while Michelle was still pregnant. Michelle described some of the work that Bill and Uncle Jim had completed in the house before she delivered Matthew.

Michelle also described the furniture and furnishings in the nursery. The crib had been hers as an infant. Her mother had purchased a crib mattress from Elkhart Bedding. When Michelle described the five drawer dresser, she said that there was an alcohol bottle on the dresser that they had used for the infant's umbilical cord.

Michelle said that the lamp on the floor had never been plugged in and never used. Then she moved to the changing table that also had a pad on it with a covering made by Jeanne Wise. Jeanne had also made the comforter, lamp shades, and other room decorations.

Bill went to birthing classes with her, as his schedule permitted. He also went to doctor's appointments, in the beginning, but when she had to go more often, he wasn't able to come as frequently.

"We thought it would be a boy so we never picked a girl's name. We wanted it to be a name that wasn't already in the family, so we decided on Matthew. Later we learned that meant Gift from God, and we just thought that was the icing on the cake. We were hoping it would be a boy."

The baby was due in February, but in January, at a doctor's appointment, it was noted that Michelle's blood pressure was high and she had swelling in her legs so a decision was made to induce labor the next day. Lukemeyer asked if Bill was at that appointment. He was not.

When Michelle got home she called her mother, Bill's mother and then Bill at work to let them know about the earlier date. She said that Bill came home early to help her pack and to reassure her. He also made sure the video camera was working. They talked all night, getting little sleep.

Bill drove her to the hospital. Her family decided to come after work on Saturday and Bill's family decided to come for a few days before their previously scheduled Florida trip.

Michelle testified about her labor, with Bill at her side. Michelle had a late afternoon epidural. Then a C-section was ordered. Bill was in the operating room with the video camera. Michelle went into lengthy and well-practiced detail about the birth and delivery. Bill was ecstatic, "five feet off the ground" at seeing the newborn.

She had six weeks maternity leave from the bank where she worked. Bill took a week off from work when Matthew was born. Michelle described how Bill cared for her during that time. She was breastfeeding. She was in charge of feeding the baby for the first few weeks. Bill had encouraged her to breast feed. Michelle went into how Matthew didn't take to breastfeeding and explained what she did to assist in that process.

Lukemeyer questioned Michelle in minute detail about how Bill helped her after she delivered Matthew. He shaved her legs. He checked her incision. He also helped with Matthew. Michelle said that Bill changed Matthew. They bathed him together. Bill clipped his toe nails.

She also included little stories about Bill and Matthew. One instance she testified to was Jeanne buying Baby Matthew a little green suit at a yard sale, but it irritated the infant's neck. Bill gave it back to his mother. Then after about three weeks, Michelle began to express milk so that Bill could feed Matthew.

She and Bill found a nearby daycare, Ten Little Indians, and enrolled baby Matthew there.

The week that Matthew died was supposed to be Michelle's first week back at work but she became ill on Wednesday. She testified that because she was ill, Bill took Matthew to the daycare and spent the entire day there with him. Matthew had only been at the daycare two or three times before he died.

Finally, after what seemed like endless testimony, Lukemeyer asked Michelle Wise about March 6, 1993. Michelle testified that she worked that day from eight a.m. until four-thirty p.m. Bill worked from noon until midnight. When Michelle got off of work, she picked up Matthew. She went to Taco Bell for dinner.

They had a Fisher Price Deluxe baby monitor at home. It was a shower gift from her mother. She kept the transmitter wherever Matthew was and the receiver part with her. She said that once, when he was in the bassinette in their room, she put the transmitter in her room. She said that Matthew slept in the bassinet a few times. She would place the transmitter under his crib in the nursery.

"Basically it would be underneath his crib," Michelle said. "Not all the way underneath, just partially underneath, by his head. We figured that's the part that, that we're going to hear, so we wanted it as, in relevance to his head."

Michelle testified that, while the baby monitor took batteries, they didn't have batteries in either one of the parts. They just plugged them in.

"As far as you were concerned, did it work well?" Lukemeyer asked about the monitor.

"Yes."

Michelle testified that Bill got home late that night, about twelve-thirty a.m. "because they were having some kind of a problem with the computers, or the communication system, or something." Matthew was sleeping when Bill arrived.

"Did he have something that he showed you?" Lukemeyer asked.

"Yes. He had a police radio with him."

"Did you guys listen to it?" Lukemeyer asked.

"No." Michelle answered.

Even though it was clear that Lukemeyer had prepared Michelle well for her testimony, she couldn't remember everything the way she was taught. She was apparently unaware or forgetting that Wise had testified to them listening to the radio together.

"Did he show you what it was for?" Lukemeyer asked.

"Yeah. He showed me how it worked and, and what it could do, and that in case they needed him, they were short-handed, that this would be a way for them to get in contact with him the quickest."

According to Michelle, Wise took the police radio downstairs when they went to bed at about one to one-thirty a.m. He put it on the nightstand next to his side of the bed. She said he did not listen to the radio.

At about two a.m. they heard Matthew crying. Her breasts were full and so she knew it was time for his feeding. Bill offered to feed Matthew, so she heated a bottle for Bill to feed him. In the meantime she expressed milk to store for future use.

Michelle didn't see Bill finish feeding Matthew.

"Okay. Did you stay up with him as he finished feeding Matthew?" Lukemeyer asked.

"No, he said, 'why don't you go ahead and go on down and get some sleep?' Bill would have had to go to work this weekend and I would be alone taking care of Matthew. And so he said, why don't you go get some sleep, I'll, I'll, I'll stay up here with him."

Michelle said this without emotion.

She said she wasn't sure which one of them had brought the receiver upstairs, but it was up there. Bill sent her downstairs but he did not come back down.

"When is the next time that you went to, or you woke up?"

"I was, I want to say it was between four-thirty, five o'clock. I remember waking up thinking, you know, Matthew should be getting hungry about now. My breasts were starting to fill a little bit. And I'm lying there, and I'm awake but I haven't gotten up, and I'm thinking that I haven't heard Bill walk across above me down the hallway into Matthew's room to put Matthew asleep in his crib, and I'm thinking, if I go upstairs, I'm going to find Bill and Matthew asleep on the couch. So I get up and, and come upstairs."

Lukemeyer showed Michelle a photograph of Bill Wise with the infant on his stomach, asleep. She asked Michelle, "Is this what you expected to find?"

Michelle acquiesced. Lukemeyer showed the photo to the jury.

Then Lukemeyer asked the same question and got a nearly memorized response. At least that was my thought. Had Michelle forgotten her lines?

Lukemeyer said, "So around, you said between four-thirty and five, you woke up. Just bring us up to speed where we are, because you thought it was time to feed?"

"My breasts were starting to get a little full. I thought it was time, getting close to time to feed Matthew. I hadn't heard Bill walk across upstairs and into Matthew's room to put Matthew to bed. I expected him to be on the, on the, on the, on the couch asleep together."

Michelle stuttered. I noticed that she stuttered infrequently. I assumed that the verbal tic indicated when she was lying or forgetting some memorized phrase.

Michelle got up and climbed upstairs. She described what she saw when she got upstairs. "I came up the stairs and I looked down the hallway toward Matthew's room. I saw the bathroom light was on, and there's an exhaust fan that comes on when you flip the light on. I could hear that and see that the light was on, and that it would shine into Matthew's room. Didn't see anything out of place. Everything was pretty quiet. Turned . . ."

But she was interrupted by Lukemeyer.

"Turned to the right . . ." Lukemeyer reminded her.

"Turned to the right, saw Bill on the couch. Came over, sat down next to him."

Again, Lukemeyer interrupted her.

"Have you ever smelled gasoline? Oil for a lamp? Rubbing alcohol?" Lukemeyer asked in rapid fire questions.

"Yes," Michelle said, adding that her mother was diabetic and used rubbing alcohol to wipe off the tops of her insulin bottles.

She asked, "When you came up to that, top of that stairway and you looked down the hallway, saw the light on, did you smell anything that resembled gasoline, lamp oil, rubbing alcohol?"

"I really didn't smell anything at all, no."

"Did you smell anything noticeable that you thought might be a liquid accelerant or anything?"

"Nothing."

"So you turned to your right . . ." Lukemeyer directed Michelle back to the scene.

"Bill was on the couch. I went over and sat down next to him. When I touched his shoulder before I actually sat down on the couch, he started awake, or started. I'm, I'm not sure if he actually had fallen asleep, or whether he was just starting to doze off. He had his back to me, so he turned over, and I sat next to him on the couch."

Michelle recalled that she and Bill sat on the couch talking for about ten minutes. They discussed how much Matthew had eaten, if he had gone to bed easily, did he fuss a little bit.

Michelle recounted and dissected the evening and her activities many times. Michelle also said that she will never forget that evening.

"After you guys talked, what did you do?" Lukemeyer asked.

"I—Bill said he was going to stay on the couch. I didn't see any, anything wrong. I covered him up with the Afghan that was on the back of the couch. I kissed him goodnight, stood up, took about two steps."

"What happened?" Lukemeyer asked encouragingly

"The alarm went off. It was just an alarm. When we bought the house we had an ADT system that was already existing in the house, and it, it was told to us that it was, was hooked up to a fire alarm, burglary, like if someone tried to get into your house, or a door opens or something, that it will sound for that. It, it's not really—I was not really familiar with it. I'd never had, been in a house, or I'd never lived in a house where it had that kind of an alarm system. It also had a smoke detector that was already there when we moved in."

Michelle described the sound as like a very high pitched tweeting sound, "like a thousand tweety birds and put them on an old record player and put it on 75, and put them up to high speed and all the way up on volume."

The smoke detector was in the hallway right at the top of the stairs on the ceiling of the hallway.

When she heard the alarm, she froze. Then she saw Bill get up and run down to the landing by the front door. She followed him. She saw that the alarm panel was all lit up. The "lights were going off, the noise was, was still going off, and I could see him trying to punch in numbers." Michelle clarified that the lights that she was describing were on the alarm panel.

" . . . then I walk, I run downstairs, and I look to see what's on the panel down there in our room, in our . . ." but Lukemeyer slowed her down by interrupting.

"What did you see down there?" Lukemeyer asked.

"Exactly the same thing."

"Did you try to punch in the code?" Lukemeyer asked.

"I never tried, no. No."

"Where did you keep the code?" Lukemeyer asked.

"On a piece of paper on the refrigerator."

"What did you do next?"

"I came back up to, to let him know, or yell at him that it's doing the same thing on that level. Bill flipped on, or turned on the light, the hanging light that's on our landing so that we could see, and that's when we saw the smoke curling around the light, and that's when we knew, really knew that there's a problem, that there was something wrong."

"When you first heard the alarm go off you didn't think there was a problem?" Lukemeyer prodded.

"I didn't smell anything, I didn't see anything. I just wanted to get the thing off so that Matthew wouldn't be afraid. I mean, it scared me. I can imagine what it did to Matthew."

"So why didn't you go get him, you bitch?" Van Buskirk snarled in a whisper.

Michelle testified that she had no idea of where the smoke was coming from, only that it was on the upper floor.

"At that point," she said, "Bill went up to get the portable telephone from the coffee table in the living room. He came back down and was trying to call 911. I could see him punching numbers."

She said they were both still standing in the foyer. Michelle said that a thousand thoughts were going through her mind and she just froze.

"Did there come a time where you went across the street? Did somebody open the front door?" Lukemeyer asked.

"I'm not sure which of us did, but someone, yes, someone opened the door," Michelle said.

"What did you do then?"

"At some point I, I grabbed my coat, and Bill told me, go across while he was punching in, he was putting . . . the phone doesn't work. I saw him try again. The phone was not working. He told me, go across the street, go call, and I'll get Matthew. So I—somehow I got my coat on and I walked across the street. I walked, because I was barefooted, I didn't have my contacts in, there was ice on the road, and all I could think of was, I can't fall, I have to get across the street."

Michelle said that it was still dark out, with some snow on the ground. Although she didn't see what Bill did after she left, she heard the screen door close. She got across the street and pounded on her neighbor's door. She was shouting, "Help us, help us, we have to use your phone, we have a fire."

"I was pounding on the door and I heard the door open from our house and I heard Bill coughing, and then I heard it slam shut again. I was screaming because I didn't know who this lady was, I didn't' know if she was awake, asleep. I assumed that she was asleep, so I was pounding and yelling, and I heard her in, I guess in her living room, and she said, 'Who is it?' and I said, 'Please, we need to use your phone, we have a fire.' And just as she was opening the door, I heard glass break behind me, and I, I turned around and I saw flames coming out of Matthew's window. They were, they were wrapping around the side and up toward the roof, I went . . ."

Lukemeyer tried to break in.

"And before you, entered that house, you heard the window breaking out in flames?"

When I objected, Lukemeyer withdrew the question because Michelle had testified that she heard the window break, not that it broke as a result of the fire.

Michelle described her call to 911. She told how she saw Bill through her neighbor's big picture window. Bill was calling her name. "I said, I'm here, where's Matthew. I don't know if he heard me or not, but I stayed, I stayed at the house. I . . ."

Michelle couldn't say how long it took the fire department to arrive. She did recall that she saw a man stop and yell something like, 'Is anyone in the house?' She couldn't see who he was, but she thought it was a male voice. Then she saw a police car pull up and a policeman get out. Then the fire trucks started to arrive.

"I didn't leave the house until after the fire was out," Michelle repeated.

"When was the next time you saw Bill?" Lukemeyer asked.

"When there were no more flames showing, at least, from his, from Matthew's window. Lois got me some slippers, because she saw that I was barefooted, and we kind of walked out, and I stopped one of the firemen and said, you know, where's my husband, we own this, you know, pointing to our house. I said, we own this house, I need to find my husband. And he directed me to an ambulance, and I walked down and I found Bill in the back of the ambulance."

When asked about Bill, Michelle continued, "He had an oxygen mask on. He was lying on a stretcher. When I went over to hug him, I could smell smoke on him. There was an attendant in the back. He asked me to sit down beside him, and asked, you know, what was Bill's name, what was his age, that kind of thing. A fireman or someone came to the back of the ambulance and opened it up and said, 'Where was the baby?' and we said he was upstairs, and then he left and came back again and said, 'Where's the baby? We found a crib or bassinet downstairs.' We were saying no, no, he's upstairs and then . . ."

Michelle was talking quickly and trying to say it all at once.

"And at some point did you learn about Matthew?" Lukemeyer asked.

Michelle spoke with minimal emotion. "Shortly after he came the second time, we heard over the radio in the front of the ambulance that they, that they had a confirmed fatality on the second floor, and we knew it was—that's when we knew, and they just left with us, and we went to the hospital."

"When you heard that, over the radio, a fatality was confirmed, did Bill react to that news?"

"He was crying, I was crying. We were hugging each other and crying."

Lukemeyer asked Michelle to describe their brief stay at the hospital. Michelle swore that she never left Bill's side. She claimed that Bill was on oxygen for four hours. She said his face was burned, parts of his hair were singed and his hands were bare of hair and red. And he reeked of smoke.

While they were at the hospital, someone named "Skip" asked them to draw a diagram of the nursery and its contents. Michelle made several calls to her family and Bill's family. Michelle also called Angela Triplett. She said that Bill couldn't talk because he had to keep the oxygen mask on his face.

Michelle began to describe going to Gary Triplett's home, but it was getting late. Michelle had been on the stand, on direct examination, for most of the day. Lukemeyer asked the court to recess for the night. I had no objection since I knew that my cross-examination of Michelle would be lengthy. We were all tired.

Katrina, my oldest, had gotten braces the afternoon before and I had not been with her at the orthodontist. I was going to make chicken soup so that she would have something soft to eat.

I told Lisa and Van Buskirk that I would see them in the morning and got into my car. It was nearly six p.m. I was late for dinner. Nothing unexpected, I feared. My phone rang and my Mother said that she had made chicken soup for Katrina.

I was glad to see Mom and Bruce. Bruce asked about the trial, but I told him that it was Katrina's night to regale us with the horrors of braces. She smiled broadly with her new plastic contraptions and told all.

When we were finished eating, chicken soup with matzo balls, home baked bread, mixed veggies, and Mom's famous lemon pound cake for dessert, I gave Bruce a brief update on the case. He and mom wanted to take Steve and me out for dinner when the trial was finally over. I happily agreed. The very thought of getting the case to the jury made me grin.

When we got home, the girls climbed into our bed. I read Harry Potter to them. By now we were on the second book. At some point I fell asleep. Steve told me later how adorable it was to watch Katrina read to her sister, until they both fell asleep. The next morning I kissed my sleeping family goodbye and left for the parking garage.

On the way in to work on day eight of the trial, I thought about Perry Mason. By the end of every one of his trials, someone, other than his client the defendant, would confess to the murder. I wondered if Michelle would be that witness, in this case. Would she go that far to protect her husband? Who knew?

Fortunately, the aiding and abetting instruction would allow us to move forward regardless of her foolishness, but this was a strange woman who had to be handled with care. Thank goodness that Perry Mason was not on the case.

The cross-examination of Michelle would be important. Cross-examination is always challenging. It is one party's opportunity to undermine the testimony of the other side's witnesses, but it can backfire. Well trained lawyers are taught never to ask a question unless the interrogator knows the answer. Also important: Resist the urge to argue with the witness. I was fairly well trained but emotions were running high. Michelle's passive-aggressiveness, self-serving memory and subservient wifeishness pushed many of my buttons. I needed to be careful.

The trial started on time. Michelle Wise retook the witness stand and Lukemeyer asked her questions for most of the morning.

Michelle recounted how, on the Saturday after Matthew died, they looked at Angela Triplett's Fisher Price baby monitor.

"I wanted to know why I didn't hear something through the receiver," Michelle said. "When they turned off the transmitter, it made a static sound. Static came over the receiver. There were a series of lights that got progressively brighter. As sound got progressively louder, it lit up more, and it would go all the way over, and static would come through it, and you'd, you'd know there was some kind of . . ."

"And did you see that happen on your receiver, or hear the static on the night of the fire?" Lukemeyer inquired.

"I didn't hear anything, so therefore, I didn't look at the monitor," Michelle said.

Then Lukemeyer asked Michelle to describe, in detail, the funeral and Bill's reaction to the funeral. Matthew was buried five days after his death at Rice Cemetery in Elkhart.

Lukemeyer continued questioning Michelle Wise. "Did you and Bill participate in planning the funeral?"

"Yes, we did."

"I want you to describe for the jury some of Bill's reactions to and, and during the funeral."

Michelle responded, "He was being very supportive of me. It was very hard for me to see the casket. It was so small. And to think of burying our child, it was very hard on me. He was there hugging me, comforting me. At the time of the funeral, during the visitation we were in tears, I was crying. Bill would try and let, have me take breaks so that I wouldn't constantly be there. Go outside, get some fresh air, come back in. During the funeral we were both sobbing."

Lukemeyer consulted with Leslie and Earnest at the defense table. She came back and asked Michelle about Amy Strati.

Michelle said that she and Strati were not close. Amy Strati was married to Angela Triplett's brother. She married into the family while Michelle was still pregnant with Matthew.

"Did you talk to her about a lawyer contacting you?" Lukemeyer suggested.

"We had been contacted after we came back to Indianapolis. We'd been contacted by a law firm from Washington, D.C. There had been a phone call, and then they had sent us material, a flyer, about their law firm, with a questionnaire in it, that they wanted us to Fed Ex back to them."

"Did you Fed Ex that?"

"No, we did not."

"So, what were you asking Amy about?"

"We wanted to know whether she had heard of this law firm, were they legit, what, what kind of questions, you know, were they trying to solicit us, or was, was there something to this."

"Was some amount of money that you could get in the forefront of your mind?" Lukemeyer asked.

"Not that I recall, no," Michelle said.

Michelle testified that she and Bill had filed a lawsuit against Fisher Price on the last day before the Statute of Limitations expired. She said a lawyer told them that if they were going to file, they had to do it then.

It was Lukemeyer who became emotional, not Michelle, as she asked, "In your opinion, or in your, your belief, can any amount of money ever replace the loss of your son?"

Michelle said, "There isn't a dollar figure. There isn't a dollar amount that anyone can put on Matthew. There isn't enough money in the world. There will never be enough money in the world."

She said that Allstate asked her questions about the fire, four days after Matthew was buried. She and Bill answered all of their questions. Then they talked to the fire department, two to three weeks later. They talked to Dave Lepper and Skip. They answered to the best of their ability.

By the time that the Statement under oath was taken, Bill and Michelle had their own lawyer present. Michelle also claimed to have been cooperating with the investigation.

Lukemeyer said, "I need to clear up a few things before I sit down. Do you recall whether that alarm continued to go off while you were over at Lois's house?"

"I believe I was still hearing it after Lois opened the door and I got in. I never stepped back outside until after the fire was out, and then going out and talking to the firemen, finding out where Bill was, I don't recall hearing it."

It had been established that at the time of the fire the Wise's were using disposable diapers on Matthew. They did not have a life insurance policy on Matthew. Then Lukemeyer asked again whether Michelle had smelled any liquid accelerant that night, when the alarm went off. Michelle said that she hadn't smelled anything unusual.

Lukemeyer's last question to Michelle Wise on direct examination was, "Would you be able to estimate the time between when you woke up and the fire was out?"

Michelle said flatly, "I can't. I, I don't know—I, I can't even hazard a guess, no."

It was the State's turn to question Mrs. William Wise. I stepped up to the middle of the courtroom. I wanted to avoid being sarcastic and disgusted, but it was tough. I knew that Michelle could garner sympathy from the jury if I treated her too roughly. I walked the tightrope.

"Mrs. Wise, you said that you'd given certain statements, am I correct?"
"Yes."

"You gave the first one to the insurance adjuster, and that was on March 15th of 1993."

"Four days after Matthew was buried, yeah."

"No law enforcement was there, ma'am?"

"No, no law enforcement."

"It was just you telling an insurance person, concerning your claim—what had happened."

"Yes."

"And in fact, ma'am, you and your husband had called Allstate Insurance Company, on the same day Matthew died, to talk to them about your claim, and let them know that the house had burned."

"Don't everybody?" Michelle said.

"You called the same day, didn't you, ma'am? Saturday?"

"It was Saturday when we contacted them, yes."

"And in addition to that first statement, on March 15, 1993, you gave a statement on March 19, 1993, to Dave Lepper."

"I don't remember the date but I did talk to him, yes."

"And you were given all the time you needed to try and answer the questions truthfully, weren't you?" I asked.

"I did answer truthfully."

"And then, you gave another statement your counsel spoke about. That was June 7, 1993, and that was to John Trimble, who's a lawyer here in town, and he was asking you questions on behalf of the insurance company, is that right?"

"Yes," Michelle said.

"And no law enforcement was there."

"No."

"You had your own lawyer there?" I said.

"We had contacted a lawyer at that time, yes."

Michelle said that she had spoken with two lawyers by the time of the sworn statement under oath. Both of those lawyers had written to the insurance carrier.

Michelle admitted that, in addition to the statements we had already discussed, she had given a deposition under oath in 1995. I asked her questions at that deposition. She also admitted that she gave testimony under oath on September 26, 1996.

"In all those statements that I've just talked about, every single one of them, the person that you just told Miss Lukemeyer about, the male voice that you'd heard, you never, ever, in any of those, mentioned that male voice, have you?"

I spoke slowly and stared at her.

"I don't know if I was specifically asked," Michelle said.

"Ma'am, have you ever told anyone, before you told this jury, or perhaps told Miss Lukemeyer, have you ever told anyone that there was purportedly some male voice out there?"

"I don't remember if I did or not." Michelle was not going to back down.

"Well, you've looked at all these statements getting ready for coming here, haven't you?" I demanded.

"I've looked through, glanced through them, yes."

"You've had them at home. You had some of them at home back in 1995."

"We do have copies, yes."

"You never mentioned it, did you, ma'am?"

"I don't remember if I did or not."

Michelle graduated from Hanover but had no fire training. She told the jury that Bill had training at the Florida Fire College. He was proud of having been a firefighter. He had a number of certificates and he may have still had his books from the Fire College. All of his certificates were downstairs in the house, the part that wasn't damaged. His computer was downstairs too.

"And your husband had a bunch of fire trucks."

"Gifts from my father."

"Ma'am, did he have fire trucks?"

"Yes."

"Now, those weren't for Matthew, those were for him, your husband."

"They were gifts from my father for him, yes."

"They were his. And all of those, ma'am, those were downstairs where it wasn't damaged."

"They were displayed downstairs, yes."

"And there weren't just the fire trucks, ma'am. There were a number of fire extinguisher lamps."

"Elkhart brass fire—antiques, yes."

"Those were downstairs."

"Yes."

"There was a fire truck wall hanging."

"I had made it for him, yes. That was downstairs."

"Downstairs. All the bedroom furniture that belonged to you and the defendant, that was downstairs and wasn't damaged."

"That's where our bedroom was, yes."

"At the time of the fire, the parrot—Molly was the parrot, is that right?"

"Lucy." Michelle corrected me.

"Lucy. Lucy was something that the defendant had purchased."

"Yes."

"And something he wanted a great deal, ma'am?"

"He'd always wanted one, yes."

"Paid about four hundred dollars for it."

"I don't know how much."

"At the time of the fire, Lucy was downstairs, too."

"As was my fish tank, yes."

"And Lucy survived the fire."

"Yes."

I asked her about Wise's firefighting. She admitted that by the time they met, Wise was no longer a firefighter, either paid or volunteer, at any department.

"But nonetheless, he kept fire coats, more than one, is that right?"

"He had one, and then had gotten another one, yes."

"And those were downstairs in the closet."

"Yes."

"He had fire boots."

"Yes."

"More than one pair," I said.

"Yes."

"And they were downstairs in the closet."

"Yes."

"He had fire hats."

"Yes," she said and yawned.

"They were downstairs in the closet?" I repeated.

"They were on the wall," she said.

"Downstairs?"

"Downstairs, but on the wall not in the closet."

"Your husband was very interested in matters having to do with fires and fire departments, wasn't he?"

"He had been a fireman, so he kept that interest, yes."

"He continued with it, ma'am. As a matter of fact, at that intimate wedding you described, your husband and his friends came to your rehearsal dinner wearing their fire coats, is that right?"

"They came in at the rehearsal for the wedding, him, the best man, and his nephew came in fire coats as a joke, yes."

I switched subjects, asking Michelle about buying their home. The house had been acquired a few months before the fire. The purchase price was fifty-five thousand dollars. Michelle worked for a mortgage company, but denied knowing anything about mortgages except "final documents that had to be in a packet in order to be put on microfilm."

After several questions, she finally admitted that they had paid less than two or three thousand dollars as the down payment on the house.

"And yet within a month of the fire, you and your husband, knowing that the bottom floor, or the downstairs hadn't been damaged, filed a claim with Allstate Insurance Company for more than eighty thousand dollars. And that was—we're not talking about Matthew, we're talking about what your claim was, is that right?" I asked.

"I believe it was the contents and the house."

"And you claimed eighty thousand dollars."

"I don't remember what we claimed."

I showed her the original claim form that she and Bill had filed with Allstate. I asked her if her signature was at the bottom. She admitted it was, but equivocated through my questions. Finally she conceded, faced with the actual claim form, "That's what it says on there, yes."

She added, "The night Matthew died we called the insurance company to let them know there had been a fire in the house."

I said, "You actually asked for a check. They came out to give you money that night, didn't they, ma'am? They met you the next day?"

"No. It—we didn't call them in order to get a check. We called them to let them know we had had a fire."

"Ma'am, did they come out and give you a check at your . . ."

I tried finishing but Michelle cut me off.

"They, they came out and talked to us, and then they said, we can give you an amount to start you out, since we had no clothes, no place to stay. Neither one of us had our contacts."

Michelle refused to tell the jury about the money they had received from Allstate that first night, but was intent on describing what Allstate allegedly told her.

Lukemeyer objected to me insisting on an answer to my question. Lukemeyer tried to testify for her client but the judge cut her off.

"I think that last question, did he give you a check? That's a very straightforward question. She can answer that question." Finally, an answer.

Michelle said, "Yes."

Michelle testified that Bill lived at her apartment in Indianapolis, off and on. When I asked if she knew he was dating other people in 1992, she claimed that they were both dating other people.

"There were no plans for a wedding."

"And you got pregnant."

"Yes."

"And the defendant pressured you to have an abortion," I said.

"No." Michelle denied it.

"He didn't pressure you to have an abortion?" I said, amazed.

"I wouldn't call it pressuring. We discussed it."

Michelle was apparently going to evade answering my questions, misrepresent, mischaracterize, and recede from her prior statements. I assumed that she had been coached to do so, but it may have been her own decision.

I had to get this cross back on track and intended to do so by referring to her prior statements.

"Well, remember that statement that you gave to your husband's lawyers? I wasn't there, right?" I reminded her of the statement that she had given to Voyles about her meeting with Van Buskirk and me.

Michelle didn't answer the question but she did correct me. She made the recording and mailed it to Bill's lawyers.

I read from the transcript of that tape-recorded statement. "'I told them that I did feel that Bill put some pressure on me before we married to have an abortion.'"

I asked Michelle, "Those were your words, weren't they, ma'am?"

"Yeah. I, I believe, so, yes."

"That he put pressure on you to have an abortion," I repeated.

"Some pressure, but I wouldn't call it pressure. It isn't what I meant to say."

"And you indicated that he advised you to have an abortion, that was your phrasing in another statement you've given, isn't it, ma'am?"

"I do recall saying those words, yes."

"And it was your decision not to."

"It was ultimately my decision, yes."

Michelle said that it was at that point that the wedding was arranged.

I then asked about Matthew; whether Bill and Michelle were unable to cope with his constant needs and crying.

"Baby Matthew, after he was born, and you had been the one who wanted to have him, is that right, that that was your decision not to abort him?"

"It was my decision, yes."

"After he was born, you considered it a mistake," I said.

"If I said that, I was mistaken."

She claimed to be confused.

I reminded her of the deposition that she gave. She had been sworn to tell the truth. No one rushed her or hurried her. Then I read her the question that I had asked and her response. "Question, 'Did you think you had made a mistake?' Your answer was, 'During that time it had crossed my mind.' Is that right?"

I asked it again having made it clear that those were her words.

Michelle wanted to see the deposition to refresh her memory. I handed her the document.

"Those are my words, but it's not the meaning I wanted to convey," Michelle said.

"I see. Was it what you wanted to convey, ma'am, on page 110, when I asked you, 'He was crying when you wanted to lay him down?' Answer, your answer, 'Right, basically.' My question, how often did this happen? Answer, 'Enough that I did not get a decent night's sleep for a long time.'"

Michelle spoke in a whiney voice without being asked a question. "It seems like he wanted to stay with me rather than be in his bassinet, but I had no experience with babies."

I said, "Baby Matthew's crying was so disturbing to both you and the defendant that the two of you went to a doctor's visit and asked the doctor about why Baby Matthew wouldn't stop crying."

"Yes, we did ask the doctor."

"And the defendant was asking those questions, too, about why Baby Matthew wouldn't stop crying."

"He knew I was concerned about Matthew's health, and yes, we did ask the doctor, and everything was fine."

"And, ma'am," I said, "in terms of your care giving, you indicated that it was you who was upstairs almost all the time with Baby Matthew, isn't that right?"

"I would be upstairs or downstairs in the family room," Michelle responded.

"The night of the fire was the very first time, ever, that the defendant had offered to stay upstairs and spend the night with Baby Matthew?"

"I don't recall if that was the first night." Michelle had repeatedly used this excuse to avoid my questions.

So, once again I went to a prior statement. I established that no one from law enforcement was present at the taking of the statement. Also, that I wasn't there. In fact, this was a recording that she made, all by herself, for Wise's lawyers.

"In the tape recording that you made, you said, 'They asked me questions about whether this was the first night Bill had stayed with Matthew. And I said, yes, it had been. I told them that in my other statements I claimed that he had done it before, because if it had been the first night, it would look bad for him.' That's what you recorded on the tape recorder, wasn't it, ma'am?"

"I know I made a recording. I don't remember what I said."

Michelle told the jury that Bill usually got home at about ten minutes past midnight but on the night of the fire he did not get home until about one o'clock in the morning.

"I don't remember the exact time, no. It was around twelve-thirty, I want to say, yes."

I was going to correct her every time until she stopped equivocating.

"Deposition, page 169. You testified, 'Usually he gets home around, like, ten after midnight or so. This was later getting home. Actually, it might have been closer to one a.m., between twelve-thirty and one a.m.'"

She stammered, "I don't know exactly. To the best of my ability it was around twelve-thirty. I don't want to say it was, it was one o'clock, but I don't remember."

I noticed whenever she was "not remembering," that she stammered. If this had been poker, that would have been her tell.

"You don't know, from your personal knowledge, where your husband was during that time, do you?"

"Not personal knowledge, no."

"He told you something about helping fix the computers at the communications department?" I said.

"He had told me there had been a problem that day with the computers, and that he had stayed, and also that they were shorthanded and he'd stayed."

"Now, there was another first that morning, because it was the first time he brought home a police/fire radio?"

"Yes."

"Not something he'd ever done before."

"I'd never seen it before, no."

"And Bill said he was bringing it home because they might need him at work, and he needed to listen to it," I said.

"He said it would be the fastest way to get in contact with him," she replied.

"Now, these things," I said, holding and showing her the police radio, "they don't ring like a telephone."

"I don't know. Do they?" she asked snidely.

"You have to have it on and listening to it, ma'am, to be called over it, don't you?" I asked.

"Yes."

"And, in fact, what he told you was that he was going to keep the radio with him, and keep it on in case they called him."

"I don't remember those exact words."

"Deposition, page 171, starts on 170. Question, 'What did he tell you?' Answer, 'He said because they were shorthanded they might have to call him in. This would be the fastest and easiest way to get ahold of him.' Question, 'Okay, so he was going to keep the radio with him and on in case they called him.' Answer, 'With him and on, I believe. I do not remember if it did get turned on. I know that was his intention. That is what he told me.'"

Again, Michelle spoke without me asking her another question.

"I know he was going to keep it with him. Whether he said he was going to have it on, I don't remember. I know that was what he told me, that they were going to contact him."

Michelle denied that Bill Wise later confessed to her that he did not have permission to have the police radio. So, I again read from a transcript of her sworn testimony.

I asked her whether she believed her husband when he told her on March 6, 1993, why he brought home the radio. She said that she did. Then I asked her if she believed him later when she found out that he had taken the radio without permission. She would not answer.

I looked at her as if in disbelief of her refusal to answer. Sometimes silence says it all. I didn't press it because the jury seemed to understand her obstinacy. I moved to another topic.

"Throughout the course of that evening that you heard it, and the morning, the baby monitor was functioning properly?"

"Yes," Michelle said.

"You were able to hear it downstairs."

"Yes."

"So, when you showed the jury the picture yesterday of your husband with Baby Matthew, and the question was, when you came upstairs what did you expect to find . . . your husband had never been upstairs in the middle of the night with Baby Matthew like that before."

Michelle said she did not understand the question.

I hoped that the jury had understood it.

So I asked about another area where Michelle had stretched the truth during her direct examination.

"Yesterday, you told Miss Lukemeyer about the time you believed it was when you came upstairs."

"I wasn't, I'm not exactly sure. I've never been sure exactly what time it was."

"Well, ma'am, yesterday you told this jury that you believe you woke up somewhere between four-thirty and five in the morning."

"Somewhere in between there, yes."

"Is that what you told them?" I asked, looking at the jury to see if that was their recollection as well.

"Yes."

"On March 15, 1993, the statement closest in time to the fire, you told investigators that you woke up between five and five-thirty, didn't you, ma'am?"

"I was believing it was closer to five, yes," Michelle admitted.

"That's what you said on March 19th when you spoke to Investigator Lepper?"

"I don't know if I—I know I have said between four-thirty and five, and I believed it was around five. I may have said five, five to five-thirty. I don't know exactly what time it was. Somewhere around five."

Michelle equivocated. Equivocation is another technique used to try to change one's story, even a tape recorded sworn statement, while trying to sound as if you're not changing it at all. But, no matter how you dress it up, equivocation like this was a lie. I hoped that the jury was getting it.

"Well, would you agree that your memory would be better closer to the event than it is some five years later?" I asked.

"That—I, I wouldn't say that exactly. I would say it depends on whether I was still in shock or not, how much I recollect. Sometimes you go back and you remember things you didn't remember then."

She just won't speak the truth, I thought.

I read clearly and carefully. "March 15, question 91. 'Can you tell me the date and approximate time of the fire?' Answer, 'It was early Saturday morning, the sixth of March, between five and five-thirty.'

"And on March 19, 1993, at page 2, 'About what time was that, if you were guessing?' Answer, 'I had set my alarm before I had went to bed for about six a.m. That's the time I wanted to get up and express some more milk. I woke up between five and five-thirty for some unknown reason.' Is that what you told them, ma'am?"

"If it's on there, yes," Michelle replied.

"Well?" I asked.

"And possibly that I, I was getting up because I thought Matthew had to be fed. I don't remember what time it was."

She looked annoyed, like she was trying unsuccessfully to swat a pesky buzzing fly.

"So yesterday, ma'am, when you told the jury the time, four-thirty to five that may not be. It may really be the five to five-thirty that you said previously."

"It could be between four-thirty and five-thirty. I cannot get specific as to what time I go up."

"And when you told the jury, ma'am, yesterday, really specifically, that you woke up because you thought you hadn't heard anybody walking in Baby Matthew's room, only a couple of weeks after the fire you indicated that you didn't know why you woke up?" Michelle repeated that she thought it was time to feed Matthew.

"And you knew, by the time you gave these statements, that someone had been up, right before you had, because the defendant, right before you walked up the stairs, had been in the bathroom according to what he told you."

"He said he had been to the bathroom. I don't remember that he told me he'd just been. I know we had discussed, talked about had he, when did he go to the bathroom."

"When you, when you came up to the couch, walked up the stairs, sometime between five and five-thirty, he was just laying back down on the couch."

"No. He was on the couch," Michelle insisted.

"Reading, from the statement of March 15, again, Question 343. 'Came upstairs and did what?' Answer, 'Came upstairs, walked upstairs, and Bill was just getting back on the couch. He had just gone to the bathroom.'"

"I didn't know that then. I didn't know at the time I was coming upstairs that he had been anywhere. He was on the couch when I came up the stairs."

She contradicted her own statement.

"Ma'am, is what I just read, is that what you told someone . . ." Again Michelle interrupted me angrily.

"And I was mistaken."

" . . . under oath in March of 1993?"

"That is what I said, yes." Michelle glared at me.

"Okay, and by the way, that statement and the one of March 19, 1993, were before you knew your husband was a suspect in the murder of your son, is that right?"

"There was no police involvement at the time."

"There was police involvement on March 19 because they took your statement, but at that time you didn't know that your husband was a suspect."

"Yeah. It was the fire department, yes."

"In the March 19 statement, the investigators asked you a question about having the receiver with you and in the course of answering that question, you said, 'So I came upstairs and I saw Bill on the couch, and I walked over to him, and he said he had just gotten back from the bathroom.' Is that what you told them, ma'am?"

"That's what I told them." She barked. By now her face was getting red and her hands were balled into fists and held across her chest.

"Later on, after he became a suspect in a murder, your statements change to where, as you told the jury yesterday, you claimed that the defendant was sleeping on the couch and you startled him."

"He was on the couch," Michelle responded.

I walked Michelle through the time that she was upstairs on the couch. She talked to Bill, then put an Afghan on him, because it was still cold in the house. She agreed that the couch was on the right of the stairs when you come up the stairs but couldn't say whether it was twelve to fourteen feet to the couch. She also said that she had no idea if the distance from the top of the stairs to the couch was slightly longer then from the top of the stairs to the nursery.

Michelle agreed that the alarm had only gone off one other time since they owned the property. That alarm had occurred right after they purchased the home. It could only be turned off by entering a code that Bill knew by heart and she had written on a paper on the refrigerator.

When I asked about her allegedly freezing Michelle clarified that she froze upstairs, before she walked down to the alarm panel. She said she couldn't move.

"And by that time, the alarm was going off, it was clear that Baby Matthew would have been woken up by the alarm?"

"Yes."

"It was shrill."

"Yes."

"But you didn't go up and get him, did you?"

"No."

"Before you even turned the light on, the alarm was ringing. The defendant didn't go up and get him."

"No."

"What you did, ma'am, is you went downstairs and looked at the panel. The defendant was standing on the landing at the main level. He was still there when you got back from having gone down and looked downstairs."

"Yes."

"Then you went downstairs again when the defendant told you to go across the street?"

"At one point I think I did go downstairs. I was looking for my shoes, couldn't find them. Came back up."

She admitted this series of priorities without a shred of doubt or remorse.

"As you were at the landing, it was the defendant who opened the door, the front door of the house and left it open."

"I don't' know who opened the door."

"Well, ma'am, do you recall testifying previously that it was the defendant who left the door open, and who originally opened it."

"I probably did say that, but I'm, at this point, I'm not sure who did."

"Before you went across the street, you tried to get the alarm off. Then the defendant went upstairs, is that right?"

"After we, after we saw the smoke he went up to get the phone, yes."

"Did you all discuss what he was going to go up to get?" I asked.

"It wasn't till he came down with the phone that I realized he'd went to get the phone," again dodging my question.

I looked into her eyes with the intensity that I felt.

"Yes, ma'am. Because he'd walked up the stairs, and all he had to do was go to the left to get Baby Matthew, but he didn't, did he, ma'am?"

"No," she said softly.

"He went to the right, all the way across the living room, to the coffee table . . ."

Michelle interrupted, "It wasn't . . ."

" . . . which is where he said he'd left the phone the last time."

Michelle tried to justify Wise's choice. "It wasn't that far, but the phone was on the coffee table."

"And he got the phone . . . is that right, ma'am?"

"He brought it down to me, yes."

"Now, he didn't take that telephone and walk down the hall to Baby Matthew's room, did he?" I demanded.

"No."

"He didn't get him."

"No."

"But when he came down with the phone, you could hear a dial tone, but your husband couldn't get through to 911. Do you remember that, ma'am?" I insisted.

"I remember saying that."

"You heard the dial tone, and you saw him punching in three numbers."

She admitted that she saw him put in three numbers, but she did not see which three. Then she said Wise told her to go across the street. She ran down to grab her coat.

The number of steps that Michelle had to go downstairs to get those shoes, were the same number of steps as going upstairs to Baby Matthew.

I waited several seconds before asking my next questions. It was all that I could think of, that this woman and her husband walked up and down the stairs several times, never going to get baby Matthew. I wanted to give the jury a chance to think about that too.

The questioning moved to Baby Matthew's room.

Michelle agreed that only two electrical items were plugged in the nursery. One was a small lamp, plugged into the west wall, the wall nearest the door. The only other electrical item plugged in was the Fisher Price 1510 baby monitor. She equivocated about the number of the monitor and so I showed her the box and she conceded that it was a 1510.

Michelle also acceded that Wise smoked cigarettes using a Bic lighter to light them. He promised not to smoke in the nursery and she had never seen him do so. She also agreed that she and her husband were the only two people with keys to the residence and that no one broke into the house that night.

We got around to the bottle of alcohol in the house. Michelle said that they had alcohol either in the bathroom or on the dresser. I read her statement from March 15, 1993.

"Question, 'Okay, how about rubbing alcohol?' Answer, 'Yes, there would be some in the bathroom.'"

Michelle asked to read the question and answer. I obliged. She was paging through the lengthy transcript. She said, "I know I had said that, and then I believe I corrected, I corrected myself and said that it was on the dresser, and I'm looking for it."

Mark Earnest decided to help her.

He called to her, "Question 500. Look at question 500."

I read. "Your answer was, "The alcohol that we did have in that room was up on his dresser in a bottle closed up. We had used it when his umbilical cord, you know, clean that, but that was the only thing we had in there. And then we had some in the bathroom.' Are you saying there were two bottles in the house?"

"It may have been at first I did not remember that we had two bottles—" she said.

She clarified that if there had been a bottle of alcohol in the nursery it would have been on the dresser on the west wall. She also told the jury that unlike the downstairs, every item of furniture in Baby Matthew's room was hers or given to her by her family.

Through Michelle's testimony, we established that the lamp in the nursery was operated by a light switch that was in the off position at the time of the fire. She also agreed that she had been asked numerous times about the baby monitor and that she had never experienced a problem with the monitor, nor had her husband, nor anyone else.

It was four to five months after the fire that Jeanne Wise first mentioned that she heard a sound coming from the baby monitor.

I asked Michelle about the lawsuit and she admitted that it was filed on the last possible day and nearly a year after William Wise was charged with murder. I showed her the interrogatories that she responded to in the Fisher Price lawsuit and she agreed that interrogatories were just written questions that she and her husband answered under oath. The Interrogatories were dated September 15, 1995 and were signed by Michelle and William Wise. I asked her to read the paragraph above the lines where she and her husband had signed the responses.

"I hereby swear and affirm under penalties of perjury that the foregoing representations are true and correct to the best of my information, knowledge and belief."

I read Interrogatory seventeen and Michelle's response. She had written that neither of them had ever had any problem with the product, nor did they ever contact Fisher Price or Wal-Mart before the fire. After the fire, Bill's mother informed them that on the night before the fire she heard some crackling coming from the area where the baby monitor was, but she didn't think much about it.

There were just a few additional issues that I needed to address about the interrogatories. Michelle had signed the responses, including those involving Wise's employment history. We started with St. Joe Hospital.

"In the answers there, you indicated that your husband was fired due to a dispute over his medical history."

"Yes."

"But, in fact, you knew, at the time that you swore to these, that the defendant had been terminated from St. Joe Hospital for making misrepresentations concerning his employment."

"At that, at this time that I filled this out, I still believed that it was due to the medical history."

By reading from the Interrogatories and comparing them with her other sworn statements, I was able to show that she knew, before she signed the interrogatories, that Wise had been fired for making misrepresentations. Then I showed her the answer to Interrogatories where they said that Wise had left the Anthony Fire Department in Ocala, Florida to move back to Indiana.

"You knew, when you answered that way, under oath, that it was false, didn't you?"

"I didn't answer the question for my husband. He answered his parts, I answered mine. We handed them in to the lawyer and they compiled this." She tried to avoid answering my very direct question.

"Did you swear to something that he (pointing to the defendant) said, that you knew was a lie?" I demanded.

"I didn't know he had said it until later."

Again I reminded her that she had testified about this previously. I reminded her that it was in August 1996. I reminded her that I had asked the same questions then.

"And you indicated that you knew the reason that he left that fire department prior to answering the interrogatories."

"I knew it, but I didn't answer for him on the interrogatories." Michelle knew that Wise had left the fire department for other reasons, and she finally admitted it.

The court took a break.

When the jury came back into the courtroom I resumed on the subject of Michelle Wise's truthfulness.

Michelle's prior animosity to me seemed to have grown exponentially. I didn't like her much either and both of us expressed those feelings in the tone of our voice, facial expressions, and general body language. Michelle glared at me, daring me to be unkind in front of the jury. She spat answers and I could see the contempt in her eyes as she responded to my questions. I was quiet and intense and my tone was disbelieving. At times I let the jury and Michelle know that I was disgusted.

I said, "While we're talking about the truth, Mrs. Wise, in that tape recording that you made on September 8, 1996, you indicated, did you not, that, and you're talking about telling them something, 'I told them that I was not going to stretch the truth like maybe I had been.' Is that right, ma'am?"

"I believe that's what I said."

"Now yesterday you were very, very clear in your recollection, apparently, about something having to do with whether or not the fan was on in the bathroom at the time of the fire. Do you remember yesterday, ma'am?" I asked.

"Yes," she said almost resignedly.

"You were asked the same questions about the fan when your deposition was taken nearly three years ago. Do you recall that?" I asked, deposition in hand.

"I, I believe I was asked about the fan."

"And in that deposition, at page 195, you said, 'I cannot recall if it was on in the bathroom when I came upstairs.' Do you remember that, ma'am?"

"If I said that, I was mistaken, because there's only one switch in the bathroom, and when you turn on the light the fan comes on."

I was ready for my final question for the witness. I stopped asking questions and looked at her, at Wise, then at the jury.

"At any time during all of the events, from the first moment that the alarm went off, after you saw the smoke, did the defendant, who you knew to be a trained firefighter, ever, and I'll be specific, did he ever make any effort to go upstairs, down the hallway, to get Baby Matthew, at any time while you were there, ma'am, did he do that?"

"Not while I was in the house, no," Michelle confessed.

I waited a few seconds, just looking at her. I shook my head sadly because it was the horrible truth. Neither she nor the defendant had even tried to rescue their son Matthew.

Then, looking at the jury and still shaking my head, I slowly walked back to the State's table and sat down.

I was repelled. She was a woman who had given birth to a healthy baby; a worthy human mother doesn't just walk away and leave her baby to die in flames. But Michelle had. And she was willing to tell the world that she had left him.

Lukemeyer tried to break the mood by stepping forward to ask more questions of Michelle.

She asked Michelle whether Van Buskirk and I had come to question her in Elkhart. Michelle said that we had and that no counsel was present. Michelle said she was terrified of the two of us. She said that we did not tape record the conversation, but each of us had note pads. Michelle said that we wanted to question her about specific instances in her statements, but that we did not have any statements with us. Michelle also conceded that her family members were present, while we asked her questions.

Lukemeyer asked Michelle why she had contacted the insurance company on the day of the baby's death. "To let them know that there had been a fire. I believe there is something, if I remember correctly, in the mortgage, that states you have some kind of fire or natural disaster you need to contact your insurance company."

"On the evening after Matthew died, what were your main thoughts that evening?" Lukemeyer asked.

"All I could think about was that Matthew was gone. It was like I was in a different world. Everything had turned upside down. Just his loss, I couldn't stop thinking about him and the fire."

After a discussion about the time she woke up, and how she just didn't think it could have been as late as five a.m., Michelle was asked about her guilt. "Do you regret not going up those stairs and getting Matthew, you've thought about this?" Ms. Lukemeyer asked.

"Yes, I feel a lot of guilt that I didn't get him at first."

"And have you played this evening over in your mind in the last five years?" Lukemeyer said, as if it were scripted.

"We've, I've gone over it so many times that now when I think of Matthew I only think of this. I can't, almost can't remember what it was like to have him. It's always since he's been gone. His life had been taken away in more ways than one. His memories have been taken away from us because we can't think of him, the joy that he brought us, how he touched our lives, without thinking about his death. And we can't, I don't know if I'll ever be able to forget and put this aside and remember him smiling, how he sounded, his touch, his smell, how he felt to hold him."

Lukemeyer tried to mitigate the differences in the versions of events that Michelle had told.

"Were what Ms. Moore categorized as changes in your statements, deviations?"

Michelle replied, "I believe through the course of the investigation certain details we were not aware of, like the time our calls were made, we did find that out and, you know, they were different from what we had previously said."

Lukemeyer sat down, having no further questions of her witness.

But I did.

I asked, "As to questions about what happened in the house that night, about when the defendant was on the couch, about the important questions that I asked you, if someone gave you more information that caused you to change those statements, there was only one other person there, the only other person that could have provided that information was the defendant?"

"Correct."

"There's a reason why you didn't go upstairs to get Matthew, isn't there, ma'am?" I asked.

"It never entered my mind," she said.

"And that's because your husband, who had talked to you about all of his skills, and all of his willingness to rescue people, and for all of the years that you knew him, he told you that he was going to get Baby Matthew."

"When he sent me across the street, he told me he would get Matthew," she said.

"But he didn't," I said bluntly.

"He was not able to get him out, no."

I had no further questions. But the jury did. The court considered the jurors' questions and then asked some of them.

The judge asked, "Why did you stay at the neighbor's instead of going back to the house?"

"I just never thought about going back to the house. I just had always been taught, if you get out of a burning house you stay where you are."

The judge asked, "The night of the fire, since it was your first week back to work, did you have to work that Saturday?"

"No. I was off that Saturday."

The judge continued, "Did Bill have to work?"

"Yes."

"When the alarm was sounding, did Matthew cry?"

"You couldn't hear anything over the alarm. So I couldn't hear if he was crying or not."

"After you both saw the smoke, what was the reason one of you didn't get to the baby immediately before even calling 911?"

Michelle said, "I froze there. I, I couldn't move. I didn't, I couldn't get anything to move to even try to get him."

"You sure got your fat ass downstairs to get your coat and to get across the street," Van B whispered.

"When did Bill start this shift?"

"It was before Matthew had been born. I want to say maybe a month before Matthew was born," Michelle replied.

"Did he request the shift he was working?"

"He thought it was a good shift in that Matthew wouldn't have, our child wouldn't have to be at daycare for so long, not for the entire week, that he would have a day off to stay home with him, that he wouldn't have to spend eight hours at daycare."

"Did you mind him not being home at night?"

"No, because he, he had done that before. The other shift he had worked had been six p.m. to six a.m., so therefore, he was gone from six at night till six in the morning, so that was kind of nice. At least I got to spend, to sleep with him a bit."

"When was, approximately what time was Allstate Insurance contacted?"

"It was Saturday evening before we, we contacted them. I can't really tell you what specific time it was."

"And who called them?"

"I believe Bill did," Michelle answered.

Michelle was asked about working fire extinguishers (none) and the extension phone in the nursery which had been there since they moved in.

The judge apparently phrased the next question as it had been written by the juror.

"Where was the bird normally at?"

"Normally downstairs. It was kind of a messy bird so we kept it downstairs in the family room."

The judge read the next juror question. "How much was the Allstate check?" Michelle wiggled in her chair.

"I really can't say at this time. I don't remember."

"Why did you need clothes and contacts? Wasn't the basement where all of your belonging were undamaged?"

"No. We, the only working bathroom was upstairs. Our contacts were stored upstairs. Most of our good clothes was kept, there was a room next to Matthew's that we stored my dresses, his suits, that kind of thing, and they were all smoke damaged."

"Were there medical problems with Baby Matthew after he was born?"

How could I have failed to consider that the jury would want to know if Baby Matthew had some chronic or deadly illness before his father murdered him?

The juror was trying to comprehend the needlessness of the killing or find some justification for the murder. Was Wise putting Matthew out of some misery?

"None. None at all," Michelle assured the juror.

Ms. Lukemeyer had no additional questions.

I asked, "At the time of the fire, you were unaware that you husband was on probation at work, is that correct?"

"I, I—correct, I did not know," she mumbled.

"I take it, in answering the juror's question, you were unaware that your husband had been switched involuntarily to TAC shift, because he was on probation."

"I was unaware of that, yes."

There were no further questions. Michelle looked at Lukemeyer hopefully and when she nodded, Michelle stepped down from the witness stand.

She did not look at the jury. She smiled at Wise and then sort of shuffled toward the back door and left the courtroom.

The jury was invited to take a break while we addressed some issues with the court.

Defense counsel took another run at the judge trying to persuade her to have evidence of the Gerry baby monitor and others admitted through their expert. The court refused and the trial would remain focused on the Fisher Price 1510 baby monitor.

I breathed a sigh of relief. Time for the defendant's uncle to testify about what a great guy he was, and then the defense would have his experts testify that the baby monitor caused the fire.

# Chapter Twenty-Four

THE CROSS-EXAMINATION FOR Mr. Berman was prepared as I would for any expert witness. I wanted first to identify if there was room to question his credentials or expertise.

Then I wanted to analyze his opinions to see if they were subject to challenge.

Therefore, I read Donald Berman's resume. I checked a legal search engine to see if Mr. Berman had been quoted in any cases. He had. I then looked up the case, read it, and contacted the lawyer for the opponent. In this instance, the other lawyer was very cooperative. He offered me some of the materials from that trial at no charge. I gratefully accepted.

Also, because Donald Berman was from California, I looked up some California law. I looked up Indiana law on the same subject. Then I put them all together as the basis for my cross examination of the witness.

I tried to do the same preparation for the defense's other expert, Gerry Mang. He was not named in any published case. His resume was not exceptional. I would have to deal with Gerry Mang on the stand, because I had little information about him, except what Lisa had uncovered at his deposition. She had gotten some interesting information during that examination and I hoped to use it to the State's best advantage. I hoped I was ready.

The next witness for the defense was James Kemnitz, who was Bill's uncle. Mr. Kemnitz was a decorated veteran who had won three bronze stars in Viet Nam and retired from the military as a major. He testified to helping William do some work around the house, including constructing a half-wall that would protect a child from falling. He had seen Wise and Matthew together a few times after the infant was born. He swore that Bill was a loving, tender father to the infant.

Lisa Swaim wisely decided not to cross-examine the man.

"The defendant, William Wise, calls Donald Berman, P.E. to the stand," Jennifer Lukemeyer announced.

I was surprised that Lukemeyer would be presenting this man's testimony since he promised to be a problem for the defense. I suspected that if the going got tough, one of the other lawyers would take over. Most judges would not allow this substitution, but Judge Magnus-Stinson was deferential to the defense team's tactics.

Sharkeyes

293

Berman introduced himself in a stereotypical New York, accent. He said he was a licensed professional engineer who did consulting in the area of product safety. He had been retained in twenty-four states to provide testimony in the area of product safety and failure analysis. He attended Carnegie Institute of Technology for three years, majoring in electrical engineering, and then transferred to New York University where he obtained a degree in industrial management. He also served in the Army for two years where he was the "live-in designer, builder, maintenance man, and operator, for the radio station that kept Fort Bragg in contact with amateur radio emergency systems."

He described his experience as "Design engineer, design engineer advanced design, engineering section head, systems assurance manager, engineering quality control, head reliability assurance, chief of components and standards, director of product assurance." He began to describe every job he had over his career.

He started by describing work he had done in the 1950s. He worked his way up to 1969, when he conducted a study on appliance electrocutions for the National Commission on Product Safety. He had also done a case for the Texas Attorney General's Office. His credentials sounded impressive. But Berman loved to expound and lecture, in response to even the most simple question.

Examples abounded, but in one instance Lukemeyer asked Berman, "Have you ever testified in any public hearings regarding product safety, or submitted analysis to be used in public hearings?"

His actual response is included in its full glory simply to confirm for the read what we all soon realized. Your life will go on beautifully if you skip it. The response should have been yes or no and perhaps a brief explanation.

Berman responded, "In about 1967, there were a number of 727 crashes. Boeing 727 crashes and fires. I submitted recommendations to the crash worthiness hearing, and those design requirements are still in effect on every commercial airliner in the U.S. The transcript of the hearings states that the recommendations were made by the Airline Pilots Association and myself. I testified in public televised hearings in Boston on refrigerator safety, and as a result, today your major appliances have three wire power cords. Before that time they didn't have it. In 1971, or 1972, I received an invitation from a congressional committee, the committee that was drafting today's product safety legislation. Three of us were invited to testify, and testified on the safety of electrical apparatus. The first one to testify was the general counsel of Electronic Industries Association, then myself, then Ralph Nader."

Humble Berman was not. He answered every question with an overly detailed response and a swagger that I found revolting. He was an unbridled egomaniac.

He explained what he meant by failure analysis. He said that he focused for many years on "electrical fires, explosions, electrical shocks, and electrocutions." He was employed by his family company, known as Product Safety Engineering Services Corporation. They divided their work half for plaintiffs and half for defendants.

"I came to the definite, definitive conclusion that the Fisher-Price 1510 transmitter definitely could have caused the fire in the Wise home."

Berman said this with grave certainty.

To reach that determination, Berman made telephone calls to Underwriters Laboratories, Fisher-Price, Structural Burn Laboratory of the National Technical Institute and the National Bureau of Standards. He also obtained documentation from the Japanese Fire Research Institute, Consumer Product Safety Commission, National Electronic Injury Surveillance System, NHITSA (National Highway Safety Administration) and the National Fire Protection Association. He also downloaded, off the Internet, information and home pages relative to what he was doing.

Berman said that he could not examine the actual transmitter, but did look at the receiver and adapter. He also reviewed the video tapes from the burn room. He reached a preliminary analysis that Lukemeyer asked him to describe.

"Well, the preliminary analysis was that there was an electrical, piece of electrical apparatus plugged into the wall in the location described by Mr. Lepper as being the origin. The origin of the fire fit with the fact that we know the transmitter uses an adapter, which was plugged in the wall at sort of one end of his origin pattern. We know that Lepper found an antenna, two-way transmitter, under the edge, what amounted to in an area under the edge of the crib," Berman said.

I objected. Lepper had never said that. The court agreed and struck Berman's response. So, Lukemeyer had Berman read the parts of Lepper's report that he had relied upon. Berman also testified that the test burn was not reputable.

"And as far as the blowtorch being utilized to demonstrate that the transformer can't melt, is that a reputable way to show that this type of plastic surrounding that adapter can't melt?" Lukemeyer asked.

Berman replied, "The answer is no, because when you get an arc in electrical circuitry you'll end up with what is, or often end up with what's called a plasma arc, where the gas ionizes and the temperature of that arc is approximately six-thousand degrees Fahrenheit, which is a bit above half of the temperature on the surface of the sun. A propane torch just doesn't do it. The propane torch test is a favorite of people to say it doesn't burn."

Again I objected to Berman's response and again the court sustained the objection and struck Berman's testimony.

He gave Judge Magnus-Stinson a "how dare you" look but said nothing.

Lukemeyer asked Berman what Underwriter's laboratory does to approve products. He described the testing that he obviously considered insubstantial.

"Is compliance, and getting the UL standard 94, is that a guarantee that it won't burn?" Lukemeyer asked.

"Absolutely not," Berman said definitively.

Berman tried, with many of his answers, to insert other electrical products and monitors. I objected each time and the court sustained those objections.

Lukemeyer showed the witness all of the pieces of the Fisher Price 1510 and asked him questions about each.

"Let's talk about this transmitter. Plastic casing, just because the adapter complied with UL 94, does that mean this plastic casing and this transmitter, this one right here, does that mean that that is compliant with UL 94?" she asked.

"Absolutely not," Berman said. "If it doesn't have UL compliant on the product, it is not UL listed or UL approved, period. The UL approval that Fisher Price got for its adapter made in Taiwan does not cover UL approval for the transmitter as far as flammability."

Berman said that UL had standards for various types of radio apparatus and baby monitors are covered under some of those sections. He could not say whether the Fisher Price 1510 was submitted, but didn't pass UL testing, or was never submitted, but he certainly implied that Fisher Price was hiding something by not obtaining UL approval.

He also denied that the transformers were class two UL approved. Although he agreed that there was a UL stamp on the step down transformers, he said that because they did not include the class two designation, the UL stamp was meaningless.

"Can a fire start in this type of step-down transformer, contained in the housing of this adapter, can a fire initiate there?" Lukemeyer wanted to know.

"Absolutely, yes. And a fire can be caused from a fault contained in this type of adapter with a step-down transformer contained in the housing."

Lukemeyer asked, "And in your experience, you have knowledge of whether this same type of adapter, as far as the step-down transformer, whether, do you have any personal knowledge about fires having been caused by faults in those?"

"Yes," Berman said.

"So," Lukemeyer continued, "if someone was to say that it's impossible for a fire to be generated with an adapter, or in an appliance with an adapter similar to that, is that an accurate statement?"

"No, it is absolutely dead wrong. Fires do start in those adapters, whether the adapters are used for baby monitors, or charging camcorders, or electric tools, or just a wide range of products."

Berman stepped down from the box to show the jury the transformer.

"All of these adapters have in common the following. What we left behind there were the two prongs that go in the wall. And there are four electrical parts in there. The, this rectangular one looks like steel, it is steel, is the transformer, I'll get back to that in a minute. Over here are two little cylinders. Those are diodes. They're rectifying diodes, rectifying semiconductors. Then this tubular thing, the blue one, that's a, what's called a capacitor, or condenser. Now, the transformer in this case takes the line voltage, and we'll use the term one-hundred twenty. It could be anywhere from one-hundred five to one-hundred thirty volts, but we'll talk about one-hundred twenty. And from the line makes a winding, lots of turns, here. And . . ."

Berman continued for several minutes describing the internal workings of the adapter. He concluded his description with the explanation that, "You could blow the capacitor, have the diodes get extremely hot and ignite the case, or you could put a higher voltage on this wire to the transmitter."

Berman testified that a secondary failure could cause the transformer to overheat, arc, and put a higher than normal voltage on the transmitter which would result in overheating of the transmitter. He described in detail why he believed that the transformer wiring was badly designed allowing maximum current to flow into the transmitter. He considered the individual wires dinky.

I was watching this man and could only think of what an arrogant snot he was. The judge was tiring of his rambling discourses as well. She interrupted him and instructed him not to interrupt Lukemeyer, or anyone else.

Berman again stepped down to show the jury an exhibit. It was a small piece of the transformer cord, which had been stripped so that some of the internal wire bunches were visible. Then it was put into some transparent, hardened plastic, like Plexiglas. Berman passed the piece of cord to the jury.

He testified that if one of the eleven wires in each bunch in the cord was to break, then it could get hot until the point where it melted and create an arc, a plasma arc where there's gas ionization and six thousand degrees Fahrenheit. Which was certainly capable of causing a fire.

Tom Leslie interrupted Lukemeyer's direct and asked to approach the bench.

"Some of the jurors are kind of nodding off," he said. I had noticed that as well. Even I was having a hard time keeping awake as this guy droned on.

"Okay," the court responded. "We'll take a break."

"Thank God," Van Buskirk whispered. "I am about to shoot myself. This guy is a fuckin' moron. Being from California is bad enough."

"Hey, if I have to sit here, so do you," I responded in my most mellifluous voice. I saw Lisa smiling, but wanted to know her thoughts.

"He's so obnoxious that I don't know how they can believe him, but he has an impressive resume. He's saying all the things that the defense needs the jury to hear. If just one juror buys into his opinions . . ." Lisa left off what we both knew.

If we lost even one of the twelve jurors, it would be a mistrial and the case would never be retried. Wise would walk.

"Too true," I agreed, hoping that the jury would sleep though the rest of the direct examination.

When the trial resumed, Lukemeyer had Berman describe again what could happen if the transmitter caught on fire, an event that he believed to be not only possible, but likely. He analyzed the solder on the transmitter and testified that it looks "awfully close together and that's another place that you get arcing."

Essentially, Berman took every item inside of the transformer and the transmitter and said that it would arc or overheat and cause a fire. Arcing can occur at any level of voltage or current, so Berman claimed.

Berman said that the demonstration by Finneran did not prove anything.

"You've got to have the exact circumstance," Berman said. "The analogy, if I'm allowed to use it, that I use is that we all know that burning lit cigarettes thrown or dropped in the forest can cause forest fires. You could probably go along a trail dropping cigarette after cigarette. Some would go out, some would cause a little fire, and finally you'll get one that'll cause a forest fire. When you realize that these kinds of problems occur with one out of ten thousand, or one out of a hundred thousand . . ."

"Mr. Berman, is there enough current to come out of an adapter like the one used with the Fisher Price 1510 to cause a fire?" Lukemeyer asked again.

"Yes."

Berman used some tiny light bulbs and showed the jury that the small wire in the bulbs would get red hot. He was showing a small halogen bulb for a flashlight to the jury. He changed that to white hot and said that one could get the electrical components inside the 1510 white hot, just like the filaments in the light bulbs.

As Berman continued to talk, the judge stopped him several times because he would argue his position without a question being asked of him.

Berman testified that the transmitter caught fire and then caught the casing on fire which caught the mattress on fire. He showed the jury mattress fire time lines that he downloaded from the internet.

"If the monitor caught fire and ignited the corner of the mattress, he droned on purportedly quoting the burn times. Once the mattress is ignited, it's Katie bar the door. That's it."

"Without the remains of this baby monitor transmitter, can you eliminate it as a cause of this fire?" Lukemeyer asked.

"Absolutely not." Berman tried to say more but was cut off by Lukemeyer.

"What's your opinion about this transmitter." She was holding the 1510 exemplar in her hand. "What's your opinion about whether or not it caused this fire?"

"There's absolutely no question in my mind but that it could have caused the fire, and, in fact, did."

"Have you been retained in any way regarding a civil suit in this matter?"
"No."

"What would it mean to you if you heard a pop from somewhere in a nursery where there was a baby monitor?"

"If I hear a pop, a popping, a crackling, snap, the sound of bacon frying, that sort of sound, you have an electrical fault occurring, and you unplug the appliance and take it to a qualified repair person. That is a specific, unique type of sound, and it's unique to an arc-over, an electrical arc."

"Does that necessarily mean it's going to burst out in flames right then?" Lukemeyer said in a tone of exasperation and concern.

"No. Might be then, the next day, a year later," Berman said, staring at the jury.

Lisa and Van B looked at me expectantly. Berman had been persuasive at times, if the jury hadn't snoozed through his testimony.

"You may cross-examine," Judge Magnus-Stinson advised me.

I said, "Mr. Berman, when you identified yourself you indicated that you are a professional engineer, is that correct, sir?"
"Yes."

"You're not a professional engineer in Indiana are you, sir?"
"No, in California."

"You don't qualify as a professional engineer in this state do you?" I insisted.

"I haven't the slightest idea. I can call, I call myself a professional engineer because I'm a licensed professional engineer in California," he said dismissively.

"In fact, you do not have a degree in engineering."

"That's correct," he said.

"Your degree is in Industrial Management?"

"Right, that was my course curriculum."

"Since graduating in 1958, you have not taken any additional course work at any university or college in the field of engineering?"

"Correct."

"Or, anything else?" I added.

"I've taken courses, some courses, miscellaneous courses in junior college, but not related to engineering." He was getting defensive.

"And, in fact, sir, in California, the way you obtained your P.E. license was to fill out an application that was essentially a listing of your resume."

Each time I said the word "California" I emphasized it, like a planet distant and bizarre to Indiana.

"It was more than that," he objected.

"And giving them references," I added.

"References, and the requirement for a test was waived based on my background, experience, and training."

"You've been asked previously what licensure in California means, haven't you?"

"Excuse me?" he said.

"You've been asked that question before about what licensure was required by the State of California, haven't you?" I asked, reminding him of his prior testimony.

I added, "Now, in Indiana, to call yourself a professional engineer, one needs to actually have a degree in engineering from a four year university or college such as Purdue or Rose-Hulman Institute."

Indiana has some top-rank engineering programs and the jury all knew it.

"I don't know what's required here, obviously." Berman was defiant.

"And you are aware that there's a national exam that's required for individuals, even after they have that engineering degree, in order to obtain licensure, call themselves a professional engineer?"

Yes, it was more statement than question.

"I'm not aware of anything of the kind," Berman snorted.

Indiana law required a person to graduate with a degree in engineering, pass a criminal background check, provide references, practice engineering for several years, and then take and pass a rigorous written examination before being designated as a "Professional Engineer." Thereafter, engineers had to take a number of continuing education credits every three years to continue to use the designation "P.E."

I asked the judge to take judicial notice of Indiana law. This means that the court told the jury what Indiana law required for a professional engineer. Coming from the judge, it was powerful.

"Mr. Berman, are you aware that there were fifteen-thousand nine-hundred and thirty-three registered professional engineers in the State of Indiana as of January first of this year, 1998?"

"I'll take your word for it," he grumbled.

"You indicated that in California, you said something about a waiver based on your experience, is that right, sir?"

"Yeah," he mumbled. "The waiver for an examination, yes."

"You said that, is that right?"

"Yes, I said that."

I asked him about some of the cases that he had testified in during the last few years. I asked him if he had been deposed in one of those cases less than a year earlier. I was holding what was obviously a transcript from that case.

"The question was, 'What did you have to do in order to obtain this license, referring to your P.E. license,' and your answer was, 'Make a written submission and obtain letters of reference.'"

"Okay," he said.

"In California, from the time you got this P.E. designation, in 1978, you have never been required to take any continuing education in order to continue to call yourself a professional engineer."

"That's correct."

"And, sir, the last time that you worked for any company, other than a family owned one, or as a consultant for hire, was in, I believe you indicated 1973?"

"Last time I worked in industry was '73. It was a period—where I worked in an unrelated situation as president of a company that was in the business of making fluoroscopes, or was supposed to be making fluoroscope detectors for bombs, in the mail."

"In all of the positions that you told the jury about, you worked for four years at one, four at another and all of the rest were six months or so. Is that right?"

I asked knowing that most of our jurors had been at the same job for decades.

"Yes," Berman admitted.

"Sir, in regard to that licensure, it not only allowed you, without an engineering degree to refer to yourself through all of these years as a professional engineer, but it also allowed you to create a company using the word engineering in it, is that correct?" I asked.

"Correct."

He agreed that he advertised his company with a website on the internet.

"Is it true that the only difference in having the California P.E. that you have used today and not having it is 'number one, I put initials after my name.' Do you recall saying that?"

"No, but I very likely did say that."

I read more. "'Number two, I'm legally allowed to use the term, "consulting engineer." California allows you to do that, is that right?'"

"That's correct," he conceded.

"And, 'Three, the company that I'm affiliated with is legally allowed to use the term, engineering, in the name of the company.' That was your testimony?"

"That's correct, also."

"And that's true, sir, even though that company has no graduate engineers involved with the company?" I asked.

"That's correct."

Berman narrowed his eyes and his expression intensified. His face was flushed. I wished I could see the steam rising from his scalp.

"Now, in coming from California, you have never previously been qualified as an expert in the State of Indiana, in any subject."

"That's correct."

"You have never been qualified to testify in regard to a criminal case in any court," I said.

"That's correct."

"And sir, in coming here today and being retained by the defendant, you have been paid not only for your hourly rate, that we'll talk about, but you also have been paid a hundred dollars an hour for your travel time. From California."

Most of our jurors made far less than I did, which was about forty thousand dollars a year (which figured to be twenty dollars an hour.) One hundred dollars an hour was a great deal of money. I asked questions to show the thousands of dollars that Berman had already billed for travel and for his hourly rate which was one and a half times his travel rate. And two-hundred and fifty dollars an hour for in-court testimony or depositions.

"You told the jury about being invited to various places to testify, and as to all of those, they occurred at least twenty-five years ago, is that correct?"

"The congressional committee and the National Commission on Product Safety, yes."

"You told counsel that you testified about a variety of subjects, and you talked about fires, is that correct? Let me remind you about your testimony in a case about a product known as Junket. Do you recall that case?"

Because Berman said that he didn't, I showed him his deposition taken on October 22, 1997, in that case.

It had been less than a year before. He suddenly began to recall the case. He said that the court permitted him to testify as an expert but excluded some of his testimony. I read from the deposition where he had listed the types of cases in which he had provided trial testimony for the proceeding five years. These included cases about automatic doors, scalding from a coffeemaker, loss of an eye from a bungee cord, an actress injured in a stunt involving an airbag, and others.

I returned to the Junket case.

"Did you, at your deposition, render an opinion preliminarily that you were, in fact, an expert in Junket, just as you told the jury today that you're an expert in certain areas?"

"Yes, My opinion was that the recipe for . . ." he began.

"No, sir, not what your opinion was, we'll get to that. The judge asked, and the question was, did you, sir, at this deposition, indicate that you believed you were an expert in analyzing the item contained in the State's Exhibit that I showed you?"

"Yes . . . yes," he stammered.

I asked to show the jury the exhibit.

First Earnest objected and then Lukemeyer in a chorus.

The judge overruled the objections, as I explained that the Exhibit was a cottage cheese recipe. I had a copy for every juror and the judge allowed me to pass them out.

The judge instructed the jury, "She is not handing this to you to prove to you the recipe for cottage cheese."

Berman said quietly, "It would be dangerous to follow it."

The Exhibit read:

## COTTAGE CHEESE

¼ Junket® Rennet Tablet

½ cup water

1 gallon skim milk

¼ cup buttermilk

1 teaspoon salt

1/3 cup cream

1.   Dissolve Rennet Tablet in water by crushing. Set aside. In large saucepan, heat skim milk to 70 F. Stir in buttermilk and Rennet Tablet solution, mixing well. Cover with towel and let stand at room

temperature 12 to 18 hours until firm curd forms. To test for a firm curd, remove a milk sample at a point near the edge of the saucepan with a spoon. The curd is ready to cut when the coagulated milk sample holds its shape and the edges are sharply defined.

2.    Cut curd into ½ inch long pieces using a long knife. Heat curd slowly over hot water until temperature reaches 110 F. Hold curd at 110 F for 20 to 30 minutes, stirring at 5-minute intervals to heat curd uniformly. Pour mixture onto fine cheesecloth in a colander and drain off whey.

3.    After whey has drained 2 to 3 minutes, lift curd in cheesecloth and immerse in pan of cold water 1 to 2 minutes, stirring and pressing with a spoon. Then immerse in ice water 1 to 2 minutes. Drain the curd until it is free from whey and place in a large bowl. Add salt and cream and mix thoroughly. Chill.

Please note: The use of any type of Lactaid milk with Junket Rennet Tablets will cause custard to not set.

Lukemeyer asked me for a copy of the exhibit, which I handed to her and her colleagues.

I turned back to Berman. "You whispered, sir, but to be sure that the jury understood, the conclusion that you rendered in regard to this recipe was that it was 'imprecise, ambiguous, and dangerous.' Isn't that right?"

"Right," Berman said ferociously. "And I'm cautioning the jury that a gentleman lost an eye and had his face scalded because he followed it, and I'd hate to see anybody else here attempt to follow this recipe."

I moved to strike his outburst. The court sustained my objection.

"What was the question again?" Berman demanded.

"Your opinion was that the recipe was 'imprecise, ambiguous, and dangerous,'" I repeated.

"That's an understatement," Berman retorted.

"You were asked to list those things that you thought were imprecise, ambiguous, and dangerous about the recipe. Is that right?"

"As I recollect," he said.

"And the recipe, by the way, so that the jurors know, is a recipe printed on a packet of Junket Rennet tablets that one can still find on any shelf, at least here in town it's at Marsh, in the Jell-O section. To your knowledge it's distributed in supermarkets, is that correct?" I asked him.

His temper was rising with the tone of his voice. "I have not checked supermarkets in Indiana to see whether that's on the shelf."

"The first opinion that you gave about the recipe that was 'imprecise, ambiguous, and dangerous,' was that the recipe referred to skim milk. Do you recall that?" I was reading from the deposition as the jury watched. Some of the jurors were trying not to laugh.

"I recall stating that I could not find skim milk in the local markets. I had to ask and be told that skim milk was the same as non-fat milk." He sneered.

"Yes, sir. And so you listed that as one of the reasons that the recipe was 'imprecise, ambiguous, and dangerous.' It was a factor that caused you to form your opinion in that case."

Lukemeyer made a long speaking objection arguing that these questions were wholly irrelevant to Berman's qualifications. The judge allowed me to ask three additional questions on cottage cheese.

"You also thought that it was 'imprecise, ambiguous, and dangerous' to refer to cream because, you indicated that, 'Well it could have been sour cream, whipped cream, could have been some other kind of cream.' In your opinion, that rendered and, in part, supported your conclusion that this recipe was 'imprecise, ambiguous, and dangerous.'"

"With respect to the cottage, to the skim milk, and the cream, that was imprecise and ambiguous, but it was not the dangerous part," he argued.

"And the dangerous part, and you said it at your deposition, page 28, was that the recipe only talked about a large pan instead of describing specific diameters. Isn't that what you said, at your deposition?"

"I don't know that I used those words, but the fact is that if I follow—if you want to know the dangerous part, I'll tell you."

He was angry now and leaning so far forward in the witness chair that I was half-prepared that if I moved closer he would try to lunge at me.

"Were all of those . . ." he roared. "And I can tell you, the fellow lost an eye."

"You've repeated that," I responded before asking the judge to strike his remark.

I collected the cottage cheese recipe from the jurors. I was trying to keep my professional face but was nearly cracking up with a couple of the jurors. If anyone still believed this guy, then I would eat my hat and go to dental hygienist school.

I moved on to some of the areas that had been touched on by Lukemeyer. My spirits were much improved.

I pointed out that, while his testimony was that he relied on photographs and the videos to render his opinions, he had given the same opinions at his deposition, long before he had the chance to see the photographs and videos.

"So, you did not rely on the photographs to render the opinions that you gave today?" I asked him.

"That's right," he admitted.

"You didn't rely on the videos?" I continued.

"Well, I relied on the videos for the opinion that the test was a sham," he retorted.

I moved to strike and again the judge struck the nonresponsive answer. Berman appeared frustrated. He was being bossed around by two women, me and the judge.

I asked him about the two studies that he had relied upon when testifying about the mattress burn time. He responded, "They both come up with the same time interval. The three to six minutes for the peak of the fire."

The judge struck his answer and looked at Mr. Berman and sternly inquired, "Sir, could you answer her question?"

I took the exhibit that he had read to the jury and gave him a copy.

"This was an experimental study. It involved containers for the storage of wood. Those containers are called cribs, am I correct?" I asked.

"Correct," he said grudgingly.

"Could you look at section 2.2, 'fire source and ignition'? It defines the type of crib that is referred to in this study, do you see that?" I asked.

"The wood crib as defined in this study, did not talk about a baby crib at all, did it?" I was reading from the document as I stood directly in front of the jurors who had seen the document.

"No."

"Didn't talk about mattresses at all."

"No, it did not."

"The study tells you what a crib is, as it's meant in this study that has nothing to do with mattresses. It says, 'the wood crib is assembled with six layers of fifty-eight pieces of cedar crib,'" I read. "The wood crib that was ignited in that case, sir, in that study, didn't involve a mattress at all, is that correct?"

"Yes."

"Liar, liar, pants on fire," I wanted to chant, but instead continued asking questions about the next study.

I did not look at the jurors. I was completely focused on Berman. I hoped that the jurors were equally focused on this man.

Berman, and therefore the defense, had misled the jury about what the study was about by playing on the word "crib." Jurors did not like to be intentionally misled. Neither did I for that matter.

"And in that situation, that you told the jury involved a mattress, there's nothing in this study whatsoever about a mattress, is there?"

I waved the study in the air and focused gimlet stares in his direction.

"That's correct, although the time of the heat peak is the same," he said.

I moved to strike and the court granted it and instructed the jury not to consider anything he said after "correct."

I asked him to confirm that the second study involved an accelerant that was used to ignite the mattress, but he refused, claiming that he did not recall. I asked him to look at the document that he had presented. He read it. I read it aloud, but he still would not concede.

"Those fires that you talked about were accelerated with accelerants, weren't they?"

"They were accelerated, because the fire may have been started with a liquid accelerant, but it was not doused, the mattress wasn't doused with accelerant. And all I was referring to was the time from point of ignition to point of peak burning."

"All of the testimony you rendered today about mattresses burning, sir, relied on your interpretation of David Lepper's materials that you reviewed, where he indicated that he'd found a glob that he believed was a baby monitor in a certain location, correct?"

"That was part of the input."

"And you were informed, weren't you, that shortly after David Lepper discovered that glob, he found out that it was not a baby monitor at all, it was a telephone?"

Berman skirted around that line of questioning, saying that Lepper found many globs and even claimed that Lepper had misplaced a glob. He evaded the question.

I had noticed several books titled *UL Standards* on the witness stand. Berman testified that he had relied upon the standards in responding to Lukemeyer's questions.

I asked Berman to permit me to review them. After looking them over, in full view of the jury, I questioned why the latest standard in the stack was 1991 when many of the standards had been replaced.

His excuse was that he also relied on his unverifiable telephone calls with United Laboratories.

"As to your demonstration with the light bulbs, Mr. Berman. There are no light bulbs in the Fisher-Price 1510, are there?"

"No. But there are thin wires inside components and elsewhere, and my demonstration dealt with the thin wire that we'll call the filament inside those bulbs, getting incandescent white hot."

I moved to strike his response after the word "no." The court granted the motion, instructed the jury and told Berman, "Again, sir, I'd remind you, Ms. Lukemeyer is here to ask you any follow-up on redirect, okay? 'Are there light bulbs in the monitor?' that's the question."

Despite the court's admonishment, he answered, "There is a light emitting diode. There is no light bulb. Or there may be a light emitting diode in there."

"The answer is no?" I asked innocently.

"No light bulbs."

"No filaments?" I asked.

"No filaments."

"In all the time that you've been preparing for your testimony, could you come up with, or did you show us in any way how this object becomes hot, the Fisher-Price transformer?"

"No, I have not demonstrated the fault that occurred in the transformer and/or wire in the transmitter."

He tried to be snide but came off puny.

Mark Earnest did the redirect of Donald Berman. He was red faced and breathing hard when he stood up.

"Mr. Berman, you've traveled a long way from California to be here with us today, that right?"

"Correct."

Then he shouted, "You've traveled a long way from California to come to this courtroom and take an oath and be called a whore."

"Your honor," I said. "I object to the question. It's improper. If anyone has used that term, it's only come from the mouth of defense counsel."

"That's exactly right, because I have the guts to say it," Earnest roared. Earnest shouted in my direction, but he was looking at the jury.

"Did you get the impression from questioning of counsel that your testimony is bought, the testimony that you gave to these fourteen strangers?"

Berman responded by looking accusingly in my direction.

"Well, I—I—let's put it this way. I think there's a difference between what the State's attorney knows and what she says here."

I moved to strike the comment with righteous indignation. "And ask for an admonishment, your honor. That is a false statement."

The court looked at Berman. "Sir, I do need to remind you, you need to answer the question that the lawyer puts to you, not the question you wish they did."

Earnest continued, "The truth is the truth, the same as it would be in California as it is in Indiana."

"Absolutely," Berman bellowed.

Berman said he would have testified anywhere in the United States for someone charged with murder where a baby monitor was involved.

"Is it your opinion in this case, based on your forty years of experience, that a Fisher-Price baby monitor, 1510, could have contributed to the fire in this case, is that your expert opinion?" Earnest asked loudly.

"Contributed and caused it," Berman responded.

"Are you lying to this jury?" Earnest said, waiting for Berman to swear to his truthfulness.

I objected. My objection was sustained. It was, as I said, for the jury to decide.

Earnest's theatrics were heightened. He insisted that Berman "Look at them so they know whether or not you're telling the truth."

Berman advised the jury. "I tell you don't use the Fisher-Price 1510 baby monitor, and put in smoke alarms with ionization circuits in it, the more expensive kind."

"Miss Marger Moore mentioned she has small children. You, yourself, have a, a five month old infant, don't you?" Earnest asked.

"Hey, Mark, I'm married and he's a cradle robber if he has a five-month-old kid," I said to myself.

"That's correct."

"Would your answer be no, or hell, no, as to whether or not you would ever use this to protect the life of your child?" Earnest asked, waving the transmitter before the jury.

"That would be hell, no," Berman said.

Earnest sat down. It looked like Berman felt better. I had a few more questions.

"By the way," I asked, "which piece of this baby monitor in the Wise residence—you've told us about three; the step-down transformer, the cord, and you've told us about the transmitter. Tell us exactly, based on your opinion that this caused the fire at the Wise residence, tell us which of those pieces caused this fire, where did it start first?"

"The—it's—okay. It is, of course, impossible to tell precisely without either the remnants or statistic, or information from the manufacturer. But the most . . ." Now he started to mutter.

"Does that mean you don't know, sir?" I asked.

"But the most likely scenario was a fault in the adapter that put excess voltage and current on the cord to the transmitter, and the transmitter ignited."

"So you're saying it happened here?" I asked, holding the transmitter by the handle.

"The fault occurred in the adapter, which may have ignited, also, but the failure, the ignition resulting from that problem occurred in the transmitter."

"So, it's your testimony that it started, it started here?"

Again, I had the transmitter in my hand showing it to the witness.

"We have to be careful about the term started. It's not that the fire started there and went down there. The initial failure was in—the most likely, the initial failure, in the adapter. It may have started ignition, but the fire, the main fire ignited in the transmitter because of the higher voltage applied to the transmitter by the adapter."

I hoped it was clear that this poseur didn't have a clue as to where the fire started. If I hadn't made my point I never would. I sat down.

Earnest then asked Berman if it is unusual for the electrical appliance that causes a fire, especially plastic, to be "totally disintegrated because it is the source of the fire?"

"This would certainly be, or could be totally vaporized, is the term I use. It would end up with very tiny parts, if any, or it would end up with plastic globs. What should have been found from the adapter was the transformer core, but it is really not unusual not to find that, to find that . . . in fighting the fire things get trashed out. That's typical."

"Vaporized?" I asked Van B.

The jurors had questions. The court asked them and Berman responded.

"If the adapter started the fire, why was it not burned or charred?"

"Well, the adapter was never found. The outlet, the, what's called a duplex outlet into which it was plugged, from the photographs at least, had burn marks, but wasn't destroyed, but, again, what usually happens is this plastic will just fall down, melt, become molten, and fall down to the floor. It was never found. The one they found belonged to the receiver, which was in the living room. I think it was the living room."

"How do you explain the lack of damage to the electrical outlet where the adapter was plugged in?" the judge asked.

"Oh, well, that, that was the, the same thing. The flames go up, and this, there really isn't much material in this plastic housing, and it, it would just fall down to the floor, which would tell why against the baseboard you had a, a char at the bottom of the baseboard."

"How do you explain the burn patterns found in the room?"

"Well, the burn pattern in the room that I'm going on is Lepper's drawing of the room, which I don't know, has the jury seen that? I can hold it up, or project it. I've got a transparency for it," Berman offered.

"They've seen it," Judge Magnus-Stinson replied.

"How do you explain the burn pattern on the floor?"

It turned out to one of those answers that gibberish is better than.

"It's my understanding that there were two layers of tile, and two layers of carpet, or something like that, and a question as to whether indoor or outdoor carpet was used, and, of course, adhesives burn, also. I asked, after going through all the data, whether there were any, what they call, well, fire people go out with hand held sensors to detect accelerants, they use dogs, and then they send stuff for gas chromatograph analysis, and I asked whether there were any of those, the hand held detectors on scene, the dogs on scene, or the, or gas chromatograph tests to determine whether there were accelerants, and I was told there weren't."

Berman rambled on. And on. And on. And on.

"Do you currently maintain a sophisticated testing lab as described in your employment history? If so, please describe."

"No. Since leaving industry, when I need something done like that little polished sample you saw, that is what, that's one of the things my lab used to do, my laboratories. They take better photographs. The State will get a bill for three hundred and seventy-five dollars, which is what it cost to have that done, but I thought it was critical because looking at the cut end of this it looks a lot different from the actual cross section as you saw in the plastic."

Berman was boastful about the State's expenditure.

"Did you personally examine the carpet samples and the east wall outlet?" the judge read.

"I saw carpet samples and outlets during my deposition. I wouldn't say I really, you know, analyzed them. I looked at them."

"Is UL Standard Number 1270, a fire safety electrical standard, or a communications related standard?"

"All UL standards are, as they call them, safety standards. If I can have that back I'll read the exact nomenclature on it. It is the standard to which some other manufacturers have submitted their baby monitors and had their baby monitors listed and approved to these standards."

The court struck his comments about other manufacturers. She told Berman, "Sir, you need to answer the question that I put to you, which is, is it a fire safety electrical standard, or a communications related standard?"

"Well, I—" Berman started.

The court interrupted him. "You said you could look at it and see the nomenclature."

"Okay. I wouldn't call it a communications—well, it's communications related in that it talks about communications equipment, radio transmitters, and receivers. It isn't what I would technically call a communications standard. All UL standards, I think all of them are really electrical/fire related. That's the type of testing UL does, is always electrical, and it'll be electrical and involve fires. If you've got a product like a . . ."

The judge interrupted him. "I think you've answered the question. Were any fires caused in exemplar transformers by you relative to this case, and I'm going to interpret the last phrase to mean exemplar 1510 transformers?"

"No. No. It would have been an impossible task."

Again, the judge lost patience and interrupted him. "Okay, you answered the question. Would a fifteen amp fuse blow if a fault occurred in one of these transformers?"

"If the fault occurred right here between these two blades, it might have, but typically not. The fuse would have blown here from shorting of an insulation being burned off electrical wiring. It is not very common necessarily for the circuit breaker to trip, or the fuse blow when a small piece of electronic apparatus has a short or a fire."

The jurors' questions had been answered. I asked some more questions about the UL standards, reading from materials that Berman had given me. Even when he read them, he disagreed with them.

It was the end of the day. The court dismissed the jury and ordered us to return in the morning for the last defense witness. Yet another expert.

# Chapter Twenty-Five

DAY NINE OF the trial, the last day of testimony. Tomorrow, Friday, would be final arguments, jury instructions and jury deliberations. One witness to go, but he was going to be enormously helpful to the defense. It had been nearly two weeks ago that the firemen, newspaper lady, and Lepper had testified. How much did the jury remember of what they said?

I drove in the dark to my parking lot downtown. I dreaded the lot. The circular drive up to the level of my reserved spot was annoying, especially as I passed empty space after empty space on the way up. In only a few days, I would have to return to this building, to my window office, and to civil litigation.

Van Buskirk and Lisa and I met in the conference room. Lisa had been working on jury instructions which were essential. We needed to convince the judge to give the aiding and abetting instruction, which would be a real fight. We also had some other instructions, about expert witnesses and credibility of witnesses that we needed to tweak. Lisa had jumped on that aspect of the case.

Van Buskirk, on the other hand, was frustrated. She had to sit and listen every day without being able to help. She had to be restrained and appear almost demure. Not an easy task, but she had been performing it admirably. Every day, for nine days, we had strolled the gauntlet of the Wise family to get to the courtroom. Jeanne, Michelle, Mrs. Davis and other family waited outside the courtroom from morning to evening to glower at us as we entered and left the courtroom when they weren't hugging Wise and his lawyers.

"The defense calls Gerry Stephen Mang," Tom Leslie, who would be examining him, said. Mang was a feisty local who worked for an Indianapolis Forensic Engineering lab.

Mang described himself as a specialist in fire and explosion causation. He had investigated hundreds or thousands of fires in the United States and abroad. He had investigated several major fires in Indianapolis that the jurors probably remembered. He was certified by the International Association of Arson Investigators and the National Association of Fire and Explosion Investigators. Mang had been a firefighter for a small Indiana department in Frankfort for about eight years. Although he had only a high school degree, Mang testified that he had attended several fire science courses at various universities and colleges. He was past president of the Indiana Arson and Crime Association.

Leslie took Mang through his process for investigating a fire. Mang discussed a time-temperature curve established by the National Bureau of Standards. He said that what he does is try to establish when a fire was extinguished or all the fuel consumed.

Mang stepped in front of the jury and lit a butane cigarette lighter. He passed his finger over the flame and explained that it was not a good heat transfer because he could nearly touch it. But the radiant heat, higher over the flame, he said, was convection heat and much hotter.

Through five hours of testimony, Mang established his credibility on the subject of fire causation. He told the jury about various kinds of heating and ignition temperatures. Mang said that a good gage of the heat temperature in a fire is any copper that can be located in the fire room. Another mathematical calculator of the time of burn is the surface area in a room and the amount of fuel. He then defined heat release rate and showed the jury a chart that he had created showing heat release rates. Mang said that the layers of tile and two layers of carpet added insulation to the floor which kept heat from passing completely through it.

Mang testified that he did not rely on the test burn because it was irrelevant to the fire. Mang claimed that, because the test burn fire was started with a torch, it could not be relied upon. He asserted that the test burn created a horizontal spread instead of the vertical spread of fire that occurred in the Wise nursery. Mang testified that a horizontal spread of fire is much slower than a vertical spread.

"Do you have an opinion, based upon a reasonable certainty, as to the area of origin of the fire which took place at the home of Mr. and Mrs. William Wise on March 6, 1993?" Leslie asked.

"Yes, I do," Mang responded.

"What is that opinion?"

"It is my opinion that the fire originated near the head of the bed at the southeast corner. I would say the north corner of the head of the bed."

"And do you have an opinion based upon reasonable certainty as to what could be the point of origin of the fire which took place in the nursery?" Leslie asked

"I don't believe that the electrical system involving the baby monitor can be eliminated as a source of ignition of this fire," Mang said.

"So, is it your opinion that all accidental causes for this fire can be eliminated?"

"No, I don't believe all accidental causes have been eliminated."

"Do you have an opinion based upon a reasonable certainty as to whether the Fisher-Price baby monitor can be eliminated as the competent producing cause of the fire which took place on March 6, 1993?" Leslie said, rephrasing the question.

"If there was a fault occurring in that baby monitor, it could have produced a fire that would involve the head of the bed, or the underneath side of the bed. That would have been a vertical and a horizontal fire burning."

"What the hell did he just say?" Van Buskirk asked me, but I ignored her as I tried to focus on the questions and answers. Besides, I didn't know.

"I take it your opinion is that the Fisher-Price baby monitor could be the source of that ignition?" Leslie suggested to Mang.

"Absolutely," Mang said.

Mang also opined that flashover occurred in the nursery. When Leslie asked him to describe the progression of the fire, Mang started, "I believe that the fire moved from the floor area . . ."

Leslie interrupted him. Mang pointed to Lepper's diagram and continued, "Fire progressed to the point that it burned the bed. Also eventually spread and, and burned off the changing table."

"And then where did it progress from that area?" Leslie asked.

"Well, fires normally burn up and out, and eventually we had a layer effect of the heat in this room until such time that enough heat was accumulated to flashover, and then all the combustibles in this room were ignited, and continued to burn until such time as the fire department extinguished it," Mang replied.

Leslie was apparently building to something. He asked, "Do you have an opinion, based upon a reasonable certainty, as to the amount of time for the fire in the nursery, after flashover, during full room involvement, until complete extinguishment?"

Mang had read all of the fire investigation reports and probably the depositions of the first-in firefighters. He testified, "I don't believe this fire could have burned any more than forty-five minutes from total starting, of an open flame, to the point that it was extinguished, at the point that I observed it in the videos and photographs."

"Forty-five minutes?" I waited for his explanation.

"Total extinguishment is that time that overhauling has occurred, where firemen have removed various debris to extinguish hot areas, the attic area was involved. There was removal of an access to the attic area. I believe that the evidence showed that that all of that could occur in forty-five minutes," Mang said.

"If the firemen reported that they came in the room with a line and sprayed water in a fog pattern, and the flames were out, is that the time you mean?" Leslie asked.

"No, that's not what I mean. At that time, they've knocked it down. The flame has been knocked down and the progression of the fire has been stopped. But complete extinguishment of the fire had not occurred at that time."

Having obtained that somewhat startling opinion from Mang, Leslie changed subjects. He handed Mang several photographs.

Mang showed the jury what he considered low burning. He said that low burning is normal to a fire.

"Do you have an opinion, based upon a reasonable certainty, as to whether a flammable liquid was used to accelerate the fire which took place at the Wise residence on March 6, 1993?" Leslie asked.

"No. No, I don't. I don't believe there was a flammable liquid used in this fire. I don't believe that there's evidence to establish that in any way," Mang asserted.

Mang said that the alcohol found in the carpet was in the area where Lepper found an alcohol bottle. Although I objected, Mang was allowed to testify that Lepper got the samples of the alcohol and that's where he found the bottle of alcohol.

The court then reconsidered. She said, "There was no testimony from Mr. Lepper as to where he got a bottle. There's actually no testimony from Mr. Lepper that he got a bottle." The judge instructed the jury to ignore that part of Mang's testimony.

Leslie asked the question another way. "Do you have an opinion as to how Investigator Lepper could find, how alcohol could be found in that room?"

Mang was prepared for this. "There was supposed to be alcohol in that room."

He showed the video taken by the Indianapolis Fire Department of the room and described even low burning. He explained that if a large amount of liquid accelerant had been poured, there would have been more effects of the radiant heat. He did not see that type of burning on the video. Mang described what he saw on the video at great length.

He pointed to the wall shared by the nursery and the landing. Mang testified that if an accelerant had been poured in that area, the wall would have burned. He said the video showed that had not happened. Mang also said that if the fire was accelerated with all of the burn patterns that Finneran identified, then that entire roof would have burned though. He said that had not happened.

Mang gave a lecture on vapors and carpet wicking and spent a great deal of time explaining why, in his opinion, the alcohol was spilled after the fire was out and not used as an accelerant. Besides, if an accelerant had been used, it would have been detected.

Mang also looked at the alcohol bottle found in the evidence boxes. He explained why it was only partially melted and assumed that it was from the Wise residence. He attacked the packaging and labeling of the evidence, which was not labeled with the room from which the evidence was taken. He also focused in on a frame from the test burn video that showed the changing table. There were a variety of items, including rubbing alcohol on that table. Mang claimed that the alcohol bottle in the burn room photograph was a different brand than the alcohol bottle that was in evidence. This was evidence, he argued, that the alcohol bottle was from the nursery.

"How does that help them?" I wondered. "The cap is on the half empty bottle."

By assuming that the bottle of alcohol was on the baby changing table, Mang explained away the alcohol smelled by Lepper and identified by the Marion County Crime Lab. Mang said it spilled and was kicked around by the firefighters.

Mang then got around to Exhibit 42, the carpeting with wires coming out. He said he observed arcing on those thin wires. He saw beading when he examined the wires under a microscope. The beading was caused either by the fire itself or a ground fault caused arcing. No one can say which occurred by merely examining the beading.

Leslie asked Mang about the effect of retardants in a fire. He said that once the fire is fully involved the retardant would have little to no effect. Mang also said that low burning can be caused not just by an accelerant but also by flashover.

This was critical because fires burn upward from their starting point. So low burning can indicate where the fire started before it began to move "up and out."

Lepper had testified that low burning was a critical factor in his opinions and the burning under the baseboard was in the same area where he smelled and sampled the alcohol laden carpet.

The difference between an accelerated fire and flashover in terms of temperature is significant. Flashover is reached at about one-thousand one-hundred degrees, while an accelerated fire is likely to exceed two-thousand degrees Fahrenheit.

Each of these topics involved many questions and answers with many of the subjects repeated. Mang testified that he had seen many charred bodies and that, in his opinion, the body of baby Matthew was consistent with a mattress fire. Mang criticized the medical examiner for failing to test the piece of diaper that remained on baby Matthew for accelerants.

Mang picked through the remnants of the evidence and identified several items. He said that some of them would have burned if the fire had been hot enough. All of this testimony led him to conclude that the fire was not accelerated. He swore that the fire was very low temperature.

Mang also said that, in his experience as a fireman, it could take minutes, up to five minutes, to reach a fire with a hose.

Mang played the Discovery Channel flashover tape that had been used in the first trial. He claimed that the mattresses in the tape were polyurethane.

Mang was allowed to play the video tape recording, without sound or his commentary.

I was allowed to question him on that testimony and he admitted that he did not know the composition of the mattresses.

Gerry Mang's testimony lasted until nearly two o'clock in the afternoon. I could tell that the jury was tired and I wanted to be quick. I was not sure that I could accomplish that.

"Mr. Mang, you've never been qualified in any court as an expert in forensic pathology, have you?" I asked sharply.

"No, I have not."

"With your high school education and some courses that you've taken, I know that you certainly didn't graduate from medical school."

"No, I did not."

"You certainly wouldn't substitute your judgment for that of a forensic pathologist, would you?"

"No, I don't believe I would."

I showed him the blow up photograph of baby Matthew's nursery. "This is the room that you describe as not having a very hot fire in it?" The skepticism was thick in my tone.

"Yes, it is," Mang responded.

I had called Mang a few months before, offering him my telephone number and assistance. He knew Dave Lepper and Jim Finneran. I asked him if he had ever called any of us to ask questions about the evidence. He responded that it would have been 'unethical to do so.' I asked him whether he knew that the court ordered us not to be present when he inspected the evidence and he denied any knowledge of that.

After Mark Earnest objected to my questioning of the witness, the judge advised the jury that she had ordered an independent inspection without anyone knowledgeable about the case being present.

I asked Mang about the materials he had reviewed to render his opinions. He admitted that he had not read everything that was available. He began working on the case in October 1997, more than four and a half years after the fire.

"When you conducted your examination of Exhibit 42, you knew that it had been moved several times, and examined by many people," I said. I was holding the glob that had tiny flecks breaking off as I asked questions. It was obvious.

"No." Mang denied that he knew this basic information.

"And each time that something has been moved, it seems to lose or change a little bit?" I wiped away some pieces that had fallen onto my suit.

"No question about it."

I asked Mang about a little newsletter that his company published in which he had written an article addressed to insurance adjusters. With his familiarity of insurance, Mang confirmed that insurance companies have to pay off the mortgage, even when the homeowner starts the fire. He also agreed with me that if an insurance company could prove that an appliance caused the fire, that they had a right of subrogation—in other words, if a homeowner's insurance company could prove that a fire was started by an appliance, that insurance company could get its money back for paying the mortgage company.

"In the article that you wrote, that your company published and sent to prospective customers, you said, 'if too much time is allowed to pass in doing a fire investigation, it can make it almost impossible for the expert to do a thorough reconstruction.'"

"That's correct," Mang agreed.

Mang said that he thought the investigation had been done poorly. Yet, it was that investigation that formed the basis for all of his opinions.

I asked whether he agreed that photographs could be deceptive, not as good as seeing in person. He agreed that sometimes that is true. Because he had testified that all of the low burning was even, I showed him a large mosaic of photographs. The photographs were of the floor and lower wall of the nursery. I pointed out a completely white area on the floor near the wall where Lepper had identified the accelerant. Mang, at first, said that the photograph did not include baseboard. When he looked more closely he conceded that the baseboard illustrated was not burned.

Mang admitted that the only thing that he was unable to rule out as an accidental cause of the fire was Exhibit 42, the wires coming from carpeting.

He also agreed that he had made up his mind as to the cause of the fire by the time he was deposed months before. At that time he had not found the beading nor looked at the wire under a microscope. He did not know that the lab had identified alcohol in the carpeting, but even he smelled alcohol when he opened the paint can that contained the carpet sample.

Although Mang was agreeing with my questions, he made every effort to evade and avoid answering. I hadn't expected that. I thought that Mang would be professional, giving the good with the bad. He was hostile and I hoped that it showed.

"At the time that you formulated your opinion, you hadn't looked at the electric outlets," I said.

"No, I did not."

"Because the source of the fire, you could tell, was not at the east wall outlet?"

"It was not in the wall."

"You were aware, you told us at your deposition, that the defendant had said that he saw the fire in the east wall outlet."

"I, I don't recall saying that."

I pointed out the page and line of Mr. Mang's deposition and read him the question that Lisa had asked him and his answer.

"Question, how did you formulate that opinion? Answer, 'because of the location of where it occurred.' What do you mean by location? Answer, 'Well, the fire, the eyewitness to fire saw the fire at the baby monitor in the location of the outlet and the baby monitor, so we have a source of ignition.' Is that what you said Mr. Mang?"

"That's what I said."

"And by eyewitness, you meant the defendant. What the defendant claimed."

"That's what I said."

"But even though William Wise indicated that there was a fire at the outlet, you didn't believe it was important to your investigation, to look at those outlets and examine them?" I asked.

"No, I did not," Mang repeated.

I wanted to show that Mang's opinions were invalid.

Part of that was to prove uncontested facts that he did not know. For example, Mang admitted that he thought that a battery found in the evidence box came from the baby monitor. He had either forgotten or never known that both William and Michelle Wise had consistently said that there were no batteries in the baby monitor. He admitted that after his deposition he found out that the battery had come from the boom box in the baby's room.

Since Mang claimed that the alcohol could have been spilled by firefighters, I asked Mang if he had read Michelle's statement about the location of the alcohol.

"In her statement of March 15, 1993, that you previously read, Michelle was asked about a variety of types of accelerants, and she indicated in the first portion of her statement that there had been an alcohol bottle in the bathroom. That's what she told the Indianapolis Fire Department investigators, isn't it Mr. Mang?"

"I believe I recall her, her saying that there was an alcohol bottle in the bathroom," he said.

"And later in that statement she was asked specifically about what was in the baby's room, and she indicated that there may have been a bottle of alcohol in the baby's room, and if so, it was on the dresser."

"Yes, I believe that's what she said."

"The dresser in Matthew's room was a six drawer highboy, right?" I asked, showing Mang the diagram of the room that he had shown the jury. "So, in your diagram, it looks a little lower, but you didn't intend to mislead that jury, right?" I asked innocently.

"No. That was not a scale thing, no."

"So we know that the dresser was actually the highest item of furniture in the nursery, a six drawer dresser," I said.

"The top of the bed could have been as high," Mang argued.

He agreed after several questions that the dresser was "one of the highest" pieces of furniture in the room.

"And the higher up an item is in a fire, the heat is going to be hotter toward the ceiling than it is toward the floor."

"That is true," Mang conceded.

"In order to confirm your opinion, that this alcohol was on the dressing table, one would have to ignore the statements of both Bill and Michelle Wise, because they said, if it was in the room at all, it was on the dresser, is that correct?"

Mang mumbled, "That's correct, but . . ."

"You would have to believe that a firefighter coming in had somehow gotten this particular item, and the purpose of this is to suggest how the alcohol got in the sample, isn't it? The firefighter would have had to kick it exactly into the very spot that this fire had begun. Is that correct?" I demanded.

He replied stubbornly, "No. I don't believe he had to kick it. He could have knocked it over with a fire hose."

"You were talking about how rooms may reignite or get hot again, is that correct?"

"Yes."

"There was no report from any firefighter, or any other person, in any of the materials that you read, that said anything other than that when Ed Barnes came in, and he said that he was there immediately, suited up, with his SCBA on, Ed Barnes said he came in the room, and the fire was out with two gallons of water, two or three gallons. Isn't that what he said, sir?"

"I believe that's that, that's what he said. I don't dispute that," Mang agreed.

"There is no evidence at all, not from any source, no one has ever said that there was a hot spot on the floor or lower area of this room, correct?"

"That's correct. I don't know of anybody."

"And firefighters indicated . . ."

I was maintaining constant eye contact with Mang and he was beginning to be responsive. Naturally Leslie objected.

"Excuse me. We're objecting to the form of the question. They don't come out as questions. It seems like they're coming out as statements," Leslie whined.

The court said, "That's called cross-examination. Overruled."

Leslie said crankily, "Thank you."

The court responded, "You're welcome."

I never said a word. My total focus was trained on Mang.

"And what you do know is that firefighters were, very shortly after this fire was put out, sifting through, with their hands, through these materials in the room, because that was also in the sworn statements you read, isn't that right."

"Well, I assumed that they, their first priority was to recover the deceased, yes."

"Yes, sir. And they testified that they sifted through it by hand, and not a one of them said that there was a hot spot or an area that needed any more fire suppression," I said.

"Ma'am, you can look at the video. You can see the hot spot. You see the steam coming off of the floor in the, in the video. That had to be, that had to be dissipated before they got in there and went through it."

"The testimony was, from the people who were there that day, that it was, in fact, steam, and it was caused by the differential of a warm house with cold air coming in the window."

"Absolutely. But that's, that prevent—that is, that's because of the hot, hot ashes that are there burning."

"Sir, let me ask you my question so that you understand it specifically. Did you read anywhere in any testimony, any deposition, any transcript, did you have any evidence whatsoever that there was a hot spot on the floor of this room, at any time after that fire was put out?"

"I never read that. It's obvious in the video. It's obvious in the heat patterns that are on the floor." Mang was getting visibly upset and argumentative.

"Sir, was that a no?" I was determined to get a yes or no from this guy.

"No. I, I said it was obvious in the video."

I then moved to the Discovery Channel video that Mang had used and asked the court to be able to play other parts of it. Just as we did before.

First, I set the stage, describing what the jury would and had seen. A room with two bunk beds, each with a foam mattress. The ear of a stuffed bunny being set on fire, other stuffed animals on the beds. The top bunk mattress was much higher than Matthew's crib and the mattresses were much thicker. I also pointed out the Teddy bear on the bottom bunk. I asked him whether the Teddy bear survived flashover. He responded flippantly that the Teddy bear may have survived, but it also had been less flammable than a baby, even though a human baby has so much water content. The judge struck his comment.

I showed the rest of the tape, but stopped it, at times, to ask Mang questions about it.

"There was paper on the floor before flashover."

"Yes."

"And it's still there." I pointed to the paper with my laser pointer so that the jury could see.

"Yes."

"Even after flashover."

"Yes," Mang conceded.

"The Teddy bear that was sitting on the mattress, is just fine. You can even tell the color of his shirt." I pointed again.

"Appears so, yes," Mang had to agree. It was right there on the television screen.

I asked Mang if he had read all of William Wise's statements. He hesitantly agreed that he had. I asked, "When he was asked about where he saw the fire at the beginning, Wise claimed to have been in the nursery, or gotten as close as he could several times. The defendant never said, never said, that he saw the baby's mattress on fire, did he?"

Mang whispered, "I don't, I don't recall that, no."

Mang, when asked about the size of the nursery, whether it was smaller than the area of the defense and prosecution tables in size, agreed that it was a pretty close comparison. I asked if he would pace it off. Mang just looked at me, without moving.

"Now, in his statement the defendant indicated that he was two feet into this room at one point. Recall that, sir?" I asked.

"Yes, I do."

I was going to pace off an area the size of the nursery for my questions. I said, "I am going to walk away from this wall. Tell me when I reach two feet, because I don't want to walk too far."

The questioning had been rapid fire and intense. I was trying to make a point about Wise's claim to have been two feet into the nursery.

"Tell me where two feet is," I continued to ask Mang. He was sort of playing with me.

"I'd say back up one step," he said. "Right there."

"Here, sir? Farther?" I asked, wandering in the center of the courtroom.

"You're a little over, you're a little over two feet," Mang said.

"If this were the baby's bed and it stood out three feet, is that right?"

"Approximately."

I was still moving. I asked again and he said I had passed it. Finally, I said, "Just tell me where to go, Mr. Mang."

He got a look in his eye that was unmistakable. Before he was able to say another word, I said, "No, you don't really get to tell me where to go."

It took the judge, who was very pregnant, a few seconds to comprehend the exchange. When she got it she threw herself on the elevated desk that we call the bench, laughing. So were the jurors.

The seriousness quickly resumed. We finally showed the size of the room and location of the dresser and crib.

In one of his later statements, Wise had claimed that he might have knocked over the dresser in the nursery spilling the alcohol.

"If the defendant said that maybe he knocked the dresser over, the one with the alcohol on it, he couldn't have done that if he was only two feet into the doorway."

"I would think not, yes," Mang replied.

I was moving from subject to subject so that I could make the important points and then sit down.

Finally, Mang also agreed that crib mattresses had to meet flame retardancy standards. He was not familiar with what those standards were or their effect on burn rates.

I had no further questions for Mr. Mang and sat down.

Tom Leslie would have another opportunity to question him. Then we would hear from the jury.

After a series of questions about Mang's ability to review the evidence, Leslie asked, "Was there anything that you felt you lost because of the time period that would not allow you to make your determination respecting the composition of the floor?"

"No."

"Did the laws of physics change with respect to insulation effect over time?" "No."

Leslie wanted Mang to reiterate the forty-five minutes that he had claimed previously for the time that the fire burned. But Mang wouldn't repeat it. Instead he responded, "It's very difficult to say. The witness indicated that the fire had vented the windows and had extended out upon police officer arrival, I believe, so it's very difficult to pin it down to a, a time. I don't know how you can go about that except in a broad sense, you know, like fifteen to twenty minutes, some—I mean, you can't—maybe twenty-five. You can't really say." He seemed considerably less cock sure than earlier.

"Based upon the observation of the damage in the room and the heat release rates of the various objects in there, can you say, with any certainty, that the damage is consistent with a non-accelerated, non-flammable liquid fire?"

"Yes, I can say that, absolutely."

The jurors had several questions. The judge asked some of them and rejected others.

"In your opinion what time was the fire extinguished?" she asked.

"I believe it was extinguished sometime between twenty-five minutes and forty-five minutes after the fire was reported."

The judge read from a slip of paper. "On what basis did you determine that the fire burned forty-five minutes? The defendant says no smoke and fire at approximately 5 a.m., and the firemen were at the scene to extinguish the fire by 5:19?"

"I'm, I'm, I'm basing, I'm basing it on from the time that there's a one foot flame in the room. I can't, I can't determine how long it could have smoldered. There's, there's just no way to predict that."

He squirmed. It was one thing to refuse to respond to my questions and another to avoid a juror's question.

"Why didn't you feel it was necessary to examine the wall outlets?" the judge asked.

"Because the wall outlet, if the fire started inside the wall, it would have a totally different burn for it to come out and cause the burning in this room. The studs, which are the two by twos, would have, would have been heavily charred in order to get enough combustion to get the fire out in the room to cause the type of burning we had here."

The jurors did not want to let go of the time frame. Sixteen minutes. But they were giving Mang an opportunity to explain his answers.

"You originally testified the length was forty-five minutes, then later said twenty to twenty-five minutes. Can you explain?" The judge asked the salient question for the juror, and probably the rest of us.

"Yes. The question was what was the maximum time, the forty-five minutes. I, I don't believe it could possibly go over that, but there's no one that can predict it down to the minute, in any case. There's too many variables. Even the moisture content of the contents itself is a variable. There's there's—so that's why I, when I talked about forty-five minutes, that's the total maximum. I believe it was extinguished sometime between, you know, twenty-five to thirty minutes after the fire was reported."

I don't know about the jury, but I didn't understand what he was rambling about. He fielded additional questions about everything from the floor to why the fire did what it did.

"How can you explain how all of the contents of the room were burned to the point of not being recognizable with the time limit that was given from the time of detection until time of arrival of firefighters, if an accelerant was not used?" Judge Magnus-Stinson asked.

"Because, because of the heat release rate, and that depends on how fast a fire will burn. And all, all this material in here has a relatively high heat release rate compared to the furnishings in this room." Mang clarified that he was comparing the nursery's contents to here—the courtroom.

The jurors asked about mastic and the characteristics of varnish. Their last question was, "Did you do any testing on baby mattresses?"

"I have done full scale house burns with baby mattresses, along with other items. Not specifically with just baby mattresses and not specifically in this case."

Leslie obviously knew that the jurors did not believe Mang's forty-five minute time frame. He asked questions to rehabilitate his witness.

"Would it be fair to say, that as we watched the video and some of the extinguishment was going on in the attic, that the involvement in the room was over?" Leslie suggested.

"Yes, it was," Mang conceded.

"When you referred to when the fire was reported, did you mean when the witnesses first saw it?"

"Yes, when it got discovered, and, and eventually the fire department got the call."

But then Mang added that he was "referring to the time that the fire department got the call, not the actual discovery."

The judge allowed me to ask Mang questions based on what the jurors had asked. I showed a blown up photograph of the nursery, taken by the fire department immediately after baby Matthew's body was found.

"Are you saying that this photograph, taken by the fire department, is not what Lt. Vernon Brown and Ed Barnes saw when they got to the Wise residence?"

"No, except for the white cloth."

"And, in fact, Baby Matthew's body, burned and cremated as it was, was found faster than the time you're talking to Mr. Leslie about as the burn time?"

I tried to demonstrate, with the transformer and the receiver, but one of the outlets in the courtroom was not working. So I asked Mang, "If the receiver was on, as Mr. Wise says it was, and the receiver was next to his head on the couch, and if there had been a short in the transmitter cord, as you suggest there was, a terrible and loud static would have come into the receiver."

"Yes."

"The defendant never said that there was any static over the baby monitor during the time that he was sitting right next to it, on the couch, before the smoke alarm went off, did he?" I had the receiver in my hand as I asked.

"I don't know whether he was even asked the question," Mang said, skirting the answer.

"Did he," I asked, looking at the William Wise, "ever say that, sir?"

"No," Mang grudgingly admitted.

"In fact, he told everyone who asked that the baby monitor was functioning properly that night, didn't he?"

"Yes, he did."

"You have no reason to doubt, when the firefighters and the fire dispatch office provided us information concerning the time that those fire engines arrived, and that being 5:15 and fifteen seconds in the morning, do you, sir?"

"No, I do not."

When I was done, the jurors had a few more questions. Some of them were better than those that I had asked. The judge again read the questions for Mang to answer. The last question of the trial was, "Mr. Mang, is it true that as lacquer finish dries that the volatile solvents are lost to the atmosphere?"

"Certain amounts of them are, but when it's heated back up there are also others extracted from the base of it."

The defense rested. We took a brief recess.

"Are we going to recall Finneran?" Lisa asked me as we considered what to do next.

I told her that I thought that Finneran had been exceptional but the jury had heard all that he had to say. Rehash on a Friday morning or keeping them late on Thursday night is going to backfire, I explained.

Van Buskirk agreed, "I think we did all we could."

It's always tempting to have the last word. Ask any married couple. But I thought it was time to see what the jury would find.

"Your honor, the State has no rebuttal witnesses. The State rests."

The jurors seemed relieved as they were released to go home for the evening with the promise that the case would be in their hands by late Friday afternoon.

The lawyers, defendant, and the judge remained in the courtroom to discuss the instructions that the court would give the jury the next day. With the evidence closed, the only things that would happen now were closing arguments from both sides, with the State giving the first and last arguments. Then the judge would instruct the jury on the law and give them proposed verdict forms for them to sign and return when, and if, they reached a unanimous verdict.

The judge agreed that we would discuss specific instructions in the morning, but she also said that she was concerned about giving the aiding and abetting instructions that the State had requested. She asked me to explain again why they should be given and I restated our position. Two people had equal access to have poured alcohol on baby Matthew: William and Michelle. The last defense lawyers had implied that Michelle could have done it and used that to raise reasonable doubt. We had a right to prevent that kind of speculation because there was proof that both of them could have been in it together.

The judge seemed at times to be teetering against giving the charge, but then would totter back. All three defense lawyers argued against the instruction, claiming surprise (the court snorted at that claim) prejudice and impropriety. Finally, Judge Magnus-Stinson said that she would do some research on her own and let us know in the morning.

I tried to keep a poker face, but this time I failed. To have come this far only to have persuaded the jury that Michelle was as culpable as her husband and having that result in his acquittal would be an unfathomable loss. I could tell that the court saw my consternation.

Meanwhile, it was on me to put all the evidence together for the jurors. It had been days since anyone, other than me, had even mentioned the name Matthew Dean Wise, Baby Matthew.

# Chapter Twenty-Six

I DROVE HOME, drained with the weight of Baby Matthew's death on my shoulders. Would Wise get away with killing his only son? If I failed to convince the jury, if I had left one stone unturned, one brick out of place, then Matthew's death would be unpunished. I was scared.

I drifted back to my first case.

When I graduated law school, I went to work for my father in Atlanta. He was a well-respected and much loved criminal defense lawyer. Dad graduated law school the year I was born. During my first few months with the firm, Dad was asked by the ACLU to represent a black inmate from Georgia's notorious Reidsville Prison, who was alleged to have killed two white prison guards. It was a black on white retaliatory killing in the racially tense South Georgia prison. To make matters worse, our client was a homosexual who was prominently featured in an Atlanta Magazine exposé of the "Maddox" prison system.

I spent six months investigating the case, along with our full time investigator, who had served as the head of drug interdiction for the U.S. Customs service in Viet Nam and elsewhere around the world. During the course of my travels to Reidsville, I had been run off the road twice and, on another occasion, someone had taken several shots at me as I drove near the prison. It probably didn't help that my license tag read "DiDi" my childhood nickname.

The trial of Jessie Mae Whittaker would be the first death penalty case in Georgia since the de facto moratorium on the death penalty imposed by the United States Supreme Court in its 1972 decision in Furman v. Georgia. As far as I knew, it was the first death penalty prosecution in the United States since Furman.

I had been out of law school less than a year when the trial began. Dad did an exceptional job selecting a jury and trying the case. There was another lawyer, an African American young man, who worked for a federal agency and had taken a leave of absence to work on the case. The two of them were trial counsel. I watched the trial, coordinating witnesses, providing Dad with legal theories and witness summaries. At the end of the second week of trial, the case was given to the jury to deliberate. When they left the courtroom, my Dad announced to the judge that he was leaving town to attend his annual party. Three hundred guests had been invited. The judge asked what would happen if the jury convicted, and Dad assured him that the other lawyer would handle the death penalty phase. I was left behind to watch the proceedings.

On Saturday morning, the jury returned a guilty verdict against Jessie Mae Whittaker. The other lawyer floundered in his opening statement. The judge told me to either take over the handling of the death phase or he would hold my father in contempt. To this day I have no idea why the judge thought that I could do any better than the other more experienced lawyer.

I called and questioned witnesses, got snookered by the prosecution at least once, but fought past it. We recessed for the night, with closing arguments set for the next morning.

I left that small courtroom in Claxton, Georgia and returned to the Miami Motel, a small single story grouping of rooms with no television, no telephone and the prosecutors staying next door. It was the only place to stay in Claxton in 1979.

I sat in my motel room alone, with little light and no experience at all. I thought about the fact that this man, who I had grown to know and almost like, and who I was convinced had not struck a single blow, could be sentenced to death if I couldn't do my job. It was more than horrifying. I spent most of the night repeating in my head, that I could be the cause of Jessie being put to death and wondering how I could convince the jury to see the evidence the way I did. I had just turned twenty-six years old.

I assured myself that after that night in Claxton, nothing could again be as terrifying.

But knowing that William Wise could walk free was sure close. I knew that there had been a lot of evidence, much of it conflicting, and that if I wasn't able to pull it together for the jury, William Wise was going to walk free.

The only things that I brought home with me were Lisa's and Van Buskirk's notes from the trial and two photographs: Where's Waldo? and the newborn photo of Matthew.

It was a long, long night. Hours after the family had gone to bed I paced up and down the short hallway between the bedrooms. I kept looking in on my daughters. Their closed eyes and quiet breathing was comforting and disturbing at the same time. The dark image of baby Matthew was etched into my consciousness.

I started giving my closing argument to myself. It wasn't good enough, so I began again. And again. And again. At about four a.m., I slipped into bed and watched Steve sleep. At some point I got dressed and drove into the office. I illegally parked out front and sat in the conference room rehearsing.

At nine o'clock the three of us headed downstairs to find out what instructions the court would give the jury. It was obvious that the judge had spent some time researching the aiding and abetting issue. She started the meeting by telling us that she would give the instruction, but would also warn the jury that if they found beyond a reasonable doubt that Wise had aided and abetted Michelle, that the jury had to be convinced that she had killed the infant.

I could live with that. When all of the instructions were assembled the judge asked if we were ready. Each side was limited to seventy-five minutes for closing argument. Both Lukemeyer and Earnest would do a part of the closing for Wise. The State would start.

The jury was led into the courtroom by the bailiff who had been in charge of them throughout the trial. They seemed more serious than they had been at any other time during the trial. I could see that the stress of making a decision was on their minds, too.

For final argument I wore flats.

I wanted to be at eye level with the jurors and, yes, my feet hurt and I wanted to be comfortable. I did not use a podium, but I did have the exhibits that I intended to show the jury piled up on a table in the middle of the courtroom. I had the television facing the jury and a tape recording ready to play. I took a deep breath and slowly approached the jury box, and I hope I looked thoughtful . . .

"The defendant—that person there," I said, pointing to Wise, moving closer to him, "killed Baby Matthew Wise in the most cruel way one could imagine. He poured alcohol over the baby, as he was lying in his crib, poured it on the floor and set him afire . . .

"William Wise was a frustrated man. He had been forced to marry Michelle, because of her pregnancy. Not planned. He didn't want to marry her. An unplanned marriage, an unwanted pregnancy. He was on probation at work because he lied, misrepresented the truth. He pressured Michelle to have an abortion, she told you that. And what happened when they had the baby, a gift from God? Complained to his friends and co-workers, 'all he does is cry.' When he finally showed anyone a picture of his son, he described him as an ugly baby.

"What about the night that Matthew was murdered? What happened that night? The defendant was at work on his probationary shift. He spoke to his co-worker. Cathy Robinson is still hurting from the pain of that conversation, her guilt. Because when the defendant complained to Cathy on that night she told him that her infant had cried for six months. What did he tell her? He said that he would not tolerate that. And he didn't. Within hours, Baby Matthew was murdered, a horrible death.

"After he left work at midnight, Bill Wise went somewhere. We don't know where. But we know that he left work at midnight and usually got home by twelve-ten or twelve fifteen. Not on the night that Matthew was murdered. Bill Wise went somewhere and didn't get home until nearly one o'clock. Michelle told you that.

"This murder didn't just happen, spur of the moment. It was planned.

"The defendant is a wannabe firefighter. Even his lawyer told you that. Bill is a wannabe firefighter. To Dave Lepper, the defendant said he had very little training about cause and origin, remember? But in this transcript (I showed them the transcript that they read) he gave himself away.

"You can infer where he went after work. Did he go to buy the accelerant? Did he get more bottles of alcohol? Why alcohol? Let's talk about that. defendant was a trained firefighter. You read that transcript over lunch one day. It was the deposition that Allstate's lawyer took of the defendant and Michelle. He testified about the courses he took about accelerants, and causes of fire. So why use alcohol? It has a very high evaporation rate. It's something that may normally be in a nursery, so if someone finds it you can say, 'Gee, it was in the room.' Just what the defendant has been claiming.

"Look at the firsts. This was the first time that the defendant didn't get home until nearly one o'clock in the morning . . . Buying alcohol? . . . This was the first time that the defendant took this (I held it) police radio home. All he had to do was push this red button. The fire department would have been there within three to four minutes. He could have keyed the speaker and spoken directly to fire dispatch. That also would have brought a quick response. As soon as the fire detector went off, or once the defendant saw smoke, that's all he had to do. No worries about the phone not working. Or calling 911.

"He said he brought the radio home because they were short handed at work, but you know that's not true. A lot of what the defendant said is not true. The defendant told Michelle that he was going to keep the police radio with him, in case they called him, he needed to have it on. Ask yourself, he had the radio there, he had it with him, he had it turned on, and we'll talk about when and how he moved it—hid it in his bedroom. A first—he had the police radio at home.

"Coincidences? Coincidences like that don't happen. On the very night that he said he wouldn't 'tolerate' Matthew's crying anymore.

"The radio is important. William Wise wants to be a hero, and in order to be a hero, he didn't want to be a hero to just anybody. He didn't care if Michelle thought he was a hero. She already thought he was a hero. He wanted the fire department to think he was a hero.

"Remember Margaret Jones? The firefighter he was dating. He thought he'd get on with IFD. No more of this having to just sit there and dispatch. He'd get on with IFD, if he went into a fire and rescued somebody, and they'd just put him in the fire department. That's what he was going to do. He brings home the radio, he's going to wait until the fire engines are arriving, then he'll pretend to retrieve Matthew.

"All of the evidence suggests that this was an intentionally set fire. Not just the evidence in the room, but all the evidence leading up to it, all the firsts. And surely you asked yourself, and one of the jurors asked the question, why for the very first time did Bill Wise decide to stay with the baby that night? He had never done it before, never.

"Michelle told you he'd never done it before and then, of course, she backed up from that, lied about it, and so then you heard from her statement that she gave to his lawyers, 'Well, I lied about it because it looked, well, it made him look guilty.' And even he, after pressure, in that same deposition, after he was asked time after time, remember how many times the lawyer kept saying, was this your first time upstairs with the baby, and he hemmed and he hawed, and he hemmed and he hawed, and finally he said, 'I don't believe I ever came upstairs while I was working and fed him in the morning like that.'

"There's no doubt that this was the first time he stayed with the baby. And the question that someone asked, which was a great one, was he had to go to work, at noon, on the day that Baby Matthew died. He had to go to work. Why was he staying with the baby? Michelle didn't have to work. She was off, it was a Saturday . . . He intended to kill the baby. From the moment he spoke to Cathy Robinson, or before.

"When I was a child, my dad took my sister and I to New York City, his home town. There were these young men on the sidewalks playing street games. People would stop and watch as they played. One young man, in particular, that we watched had three small cups with a pea in one of them. The point of the game was to see whether you could keep your eye on the cup with the pea in it. It wasn't easy because the guy did all sorts of things to distract you from watching the cup with the pea in it. I was fascinated by the game, but I could never guess which cup had the pea in it.

"Do you think you've kept your eyes on the evidence? Because in this case you need to keep your eye on what the defendant did, and you need to keep your eye on what this case is really about. It's not about a baby monitor. It's not about an alcohol bottle. This case is about the murder of Baby Matthew. And you've gotten a bit of a shuffle, and you'll have to decide, and I know that you'll focus on the issue, which is the defendant. He's alone with Baby Matthew. Keep that in mind.

"This is the first time he's alone with baby Matthew. He has this radio. He's the last person to see the infant alive. He admits that he was in the baby's room at five o'clock in the morning. You can shuffle the times the way Mr. Mang did, but the defendant said that he looked in the room, there was no problem at five o'clock. Despite Mr. Mang's attempts, there can be no hedging on the times. Bill Wise said he was there, in the room and there was nothing amiss. He didn't see anything and he sure didn't hear any popping. He returned to the couch where the receiver was on volume level three, remember how loud that was? There was no static on the receiver.

"We also know the time when the fire started was after the defendant was in Matthew's nursery because of what the newspaper lady told you. She was amazing. She knew the streets she drove on, where she turned around. She remembered every address she delivered a newspaper to, and she told you that at 4:58 a.m. she drove by the Wise house, she was out of her car, she was very conscious of the neighborhood and her surroundings. At 4:58 a.m. there was no problem at that house. Defendant looked at his watch, he knew it was five o'clock when he was in the bathroom. He claims that he goes back to the couch and falls asleep.

"But then the defendant starts to change his story. Why? The versions change. He changes the versions because the timing is just right. He'd just come back from setting the fire. And what he didn't expect was Michelle. She had set her clock for six o'clock. He didn't expect Michelle to come up the stairs. He's in the baby's room, which backs onto the stairs. Michelle didn't remember what woke her. He (I again pointed at Wise) was in that room pouring the alcohol on baby Matthew. Had Baby Matthew been crying? We know the monitor worked. We know where the monitor was at the time. You saw the photo.

"Defendant, who was going to 'take care' of the baby for the first time, he had that monitor laid down so he didn't have to hear the crying. And then when not hearing the crying, he could still hear it from the baby's room, he decided to resolve his problem. The defendant thought that Michelle should be well asleep by that time. She was exhausted from work, from taking care of the baby, which was her primary responsibility. But she came upstairs. And so he wanted to be asleep. But he wasn't. Because, although Michelle lies for him later, Michelle confirms, again in a statement to his lawyers, that no, he was awake on the couch when she came upstairs. He's just gotten back from what he told her was the bathroom. He'd gotten back from Baby Matthew's room where he poured the accelerant.

"That's where all of this becomes so clear. Because the alarm goes off shortly after that, as alarms do. He set the fire at five o'clock. And if you have any doubt, consider what the defendant does next. The fire was out by 5:16. When he heard the alarm go off, and he couldn't shut the alarm off.

"What he did, was he walked up six stairs, and his child was as close to him as the back row of jurors are to me, and he left Matthew there. And he walked to the right, as far over as he is now, and he picked up a telephone, a portable telephone. And as he walked back down the hall, did he take the phone, dialing 911 and go to Baby Matthew? He did not. Can you infer from that that he wanted Baby Matthew dead? He takes the telephone downstairs, and he tells you he doesn't get a dial tone, and Michelle, at one time, she said she heard a dial tone.

"One way or the other we know what he didn't use. We know what he'd been trained to use. This wasn't the first time he was a dispatcher.

"You heard that he'd been a dispatcher at other facilities. He was an EMT. He knew what this was (showing the police radio). He didn't use this.

"And I thought, well, okay could he have been in a panic? And then you ask yourself, he didn't know there was any big fire, he knew there was smoke, but he wasn't so panicked that he didn't go upstairs and remember where the phone was. He wasn't so panicked that he was afraid to go up into that area. It wasn't that they were going to wake the baby, because the baby was sure awake from that shrilling alarm, and undoubtedly terrified as he lay in his crib.

"No, the defendant waited, stayed downstairs at the landing. What did you hear next? Michelle said they couldn't get through to 911, so he told her to go downstairs. She walks down six steps, the same number of stairs as there are to get upstairs, to where Baby Matthew is, and she goes toward her bedroom, all the way at the other end of the house. And she couldn't find her shoes, so she comes back up the flight of stairs.

"Know where the defendant still was? Still standing at the landing. It's not just that he didn't take the left the first time, it's that while she went downstairs to get her shoes, while she had the time to look for her shoes while her baby's room was on fire, and perhaps him, too, this man stood and waited at the landing. He didn't go upstairs and get that child. And you tell yourself, why not?

"The answer is very clear.

"And then Michelle goes back downstairs to get her jacket and goes outside to call 911.

"The defendant, in his statement, claims that he tried to save the baby. He didn't try to save the baby. You learned from Lewie-Bob Hiatt, the first call, that was from her. (Michelle was in the courtroom and I pointed at her.) Michelle calls at 5:09:39. Twenty-seven seconds later he calls. Twenty-seven seconds later. What did he do in the twenty-seven seconds? Well, we know that he had to have gone downstairs because defense witness, Wayne Edwards—you remember him, the gentleman who was the neighbor, the person that Bill called 911 from his house, do you remember him? He said that when the defendant got to his house, he was wearing his fire gear. Where was it kept? Downstairs. So in that twenty-seven seconds, between the two calls, the defendant took six steps downstairs, which tells you what he didn't do, because he sure didn't take those six steps upstairs. He gets on his fire gear. At that point he may or may not have come upstairs, seeing that the fire wasn't burning fast enough, and threw that stool through the window.

"But we know that once he has his fire gear on, he runs out of the house. Now, remember he only had the twenty-seven seconds, and he claims that he's been rescuing Matthew. In twenty-seven seconds he gets on the fire coat, and where does he go? To Tamara Snyder's house. Remember her, blonde lady in a black pants suit? She said that the defendant came to her house, knocked on the door, said he had a fire, but didn't wait for her to open the door. Ladies and gentlemen, that took time.

"The defendant, who wants you to believe he was trying to save Baby Matthew, who he didn't try and save at all, he killed him. (I showed the diagram of the houses on the street.) He went from this house, over to here. Is there a reason he wanted to wake some of the neighbors? You betcha. To be a hero, people need to see you do something. In that same twenty-seven seconds he goes from her house, across the street to Mr. Edwards house. All in twenty-seven seconds. What he doesn't do is very clear.

"So, ladies and gentlemen, when you think about him going up the stairs and getting the phone instead of getting the baby, don't forget it. When you think of Michelle getting her shoes, think of the defendant standing there while she's got time to do that, not getting Baby Matthew. And when he tells you in his statements that he tried to rescue baby Matthew, think of the time he had to go downstairs and get his own fire coat before he ran across the street to go the Snyder's and then Mr. Edwards house to call 911.

"And what else was downstairs, allegedly? If it wasn't upstairs on the couch with him, Michelle told you this police radio was downstairs within steps of where the defendant went to get his fire gear. This man is a firefighter nut. He has information everywhere about fire trucks, fire-fighting. He is a wannabe. He knew that radio was there, and he didn't use it.

"We know that the firefighters got there at 5:15. Fifteen minutes. This isn't something subject to dispute. This is not the speculation of Mr. Mang. 'I wasn't there, I didn't see it, and no one said it, in any of their statements, but I can render an opinion.'

"We don't need opinions. We have tapes. The firefighters arrived at 5:15:15 exactly. And Barnes told you, he had his SCBA on the truck, it was a tanker, which meant it had its own water, they didn't' have to go to a hydrant. The hose was pulled out for him by the guys on the street closest to the house. Ed Barnes, all he had to do was jump off that truck and run in that house, and that's what he did, and he told you he had the fire out within seconds.

"Notwithstanding this whole 'what does the fire out mean,' Mr. Barnes, who has been a firefighter for twenty-seven years, knows pretty well what 'fire out' means. So does Lt. Vernon Brown. This man (pointing to William Wise) wants the baby to burn to the extent that you've seen him, so that he could get a crowd and make sure the fire department got there, and just in time, right before they arrived, he was going to go into the house, pretend to rescue the baby and be a hero. And then there was an added bonus. He could collect a million dollars later . . .

"Keith Williams, the police officer, willing to risk his life to save a baby that he'd never met, told you that Wise wasn't coughing, no stridor, he didn't even claim that child as his own.

"Ed Barnes, the first in firefighter. He's twenty-seven years with the department. Think about him and Officer Williams. Think about what people's motivations are, biases. Ed Barnes is a first-in firefighter. His job, his career, his dedication is to save lives. He's not a ranked officer, he's not a politician. He is, for twenty-seven years, a corporal, who goes in and tries to save lives and property. It's pretty humble. He told you he went into that house and saw this (showing the photograph of the room with only five or six inches of black charred debris). Ed Barnes saw nothing. He saw rubble in a fire that could not have lasted more than sixteen minutes. This isn't some, 'Oh, what did the room look like forty-five minutes later.' This photograph is what Ed Barnes told you the room looked like at 5:16. And he wasn't the only person who told you that.

"He described it to you verbally, too. He said, 'There was nothing left.'

"So, defense counsel asked him, 'Well, that's not unusual, is it?'

"Ladies and gentlemen, in his twenty-seven years and his hundreds of fires, he had never seen anything like this. Now you know he's been in fires with mattresses, I mean most accidental fires are caused by smoking in bed. Common sense. He'd been in mattress fires involving foam rubber. Think about it. Every bedroom has foam rubber, or some sort of mattress components and almost all of them bigger than a little flame retardant baby mattress.

"Ed Barnes told you, in twenty-seven years' experience fighting fires, he told you that what he saw wasn't right. He'd seen accidental fires. He's not paid by anybody, except to go out and save lives and property. And he told you, this (the photograph of the nursery) is not what one expects to see in a fire of this length."

I played the test burn video, pointing out the time that it started, and telling the jury that we would stop it when it had burned for sixteen minutes.

"The next witness to testify was Lt. Vernon Brown. Do you remember him? It seems like a long time ago. He was also a firefighter. Motive, bias? Was he representing one side or the other? No, he was there to try to save lives and property. That's what he does. What did he tell you? 'There was nothing in that room.' From the moment he walked in that room it was suspicious because this was a fire, in an occupied house, and within four and a half minutes, or five minutes of the call to the fire department, in a house with smoke detectors, this is what he saw. And when Vern Brown walked into that room, having been a former investigator, he had them call arson. 5:19 in the morning was when Lepper was dispatched. Why? Because no matter what Mr. Mang or Mr. Berman say, those firefighters knew that this is not what a room looks like after an accidental fire.

"Remember the video that the defense showed you yesterday. The two bunk beds on fire? And after flashover? You knew they were bunk beds. Did you notice you could even see the little wooden knobs that held the bed together? You could see the teddy bear, his clothes, the dresser, everything. Not here. There's a reason. Here there was a liquid accelerant, poured on the floor, and, as you heard from a forensic pathologist, the assistant director at I.U. Medical School, in his opinion it was poured directly on Baby Matthew."

In the meantime, the test burn tape was running. I talked about David Lepper and his opinions. He knew the same things that the other firefighters knew. He knew the facts. The smoke detector would have gone off within four minutes of the fire igniting. He knew when the fire department arrived. He concluded that the fire had burned too fast for the fuel load.

"It was a total destruction of the room contents and no one can contest that. Oh, I forgot. They tried. Mr. Mang came in and said, there's forty percent of a rocking chair left. Remember that? This is what's left of the room. We spread it out once. Dresser, stool, hamper, forty percent of a rocking chair? (I showed the six inch piece of the bent wood) Floor level burning—again Mr. Mang said there is no floor level burning. I pointed out to him, I said, well sir, let me show you States Exhibit 132, the montage.

"Now remember, David Lepper showed you, in this area of origin, that there was no burning low here. And there's no low burning because fire goes up. So you don't expect it right at floor level. And he said, look, nothing here. And then you get to that area, the area of origin and because David Lepper was there, he was able to look under the baseboard, and he said that there was burning under the baseboard, which should have been protected. That's where it's not burned, (I showed them on the photographs) and that's where it is burned.

"Now Mr. Mang, who relied on photographs, who told you he could render opinions based on careful observations of photographs, he testified, 'Oh no, there was no baseboard' there, you remember that? Then I said, well, yes, sir, I believe there is. And I showed him that all along the east wall there was no low burning under the baseboard. (I stepped forward with the collage and showed each juror) You see, here's the top of the baseboard. There's no low burning. You can see the wood there until you get to the one point where David Lepper said there was a liquid accelerant poured.

"Let's talk about Mr. Mang's ability to observe, because he told you some pretty, well, some pretty contrary information to what you'd been given earlier. And his ability to observe and to testify honestly to you is crucial to that, so I want to ask you to look at something and remember what he said.

"Yesterday, on the stand, Mr. Mang was asked to look at one of the autopsy photographs. Now think about this. He was asked to look at it, and Mr. Leslie asked him whether he could look at the material by the leg of the baby, what was left, and identify it. Do you remember that? And Mr. Mang said, oh, it was diaper. Mr. Mang, under oath told you that what he saw in that photograph was paper, this. (I showed the infant Pamper that the defense had introduced.) I'm not going to ask you at this point to look at Baby Matthew again, but I want you to look closely at the material, because Mr. Mang gave an answer that was convenient to the defendant's theory, that wasn't true, because when you look at this material closely you're going to see that it's a knit material, and if you look closely you can actually see the stitches and thread on this material. Take a look at it and I'll show you where I'm talking about."

I took the photograph that was blown up and showed every juror what I meant and gave them time to look carefully.

"Do you see the stitching? You see the texture in the cloth that looks like it's a knit?

"By the way, while the other jurors are looking at the photograph, look at the video. We are at ten minutes. (The test burn room was barely doing anything at that point. There was fire certainly, but nothing was destroyed.) Remember Mr. Berman told you that if this cord shorted then the fire would go to the transmitter. Look at the transmitter in the video. Do you see what's happening? Nothing. It's not on fire until, and you'll see this in a few minutes, this fire comes over and somehow catches the transmitter on fire.

"Catastrophic failure in this, the transformer, does not, like a lightning bolt, go down the wire and somehow catch the transmitter on fire. That cannot happen.

"David Lepper told you that it was accelerated by a liquid accelerant because of the low burn in an uneven area, and because of burn patterns on the floor. And Mr. Finneran confirmed that.

"Yesterday Mr. Mang said that, 'Oh, no, that was just scorching.' Do you remember, one of the jurors asked a question and Mr. Mang said, oh, no, that's just normal scorching?

"So, I was trying to think of a way to explain this while I was driving here today. And, of course, being one of the worst housekeepers in Indiana, I've scorched my husband's shirts on numerous occasions. And you know what you find when you scorch something? After the scorch you can tell what was on top. With his shirts, it looks like an iron. You can see the details. I have a steam iron, and so I know for sure, because you can see the little ring. Scorching is uniform. If you haven't burned someone's shirt, or your own shirt, think about if you've ever put a pot that was hot, on your counter and scorched your counter. When you picked it up you could see the entire area was scorched. That's what scorching does. This (showing the photograph) isn't scorching. This is pouring. This is dripping. This is pouring on the baby and the floor, and then going out of the room, leaving the accelerant trailing behind. That's what this is. "And that's exactly what Mr. Lepper told you it was, and exactly what Mr. Finneran told you it was."

I looked at the television screen and the clock in the courtroom.

"At this point Keith Williams is already at the house trying to get in. This is the fire that would have been occurring if it had not been accelerated. That's not what was, because in a minute and a half is when the fire department arrived.

"What's this all about? Wanting to be a firefighter for sure. What about the million dollars? Were you shocked when Amy Strati came in and said, at another relative's funeral, talk about cold, another relative's funeral a few weeks after Matthew's death, the conversation wasn't the way the defendant tried to characterize it, well, should we bring a lawsuit. A million dollars. Amy Strati was struck by that. A million dollars. Do you think we can get a million dollars from Fisher-Price? That's what this is about."

I looked at the video drawing the jury's attention to the screen, the test burn room was now in flames, but all of the furniture was standing. I show them the time stamp on the video. Fifteen minutes in.

"At this point the fire trucks, they're out front. But at the Wise residence they don't see what an accidental fire would show. No. There's fire coming out the window. Not this (pointing to the video).

"Ladies and gentlemen, hopefully you want to see it to believe it. Jim Finneran sat here and showed you. He showed you and no one seemed to dispute (I had plugged in the transformer with the stripped wiring and held it between my fingers) and I can hold this from now until the end of my closing. This doesn't get hot. This doesn't get hot."

I looked at the video.

"Ladies and gentlemen, the fire at the Wise home is now out. It is sixteen minutes into the fire. Look at what an accidental fire room would have looked like. And in case there's any question about the heat, do you see that guy's knee in the video, right there. He's wearing a golf shirt.

"Mr. Berman, who spent three hundred fifty-seven dollars of someone's money on this (I held the Plexiglas covered transformer cord) couldn't show you what he claimed. This item (the transformer in my hand) uses fifteen milliamps of power. Nothing more, nothing less. This is what they tell you caused the fire (showing the transformer). Can't happen. It cannot happen.

"We know you have listened carefully and on behalf of the State, we appreciate that attention.

"The first Count charged in this case is Murder. The elements of the crime are that the defendant did knowingly kill another human being.

"You can't set a fire on a baby and not know it. Don't forget what Dr. Pless said. He gave you his opinion: That a fire was set on the baby. And do you know what? Mr. Mang's quick and easy coming up with, 'oh, yeah, the mattress could have caused it,' but he doesn't explain to you how there's a protected area. Do you remember it? You can't see this child whose arms are burned off, his head is exploded, but you can see his soft tissue genitals remaining. Why? Because they were protected with a liquid accelerant. Because it's the fumes, not the liquid, that burns. And because it's the fumes that burn, the liquid remains.

"In Count II, we've charged Felony Murder. And felony murder is killing during the course of committing an arson. And you've heard the elements of felony murder and the judge will read them to you again.

"That the defendant, that's the defendant (I pointed at Wise), killed Matthew Wise while committing or attempting to commit arson. And the last element is that it resulted in serious bodily injury. And of course, in this case, death.

"And finally, Arson. Arson is to knowingly by use of fire—there was surely fire in this case—damage property, that's their home, under circumstances that endangered human life, and it did, which resulted in serious bodily injury."

I still had the three cups in front of the jury with a pea under one of them. I had been shuffling them while describing the elements of arson. I shuffled one more time and then stopped.

"Ladies and gentlemen, when you look at all of the evidence, you know, you know that that man killed, he murdered his child. And in terms of the other parts of the game, the baby monitor (I lifted a cup and there was nothing under it), and the alcohol (another cup and nothing.)

"If there had been alcohol spilled in that room after the fire, then the firefighters would have smelled it. It would not have burned the wood under the baseboard.

"The defendant (I lifted the third cup with the pea) killed his baby, and today is the day for justice."

There was complete silence in the courtroom as I finished. Van Buskirk and Lisa Swaim were watching me but made no movement as I finished. Their faces were expressionless.

The judge said, "Thank you."

The jury waited without speaking or taking notes. They were doing as the court had instructed, trying to be neutral until the case was given to them to deliberate. No notes, because closing arguments are not evidence. No facial expressions because being neutral is a sacred and difficult task, especially at this stage of a trial.

As I sat down, I closed my eyes hoping that I had convinced every one of the twelve jurors. I had little time to consider the closing because it was my job to respond to whatever the defense said in their closing. I put any feelings aside and listened intently.

The judge continued, "Does the defendant care to make a closing argument?"

Jennifer Lukemeyer stood.

"Counselor, ladies, and gentlemen, the facts are what are important in this case, and the fact is that this morning the sun rose from the east. Sun rose from the east, as it does every day—a fact. And that sun rose over a small grave about three hours north of here. A small grave where almost five years ago to the date, Michelle Wise and Bill Wise had to rest their child, a child they loved. And the fact is, that sun will rise every day from the east over the small grave that they maintain and upkeep.

"Fact is, that here in Indiana we don't play games. It's a con game, and that's not what we're doing here. We're not in the courtroom to play a con game. We're here to deal with the facts.

"I'm not going to sit here and shuffle stuff around and try to divert your attention. Number one, that's not my job. But it's the facts that are before you. I'm not going to shuffle anything around for you and ask you to, try to trick you into picking the wrong cup. The fact is that Bill Wise did not kill his child, did not set that nursery on fire March 6, 1993. The fact is that the State cannot and did not eliminate all accidental causes, as is their burden, and the fact is, ladies and gentlemen, that you cannot eliminate what you can't find. David Lepper, March 5, 1998, Marion County Criminal Court, Room Six. (Lukemeyer read from what looked like a transcript.)

"The State has summarily claimed that the facts support arson. A fact is something that is put forth as objectively real. And, ladies and gentlemen, there is no objectivity in this investigation. There's no factual support for the allegations. It's a terribly lax investigation. As Mr. Mang told you, in all his experience, it's one of the worst investigations he's ever seen.

"And you've sat in this courtroom for two weeks, as we have. You know how to come to an inference, you know how to interpret the facts, but let's look at the facts.

"After the judge finishes final instructions and you go back through that door and into that room where you guys probably sat around, you've talked, you probably know each other, how many kids you have, where, what you do for a living, what your hobbies are. And in that room you won't be talking about hobbies. You'll be talking about whether or not to find this man guilty. (She had walked behind her client and touched his shoulder.)

"This is a huge, huge obligation, and you've promised everyone in this courtroom, including the State of Indiana, that you would follow your oath and you would not compromise those principles, you would not shift the burden, you would not hold us to any obligation, and you would look straight to that table for the facts. To compromise undermines the entire system, and the system is set up to prevent innocent people from going to jail. The system is designed to protect everyone, and to compromise that, to compromise it by deciding on admittedly heinous pictures, horrible pictures of Matthew, to be decided on inferences and speculation and rumors, if you compromise, the risks are huge.

"One of those principles that the judge will instruct you, you can't consider that Bill Wise did not testify. You look at him in the court, in the jury room and say, well, defendant didn't testify. That's a compromise, because the defendant has answered and you've heard. Bill Wise has answered over seven hundred questions that have been put in front of you. Seven hundred questions that you've heard, and you've read. But the two most important words that he's uttered in the last five years are, not guilty.

"It's a principle you cannot compromise back there in that jury room. Talk to each other, listen to each other. Don't let any other juror compromise.

"I'm going to talk about the facts of the fire, because that's what's important here. One of the first compilation of the facts generated by the State's witnesses was Detective Lepper's diagram of the nursery. Most important he's got the point of origin right here, the head of that bed where that transmitter, or the monitor is.

"The fact is, that you have a fast fire. You have a fast fire, an accelerated fire. But as defined in accelerated, it means to speed up, to speed, does not equate with having a flammable liquid there. And fire can be accelerated by looking at the contents in the room, and that brings me to the heat release rate. That's what is important, is the heat release rate. You look at the contents of the room and this terribly flammable polyurethane foam mattress and look at its heat release rate.

"Flashover means that everything in the room is engulfed. And the time from full room involvement to suppression is crucial, because there's where you'll have your damage. And that is exactly why this room looked like it did after that fire. It is completely consistent, the time given, the heat release rate, the flashover, and the time of full room involvement. That's exactly why that room looked like it did.

"Now we've got the times. Got to look at the times. We've got the fire out, initial suppression, the room involved, the fire is, is out, and they're still looking for hot spots at 5:16. It's the State's contention that at five a.m., five a.m. exactly, Mr. Wise was up going to the bathroom and getting back on the couch. Funny thing is, that all the statements that Bill and his wife, Michelle, gave, in all the statements, the State managed to pick the points they want you to believe, and pick the points they want you to disbelieve.

"And to be honest with you, in looking at the statements, to look at those statements, that is the only thing that the State has treated as a scientific specimen. What have they done with these statements of Bill and Michelle, the statements that they gave to police investigators, fire investigators, insurance agents, lawyers? What have they done? They've put them under a microscope, they've dissected them, they've analyzed them, they've highlighted the bad and they've sort of shoved aside the good. They have dissected the product of just two human beings sort of reiterating what they thought had happened. That is the only scientific approach they took in this case, was to dissect, retrospectively, the statement of Bill and Michelle, and that's what they want you to rest on.

"So they're going to say it's five o'clock. There's other statements indicating Michelle had testified that she had woke up at approximately between four-thirty and five. Well, then, the State asked her, well, didn't you say at one time that you woke up at five-thirty, Mrs. Wise? And she says, well, yeah, I probably did. Well, through the investigation of this case we all know she didn't wake up at five-thirty. Not like the firemen found her downstairs sleeping. Their accuracy and their reiteration of what had happened was the best they could do, when they were talking to an insurance agent, four days after they had buried Baby Matthew in that small grave up in Elkhart."

Lukemeyer told the jury that "Michelle woke between four-thirty and five and she was going to check on Matthew to see if he had eaten enough. She went upstairs and went over to talk to Bill, on the couch for about five to ten minutes. As she was getting to the stairway, she heard the alarm, she panicked and the next ten to fifteen minutes of her actions and her husband's are going to be broken down for more than five years. They're going to be stretched out, they're going to be slowed down, they're going to be questioned for five years. Their actions, in that ten minutes, are going to be dissected, torn apart, criticized and commented upon.

"We've made ten minutes into a two week trial. We know that the fire and the intensity of it could have happened in the time frame between quarter till five until the initial extinguishment and initial suppression, at 5:16. How do we know that? You've got a foam polyurethane mattress with an incredibly high heat release rate. That's twice as fast as gasoline."

Lukemeyer claimed that, in the test burn room, it was two minutes before the foam mat on the changing table caught fire due to the high heat release rate in the foam product. Lukemeyer described the furnishings in the nursery as flimsy pressboard and said that the room itself was well insulated from the double carpeted floor.

"The pressure was building up in the room," she argued, "even with the door open. It's not the temperature, she said, it's the rapidity, it's fast, and the heat release is, it's building up to that flashover threshold.

"Each wall, ceiling, and floor, every part of that room is serving as an insulator for that pressure build-up. Very quickly, because of the heat release rate ratio or rate. The gases build up to the point where everything becomes combustible, especially those gases that have built up in the room. You saw it. Everything explodes. The room is engulfed in flames. And this is a fact, ladies and gentlemen.

"Now the State would like you to believe that it's this flashover that the State's witnesses concede happen, is what blew out the window. And then the State would like you to believe that it was the stool that broke open that window. Well, ladies and gentlemen, we've got a three legged stool right here just burned. This didn't go through the window. This remained in that room. This did not break the window. What broke the window was the pressure of the fire buildup in that room, and we know that happened before Michelle Wise's call came in. We know that happened before 5:09 when that call came in.

"David Lepper came in and said total destruction. Look at this box of debris they waived around. But if you look at the photographs there's cloth, there's pieces, big pieces of wood. And the video, you saw a big old pile, up to the knees of debris sitting outside that window. That is what you have in front of you.

"It's one of the worst investigative cases, because you've got all this debris and that's what you are given. And who knows where exactly this came from?

"Afterward, you have floors that are cleaned up, the carpet samples are thrown out the window. Now later, somebody says that they came in, they put, the, arranged the carpet back in the room to sort of try to re-create it. Where are those photographs? How much of that was left? Where are they? You've got low burning, which is consistent with a flashover and full room involvement. You've also got the low burning. You've got the contents of the room."

Lukemeyer described everything in the nursery that she considered flammable including the mastic on the floors. She asserted that Dirk Shaw testified that the mastics could cause the burning under the baseboard. She said that Mang explained that the construction of the room and the drafts between the floor and baseboard would account for the burning under the floorboard.

"There was no flammable liquid used in this fire. Why? Because none was found. Yeah, you have the sample of alcohol. Let's talk about that. Mr. Finneran got up there and said, I don't know what flammable liquid was used, but one was used, I know that. And you have a bottle that the State does not want in that room, and you've got a bottle that had to have been almost full, because it was protected. The bottle was not burned. I know Mr. Earnest is going to talk a lot about that bottle. I tell you what, we did our darndest to get that in, and he'll tell you about that bottle and what its significance is. There would have been just more damage, if there would have been a flammable liquid. This is the alcohol du jour that the State is going to use, as being their flammable liquid. You would need a lot of it. You would need a lot of it, because it is extremely volatile, and to make these pour patterns that cover this much of the room, you would need a lot of it because of its volatility. You would need a lot of it.

"No receptacles were found from which this supposedly flammable liquid came from."

Lukemeyer described the wall joists in the room. She argued that the vapors from an accelerant would have had an effect on the HV/AC unit. No evidence of that.

Lukemeyer now spoke in broken sentences. "Mang found evidence of beading, he counted the wires and you have twenty two strands that he found. Eleven per side. What did Mr. Berman count for the Fisher-Price conductors? He counted twenty-two. You've got pointers . . . This is not a hot fire, it's a fast fire. You've got a lamp not bent over. Indication of normal heat."

She reviewed photographs and continued to argue that the fire was fast but not hot—not arson, not accelerated.

"You've got the area of origin at the baby monitor and you cannot rule out what you can't find," she repeated. "Mr. Berman never said that if you start a fire in there, that fire would shoot down the cord. He said that it could send extra current and voltage down that line. No, he couldn't recreate it. The fact is the potential is there. You cannot rule it out.

"I'm going to let Mr. Earnest talk to you. Stick with the facts. This man did not kill his child."

Lukemeyer walked to the defense table, smiled at Wise, and sat down. As she did, Earnest shot from his chair.

"I've got thirty-eight minutes that has to last a lifetime, and I need to begin by talking to all of you, and you talking to me through your eyes, and we can enter a pact, we can agree on something, because it's very important, and everything this courtroom stands for requires it. We need to enter a pact that you will agree that your verdict, when you reach it, will not be based on the gruesomeness of the photos, because I've seen your faces for the last two weeks, and I understand how you feel. Because if that's the case, I don't have a chance, we don't have a chance. The pictures are Matthew Dean Wise in one sense, but in another real sense they're not. They're a picture, and they're a fact. It's not to minimize him or his life. They're a fact that we can look at and try to determine things. But Matthew Dean Wise lived on this earth for seven weeks and one day. And there's another fact. During that time he was loved, he was held. And he was a gift from God.

"The State knows it. It's the bottle. It's the bottle. The State's scared of the bottle . . . Why? The State's scared of the bottle because the bottle is truth."

Earnest held the partially melted plastic bottle of alcohol.

Earnest reenacted Finneran saying that various items in the exhibit boxes came from the test burn room. He was reading from a transcript. Finneran said that "the bottle came from the test burn room," but Mr. Mang said it did not come from the test burn room. This is the bottle from the test burn. (He showed the jury a still frame from the test burn video.) And you saw it, and you held it, and it's different. So somebody did try to suggest that it was in the test burn. Why is this important? I want you to hold that. I want you to pass it down amongst yourselves, and I want you to feel it, because it's solid.

"And it's solid because it's solid like the truth. Please just touch it one last time. It's solid. And the truth is solid. And what I'm telling you now is what you know. What you know is that was in the room during the fire.

"Do you remember the State, on its cross examination of Mr. Mang, asked him to look at the photographs and see if he saw that bottle in the room. And she had a picture in her hand. He says, I looked at all the pictures, but I don't recall seeing that bottle anywhere else. And we know by now that if she would have had the pictures she would have shoved them in his face.

"This bottle was in the room, and this bottle is the truth, because what this bottle tells us is that when that room was on fire, this bottle was protected because it was full. Look how good of shape it's in. And, what it tells us is, if it was full, it wasn't used as an accelerant to kill Matthew Dean Wise, because it was inside there, full, like that. And that's the truth. The truth."

Earnest implored the jury to consider after two weeks of trial. "Do any of you believe, do any of you honestly believe that the way this case has been investigated under a microscope for five years, the lengths that the State has gone to get depositions of our expert from some obscure place in California, to, to talk to everybody that he worked with. All of those lengths. Do you believe for a second, when they can refer by memory to numbers one through one-hundred on exhibits, do you believe for a second they don't know where that came from? Well (holding the bottle of alcohol) this is a witness you can't make fun of, you can't have jokes about cottage cheese with, and you can't impeach this truth because it doesn't lie. They found no other containers of alcohol anywhere in that house and she's told you now (pointing at me) that it's alcohol. That's your truth . . .

"Miss Lukemeyer is right. I counted them. There's seven hundred and two questions. He answered one within a week or so after he buried his child, another one voluntarily a month later, and another one four months later without attorneys present, except for the one with the insurance company.

"And people communicate in different ways, as we've seen. People communicate sometimes not only with words, but with their eyes. I'm going to ask you, after I sit down, to communicate with your eyes to her (staring at me) in different ways, and ask questions of her with your eyes, because you deserve to know the answers."

Now Earnest changed gears, reminding the jurors about the testimony of James Kemnitz, how much Wise loved the baby. "She (looking at me) didn't ask a single question of him and I'd like somebody to ask her, and I will select you, ma'am, to ask her with your eyes when she comes to talk to you again, to tell me, representative of the State, why is James Kemnitz lying?"

Earnest apologized for skipping around, but talked about the test burn room "that we all know has nothing to do with the actual room, because of all the various conditions. I will select you, ma'am, to ask her this question with your eyes. If you're so sure about how this happened, if you are sure, beyond a reasonable doubt, how this happened, and you want to convince me beyond a reasonable doubt exactly how this happened, ask her this question with your eyes. When you built the mockup, why the hell didn't you just do it the way you thought it happened, the way that you know it happened? Why didn't you put accelerant in it? Why didn't you just do it the way you said it happened, and show us that the contents after the rooms are exactly the same. That will prove it to me . . .

"Why did you play with a blow torch? See, it's the burden, the State's burden. And she was asking Mr. Berman, can you start a fire with one of these things. (He pointed to the transmitter.) Mr. Berman doesn't have to start a fire. Ask her that question and have her answer that to your satisfaction."

Van Buskirk leaned over. We were trying to be polite, but I leaned toward her as well. "Speak to her with your eyes," she said sarcastically, "this asshole is creeping me out. Where's the hand sanitizer, I'm gonna take a gulp."

While I agreed, I didn't want to encourage Van Buskirk. Well, I did want to encourage her, just not now.

"Ma'am, you can ask her about Cathy Robinson, who he worked with, about the ugly baby comment and the 'I won't tolerate that' comment."

Earnest was focusing on a juror who looked extremely uncomfortable with the attention.

"Ask her why Cathy Robinson only appeared a few months ago when this case was five years old and he was charged with murder four years ago. You can ask her that and see what she has to say to you . . .

"Wise's supervisor on the night before the fire was Robert Temple."

He looked at another juror. "You ask her, please, why didn't we hear from Robert Temple on the witness stand? Why didn't he tell you that Wise didn't have permission to take that police radio?"

Earnest went through several other witnesses in the same way. Kathy Roberts' testimony, Earnest implored, "What the hell, who cares?"

I was pretty astounded. I had never heard a lawyer using foul language in court. Maybe a witness would recite what the defendant said that included curse words, but from a lawyer? Okay, so I am old fashioned, but it just was not the place. I had no idea if the jury shared my aversion to the base expressions.

Earnest was still raging. His complexion was red peppermint. "They weren't invited to the wedding. He's a murderer. Ask her this question now, I'll ask you to please ask her this question with your eyes, why the hell did you even ask that question about did he get e-mail on his computer from somebody named Julie, across the hall. Ask her what she meant by that. Ask her if that's something about proving this guy committed murder or just trying to make him look bad. What the hell did that mean?

"You know, defense attorneys, like us, are accused all the time by prosecutors of doing smoke screens, red herrings. Well, I suppose that means he's a philanderer, and he was out there having lots of girlfriends, and Julie, who obviously didn't testify about that, didn't come to court. Ask her (looking at me) why's she's not being straight with you."

Earnest read from a transcript. He quoted some of my opening statement.

"Figure out, you try to figure out what the hell these questions are about, the one's she asked Wayne Edwards."

Earnest mocked the testimony about Wise going to Tamara Snyder's house and then to Mr. Edwards house.

"So what? He ran because it seemed like an eternity before Tamara Snyder answered the door. Edwards said that Wise was covered with soot . . .

"He was pretending, but we know he had tried to rescue the child in the fire. How do we know that? Because Mr. Edwards told you, when he left my phone it had soot on it, and he was so hysterical and panicky that he could hardly dial 911. So proof positive, beyond a shadow of a doubt, he tried to save the child before he made the 911 call."

Earnest's voice was thick with sarcasm and mockery as he talked about Gary Triplett, too.

"Gary Triplett met Bill four or five times. He's a psychologist, he's an expert on grief, he knows that he wasn't very real, he was just a sham, he didn't mean it. What Triplett tells us, really, is a little bit different than Doris Gilbert in the back of her well-lit ambulance. He says that coat reeked of so much smoke, I had to get it out of my house."

Earnest mocked Doris Gilbert's testimony that Wise had some minor redness on his hands. "He (pointing at Wise across the room) was just pretending to be a hero!

"We made promises in this courtroom. When somebody makes a promise in this courtroom, that somebody is the State of Indiana, they have to keep their promise. They have to keep those promises.

"Keith Williams, he says, sure Bill doesn't go up the stairs until Williams orders him to, right. I'd crawl to hell and back to try to prove to you the truth. But the truth is that he gets this far down the hall, this big man, this ex-Marine, this firefighter, this police officer, stops, because in his mind he says 'I've got to continue to live,' and he knows that if he doesn't stop he's going to be overcome with the smoke and he could die.

"And so this big ex-Marine, on the heels of Bill Wise, says, what'd he say, 'I've got to go home.' And Bill Wise is crawling in the other direction in the smoke, and he disappears and he's going toward home, he's going toward his child. But that's just pretending.

"And the flames on the hair are just pretending. Well, that's what she (looking at me at the State's table) told you, also. Officer Williams will tell you that it appeared to him that Mr. Wise had not been in that house previously. I'm not calling him a liar. I know better than to call cops liars, but I can say they can certainly be mistaken.

"Dr. Pless doesn't give her what she wanted, which was definite alcohol in the diaper. He said it could have been urine, so he did not give her what she wanted so badly. Because he's a doctor and he's medical, he had to tell the truth, what his opinion was. And what he says also, twice under oath, is that certainly the burning of a foam mattress can serve as an accelerant substance.

"Now, she's got this convenient theory, after I did my demonstration with Dr. Pless, where now the alcohol is poured underneath the diaper, okay? Do any of us believe for a minute, just use your common sense, that there wouldn't be more burns there than there were. I mean, is it going to be that protected when everything else was so burned up? I don't think, and you don't think, that he poured alcohol down, because there was none to pour. He didn't pour alcohol down that child's diaper."

Earnest disputed Lewie-Bob's testimony about Wise's ability to be calm under stress. He told the jury that the matches in the next room were so unimportant that the State didn't even have the matchbook, only a photograph of the matchbook.

"Ask yourselves why Jeanne Wise is a liar, why Joanne Davis is a liar. Well, obviously it's because they love him, that's why. And if you find him guilty, you can feel free to write on the verdict form, we also think they're liars. You can do that. You can infer that there's some bias there because they're family. But you can infer something else, too. You can infer that they know him better than anybody else in the world and they've known him all his life. And they're here, and they were there. And they told you that he loved that child, that he held the child, that he was proud of the child when the child was born. Matthew Dean Wise. That's evidence which maybe had more substance to it that some employee who doesn't come up 'till four years after the fact and all of a sudden remembers a conversation.

"Doris Gilbert? I don't even want to waste my time . . .

"This is the law. To prove the defendant guilty of arson the State must prove beyond a reasonable doubt that all accidental and natural causes for the fire have been eliminated."

Earnest appeared to have been reading from a transcript. State's expert in cause and origin, David Lepper. "You can't rule out what you don't have."

Earnest went into detail about the investigation, how bad it was, and, using my full name, said that I failed to produce what I had promised the jury.

"It's a murder case, the most serious crime that we have, and I think that you would want, that you would expect that for every individual piece of evidence there should have been a box, and it should have been labeled, who found it and where it was found."

Earnest spoke at length about Lepper not having the evidence properly marked or documented. While he addressed the jury he toyed with the debris in one of the evidence boxes.

"Mr. Berman differed in his opinions from what Finneran told you," Earnest argued, "because he was telling the truth."

He went on. "Motive. No evidence of arson for profit. Allstate, the helping hands, you know, give you a check to get by. That's the motive to kill here? You know, if there was some arson for profit going on here, they would have found it. They would have crawled around the room on their hands and knees to find it. But instead, with that check from Allstate, they bought clothes, emergency provisions, and they bought something to bury Baby Matthew in."

Earnest spoke faster and faster. The filing of the lawsuit two days before the Statute of Limitations ran was normal.

"Any of us would sue the hell out of some corporation that had a product that killed your only child. Fault him for that and call him a murderer."

Earnest talked about the downstairs and that all of Wise's things, including the bird, survived. "So, he's so brilliant in one way that he masterminded this fire, but so stupid not to know what to expect afterward?

"And if you want to kill a kid, but you've got to think, you don't want to bring attention to yourself, can you just suffocate him with a pillow? Unfortunately, I think that happens.

"You have an instruction now on accomplice liability, and the reason you have that is because now the State can say, when she gets up next, if she chooses, that if you think that Michelle caused the fire, committed the arson, or Bill knew about it and he participated in it, you can find him guilty as an accomplice. You see, because that widens the net. You see, that widens the net, now, for her to get Bill. But I want you to ask yourself, ask yourself, please, the integrity of the State's case, the theory, look closely at the information and you'll see that Michelle is listed as a victim of these crimes, Michelle and Matthew, and now they want to make her out as a perpetrator, the principal, just in case, so they can get him."

"Ask yourself, if she wants to argue that to you now, why she didn't say a damn thing about that in her opening argument. Ask her that."

Lisa leaned over Van Buskirk. "You couldn't argue that in opening because the judge hadn't decided whether to give the instruction yet. That's not right. Are you going to object?"

I shook my head. I was going to let Earnest have his say.

"Make her show you where she told you in opening that Michelle was a killer. Invite her to do that. Ask her that. Ask her to explain that. Ask her why she's afraid of that. There's too much at stake here. He tried to save his child. He made a bad mistake, one that he'll—a judgment call. But that's not a crime. That's not the crime.

"If justice is to mean anything, when you hear the instructions on beyond a reasonable doubt, in the jury room you can talk yourselves into anything you want to, but you're required to talk yourselves into the right thing. Promise me that it's not based on emotion, but the facts, and you know all about the accelerants and what happened after it fell down, it's opened . . . I have a lot more to say, but I leave that to you to ask the questions now. It's not there. Doesn't make sense."

Earnest had worked himself into such a frenzy, his face was flushed and there was sweat running down his cheeks in the cold courtroom. I watched as he slammed into his chair and put an arm around William Wise.

I stood up, and, still at my table, said quietly, "All of a sudden I'm on trial. Mr. Earnest is so angry, I'm concerned that he's going to have a heart attack. What he doesn't want to talk to you about is the evidence. There's an old saying, 'If you can't argue the facts, argue the law. If you can't argue the law, argue the facts, if you can't argue the facts or the law, then call the other lawyer names.' Arguments can be made, in law, without curse words, without personal attacks, and while I'm flattered that I'm quoted, I am proud and stick by what I've said. My job is not to defend myself. My job, and one that I undertake proudly, is to show you the evidence, because Matthew Dean Wise is dead."

I stepped to the jury box, whispering, but getting louder with each repetition. "Seconds save lives, seconds save lives." That's what is drummed into them at fire dispatch. Get that fire dispatched. You get a call, seconds save lives.

"What the defense did not want to talk to you about is all the times that the defendant could have saved the baby. Why did he take a right to get the phone instead of a left? Why did he sit there as his wife got her shoes and not get the baby? He had time to go downstairs to get his fire coat on but not go up and get his child.

"We never said that the defendant wasn't in a fire. There was a fire in the house. He started it. We didn't say he wouldn't have any soot on him. Of course he had soot on him. There was a fire and he was standing there on the landing watching it. He opened the door and let more oxygen feed the fire in his baby's room."

I reminded the jury that Michelle was an admitted liar and discussed the alcohol and where it was in the room. I told them about Finneran's examination of the outlet where the baby monitor had been plugged in. That there was no fault at the outlet, which made Berman's theory impossible. I also recounted that neither Mang nor Berman even looked at the wall receptacle because they knew the fire did not start there.

I reiterated what Michelle swore about the alcohol bottle location. The alcohol bottle was a distraction from the real evidence.

"How do they excuse the very strong testimony of Dr. Pless? Yes, Dr. Pless is a professional, unlike some paid witnesses who, like, say, Mr. Berman, will make absolutes about everything, including the dangerousness of a recipe for cottage cheese. Dr. Pless told you, when asked 'Could it have been that,' and he said, 'Well, it could have, but it's my opinion that it was not.'

"Dr. Pless was fair and professional. He explained that this part of Baby Matthew's body was protected because of the accelerant poured on him. Matthew's body had significant water content. The diaper wasn't much more. What preserved it was that the fire was burning above his body, in the area where the alcohol was. It was the alcohol fumes that burned, not the liquid. The liquid alcohol protected his groin. That's what this is about . . .

"Dr. Pless said, and I asked him specifically, 'In your opinion could a non-accelerated or accidental fire, in a period of fifteen to twenty minutes, have caused the type of destruction and incineration of that infant that you observed?' He said, 'No.'

"There are two things you should take from Dr. Pless' testimony. It was a protected area, and he told you, in his opinion, that it was caused by the pouring of a liquid accelerant on Baby Matthew. That was his opinion, and it's based on his experience and training. And number two, he said that this damage and destruction could not have happened to Baby Matthew without a liquid accelerant. It could not have happened in an accidental fire.

"Even after I reminded Dr. Pless about the foam mattress, the infant's size and his age, Dr. Pless rendered his opinion that the damage to this infant's body, the damage to that child, could not have been caused unless the fire was accelerated.

"Dr. Pless didn't know Ed Barnes. He didn't know Lt. Vernon Brown and what did they tell you? What possible reason do they have to deceive you? They told you that, having seen hundreds of fires, they knew that this fire was accelerated.

"And as angry as Mr. Earnest wants to be, and whatever questions he may care about, we believe ladies and gentlemen, that you've listened to and seen the evidence.

"Mr. Earnest says he doesn't want you to rule on emotion, but he does. If he can get you mad at me, if he can have you looking at other things, then you won't think about why the defendant didn't go upstairs, when the alarm was screeching, to get his baby. And you won't think about why Michelle went to get her shoes, instead of getting the baby, while the defendant stood at the landing, and why he didn't get the baby then. You won't think about this." (I held the police radio.)

"And this police radio is important because between that evening and sometime before the police and fire department came, this radio was hidden. You know what? The evidence was that the defendant would not have gotten in big trouble for having it. I mean, he wasn't allowed to have it, it was a bad thing, but he wouldn't have gotten in big trouble for it. He hid it because it was evidence of what he was doing.

"Rely on the evidence, all of it that you've heard. The defendant killed his baby, and it may be his day in court, and it is, but it's also Matthew's only day in court."

Every person in the room seemed to inhale a breath and let it out at the same time.

Then everyone focused on the bench. All eyes were on Judge Magnus-Stinson as she read the final instructions to the jury. She gave the bailiff three pages to give the jurors and then excused them to deliberate.

I watched as they silently filed out of the courtroom. The documents that they each had been given were the verdict forms. There was one page for each charge against William Wise: Murder, Felony Murder, and Arson with Bodily Injury.

I felt an enormous sense of relief. I looked at Van Buskirk as the Wise defense team, hugging and talking, left the courtroom.

"Let's go. I need a drink." I sighed.

"What'd you want, a milkshake?" Van Buskirk sneered jokingly. I really didn't drink. No moral compunctions. I preferred to take my calories in chocolate form.

Lisa asked me how long I thought it would take the jury to make a decision.

"We put on a lot of evidence and it was a two week trial. Some people think that a quick verdict is more favorable to the State, but I've had juries take days to convict. I have also had a record thirteen minute guilty verdict. In other words, I don't have a clue."

"Let's go to Fridays," Van Buskirk suggested. She and I laughed but Lisa just looked at us curiously. Lisa had not been part of the team when we had almost dined at Fridays following the first trial.

# Chapter Twenty-Seven

ALMOST UNBELIEVABLY, I had mixed emotions as Van Buskirk drove us to Fridays. It was about two miles from the courthouse, but there was a light on almost every corner so it took us about ten or fifteen minutes to get there.

I sat in the back seat listening to Van Buskirk and Lisa discuss various aspects of the trial, their estimates of the time it would take the jury to reach a verdict and a variety of other things.

Although it was a short ride, they both had much to discuss. Since I had been talking, pretty much nonstop for two weeks, I was relieved to be able to be quiet and listen.

When we left the courthouse, we had seen a number of news vans, antennae out, ready to report the story. I was uncomfortable speaking with the press. One never knew their angle or if your words would be taken out of context. The press had been kind to me in Indianapolis, but that did little to alleviate my discomfort.

What I needed was a peaceful weekend with my family. Maybe we would go to the zoo, our favorite place to stroll with the kids.

I called Steve to let him know that the trial was over. He also seemed relieved. I asked him to call Mom and Bruce to let them know. Steve told me that the news was already covering the case and had broadcast that the jury was deliberating. He told me that Bruce wanted to take us to dinner after the verdict. I asked him to call and beg off. I was completely exhausted and wanted to do absolutely nothing except watch the family and maybe some mindless TV.

"Honey, please tell Mom and Bruce that we'll have dinner with them tomorrow or Sunday."

He agreed to make the call.

We arrived at Fridays and got a corner booth. It was late for the lunch crowd and too early for the after-work bar flies. Lisa and Van Buskirk urged me to order something stronger than a diet coke, but we still had issues that could arise.

"You may recall that things sometimes come up during jury deliberations," I said pointedly to Van Buskirk, who just laughed. Neither of us had forgotten the mistrial.

"Yeah, but Judge Magnus-Stinson doesn't let the jury have the exhibits during deliberations, so we shouldn't have a problem," Van Buskirk chided playfully.

Our waitress appeared and we ordered. As soon as the waitress walked away, Lisa's pager buzzed.

"Fuck all," Van Buskirk's responded. Then her pager began to wildly vibrate.

I was thinking how grand it was not to have a pager. "The jury must have a question," I thought. I waited for Lisa and Van Buskirk to get off of their respective phones.

"Well?" I asked.

Lisa said blankly, "The jury has a verdict."

Van Buskirk nodded. Her office had contacted her to tell her to get back to the courtroom.

"A verdict? This quickly? After a two week trial?" I was stunned. And hungry. I put a twenty on the table, cancelled our order and we walked out of the restaurant. I was not really in a hurry. They weren't going to start without us. I was breathing slowly to calm my nerves.

As we approached the City County Building, we saw that the reporters were speaking with Wise and the defense team. There were several Wise family members standing with them.

"Let's go in the back way," Van Buskirk suggested.

We reached the courtroom, having successfully avoided the news folks, to find several deputy prosecutors and Scott Newman waiting outside the courtroom. I could tell that Scott was annoyed that I was not in the building when the call came in. But, technically, I didn't work for him any longer, so I didn't have to explain myself.

He took me aside and said, "I will handle the press after the verdict. Just stand next to me."

Scott Newman was about my height. "Glad I wore flats. I should be a comedian," I thought, stalling to gain control. I was glad that Scott would deal with the press. He was the elected prosecutor and if we lost this case, he would take the heat. Fairness required that if we won, he could take the credit. I had no problem with that. Besides, I never liked the way I looked on camera.

As we walked into the courtroom, we saw that it was jammed, with every seat taken. I didn't know how the word had gotten out so quickly. It must be court staff or something. I wondered whether they had the television stations on speed dial. I was longing for our appetizers.

Lisa Swaim, Leslie Van Buskirk, and I sat at the State's table to await the verdict.

A few minutes later, Mark Earnest led the rest of the defense team, William Wise and the entire Wise crew into the courtroom. They sat down noisily and continued talking until Judge Magnus-Stinson was about to enter the courtroom.

Her bailiff barked, "All rise."

We did and then the judge directed us to take a seat. She also asked the bailiff if he knew anything of the jury. He said that they had advised him that they had reached verdicts in the case.

The judge instructed, "Ladies and gentlemen in the audience, there will be no outbursts when the verdicts are read. If you are not capable of controlling yourself, then please wait outside."

The jury entered the courtroom somberly. None of them looked at me. Several of them looked at William Wise.

"What does that mean?" I wondered urgently. I didn't know if it was a good sign or a bad sign. Heck, I'd tried more than two hundred jury trials, and I still never knew what they were thinking until the verdicts were read. Time was in slow motion.

Judge Magnus-Stinson said to the jury, "Ladies and gentlemen, I understand that you have reached a verdict."

There were only twelve jurors now, because the two alternates had been excused.

"Mrs. Little, I see that you have some papers in your hand. Are you the foreperson of the jury?"

The juror responded that she was the foreman.

"Has the jury reached a unanimous verdict?"

Mrs. Little said that they had reached three unanimous verdicts.

The judge asked her to hand the forms to her bailiff. The bailiff took the three pages and gave them to the judge who carefully and slowly reviewed each page. She asked Mr. Wise and his lawyers to rise as she read the verdict.

The judge read clearly, "Verdict. We, the jury, find the defendant, William J. Wise, guilty of murder, a felony, as charged in Count I. It is signed by Ms. Little and dated with today's date."

There was a sob from behind Wise. The judge looked at Jeanne Wise, who loudly slammed out of the courtroom.

"Verdict. We, the jury, find the defendant, William J. Wise, guilty of felony murder, a felony, as charged in Count II. It is signed by Ms. Little and dated with today's date."

The judge turned to the third page. "Verdict. We, the jury, find the defendant, William J. Wise, guilty of Arson with serious bodily injury, a felony, as charged in Count III. It is signed by Ms. Little and dated with today's date . . .

"Mr. Wise, the jury has found you guilty of all counts of the charging documents. Are there any requests, Mr. Earnest?"

"Yes, your honor. We wish to poll the jury."

I looked at Wise, sitting ramrod straight at the defense table emotionless. He looked directly ahead, his black eyes were dark. If he felt any emotion, it was hidden in some deep recess of his being.

To poll the jury means to ask each juror if the verdicts were his or her individual verdict.

The judge started with Mrs. Little. "Mrs. Little, are these your verdicts?"

"Yes, your honor," Mrs. Little said.

The judge then repeated this question of every juror. Each confirmed that each verdict was his or her verdict. The judge thanked them for their service. Then she excused the jury to return to the jury room.

Van B had actually grabbed my hand and squeezed it hard under the table. Lisa was grinning from ear to ear. I was trying to remain as professional as I could. I had to look down at the table so that my relief could not be seen by anyone. I did not look back to see Scott's reaction but there was some positive hum emanating from the rows of seats behind us.

As soon as the jury left the courtroom, Earnest was on his feet asking the court to allow the defendant to remain on bond pending sentencing. Before I could respond, the judge denied the request.

"Mr. Wise has been convicted of killing his eight week old son. He will be taken into custody immediately and I will set a date for sentencing, unless you want to waive a presentence investigation."

The defense did not want to waive a presentence investigation. They did ask the judge to overrule the decision of the jury on a variety of grounds. She denied the request.

The judge asked if the State had any requests. We did not. The judge set the sentencing for May 1, 1998. She asked that the State and its audience allow the Wise's family to leave first. They walked out noisily. Michelle was sobbing and grabbing out for Wise, who the bailiff whisked off to the holding cell behind the courtroom.

I was numb, and dumb.

How could one vociferously celebrate the death of a child at the hands of his father? As we sat there, two women approached Lisa. She walked to the side of the courtroom with them, while I waited in the emptying courtroom.

Scott jumped up from out of some stray slow-motion frame and congratulated Van Buskirk and me. He wanted to speak to the press, so I steeled myself and headed out into the hallway. Although all of the questions were directed to me, I was very content to listen to Scott respond. Van Buskirk stood behind us waiting. She would not allow any photographs to be taken of her. I tried to pull Lisa into the Q and A session, but she stood next to Van Buskirk, watching.

I saw George McLaren, the newspaper reporter, standing patiently near the stairwell. Once Scott released me, I walked over to George. He asked me a few questions. I was glad to answer. I also asked Van Buskirk if she wanted to add anything and she gave him a few quotes as well.

I sat on the bench after Scott, the press, and everyone else had cleared out. Only Lisa, Van Buskirk, and I remained.

"What did those women say to you, Lisa?" I asked.

"They were some of Michelle's family members. They asked me to thank you for saving Michelle's life. They said that even though Michelle hates you, they believe you saved her from a monster."

"That's good to know." I meant it.

No one, not one reporter, except for George, asked or said a word about Baby Matthew. I walked toward the elevator.

"Let's go back to Fridays," Van Buskirk suggested. She was in a celebratory mood. I told her to take Lisa and have a blast. I was headed home.

On the way, I got a call from Mom. She and Bruce were going out to celebrate my victory, whether I wanted to go or not.

"Bruce really wants to take you, Di. He is really proud of you," Mom said. I told her that we would do it over the weekend. All I wanted was my bed and some cartoons with the kids.

I drove home. I had dinner with Steve and the girls. We watched the evening news and they teased me about my photograph on the screen. I was in bed by nine p.m. I was worn out. I think I got the first good night's sleep that I'd had in a month.

In fact, I was sound asleep when the phone by my bedside rang at five-thirty a.m. "Who calling at this time of morning?"

I tried to get the phone before it woke Steve.

"Diane, this is Dennis Buckley, Beech Grove Fire Department," a male voice said. Dennis was the investigator on an arson murder case that I had prosecuted. I considered him a friend.

"Hi, Dennis. You're calling pretty early. What's up?" I asked.

"Diane, I need you to come over to your mother's house right away. Will you do that please?"

He was calm but authoritative.

"Is everything okay?" I asked getting out of bed.

"Just come now, please. By the way, congratulations on convicting Wise."

He hung up.

I threw on a pair of jeans and a tee shirt, and, once again, left my sleeping family. My Mother and Bruce lived in Beech Grove which was a twenty minute drive from our home. I made it in ten.

When I arrived, there were a variety of fire department vehicles in the yard, but I was thankful that there was no fire or fire damage that I could see. When I walked in, there were no wonderful smells from the kitchen. My mother was in her robe sitting on the couch, crying. She looked up when I walked over to her, but didn't speak. I looked at Dennis who had been promoted to fire chief. Dennis took me by the arm. He walked me down the hall. Their bedroom door was closed.

"Is something wrong with Bruce?" I asked looking suspiciously at the closed door. Bruce was always up by this time. He got up much earlier than Mom on most days.

"It appears that Bruce died in his sleep. Your mother said that they went out to celebrate last night, and then went to bed. He never woke up. We need you to identify the body."

# Chapter Twenty-Eight

ON MAY 1, 1998, William J. Wise was sentenced for the murder of Baby Matthew.

Van Buskirk, Lisa Swaim, and I represented the State.

Wise presented two family members who testified about what a great guy he was. His uncle testified that he was a 'fine young gentleman.' During the cross examination of James Kemnitz, I asked about the stolen fire truck, the burglary conviction, the fire at Jeanne's house, William shooting himself and the other misdeeds and crimes that he had committed. The rules of evidence do not apply to sentencing, and so I gave the judge all of the reports that we had accumulated from Wise's juvenile records and elsewhere.

After the trial we'd also learned that Wise had petitioned to receive money from the State victims' compensation fund. He'd applied, despite the fact that he had shot himself and hidden the gun in his mother's garage. I asked Mr. Kemnitz if he was aware of that. He was not, he said.

I also asked Uncle Jim about the situation in Florida where Wise tried to hide his medical records. When Mr. Kemnitz said he was unaware of that situation, those documents were provided to the judge. Mr. Kemnitz did not know that William Wise had lied, misrepresented and mislead law enforcement, fire departments and others. But at this hearing, the judge reviewed all of the records related to these crimes.

Jeanne Wise testified about her son as well. It was heartfelt but dishonest. Mrs. Wise said that her divorce in 1973 adversely affected William. She described her observations and took blame for his conduct. She told the court that she knew that Bill did not kill "that baby" and that he loved "that baby." She testified that Wise had an actual hole in his heart and was small, but had overcome all of that.

When I cross examined Jeanne, I asked about the fire at their home. She denied that it was in Bill's closet, instead correcting that it was in the pantry and found when he was home alone. She also said that she was familiar with many of Bill's girlfriends including Rae Ann Symons. Jeanne had met Rae Ann, and several other young women.

I asked her, "And you were aware that your son was with her the last time anyone saw her, before her disappearance." She said that Bill was with Rae Ann that night and something about Rae Ann not having a prom date. I interrupted her. "Ma'am, were you aware that she was pregnant with twins?" Jeanne said she learned about it later.

She expressed not an ounce of concern about a dead young woman. Jeanne said that she later learned that Rae Ann was pregnant with twins at the same time that Michelle was pregnant with the fetus that she later aborted.

When I asked Jeanne Wise if Bill was twenty-five and Rae Ann Symons seventeen at the time, she said, "Well, she was a senior and needed a date to the prom, and Bill had a sports car and was a handsome young man and agreed to take her."

The State introduced the testimony of Investigator Miles Stacey. He was the lead investigator for the State Police and responsible for the Rae Ann Symons murder investigation. He testified, at length, about Wise and how he was the only suspect in the case. Investigator Stacey also gave his opinion that Wise killed Rae Ann Symons. On cross-examination by Mark Earnest, Investigator Stacey admitted that no charges had been filed against William Wise in that case.

The State had no other witnesses. I did introduce Dixie Norman, Rae Ann Symons grandmother. Ms. Norman had been present every day of the trial and was here to see Mr. Wise sentenced. I also introduced Jerry Shulte, the Allstate Insurance Company adjustor who had conducted the investigation for Wise's homeowner's insurance company.

Both sides were permitted to make arguments to the court as to the appropriate sentence. Mark Earnest urged the court to impose minimum sentences.

I argued briefly, but knew that the court had heard the evidence and listened to every word. I urged the court to sentence Mr. Wise as she saw fit.

The court spent nearly an hour explaining her sentence.

"One factor that the court must consider is the risk that you will commit another crime. While you have no formal criminal history, and no one could have predicted the crime of which you were convicted, that crime discloses a side of your character that causes me concern about the safety of the community and the risk that you'll commit another crime. The evidence about you and the fire truck as a juvenile, the fire in your mother's home, all these things fire related which cause the court concern about your clear fixation with fires and fire-fighting or being a paramedic. You twisted that, what could have been a noble goal, into something evil."

" . . . I also find that there is a risk that you will commit another crime. I do not afford much weight to the murder of Rae Ann Symons, because you were not charged with that crime, and I don't have a desire to have my sentence reversed on appeal. But you do have a history of delinquent activity and doing what you want to do to suit your own purposes."

Judge Magnus-Stinson described Wise's life as indulged. She believed that Michelle was under Wise's control, doing anything she could to please him. "Your character is complicated, but there's a side to it that causes me great concern for the safety of others in our community.

" . . . And then I will turn to the nature and circumstances of the crime committed. Mr. Earnest, I must disagree with your argument, being a murder is a murder is a murder. I have to consider what a little baby went through for seven and a half, at seven and a half weeks for the time that it took for his body to become incinerated beyond recognition. Even at seven weeks kids are getting to the point where they respond to their parents, they know who's there, they cry out when they want things.

"They're beginning the stages of cognition and knowing that there could be people out there to take care of them, because that's why they cry. They tell us, I'm wet, I'm hungry, I'm tired, I want to be held. And it's primitive, but it works. And the doctor's testimony supports a conclusion that the baby himself was the subject of the fire, in addition to what the firefighters found on the floor. These are all circumstances that do make this the worst of the worst. And if people could choose ways not to die, I think the number one way not to die would be to be burned to death."

The court found several aggravating factors and no mitigating factors.

"The court believes that an aggravated sentence is warranted. I think the most compelling fact for the jury is, was, and it certainly is compelling for me. I would sooner burn to death than know that my baby is up in a room from which I am twelve, fifteen, twenty feet away. I would never leave my house and none of those jurors would ever leave their house without getting that baby out of there. And that was one of the most compelling facts, in addition to all the physical evidence about the fire and how it was started. I mean, the bottom line is, parents walk through fire for their children. That's their responsibility, and that's their instinct, and because of that, I have to say that this is the worst of the worst that I've seen."

With those words, the court sentenced William Wise to the maximum sentence of sixty years incarceration for murder.

She also sentenced him to the maximum sentence for arson, saying that "I do want to say that it's a most brutal and gruesome way to kill your baby, to kill anybody, but your own baby, it's almost unfathomable." That sentence was fifty years. The judge ordered the sentences to run consecutively, for a total sentence of one-hundred and ten years.

As we walked out of the courtroom and hugged, Lisa handed me a small gift wrapped package. It was a cassette tape. The name of the recording was "Time to Say Goodbye" by Sara Brightman and the London Symphony Orchestra. I had never heard the song or the artist. I popped it into the player in my car.

Tears rolled down my face as Sara Brightman sang those four words. I said goodbye to Wise, glad that he would be in prison for a long time. I said goodbye to my dedicated team. I pulled over, put the top down on my little ancient V.W. Cabriolet convertible, and mourned for Baby Matthew. I was also sure that I would never prosecute another case. I quietly sang along until I regained the spirit to drive home.

# Epilogue

WILLIAM WISE IS currently incarcerated in the Indiana Department of Corrections at the Pendleton Correctional Facility. His earliest release date is June 6, 2037.

No one has been prosecuted for the murder of Rae Ann Symons or her unborn twins.

Michelle Wise Takerer still lives in Elkhart, Indiana. She has not been charged with any crime.

Matthew Dean Wise is buried in a tiny grave, marked only with a small stone, in the baby section of the Rice Cemetery in Elkhart, Indiana.

Sgt. Leslie Van Buskirk is still a detective with the Indianapolis Metropolitan Police Department. She is one of the most decorated and successful detectives in the history of the department.

Lisa Swaim is the elected prosecutor in Cass County, Logansport, Indiana.

Diane Marger Moore continues to practice law.

Diane Marger Moore has been a lawyer for nearly forty years in both private practice and government service. She has been a federal public defender, deputy attorney general, chief arson prosecutor, felony court supervisor and a judicial officer in the major felony division of the Marion County, Indiana, Superior Court. Diane has taught trial practice to other lawyers for decades and has written and published legal articles and chapters but this is her first book. She tells the story of a true life murder prosecution. Her self-described greatest achievement is having raised strong, opinionated children who care about the world and work to improve it.